INJUSTICE

GODS AMONG US: YEAR FIVE

VOLUME 3

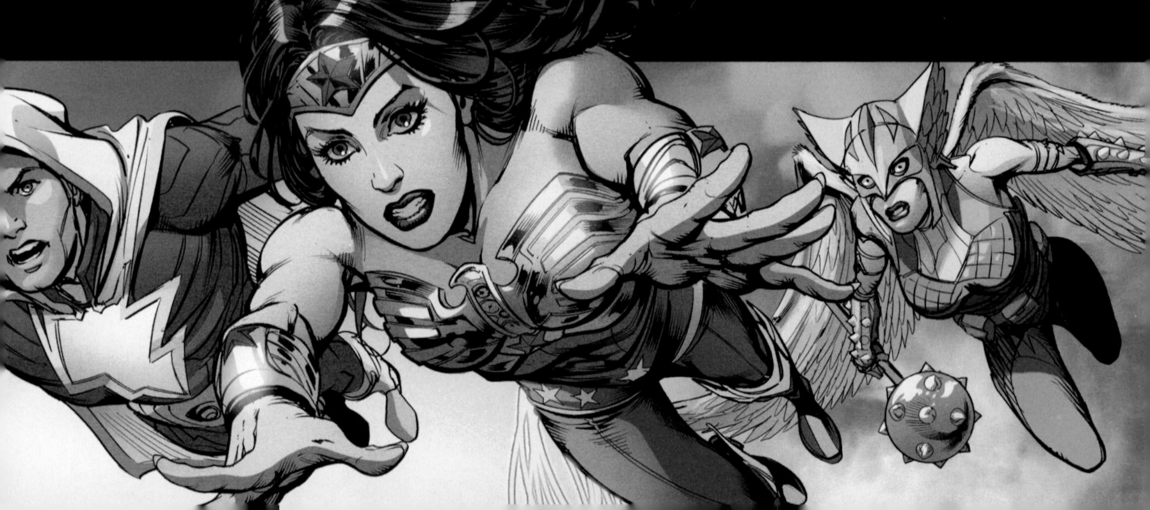

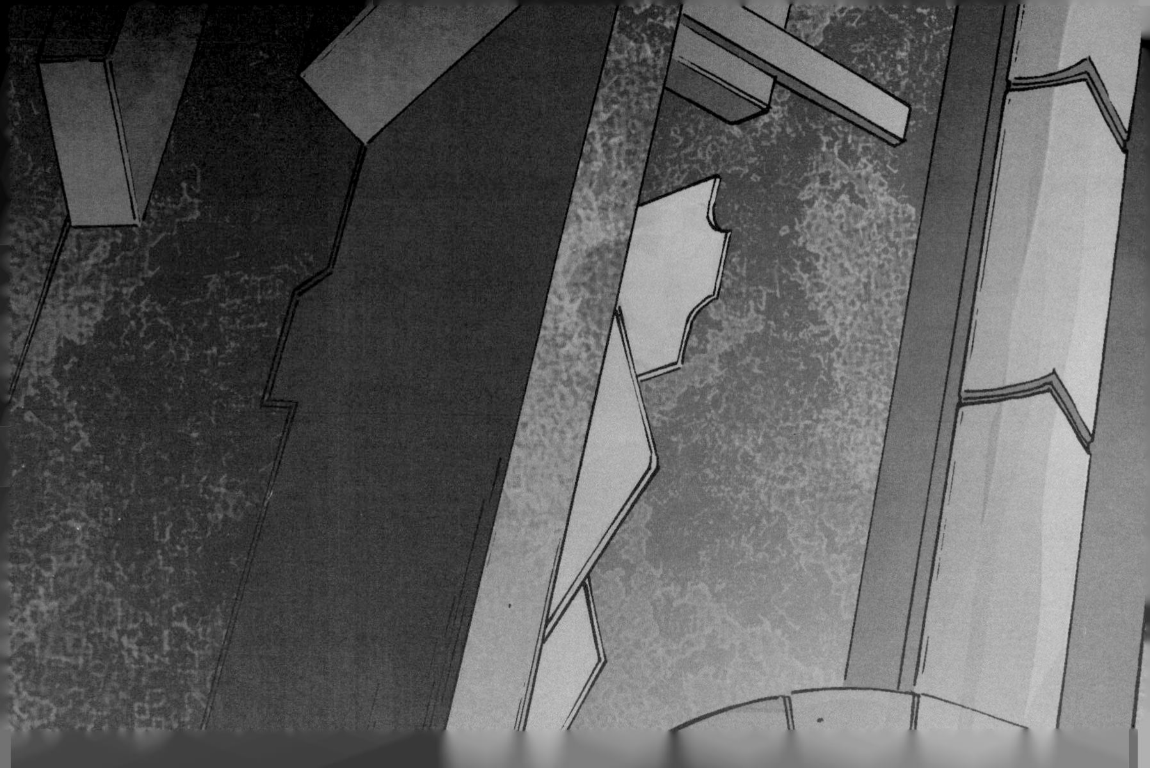

STICE

US: YEAR FIVE

VOLUME 3

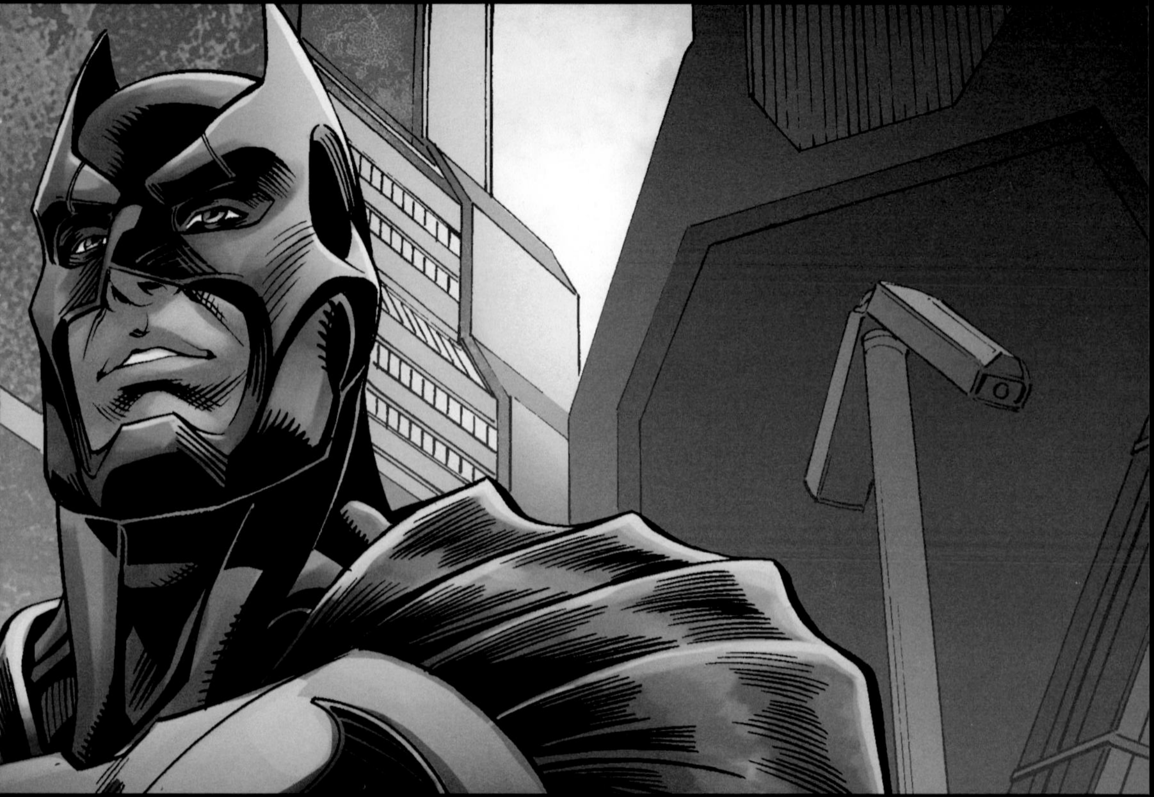

SUPERMAN created by JERRY SIEGEL and JOE SHUSTER.
By special arrangement with the Jerry Siegel Family.

JIM CHADWICK Editor – Original Series
DAVID PIÑA Assistant Editor – Original Series
JEB WOODARD Group Editor – Collected Editions
PAUL SANTOS Editor – Collected Edition
STEVE COOK Design Director – Books
AMIE BROCKWAY-METCALF Publication Design

BOB HARRAS Senior VP – Editor-in-Chief, DC Comics

DIANE NELSON President
DAN DiDIO Publisher
JIM LEE Publisher
GEOFF JOHNS President & Chief Creative Officer
AMIT DESAI Executive VP – Business & Marketing Strategy,
    Direct to Consumer & Global Franchise Management
SAM ADES Senior VP – Direct to Consumer
BOBBIE CHASE VP – Talent Development
MARK CHIARELLO Senior VP – Art, Design & Collected Editions
JOHN CUNNINGHAM Senior VP – Sales & Trade Marketing
ANNE DEPiES Senior VP – Business Strategy, Finance & Administration
DON FALLETTI VP – Manufacturing Operations
LAWRENCE GANEM VP – Editorial Administration & Talent Relations
ALISON GILL Senior VP – Manufacturing & Operations
HANK KANALZ Senior VP – Editorial Strategy & Administration
JAY KOGAN VP – Legal Affairs
THOMAS LOFTUS VP – Business Affairs
JACK MAHAN VP – Business Affairs
NICK J. NAPOLITANO VP – Manufacturing Administration
EDDIE SCANNELL VP – Consumer Marketing
COURTNEY SIMMONS Senior VP – Publicity & Communications
JIM (SKI) SOKOLOWSKI VP – Comic Book Specialty Sales & Trade Marketing
NANCY SPEARS VP – Mass, Book, Digital Sales & Trade Marketing

INJUSTICE: GODS AMONG US – YEAR FIVE VOLUME 3

Published by DC Comics. Compilation and all new material
Copyright © 2017 DC Comics. All Rights Reserved. Originally
published in single magazine form in INJUSTICE GODS:
AMONG-US YEAR FIVE 15-20.and INUSTICE GODS AMONG
US YEAR FIVE ANNUAL 1 Copyright © 2016 DC Comics. All
Rights Reserved. All characters, their distinctive likenesses and
related elements featured in this publication are trademarks of
DC Comics. The stories, characters and incidents featured in
this publication are entirely fictional. DC Comics does not read
or accept unsolicited submissions of ideas, stories or artwork.

DC Comics, 2900 West Alameda Ave., Burbank, CA 91505
Printed by LSC Communications, Salem, VA, USA. 5/12/17.
First Printing. ISBN: 978-1-4012-7246-3

Library of Congress Cataloging-in-Publication Data is available.

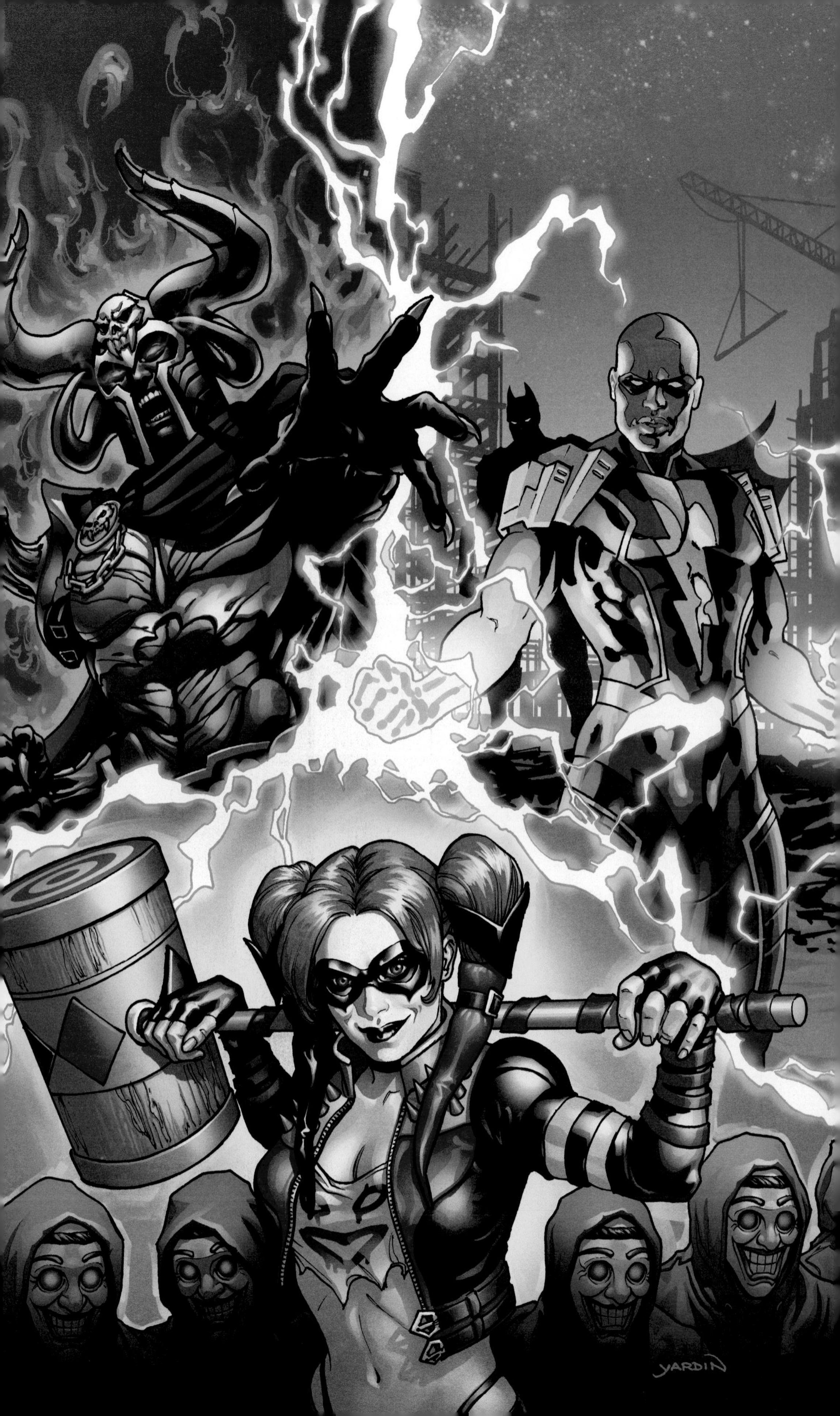
YARDIN

"The Clan" **Mike S. Miller** Artist **J. Nanjan** Colorist
"Ares" **Xermanico** Artist **Rex Lokus** Colorist
"Reconstruction" **Marco Santucci** Artist **Rex Lokus** Colorist

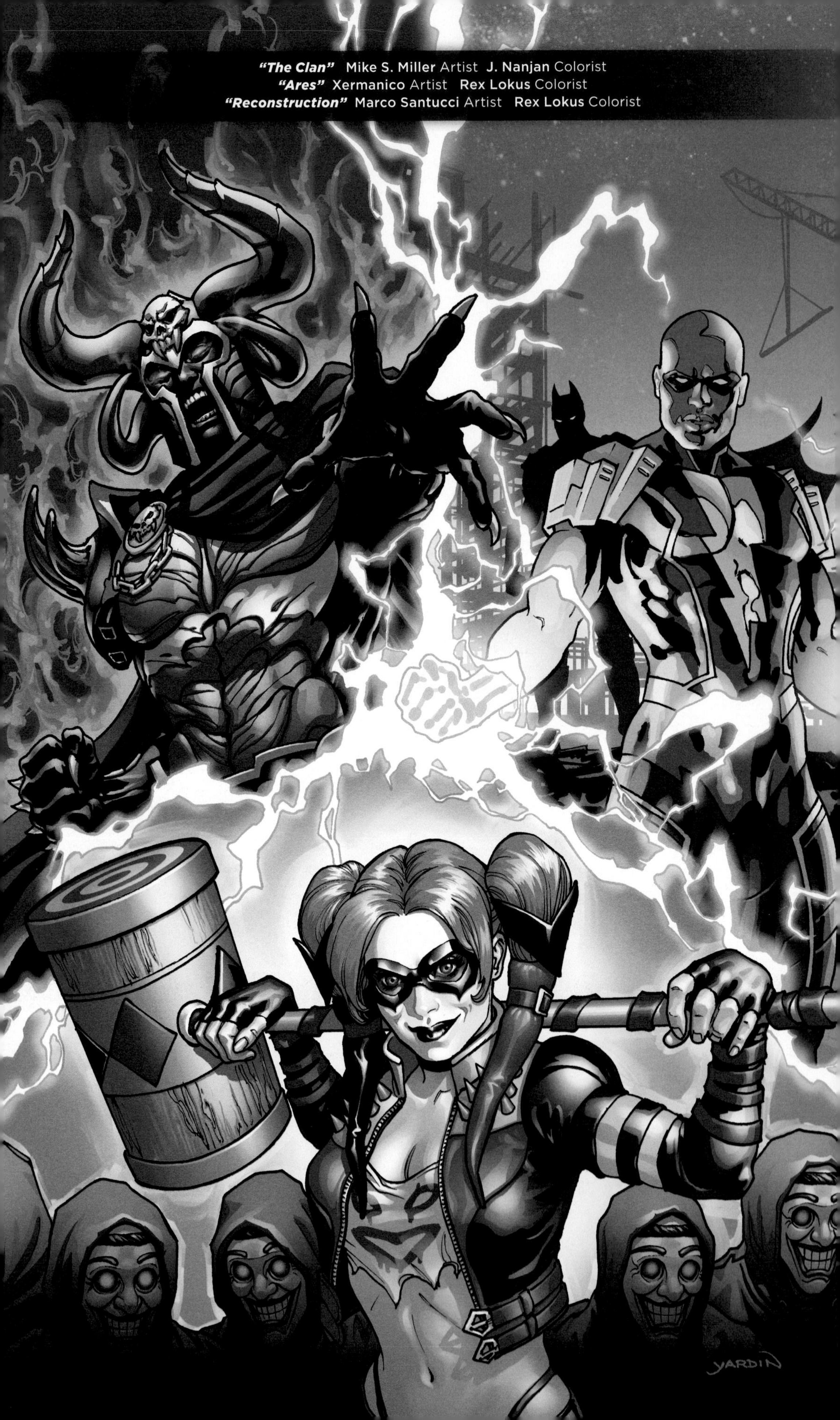
YARDIN

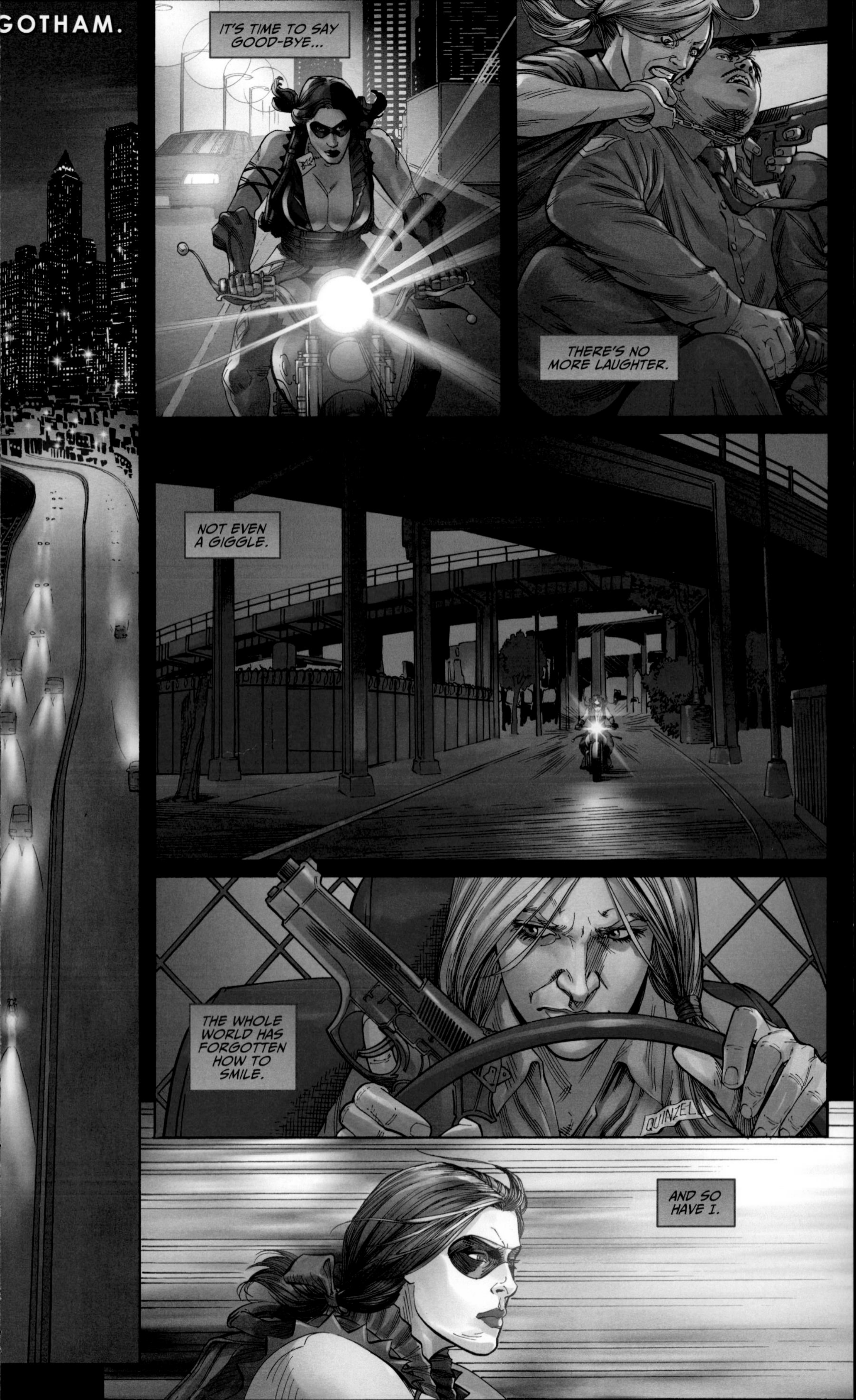
GOTHAM.
IT'S TIME TO SAY GOOD-BYE...
THERE'S NO MORE LAUGHTER.
NOT EVEN A GIGGLE.
THE WHOLE WORLD HAS FORGOTTEN HOW TO SMILE.
QUINZEL
AND SO HAVE I.

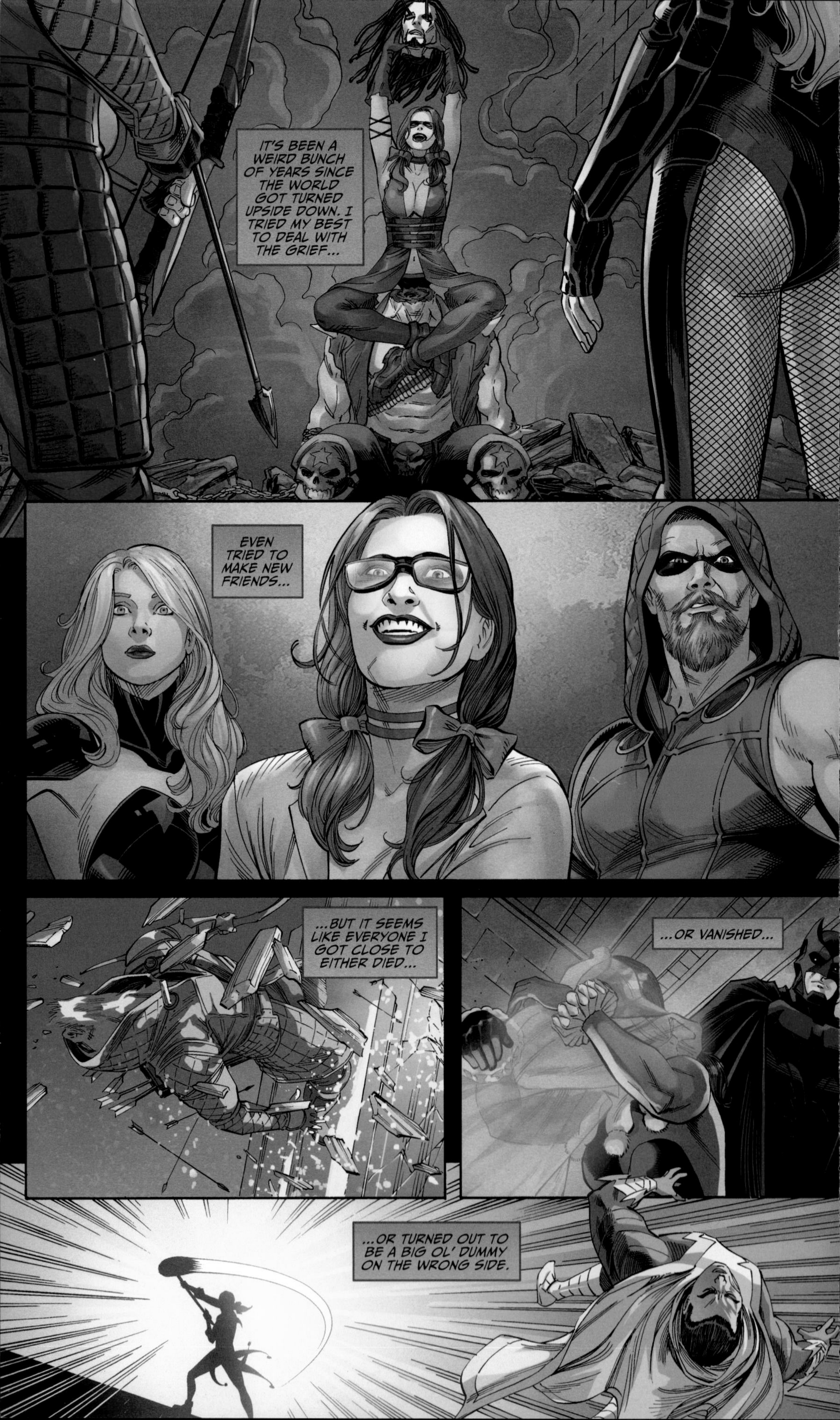
IT'S BEEN A WEIRD BUNCH OF YEARS SINCE THE WORLD GOT TURNED UPSIDE DOWN. I TRIED MY BEST TO DEAL WITH THE GRIEF...
EVEN TRIED TO MAKE NEW FRIENDS...
...BUT IT SEEMS LIKE EVERYONE I GOT CLOSE TO EITHER DIED...
...OR VANISHED...
...OR TURNED OUT TO BE A BIG OL' DUMMY ON THE WRONG SIDE.

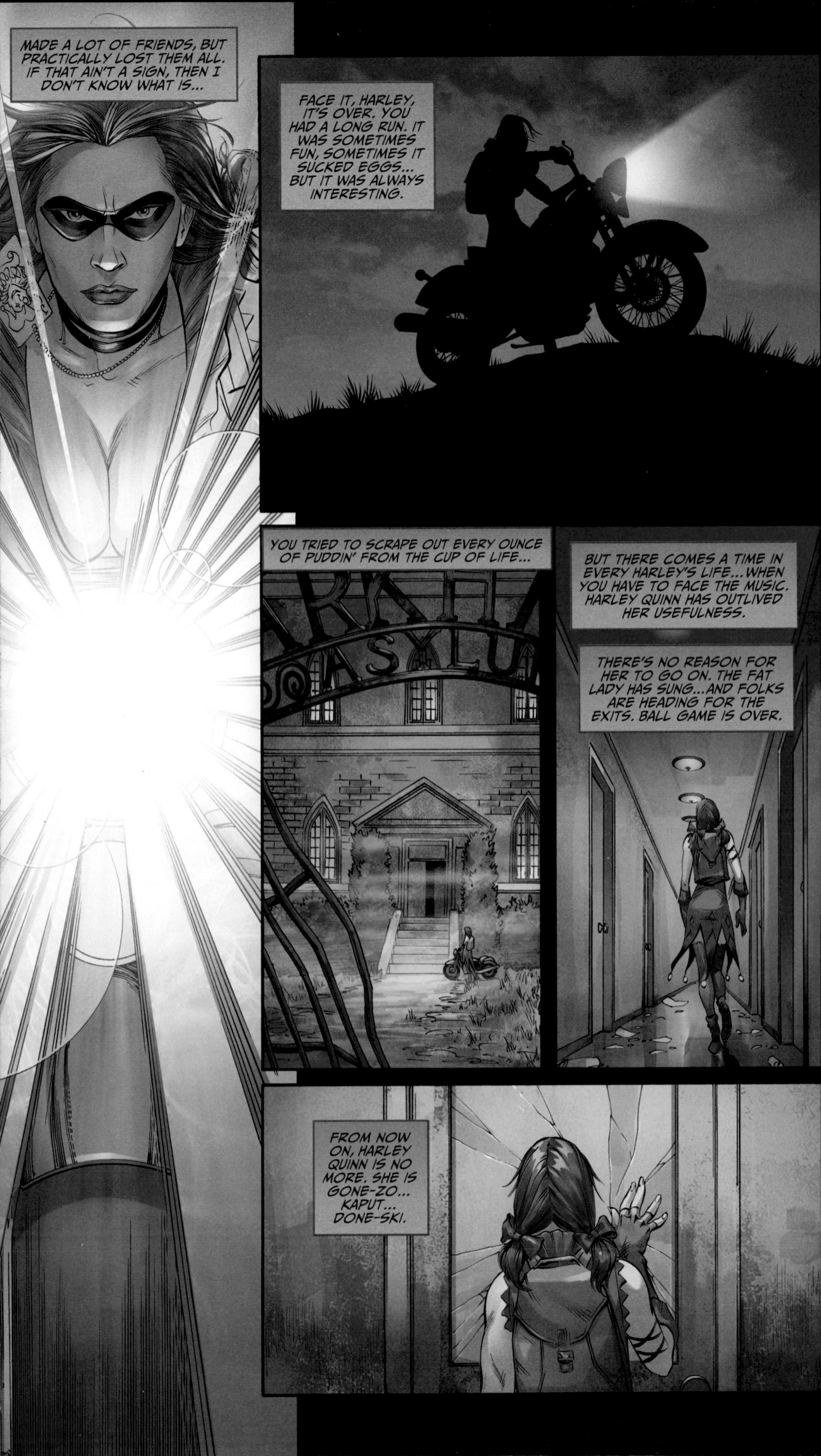
MADE A LOT OF FRIENDS, BUT PRACTICALLY LOST THEM ALL. IF THAT AIN'T A SIGN, THEN I DON'T KNOW WHAT IS...
FACE IT, HARLEY, IT'S OVER. YOU HAD A LONG RUN. IT WAS SOMETIMES FUN, SOMETIMES IT SUCKED EGGS... BUT IT WAS ALWAYS INTERESTING.
YOU TRIED TO SCRAPE OUT EVERY OUNCE OF PUDDIN' FROM THE CUP OF LIFE...
ASYLU
BUT THERE COMES A TIME IN EVERY HARLEY'S LIFE... WHEN YOU HAVE TO FACE THE MUSIC. HARLEY QUINN HAS OUTLIVED HER USEFULNESS.
THERE'S NO REASON FOR HER TO GO ON. THE FAT LADY HAS SUNG...AND FOLKS ARE HEADING FOR THE EXITS. BALL GAME IS OVER.
FROM NOW ON, HARLEY QUINN IS NO MORE. SHE IS GONE-ZO... KAPUT... DONE-SKI.

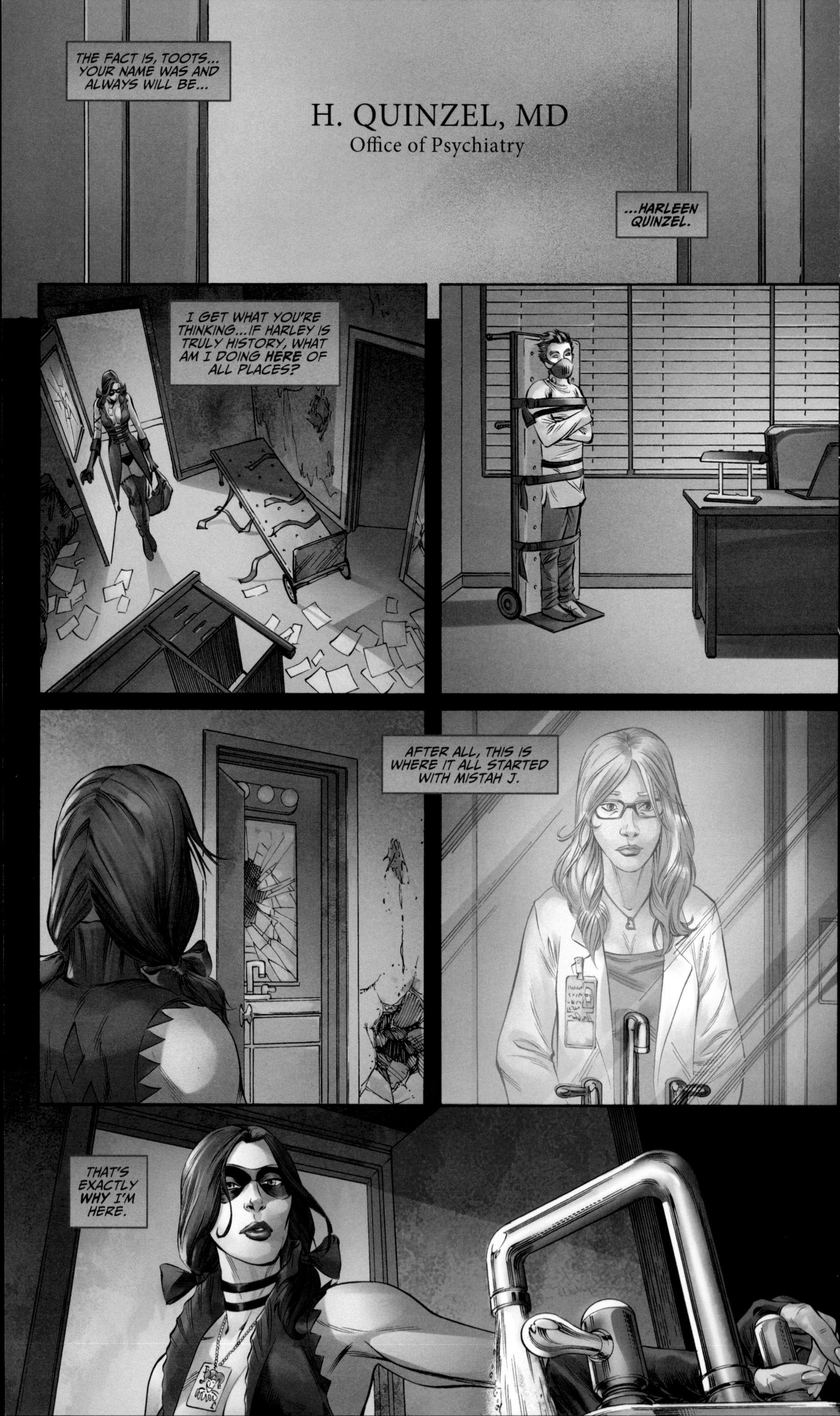
THE FACT IS, TOOTS... YOUR NAME WAS AND ALWAYS WILL BE...
H. QUINZEL, MD
Office of Psychiatry
...HARLEEN QUINZEL.
I GET WHAT YOU'RE THINKING...IF HARLEY IS TRULY HISTORY, WHAT AM I DOING HERE OF ALL PLACES?
AFTER ALL, THIS IS WHERE IT ALL STARTED WITH MISTAH J.
THAT'S EXACTLY WHY I'M HERE.

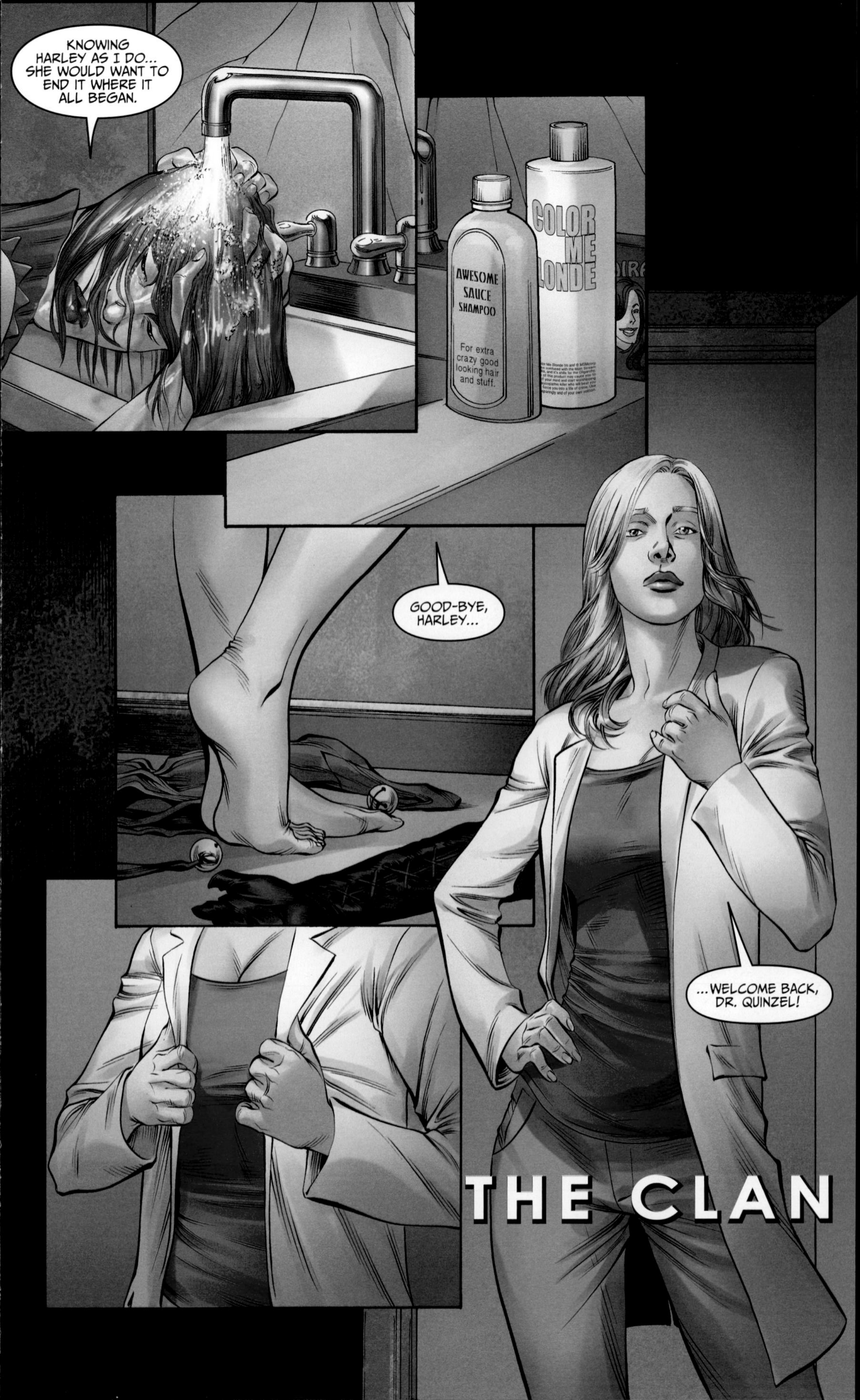
KNOWING HARLEY AS I DO... SHE WOULD WANT TO END IT WHERE IT ALL BEGAN.
AWESOME SAUCE SHAMPOO
For extra crazy good looking hair and stuff.
COLOR ME LONDE
GOOD-BYE, HARLEY...
...WELCOME BACK, DR. QUINZEL!
THE CLAN

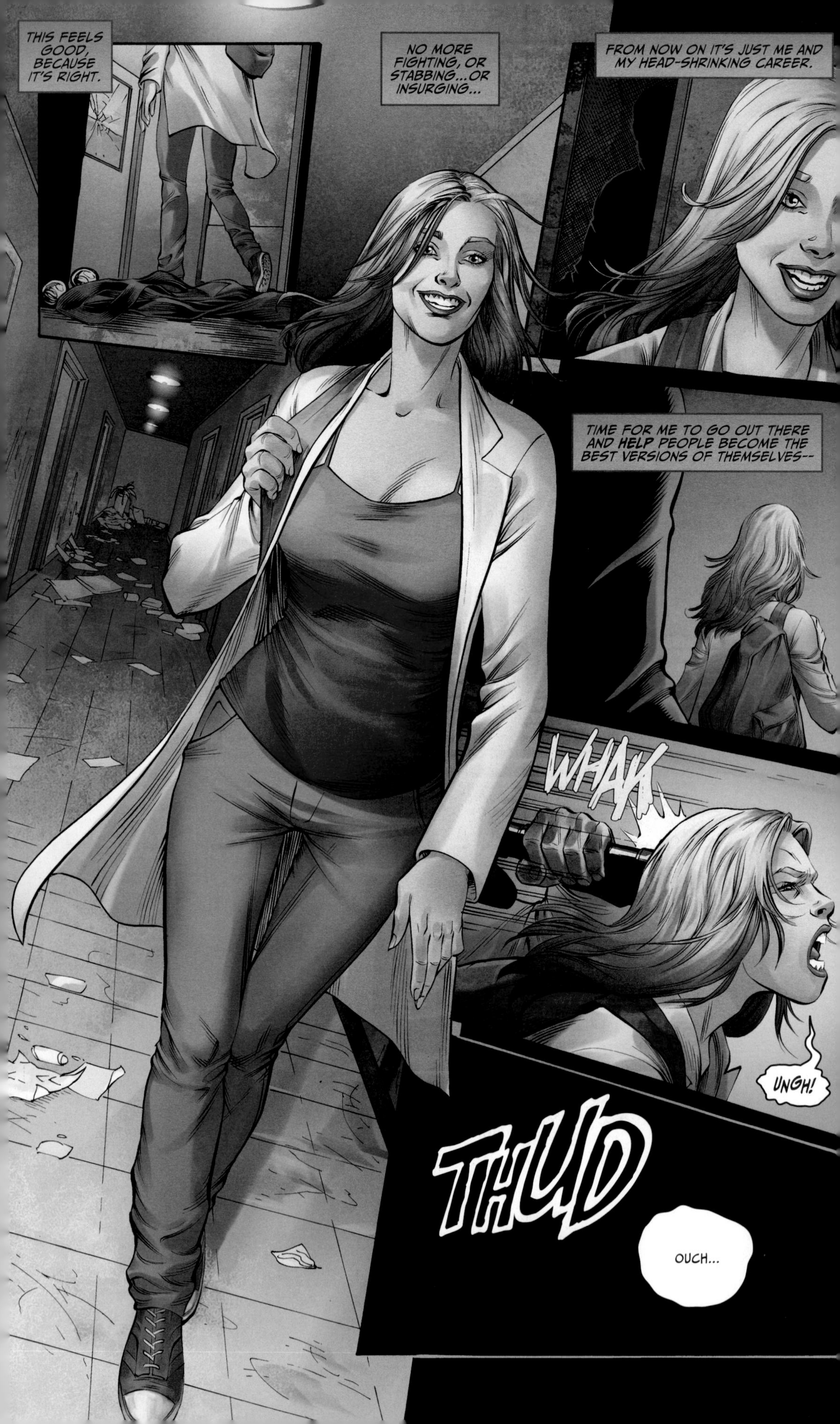

THIS FEELS GOOD, BECAUSE IT'S RIGHT.
NO MORE FIGHTING, OR STABBING...OR INSURGING...
FROM NOW ON IT'S JUST ME AND MY HEAD-SHRINKING CAREER.
TIME FOR ME TO GO OUT THERE AND HELP PEOPLE BECOME THE BEST VERSIONS OF THEMSELVES--
WHAK
UNGH!
THUD
OUCH...

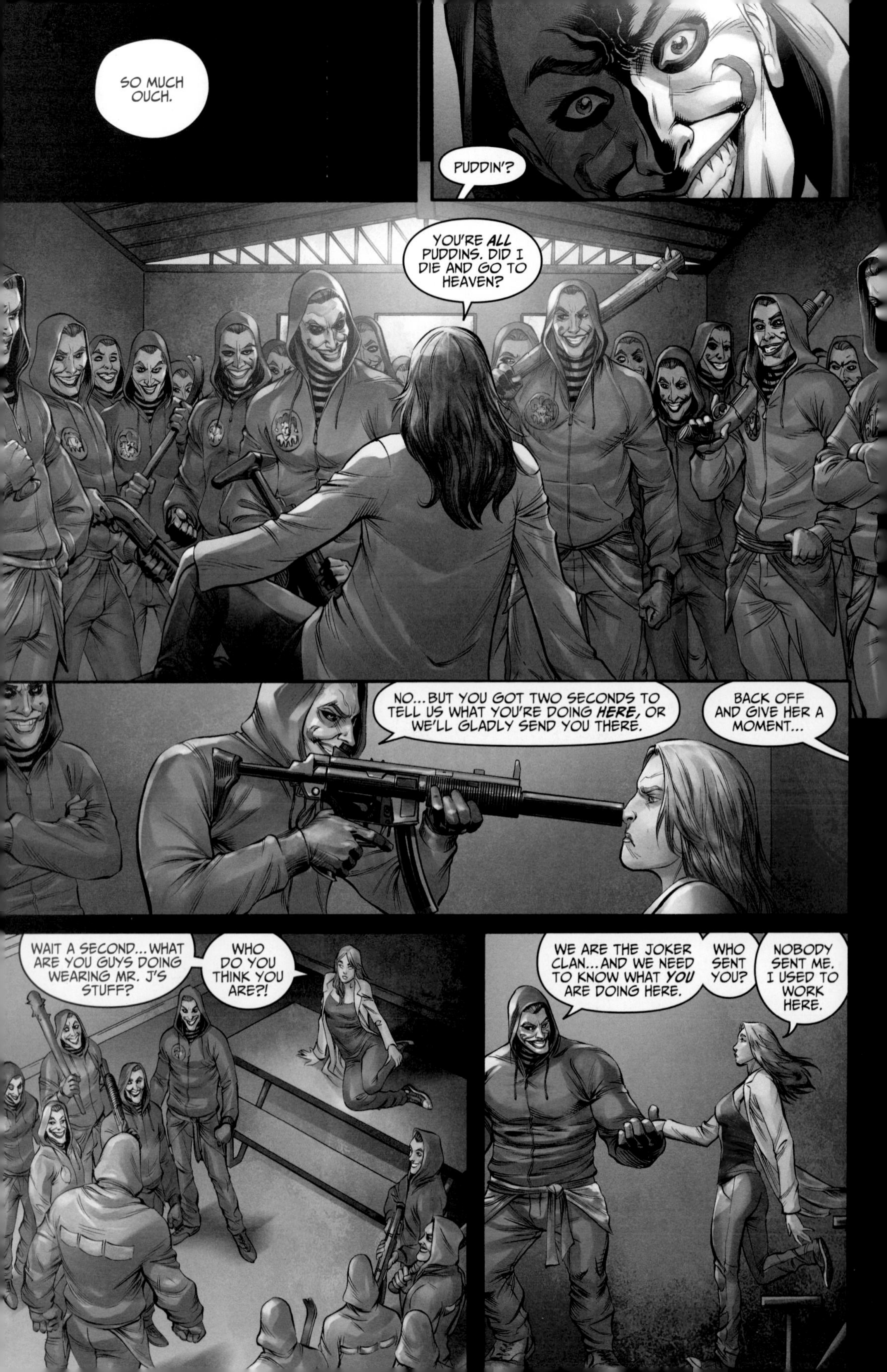
SO MUCH OUCH.
PUDDIN'?
YOU'RE **ALL** PUDDINS. DID I DIE AND GO TO HEAVEN?
NO... BUT YOU GOT TWO SECONDS TO TELL US WHAT YOU'RE DOING **HERE,** OR WE'LL GLADLY SEND YOU THERE.
BACK OFF AND GIVE HER A MOMENT...
WAIT A SECOND... WHAT ARE YOU GUYS DOING WEARING MR. J'S STUFF?
WHO DO YOU THINK YOU ARE?!
WE ARE THE JOKER CLAN... AND WE NEED TO KNOW WHAT **YOU** ARE DOING HERE.
WHO SENT YOU?
NOBODY SENT ME. I USED TO WORK HERE.

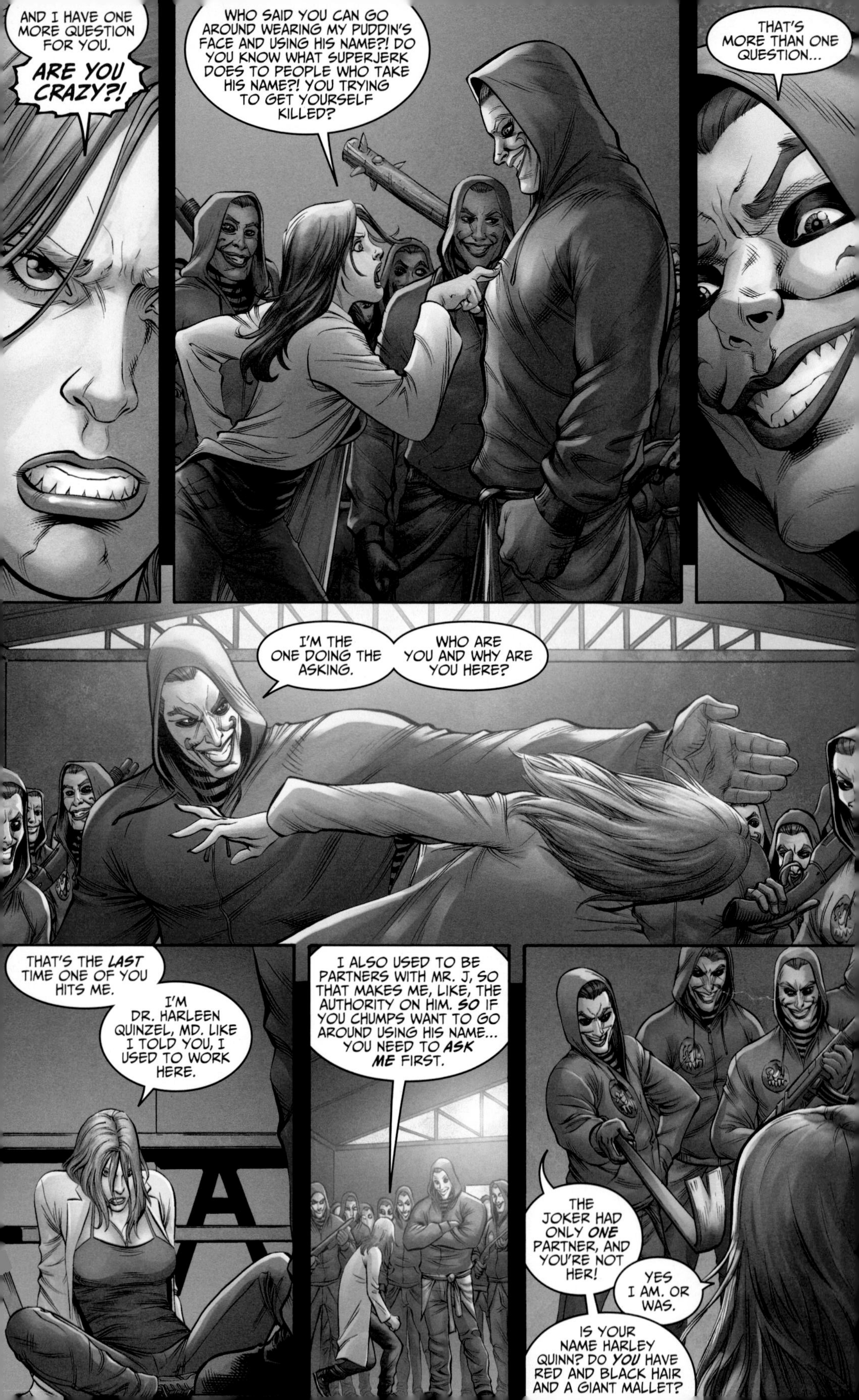
AND I HAVE ONE MORE QUESTION FOR YOU.
ARE YOU CRAZY?!
WHO SAID YOU CAN GO AROUND WEARING MY PUDDIN'S FACE AND USING HIS NAME?! DO YOU KNOW WHAT SUPERJERK DOES TO PEOPLE WHO TAKE HIS NAME?! YOU TRYING TO GET YOURSELF KILLED?
THAT'S MORE THAN ONE QUESTION...
I'M THE ONE DOING THE ASKING.
WHO ARE YOU AND WHY ARE YOU HERE?
THAT'S THE LAST TIME ONE OF YOU HITS ME.
I'M DR. HARLEEN QUINZEL, MD. LIKE I TOLD YOU, I USED TO WORK HERE.
I ALSO USED TO BE PARTNERS WITH MR. J, SO THAT MAKES ME, LIKE, THE AUTHORITY ON HIM. SO IF YOU CHUMPS WANT TO GO AROUND USING HIS NAME... YOU NEED TO ASK ME FIRST.
THE JOKER HAD ONLY ONE PARTNER, AND YOU'RE NOT HER!
YES I AM. OR WAS.
IS YOUR NAME HARLEY QUINN? DO YOU HAVE RED AND BLACK HAIR AND A GIANT MALLET?

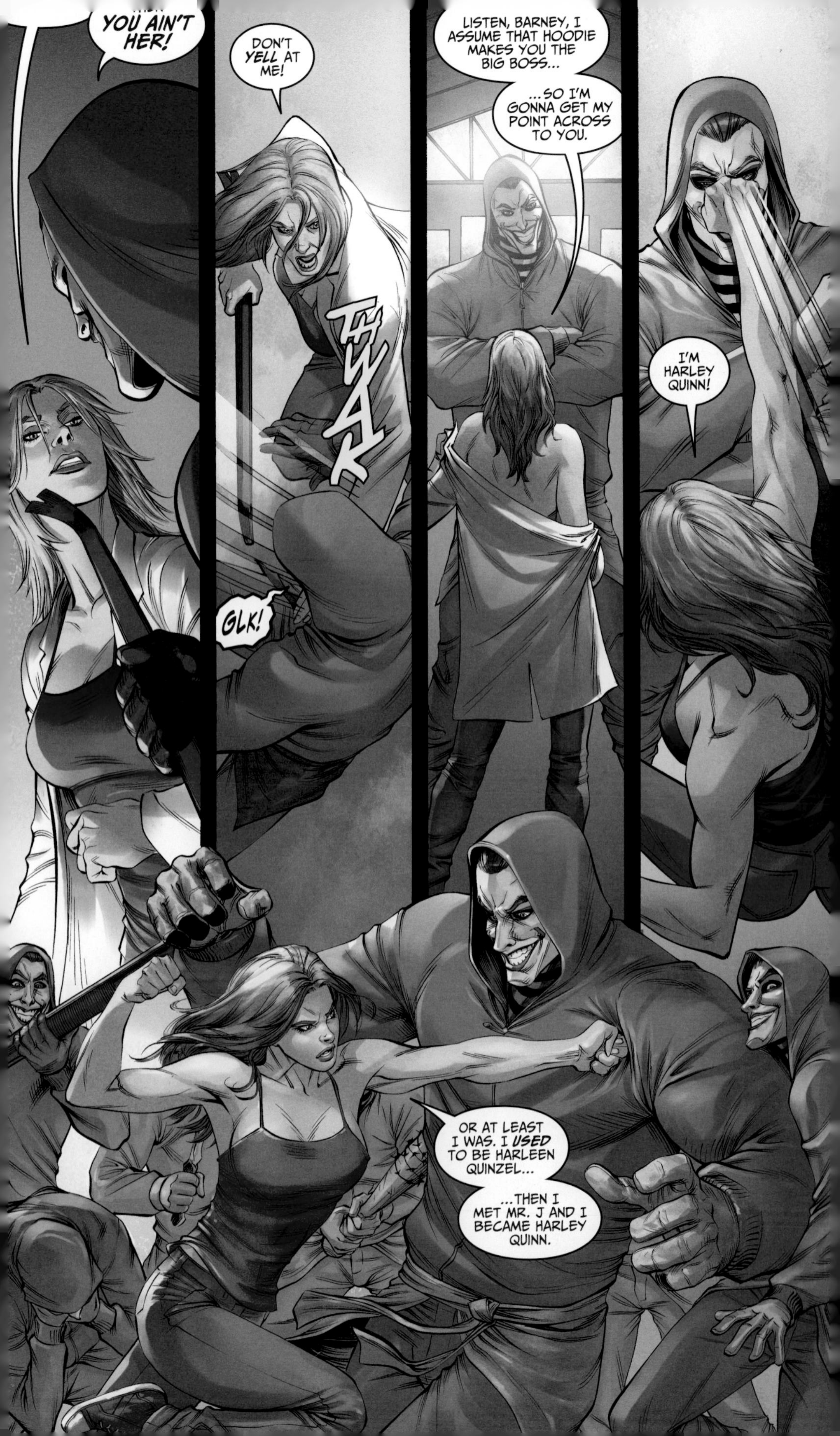
YOU AIN'T HER!
DON'T YELL AT ME!
THWAK
GLK!
LISTEN, BARNEY, I ASSUME THAT HOODIE MAKES YOU THE BIG BOSS...
...SO I'M GONNA GET MY POINT ACROSS TO YOU.
I'M HARLEY QUINN!
OR AT LEAST I WAS. I USED TO BE HARLEEN QUINZEL...
...THEN I MET MR. J AND I BECAME HARLEY QUINN.

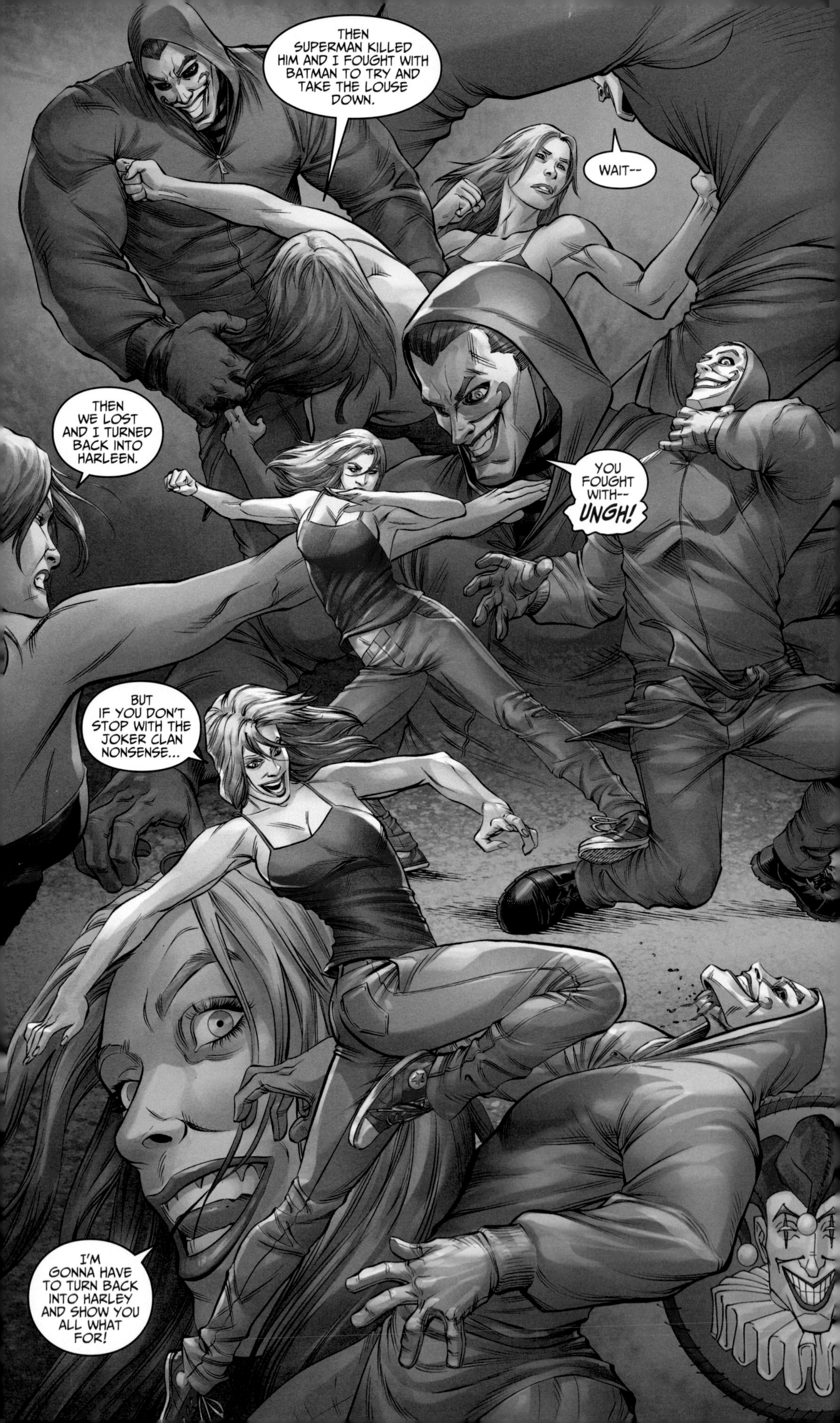
THEN SUPERMAN KILLED HIM AND I FOUGHT WITH BATMAN TO TRY AND TAKE THE LOUSE DOWN.
WAIT--
THEN WE LOST AND I TURNED BACK INTO HARLEEN.
YOU FOUGHT WITH-- UNGH!
BUT IF YOU DON'T STOP WITH THE JOKER CLAN NONSENSE...
I'M GONNA HAVE TO TURN BACK INTO HARLEY AND SHOW YOU ALL WHAT FOR!

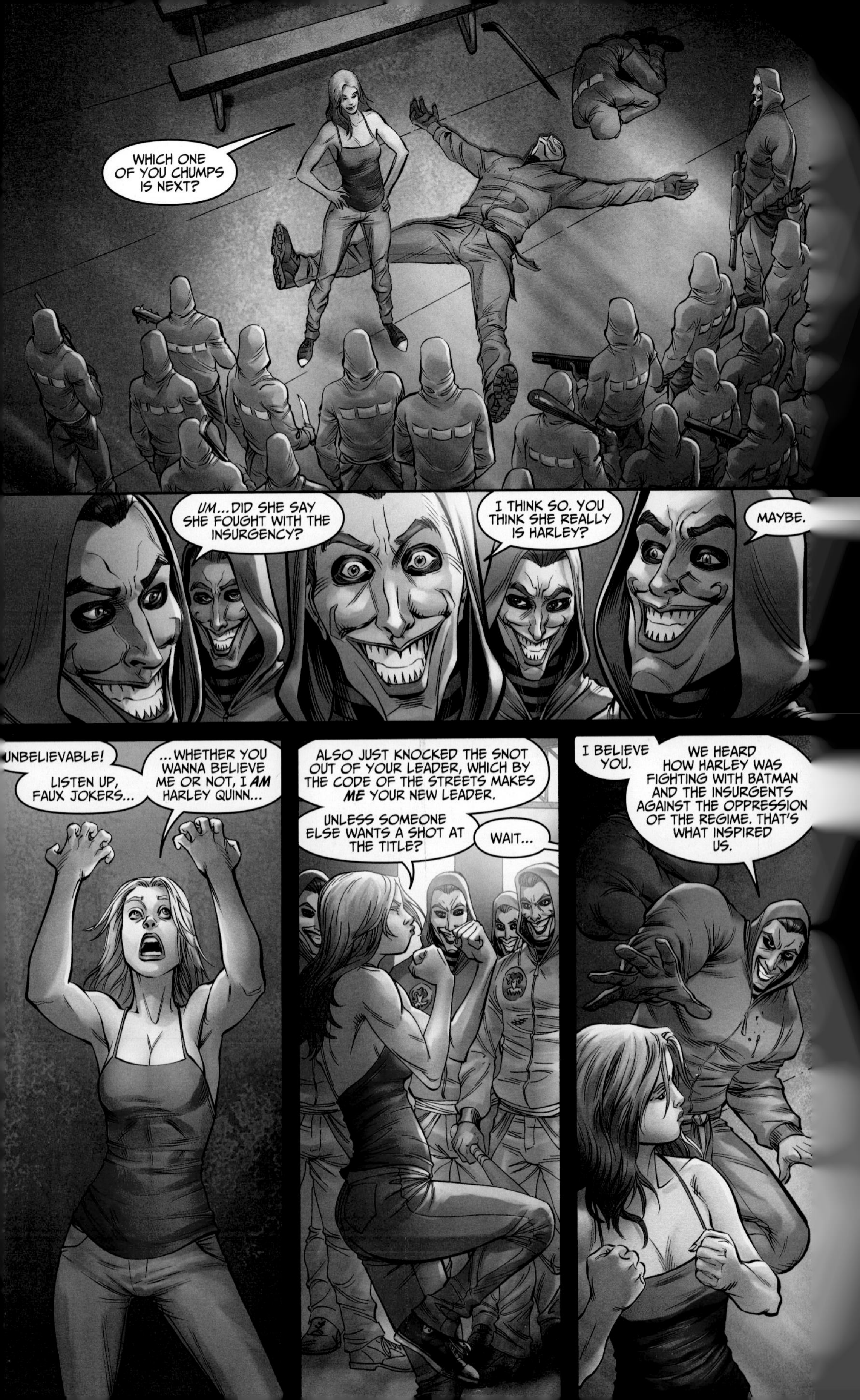
WHICH ONE OF YOU CHUMPS IS NEXT?
UM...DID SHE SAY SHE FOUGHT WITH THE INSURGENCY?
I THINK SO. YOU THINK SHE REALLY IS HARLEY?
MAYBE.
UNBELIEVABLE!
LISTEN UP, FAUX JOKERS...
...WHETHER YOU WANNA BELIEVE ME OR NOT, I AM HARLEY QUINN...
ALSO JUST KNOCKED THE SNOT OUT OF YOUR LEADER, WHICH BY THE CODE OF THE STREETS MAKES ME YOUR NEW LEADER.
UNLESS SOMEONE ELSE WANTS A SHOT AT THE TITLE?
WAIT...
I BELIEVE YOU.
WE HEARD HOW HARLEY WAS FIGHTING WITH BATMAN AND THE INSURGENTS AGAINST THE OPPRESSION OF THE REGIME. THAT'S WHAT INSPIRED US.

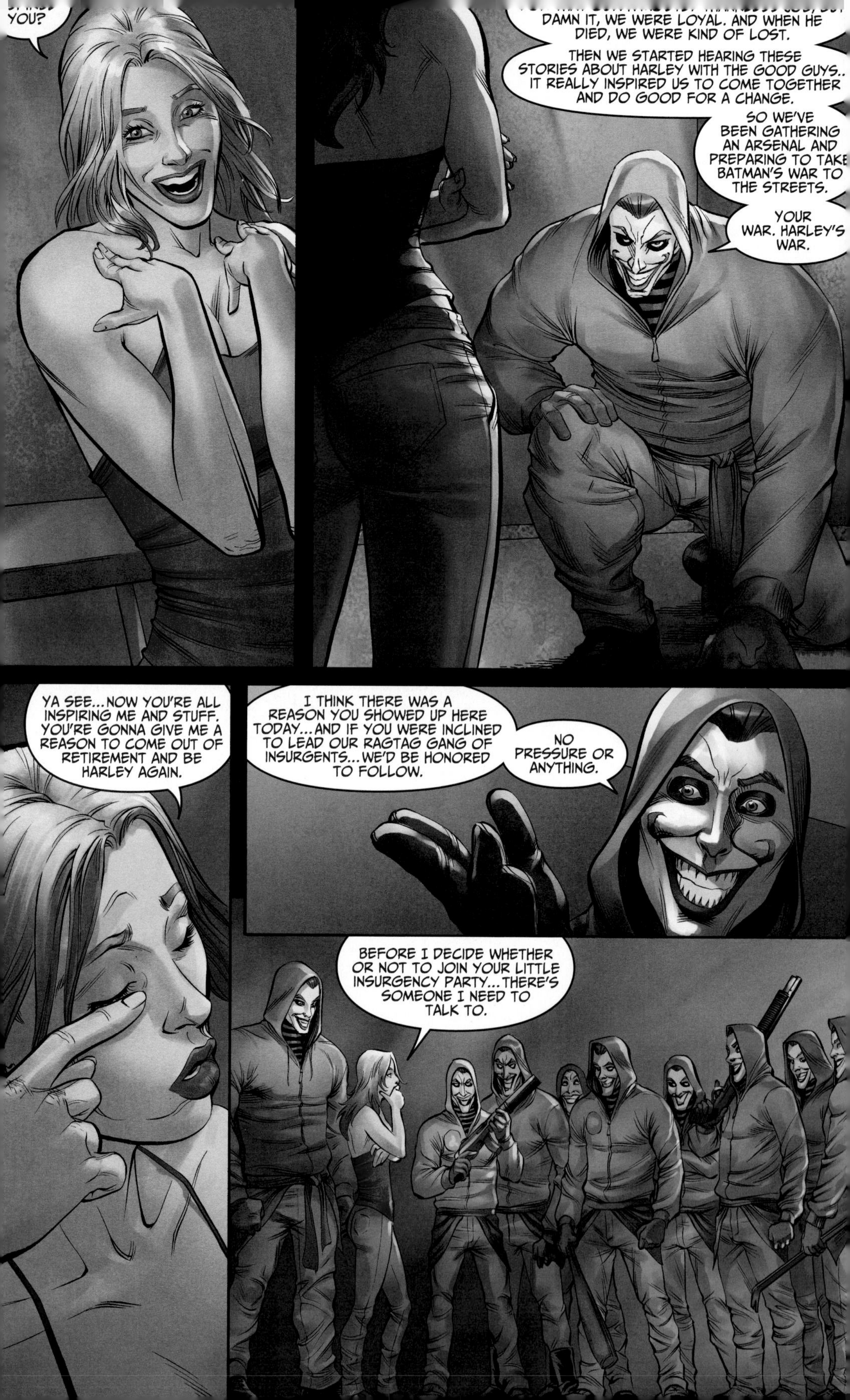
YOU?
DAMN IT, WE WERE LOYAL. AND WHEN HE DIED, WE WERE KIND OF LOST.
THEN WE STARTED HEARING THESE STORIES ABOUT HARLEY WITH THE GOOD GUYS... IT REALLY INSPIRED US TO COME TOGETHER AND DO GOOD FOR A CHANGE.
SO WE'VE BEEN GATHERING AN ARSENAL AND PREPARING TO TAKE BATMAN'S WAR TO THE STREETS.
YOUR WAR. HARLEY'S WAR.
YA SEE...NOW YOU'RE ALL INSPIRING ME AND STUFF. YOU'RE GONNA GIVE ME A REASON TO COME OUT OF RETIREMENT AND BE HARLEY AGAIN.
I THINK THERE WAS A REASON YOU SHOWED UP HERE TODAY...AND IF YOU WERE INCLINED TO LEAD OUR RAGTAG GANG OF INSURGENTS...WE'D BE HONORED TO FOLLOW.
NO PRESSURE OR ANYTHING.
BEFORE I DECIDE WHETHER OR NOT TO JOIN YOUR LITTLE INSURGENCY PARTY...THERE'S SOMEONE I NEED TO TALK TO.

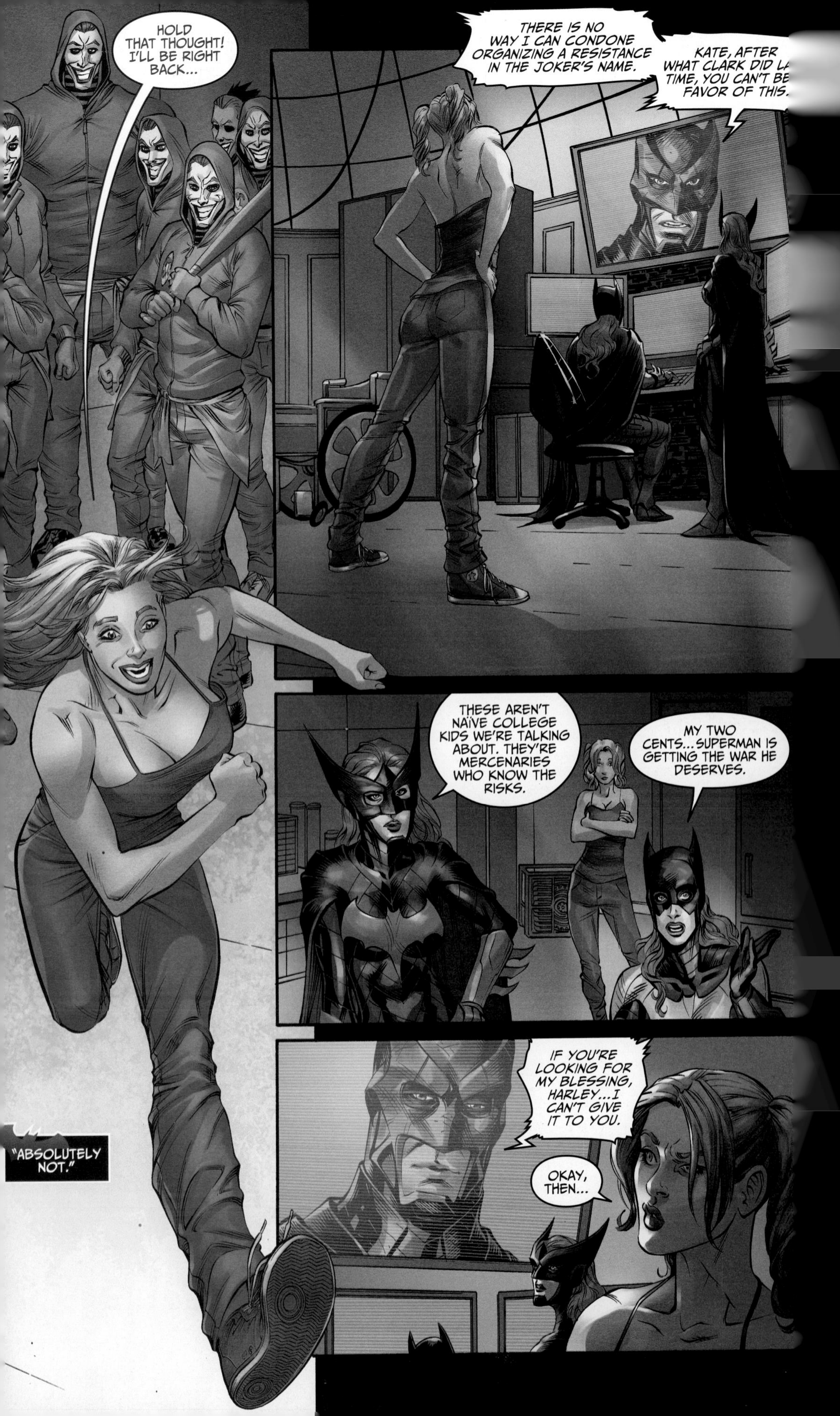
HOLD THAT THOUGHT! I'LL BE RIGHT BACK...
THERE IS NO WAY I CAN CONDONE ORGANIZING A RESISTANCE IN THE JOKER'S NAME.
KATE, AFTER WHAT CLARK DID LA TIME, YOU CAN'T BE FAVOR OF THIS.
THESE AREN'T NAÏVE COLLEGE KIDS WE'RE TALKING ABOUT. THEY'RE MERCENARIES WHO KNOW THE RISKS.
MY TWO CENTS...SUPERMAN IS GETTING THE WAR HE DESERVES.
IF YOU'RE LOOKING FOR MY BLESSING, HARLEY...I CAN'T GIVE IT TO YOU.
OKAY, THEN...
"ABSOLUTELY NOT."

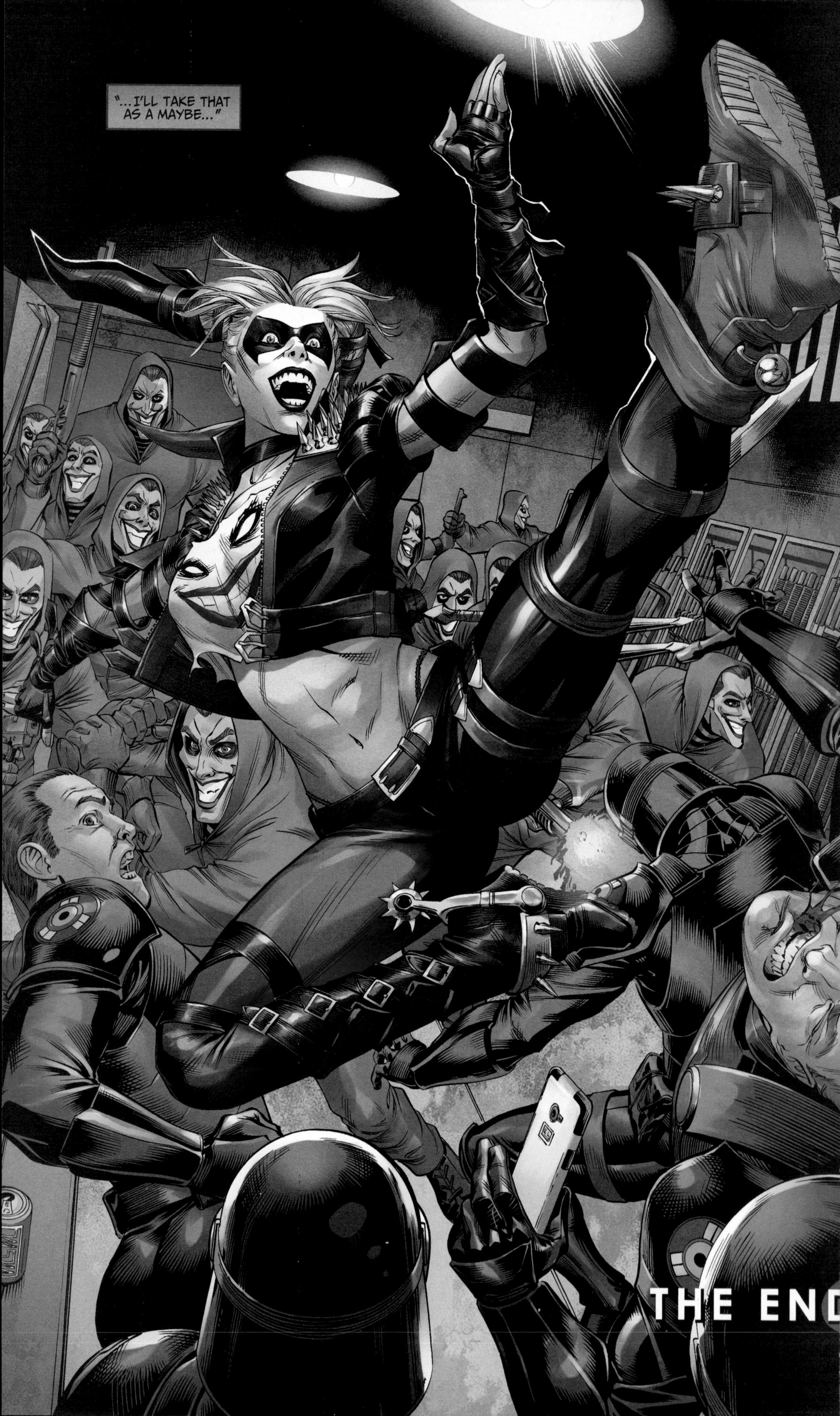
"...I'LL TAKE THAT AS A MAYBE..."
THE END

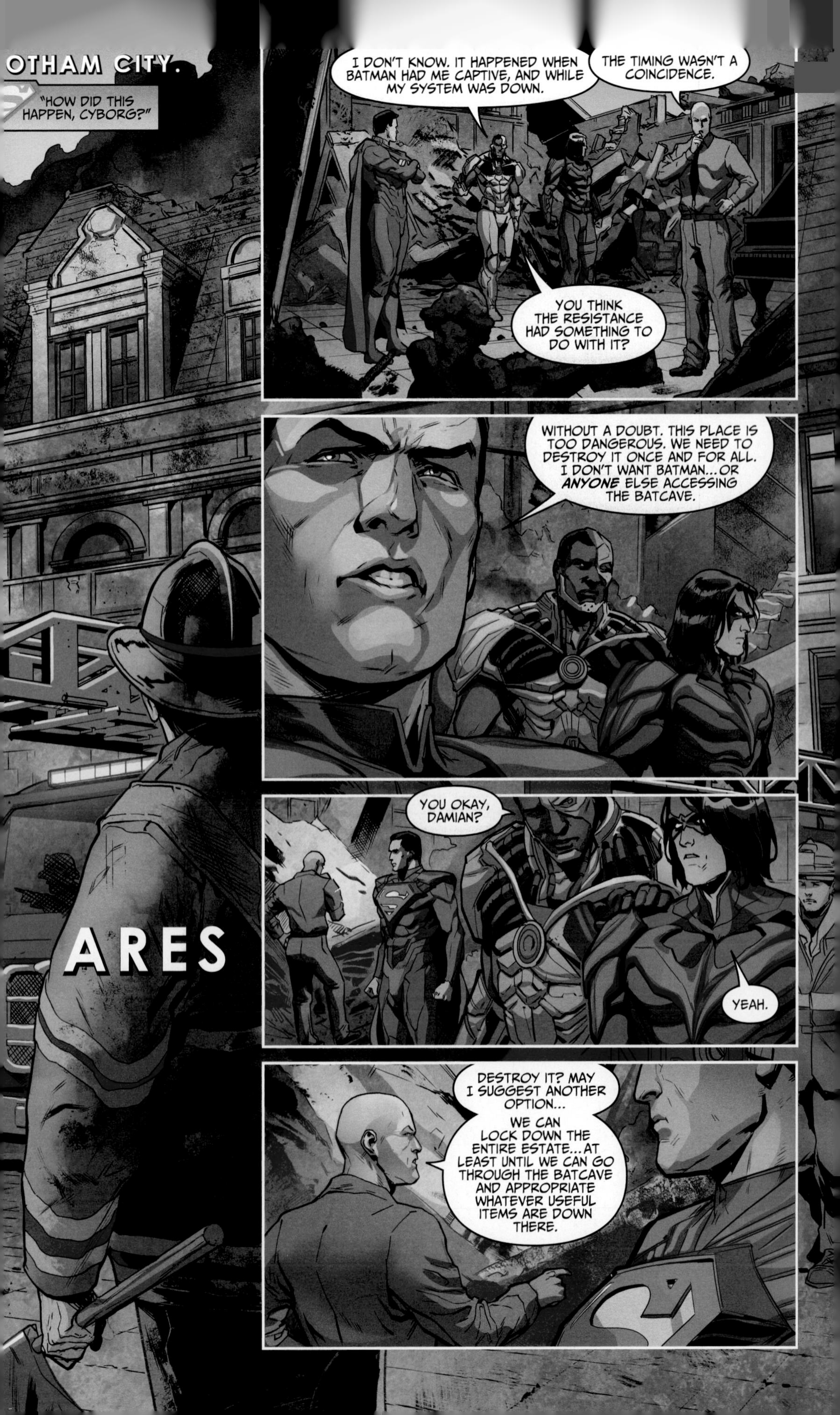

OTHAM CITY.
"HOW DID THIS HAPPEN, CYBORG?"
I DON'T KNOW. IT HAPPENED WHEN BATMAN HAD ME CAPTIVE, AND WHILE MY SYSTEM WAS DOWN.
THE TIMING WASN'T A COINCIDENCE.
YOU THINK THE RESISTANCE HAD SOMETHING TO DO WITH IT?
WITHOUT A DOUBT. THIS PLACE IS TOO DANGEROUS. WE NEED TO DESTROY IT ONCE AND FOR ALL. I DON'T WANT BATMAN...OR ANYONE ELSE ACCESSING THE BATCAVE.
YOU OKAY, DAMIAN?
YEAH.
DESTROY IT? MAY I SUGGEST ANOTHER OPTION...
WE CAN LOCK DOWN THE ENTIRE ESTATE...AT LEAST UNTIL WE CAN GO THROUGH THE BATCAVE AND APPROPRIATE WHATEVER USEFUL ITEMS ARE DOWN THERE.
ARES

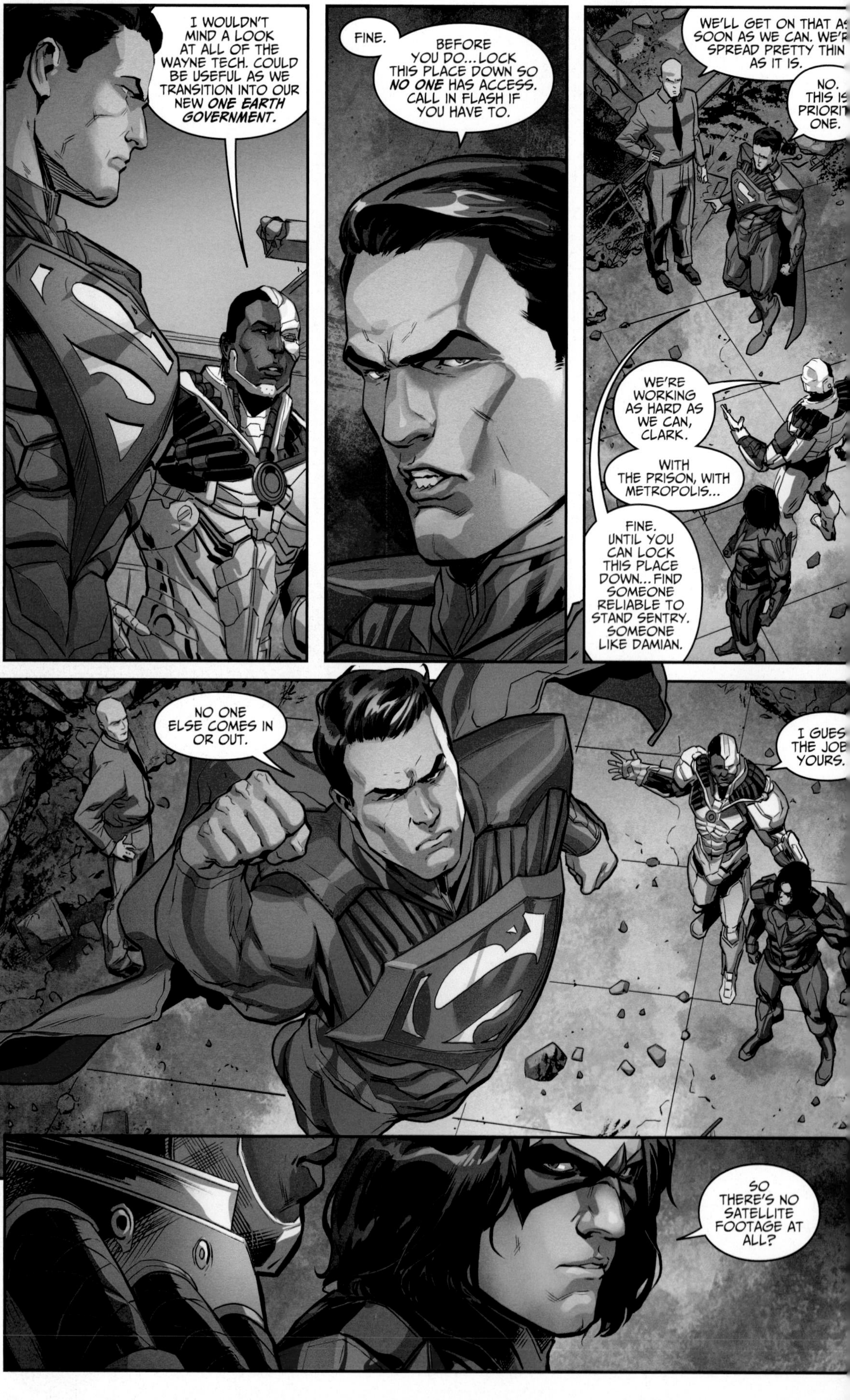
I WOULDN'T MIND A LOOK AT ALL OF THE WAYNE TECH. COULD BE USEFUL AS WE TRANSITION INTO OUR NEW ONE EARTH GOVERNMENT.
FINE.
BEFORE YOU DO...LOCK THIS PLACE DOWN SO NO ONE HAS ACCESS. CALL IN FLASH IF YOU HAVE TO.
WE'LL GET ON THAT AS SOON AS WE CAN. WE'RE SPREAD PRETTY THIN AS IT IS.
NO. THIS IS PRIORITY ONE.
WE'RE WORKING AS HARD AS WE CAN, CLARK.
WITH THE PRISON, WITH METROPOLIS...
FINE. UNTIL YOU CAN LOCK THIS PLACE DOWN...FIND SOMEONE RELIABLE TO STAND SENTRY. SOMEONE LIKE DAMIAN.
NO ONE ELSE COMES IN OR OUT.
I GUESS THE JOB'S YOURS.
SO THERE'S NO SATELLITE FOOTAGE AT ALL?

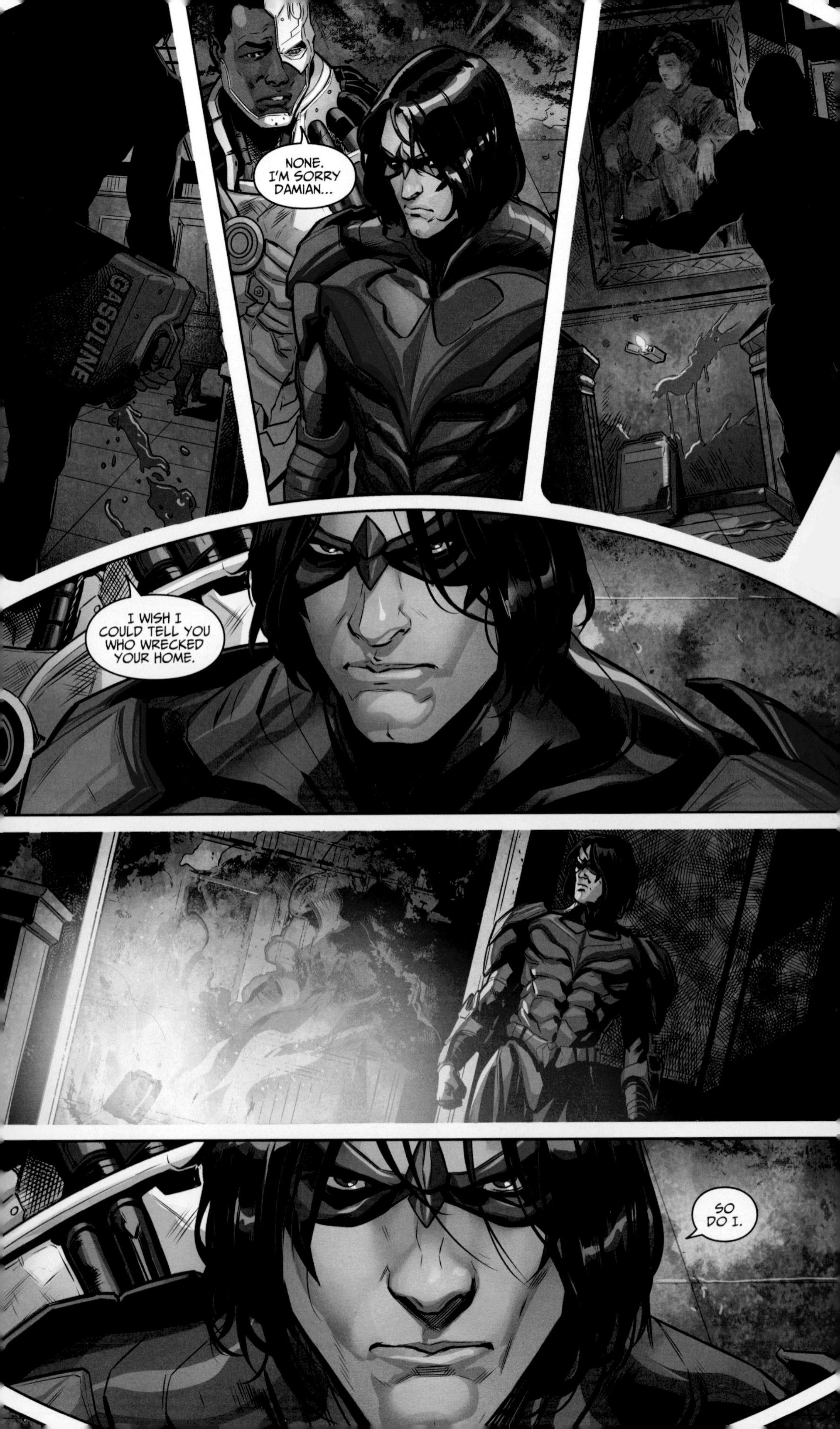
GASOLINE
NONE. I'M SORRY DAMIAN...
I WISH I COULD TELL YOU WHO WRECKED YOUR HOME.
SO DO I.

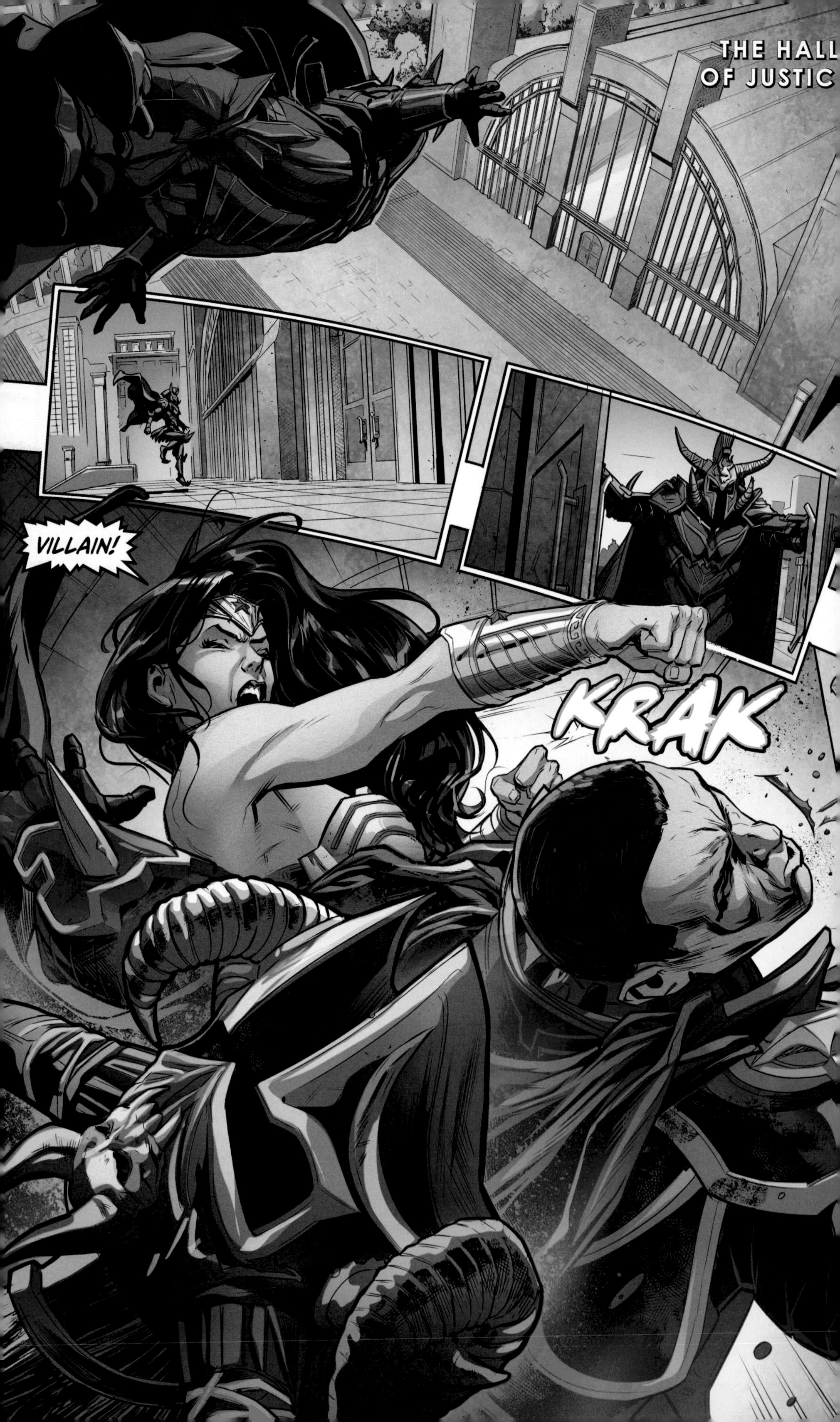
THE HALL
OF JUSTIC
VILLAIN!
KRAK

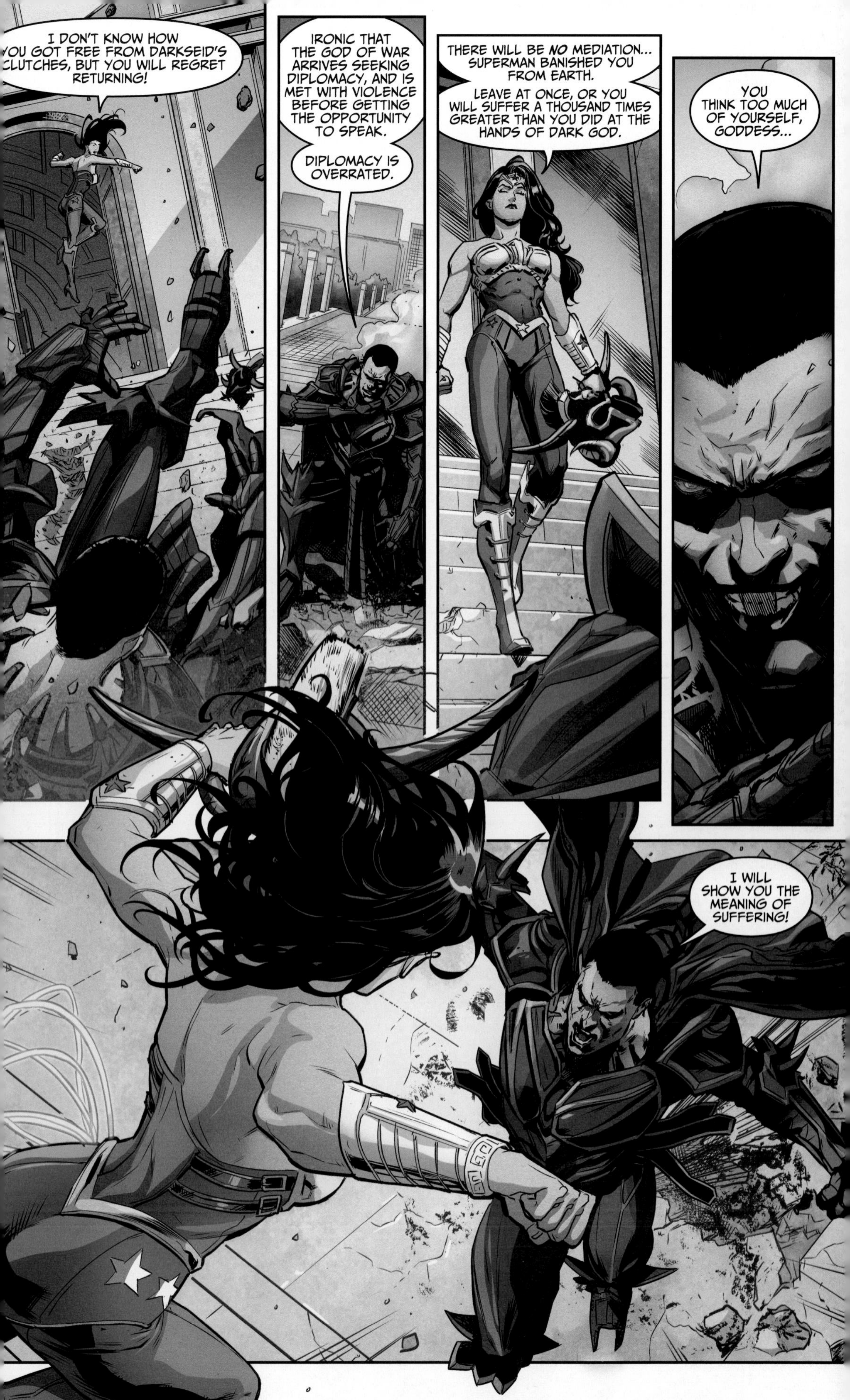

I DON'T KNOW HOW YOU GOT FREE FROM DARKSEID'S CLUTCHES, BUT YOU WILL REGRET RETURNING!
IRONIC THAT THE GOD OF WAR ARRIVES SEEKING DIPLOMACY, AND IS MET WITH VIOLENCE BEFORE GETTING THE OPPORTUNITY TO SPEAK.
DIPLOMACY IS OVERRATED.
THERE WILL BE *NO* MEDIATION... SUPERMAN BANISHED YOU FROM EARTH.
LEAVE AT ONCE, OR YOU WILL SUFFER A THOUSAND TIMES GREATER THAN YOU DID AT THE HANDS OF DARK GOD.
YOU THINK TOO MUCH OF YOURSELF, GODDESS...
I WILL SHOW YOU THE MEANING OF SUFFERING!

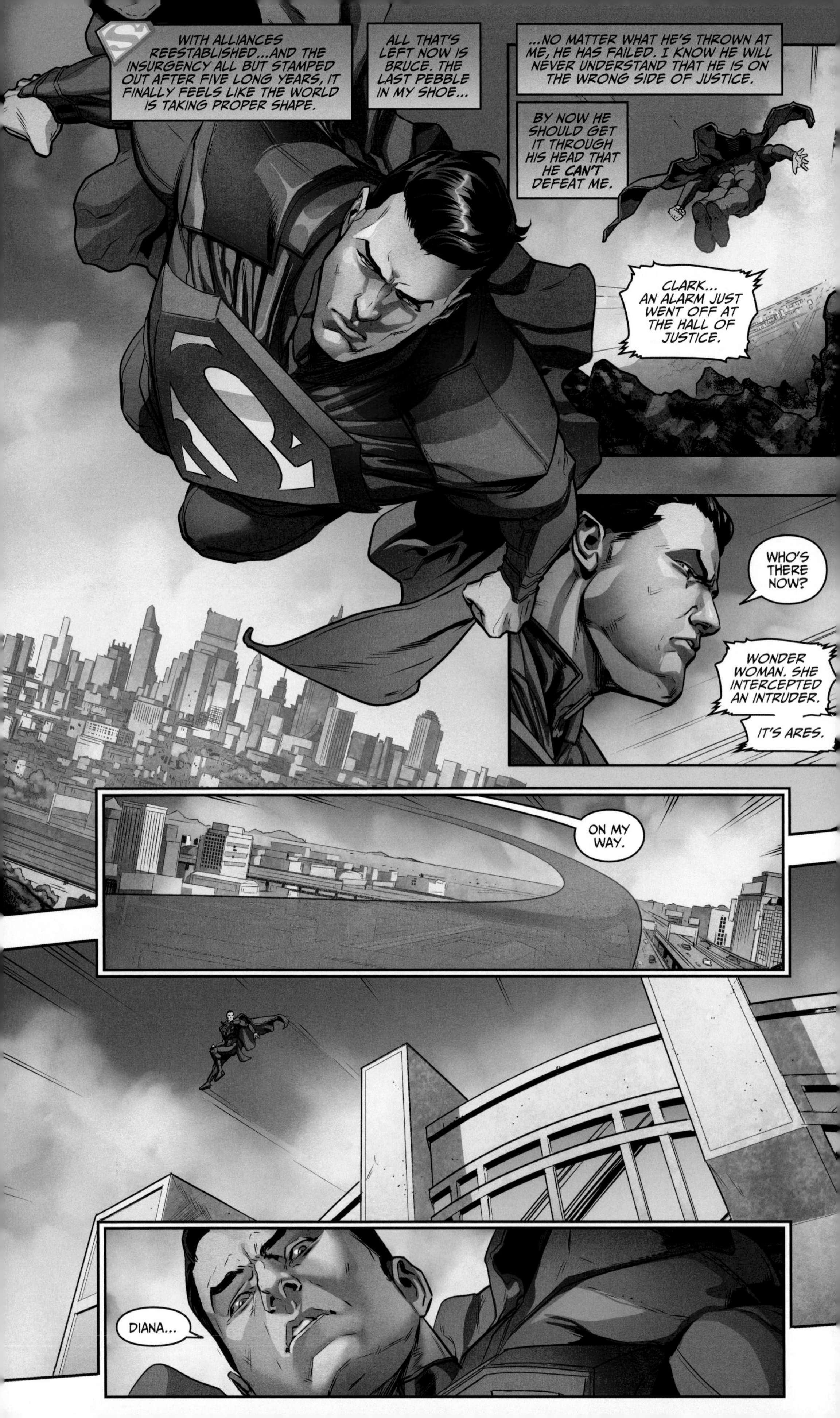
WITH ALLIANCES REESTABLISHED...AND THE INSURGENCY ALL BUT STAMPED OUT AFTER FIVE LONG YEARS, IT FINALLY FEELS LIKE THE WORLD IS TAKING PROPER SHAPE.
ALL THAT'S LEFT NOW IS BRUCE. THE LAST PEBBLE IN MY SHOE...
...NO MATTER WHAT HE'S THROWN AT ME, HE HAS FAILED. I KNOW HE WILL NEVER UNDERSTAND THAT HE IS ON THE WRONG SIDE OF JUSTICE.
BY NOW HE SHOULD GET IT THROUGH HIS HEAD THAT HE CAN'T DEFEAT ME.
CLARK... AN ALARM JUST WENT OFF AT THE HALL OF JUSTICE.
WHO'S THERE NOW?
WONDER WOMAN. SHE INTERCEPTED AN INTRUDER.
IT'S ARES.
ON MY WAY.
DIANA...

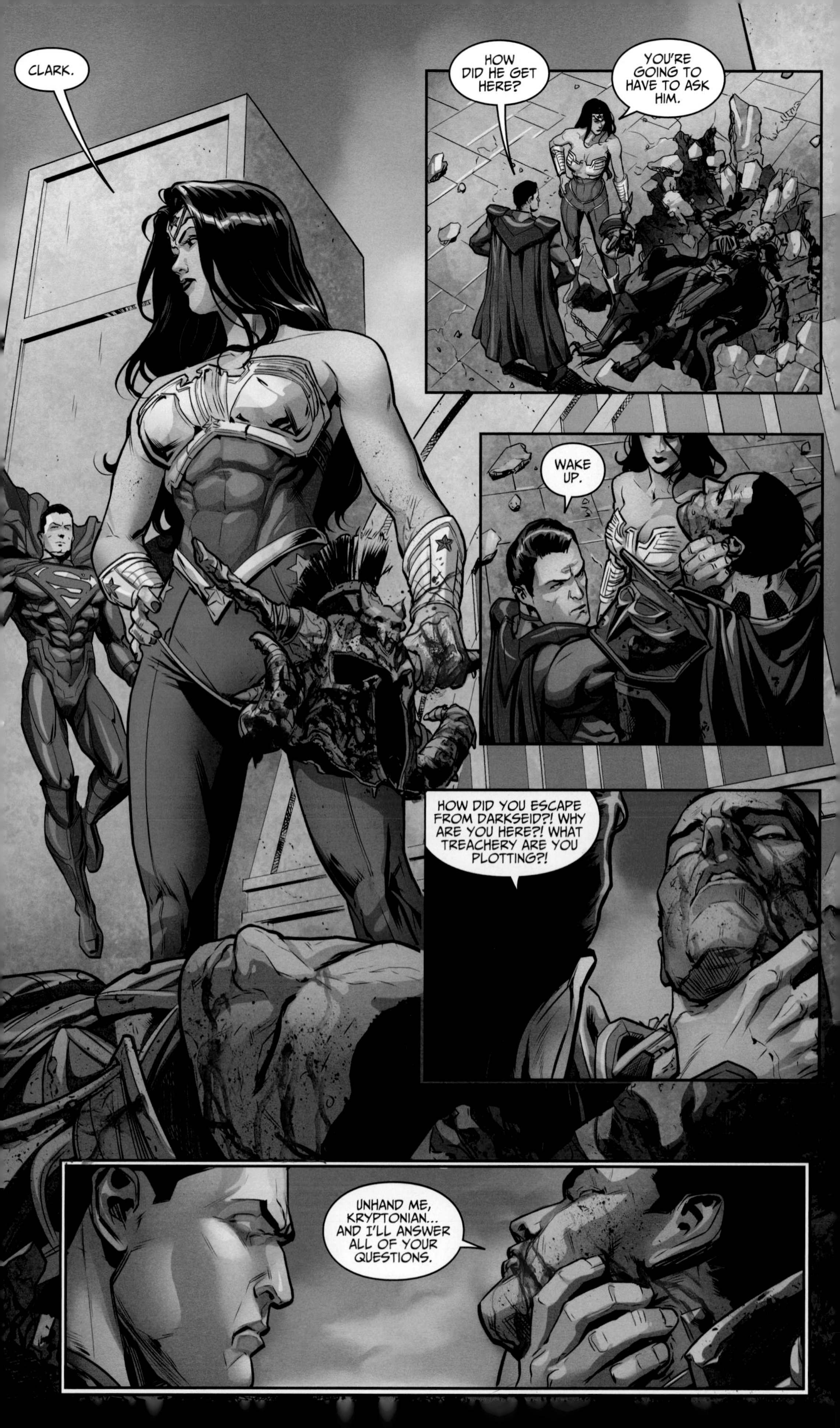
CLARK.
HOW DID HE GET HERE?
YOU'RE GOING TO HAVE TO ASK HIM.
WAKE UP.
HOW DID YOU ESCAPE FROM DARKSEID?! WHY ARE YOU HERE?! WHAT TREACHERY ARE YOU PLOTTING?!
UNHAND ME, KRYPTONIAN... AND I'LL ANSWER ALL OF YOUR QUESTIONS.

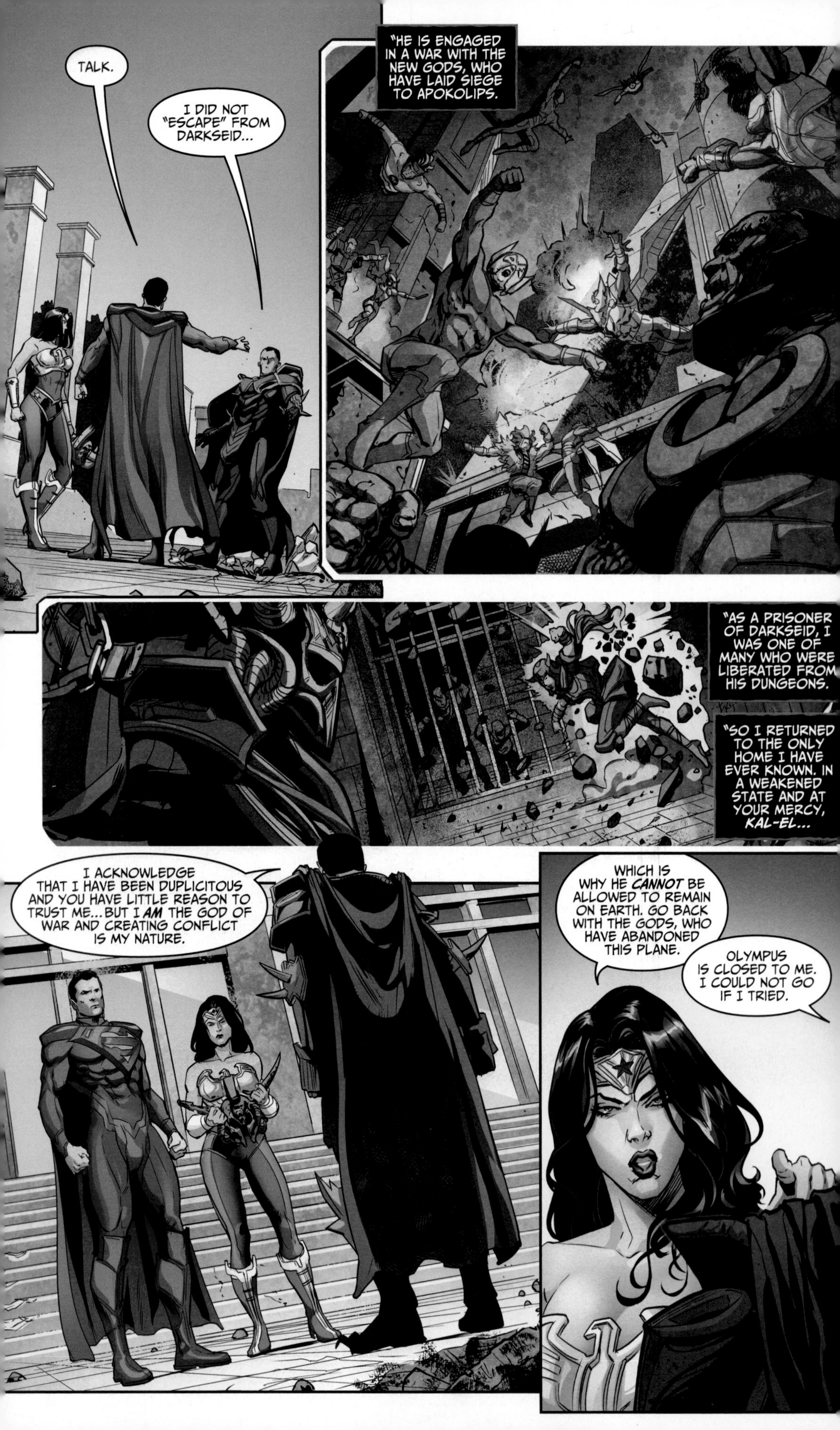

TALK.
I DID NOT "ESCAPE" FROM DARKSEID...
"HE IS ENGAGED IN A WAR WITH THE NEW GODS, WHO HAVE LAID SIEGE TO APOKOLIPS.
"AS A PRISONER OF DARKSEID, I WAS ONE OF MANY WHO WERE LIBERATED FROM HIS DUNGEONS.
"SO I RETURNED TO THE ONLY HOME I HAVE EVER KNOWN. IN A WEAKENED STATE AND AT YOUR MERCY, *KAL-EL*...
I ACKNOWLEDGE THAT I HAVE BEEN DUPLICITOUS AND YOU HAVE LITTLE REASON TO TRUST ME...BUT I *AM* THE GOD OF WAR AND CREATING CONFLICT IS MY NATURE.
WHICH IS WHY HE *CANNOT* BE ALLOWED TO REMAIN ON EARTH. GO BACK WITH THE GODS, WHO HAVE ABANDONED THIS PLANE.
OLYMPUS IS CLOSED TO ME. I COULD NOT GO IF I TRIED.

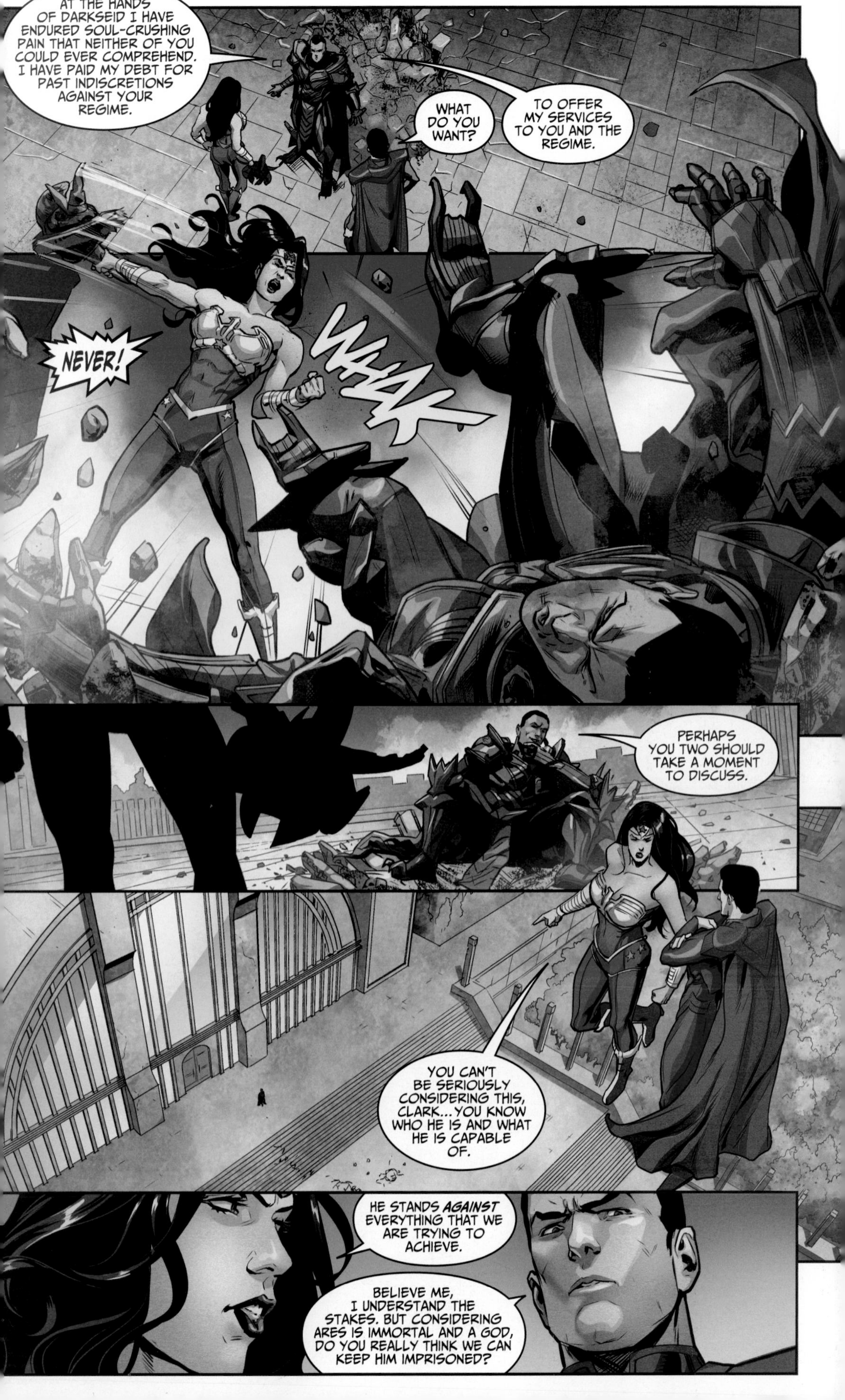
AT THE HANDS OF DARKSEID I HAVE ENDURED SOUL-CRUSHING PAIN THAT NEITHER OF YOU COULD EVER COMPREHEND. I HAVE PAID MY DEBT FOR PAST INDISCRETIONS AGAINST YOUR REGIME.
WHAT DO YOU WANT?
TO OFFER MY SERVICES TO YOU AND THE REGIME.
NEVER!
WHAK
PERHAPS YOU TWO SHOULD TAKE A MOMENT TO DISCUSS.
YOU CAN'T BE SERIOUSLY CONSIDERING THIS, CLARK... YOU KNOW WHO HE IS AND WHAT HE IS CAPABLE OF.
HE STANDS *AGAINST* EVERYTHING THAT WE ARE TRYING TO ACHIEVE.
BELIEVE ME, I UNDERSTAND THE STAKES. BUT CONSIDERING ARES IS IMMORTAL AND A GOD, DO YOU REALLY THINK WE CAN KEEP HIM IMPRISONED?

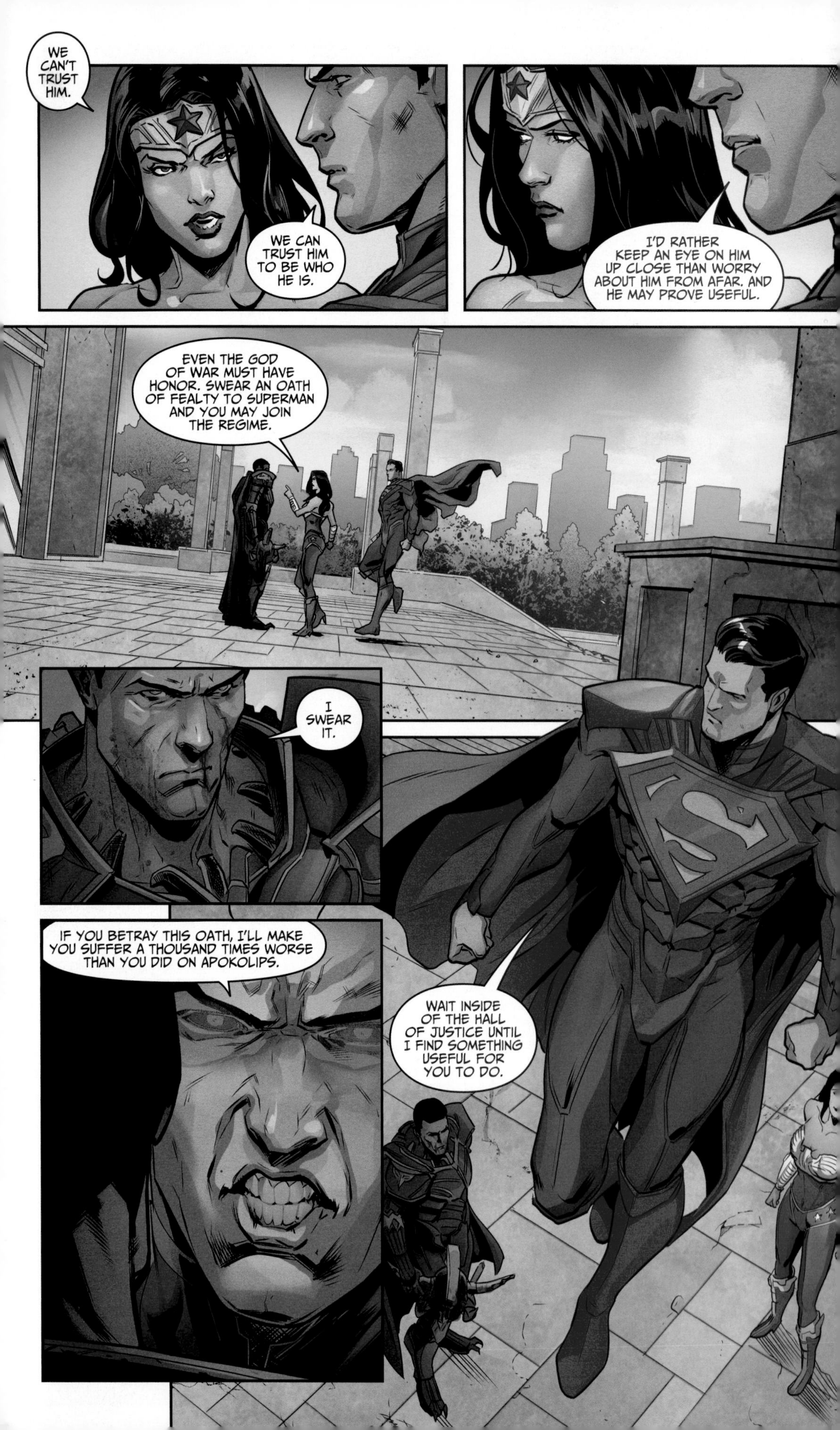
WE CAN'T TRUST HIM.
WE CAN TRUST HIM TO BE WHO HE IS.
I'D RATHER KEEP AN EYE ON HIM UP CLOSE THAN WORRY ABOUT HIM FROM AFAR. AND HE MAY PROVE USEFUL.
EVEN THE GOD OF WAR MUST HAVE HONOR. SWEAR AN OATH OF FEALTY TO SUPERMAN AND YOU MAY JOIN THE REGIME.
I SWEAR IT.
IF YOU BETRAY THIS OATH, I'LL MAKE YOU SUFFER A THOUSAND TIMES WORSE THAN YOU DID ON APOKOLIPS.
WAIT INSIDE OF THE HALL OF JUSTICE UNTIL I FIND SOMETHING USEFUL FOR YOU TO DO.

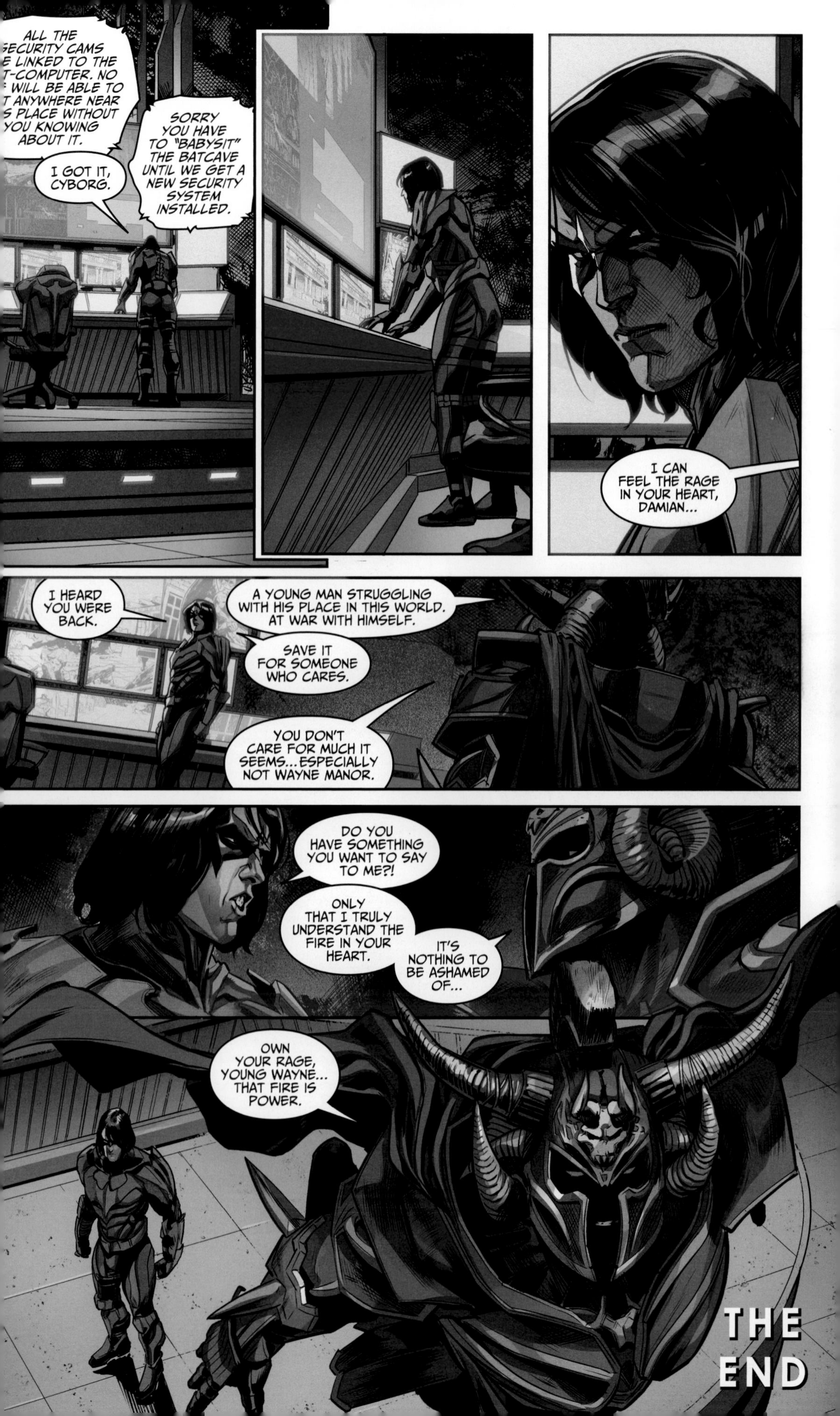

ALL THE
ECURITY CAMS
E LINKED TO THE
T-COMPUTER. NO
E WILL BE ABLE TO
T ANYWHERE NEAR
S PLACE WITHOUT
YOU KNOWING
ABOUT IT.
SORRY YOU HAVE TO "BABYSIT" THE BATCAVE UNTIL WE GET A NEW SECURITY SYSTEM INSTALLED.
I GOT IT, CYBORG.
I CAN FEEL THE RAGE IN YOUR HEART, DAMIAN...
I HEARD YOU WERE BACK.
A YOUNG MAN STRUGGLING WITH HIS PLACE IN THIS WORLD. AT WAR WITH HIMSELF.
SAVE IT FOR SOMEONE WHO CARES.
YOU DON'T CARE FOR MUCH IT SEEMS...ESPECIALLY NOT WAYNE MANOR.
DO YOU HAVE SOMETHING YOU WANT TO SAY TO ME?!
ONLY THAT I TRULY UNDERSTAND THE FIRE IN YOUR HEART.
IT'S NOTHING TO BE ASHAMED OF...
OWN YOUR RAGE, YOUNG WAYNE... THAT FIRE IS POWER.
THE END

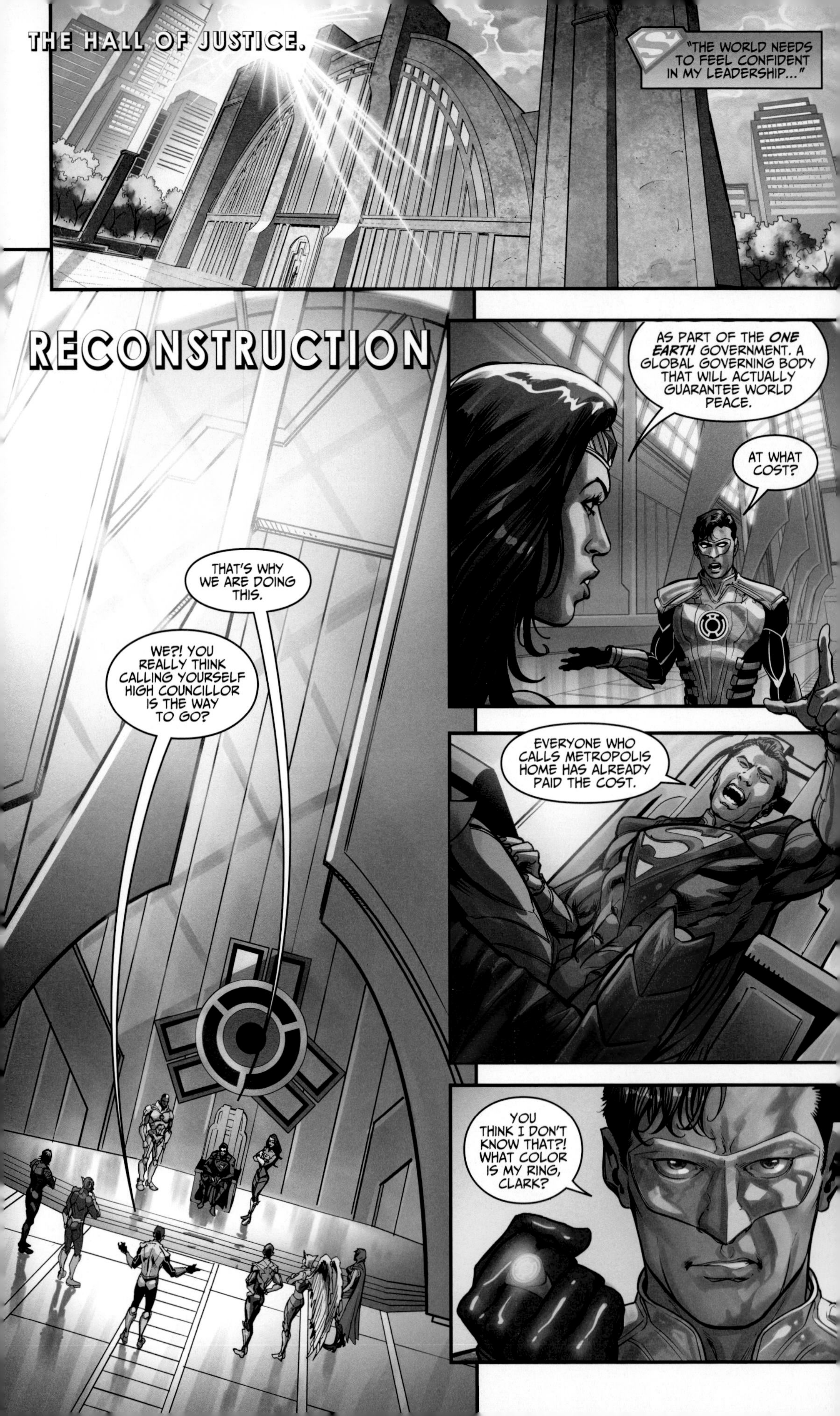
THE HALL OF JUSTICE.
"THE WORLD NEEDS TO FEEL CONFIDENT IN MY LEADERSHIP..."
RECONSTRUCTION
AS PART OF THE *ONE EARTH* GOVERNMENT. A GLOBAL GOVERNING BODY THAT WILL ACTUALLY GUARANTEE WORLD PEACE.
AT WHAT COST?
EVERYONE WHO CALLS METROPOLIS HOME HAS ALREADY PAID THE COST.
YOU THINK I DON'T KNOW THAT?! WHAT COLOR IS MY RING, CLARK?
THAT'S WHY WE ARE DOING THIS.
WE?! YOU REALLY THINK CALLING YOURSELF HIGH COUNCILLOR IS THE WAY TO GO?

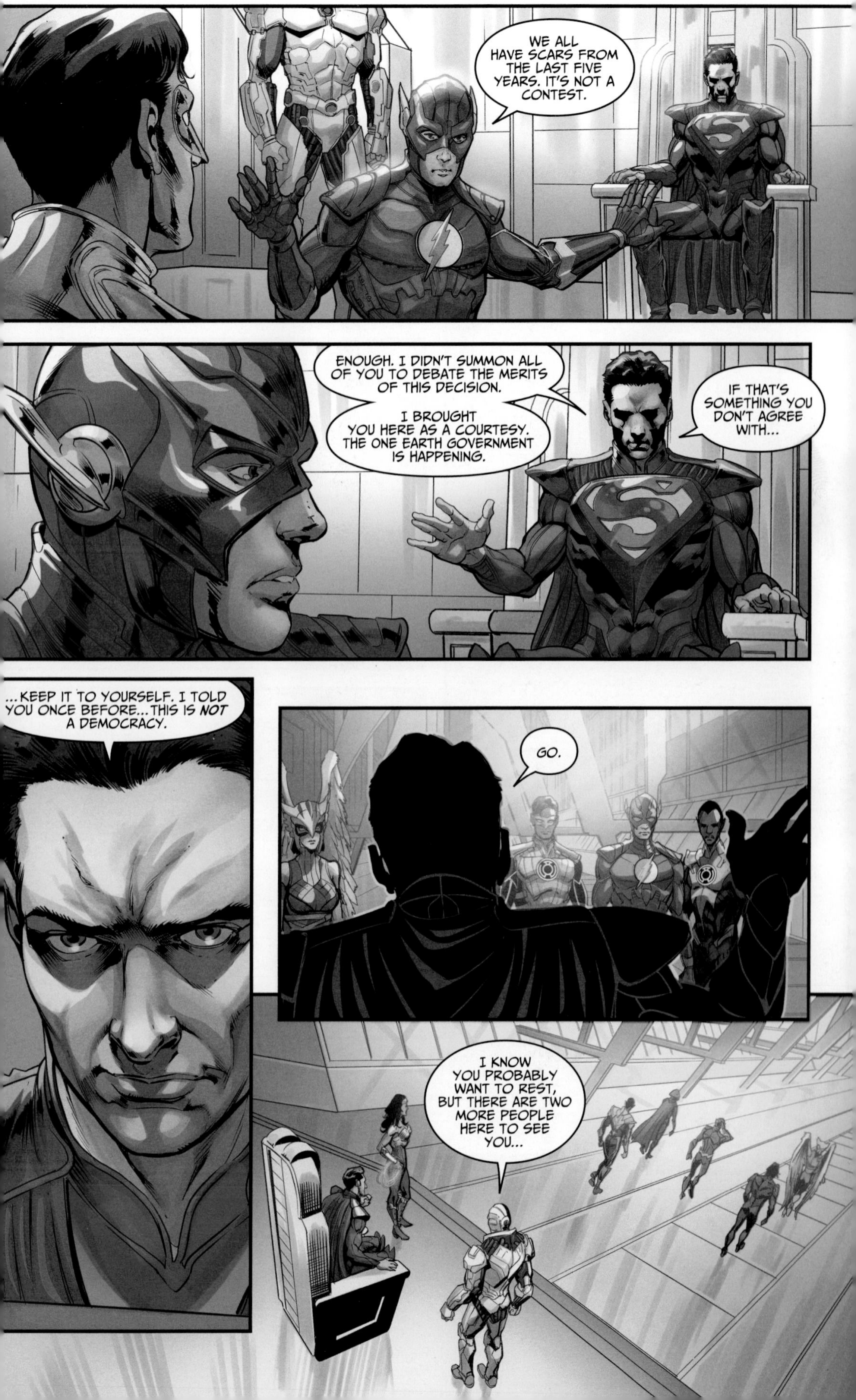
WE ALL HAVE SCARS FROM THE LAST FIVE YEARS. IT'S NOT A CONTEST.
ENOUGH. I DIDN'T SUMMON ALL OF YOU TO DEBATE THE MERITS OF THIS DECISION.
I BROUGHT YOU HERE AS A COURTESY. THE ONE EARTH GOVERNMENT IS HAPPENING.
IF THAT'S SOMETHING YOU DON'T AGREE WITH...
...KEEP IT TO YOURSELF. I TOLD YOU ONCE BEFORE...THIS IS *NOT* A DEMOCRACY.
GO.
I KNOW YOU PROBABLY WANT TO REST, BUT THERE ARE TWO MORE PEOPLE HERE TO SEE YOU...

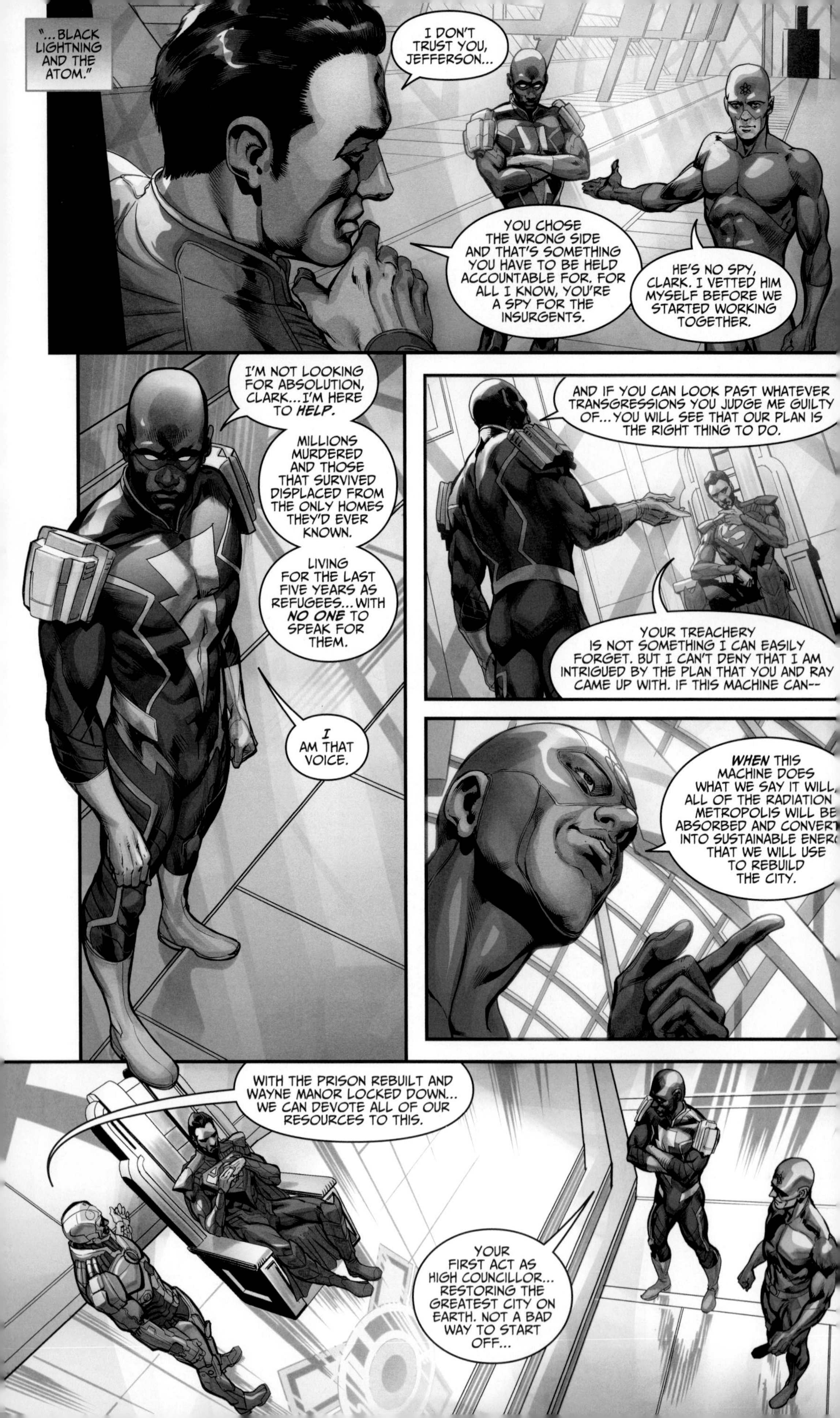

"...BLACK LIGHTNING AND THE ATOM."
I DON'T TRUST YOU, JEFFERSON...
YOU CHOSE THE WRONG SIDE AND THAT'S SOMETHING YOU HAVE TO BE HELD ACCOUNTABLE FOR. FOR ALL I KNOW, YOU'RE A SPY FOR THE INSURGENTS.
HE'S NO SPY, CLARK. I VETTED HIM MYSELF BEFORE WE STARTED WORKING TOGETHER.
I'M NOT LOOKING FOR ABSOLUTION, CLARK...I'M HERE TO *HELP.*
MILLIONS MURDERED AND THOSE THAT SURVIVED DISPLACED FROM THE ONLY HOMES THEY'D EVER KNOWN.
LIVING FOR THE LAST FIVE YEARS AS REFUGEES...WITH *NO ONE* TO SPEAK FOR THEM.
I AM THAT VOICE.
AND IF YOU CAN LOOK PAST WHATEVER TRANSGRESSIONS YOU JUDGE ME GUILTY OF...YOU WILL SEE THAT OUR PLAN IS THE RIGHT THING TO DO.
YOUR TREACHERY IS NOT SOMETHING I CAN EASILY FORGET. BUT I CAN'T DENY THAT I AM INTRIGUED BY THE PLAN THAT YOU AND RAY CAME UP WITH. IF THIS MACHINE CAN--
WHEN THIS MACHINE DOES WHAT WE SAY IT WILL, ALL OF THE RADIATION METROPOLIS WILL BE ABSORBED AND CONVERT INTO SUSTAINABLE ENER THAT WE WILL USE TO REBUILD THE CITY.
WITH THE PRISON REBUILT AND WAYNE MANOR LOCKED DOWN... WE CAN DEVOTE ALL OF OUR RESOURCES TO THIS.
YOUR FIRST ACT AS HIGH COUNCILLOR... RESTORING THE GREATEST CITY ON EARTH. NOT A BAD WAY TO START OFF...

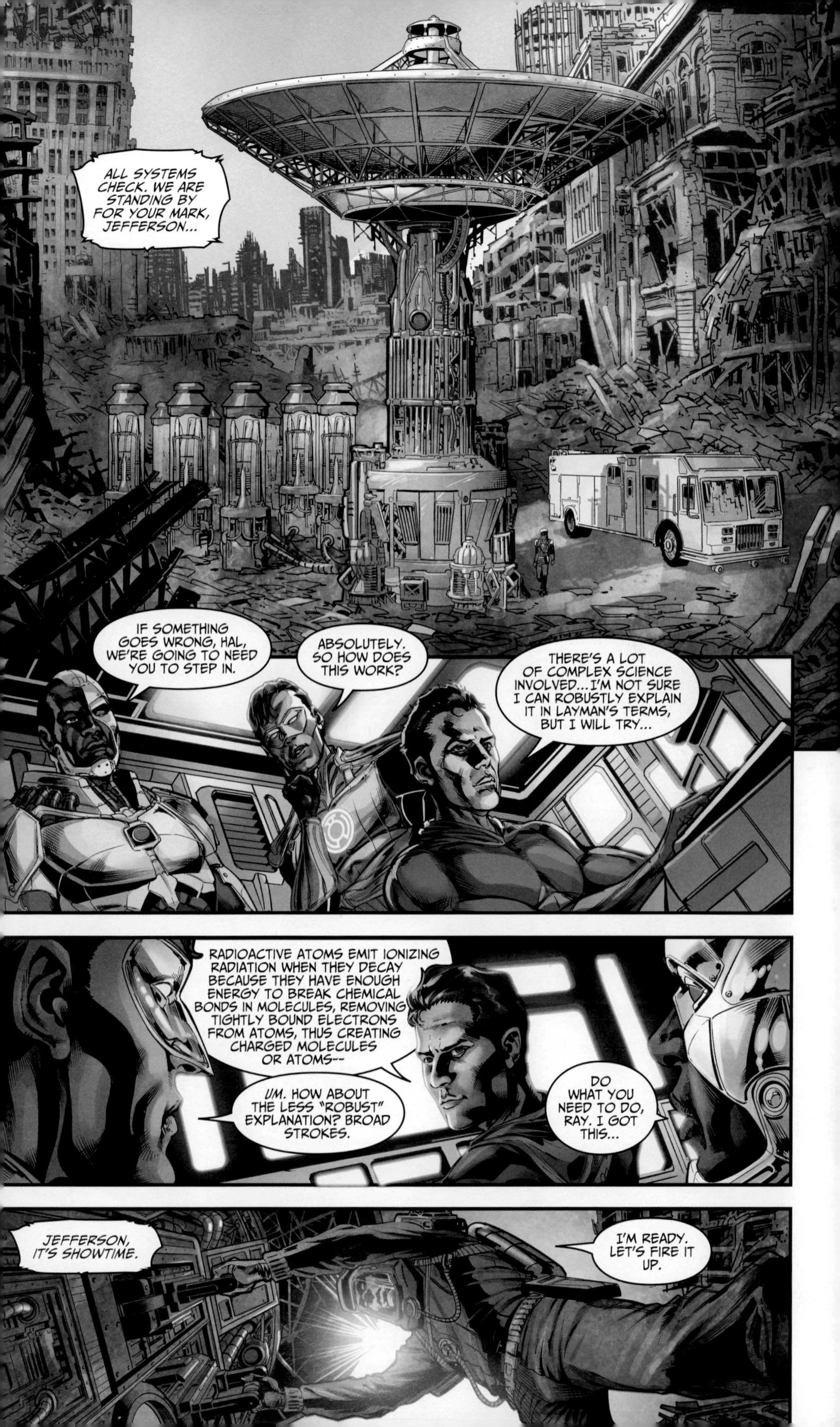
ALL SYSTEMS CHECK. WE ARE STANDING BY FOR YOUR MARK, JEFFERSON...
IF SOMETHING GOES WRONG, HAL, WE'RE GOING TO NEED YOU TO STEP IN.
ABSOLUTELY. SO HOW DOES THIS WORK?
THERE'S A LOT OF COMPLEX SCIENCE INVOLVED...I'M NOT SURE I CAN ROBUSTLY EXPLAIN IT IN LAYMAN'S TERMS, BUT I WILL TRY...
RADIOACTIVE ATOMS EMIT IONIZING RADIATION WHEN THEY DECAY BECAUSE THEY HAVE ENOUGH ENERGY TO BREAK CHEMICAL BONDS IN MOLECULES, REMOVING TIGHTLY BOUND ELECTRONS FROM ATOMS, THUS CREATING CHARGED MOLECULES OR ATOMS--
UM. HOW ABOUT THE LESS "ROBUST" EXPLANATION? BROAD STROKES.
DO WHAT YOU NEED TO DO, RAY. I GOT THIS...
JEFFERSON, IT'S SHOWTIME.
I'M READY. LET'S FIRE IT UP.

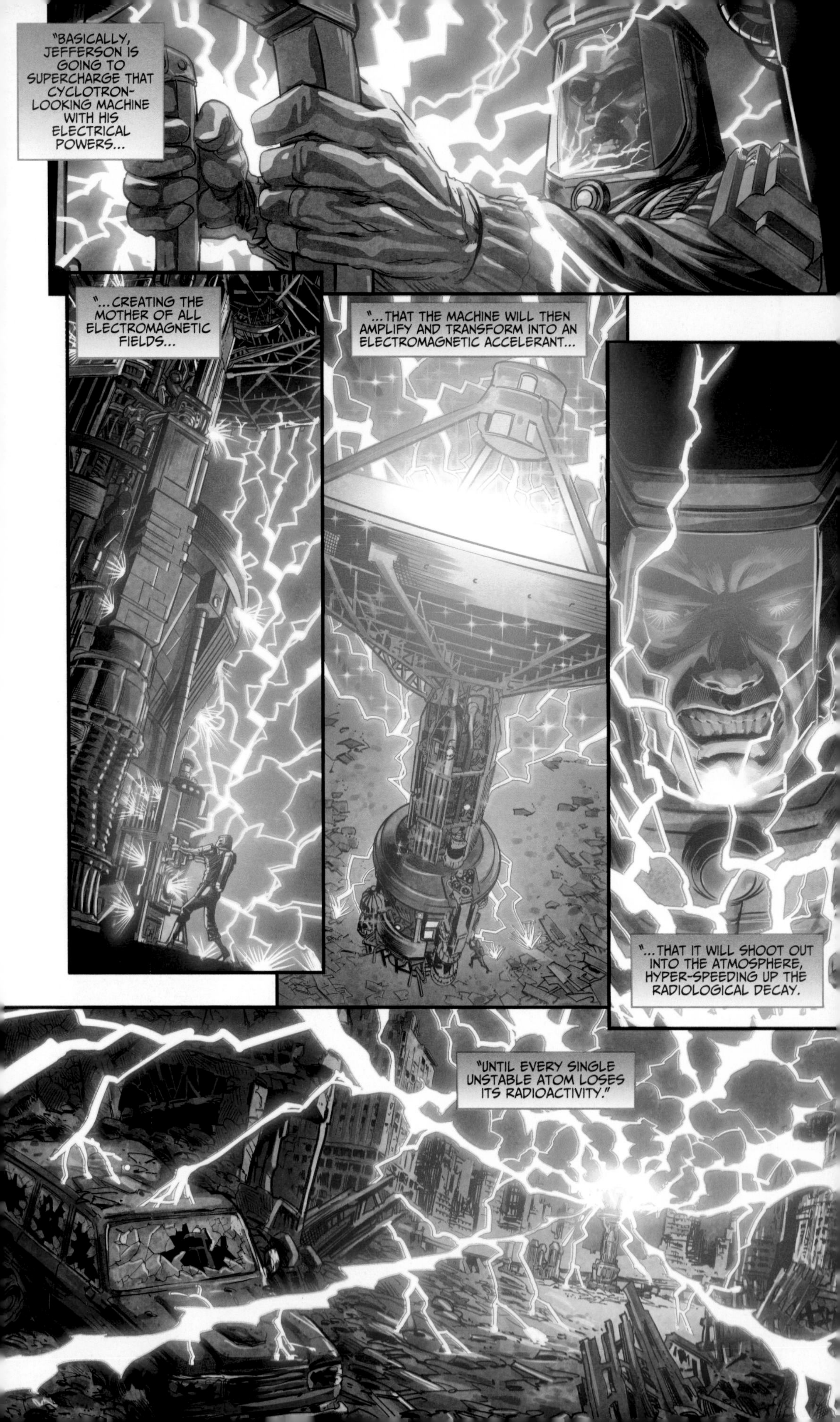
"BASICALLY, JEFFERSON IS GOING TO SUPERCHARGE THAT CYCLOTRON-LOOKING MACHINE WITH HIS ELECTRICAL POWERS...
"...CREATING THE MOTHER OF ALL ELECTROMAGNETIC FIELDS...
"...THAT THE MACHINE WILL THEN AMPLIFY AND TRANSFORM INTO AN ELECTROMAGNETIC ACCELERANT...
"...THAT IT WILL SHOOT OUT INTO THE ATMOSPHERE, HYPER-SPEEDING UP THE RADIOLOGICAL DECAY.
"UNTIL EVERY SINGLE UNSTABLE ATOM LOSES ITS RADIOACTIVITY."

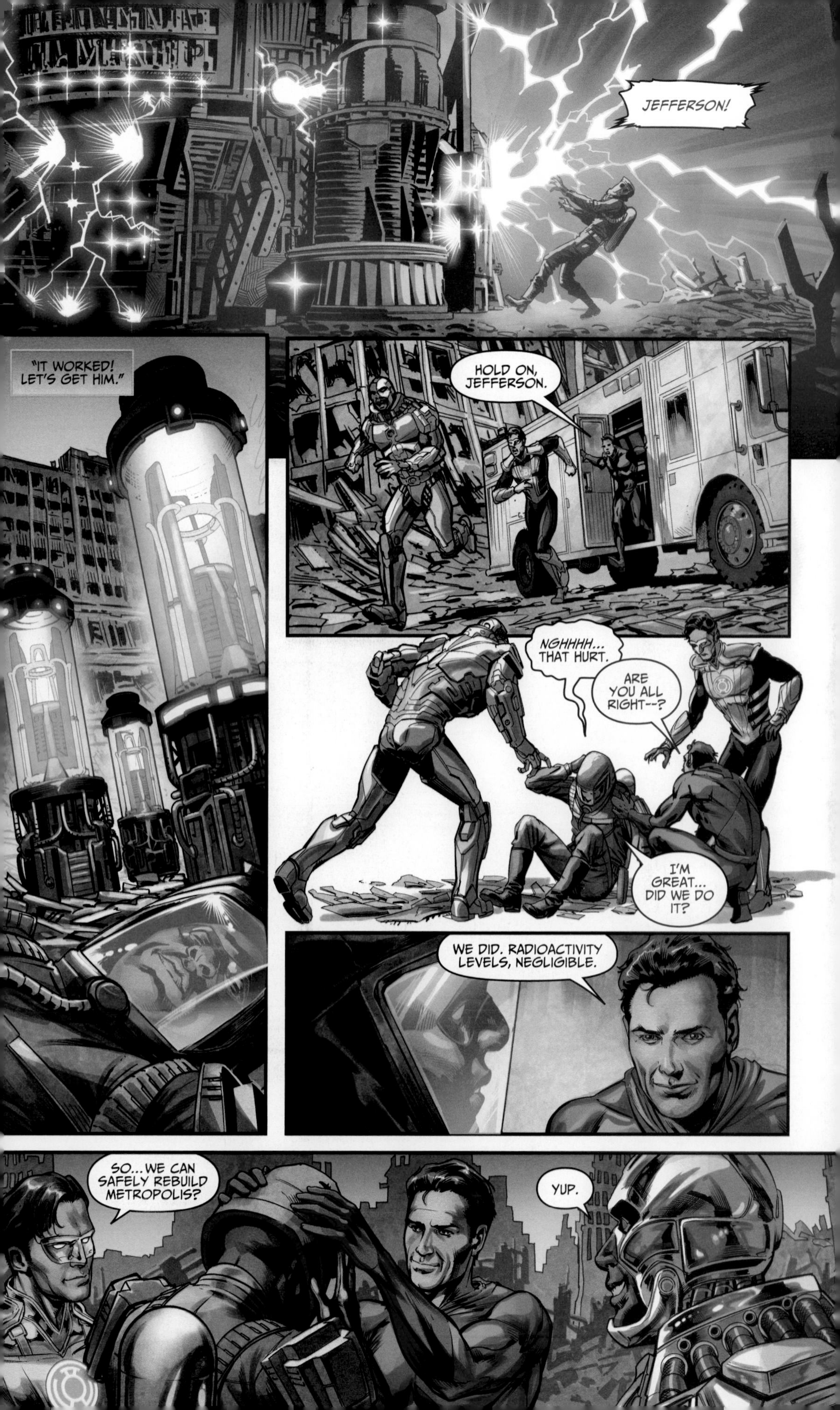
JEFFERSON!
"IT WORKED! LET'S GET HIM."
HOLD ON, JEFFERSON.
NGHHHH... THAT HURT.
ARE YOU ALL RIGHT--?
I'M GREAT... DID WE DO IT?
WE DID. RADIOACTIVITY LEVELS, NEGLIGIBLE.
SO...WE CAN SAFELY REBUILD METROPOLIS?
YUP.

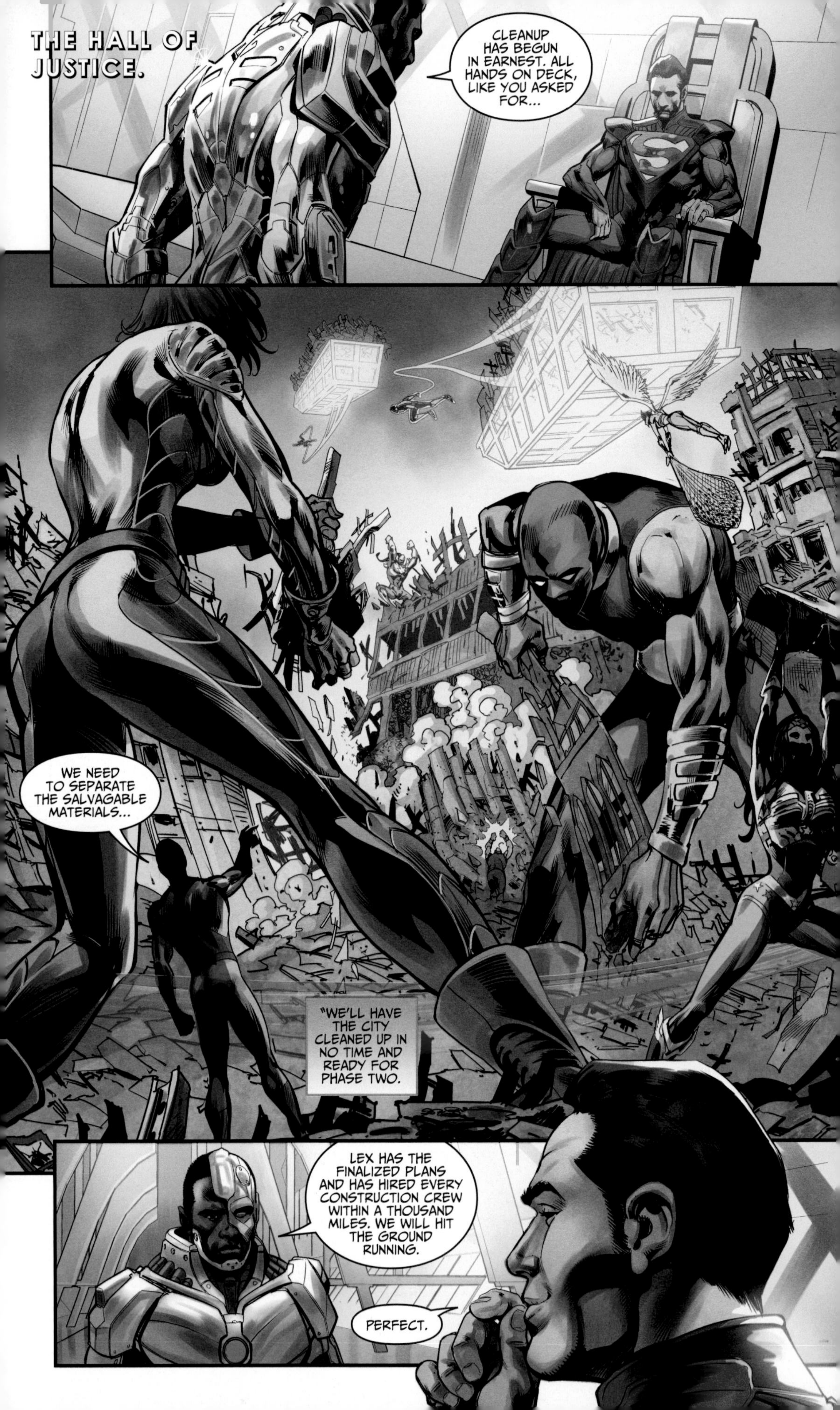
THE HALL OF JUSTICE.
CLEANUP HAS BEGUN IN EARNEST. ALL HANDS ON DECK, LIKE YOU ASKED FOR...
WE NEED TO SEPARATE THE SALVAGABLE MATERIALS...
"WE'LL HAVE THE CITY CLEANED UP IN NO TIME AND READY FOR PHASE TWO.
LEX HAS THE FINALIZED PLANS AND HAS HIRED EVERY CONSTRUCTION CREW WITHIN A THOUSAND MILES. WE WILL HIT THE GROUND RUNNING.
PERFECT.

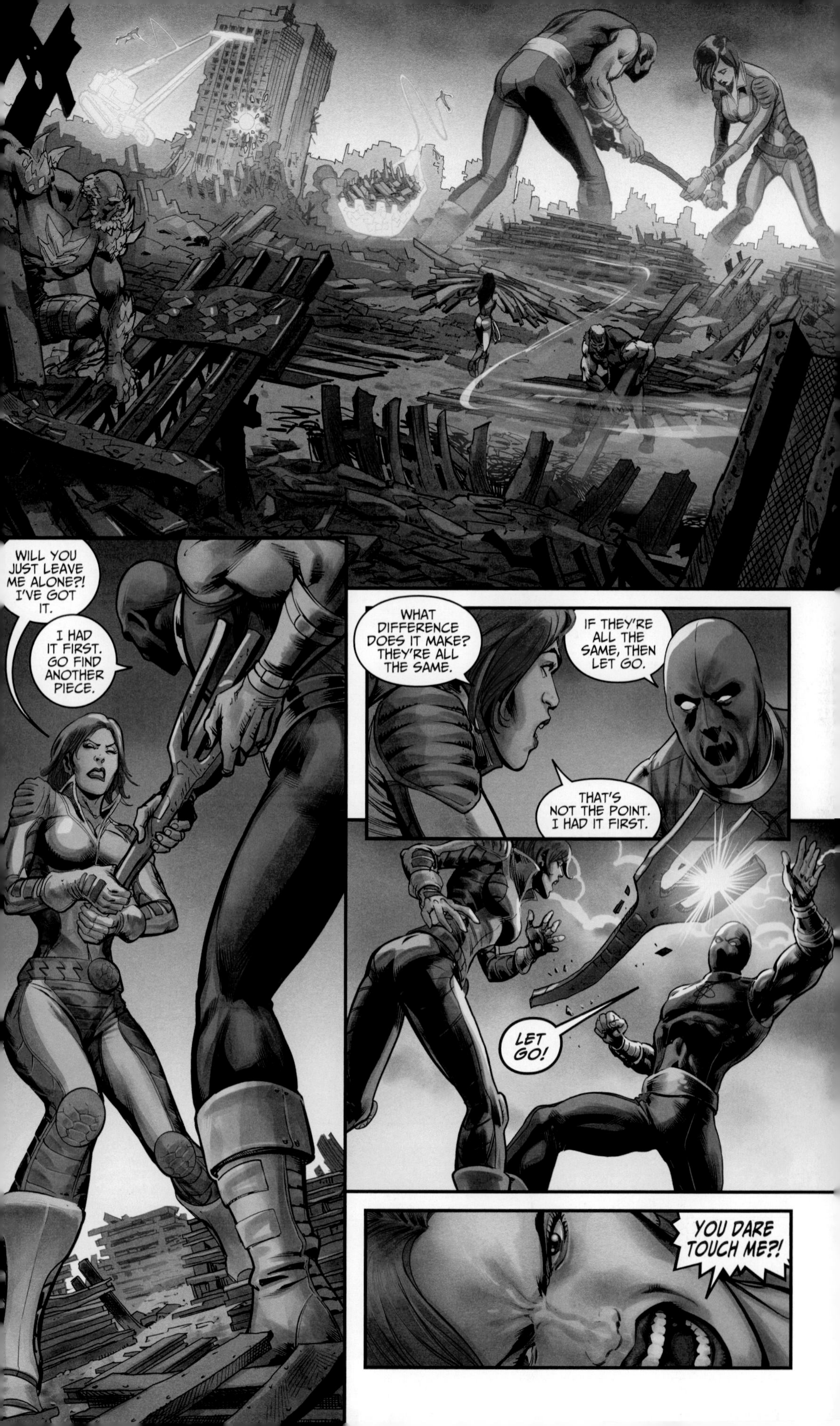
WILL YOU JUST LEAVE ME ALONE?! I'VE GOT IT.
I HAD IT FIRST. GO FIND ANOTHER PIECE.
WHAT DIFFERENCE DOES IT MAKE? THEY'RE ALL THE SAME.
IF THEY'RE ALL THE SAME, THEN LET GO.
THAT'S NOT THE POINT. I HAD IT FIRST.
LET GO!
YOU DARE TOUCH ME?!

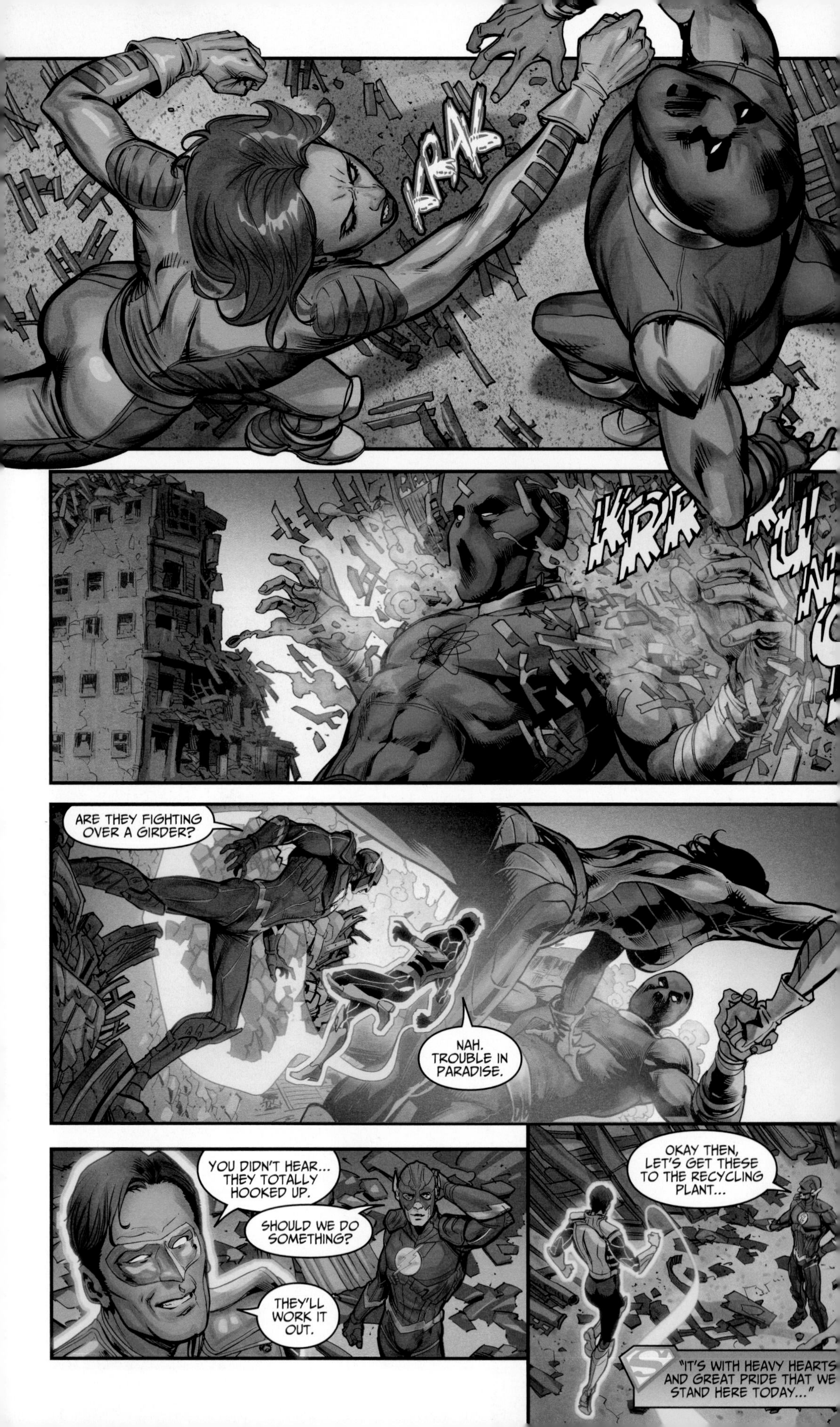
KRAK
KRAKUNCH
ARE THEY FIGHTING OVER A GIRDER?
NAH. TROUBLE IN PARADISE.
YOU DIDN'T HEAR... THEY TOTALLY HOOKED UP.
SHOULD WE DO SOMETHING?
THEY'LL WORK IT OUT.
OKAY THEN, LET'S GET THESE TO THE RECYCLING PLANT...
"IT'S WITH HEAVY HEARTS AND GREAT PRIDE THAT WE STAND HERE TODAY..."

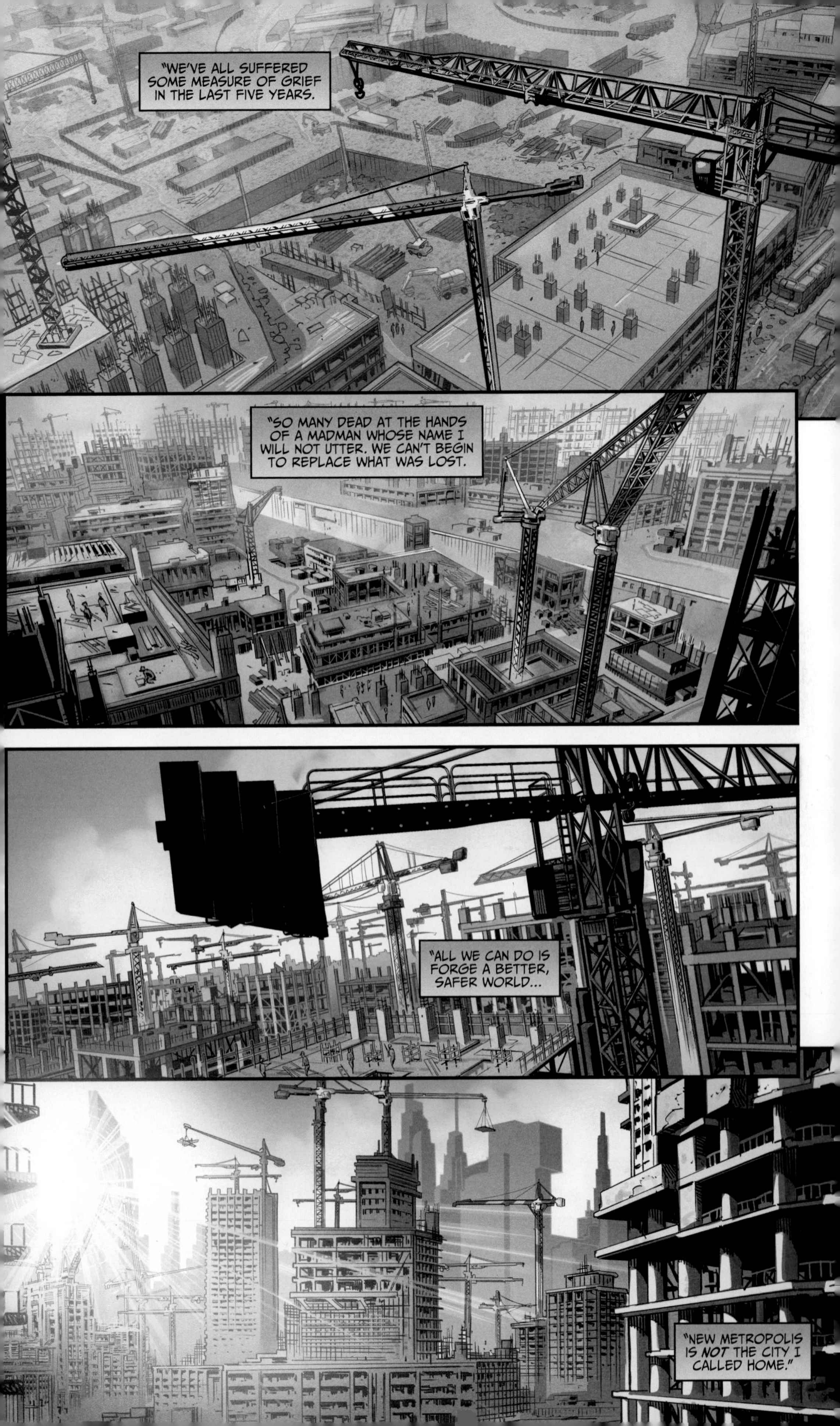
"WE'VE ALL SUFFERED SOME MEASURE OF GRIEF IN THE LAST FIVE YEARS.
"SO MANY DEAD AT THE HANDS OF A MADMAN WHOSE NAME I WILL NOT UTTER. WE CAN'T BEGIN TO REPLACE WHAT WAS LOST.
"ALL WE CAN DO IS FORGE A BETTER, SAFER WORLD...
"NEW METROPOLIS IS *NOT* THE CITY I CALLED HOME."

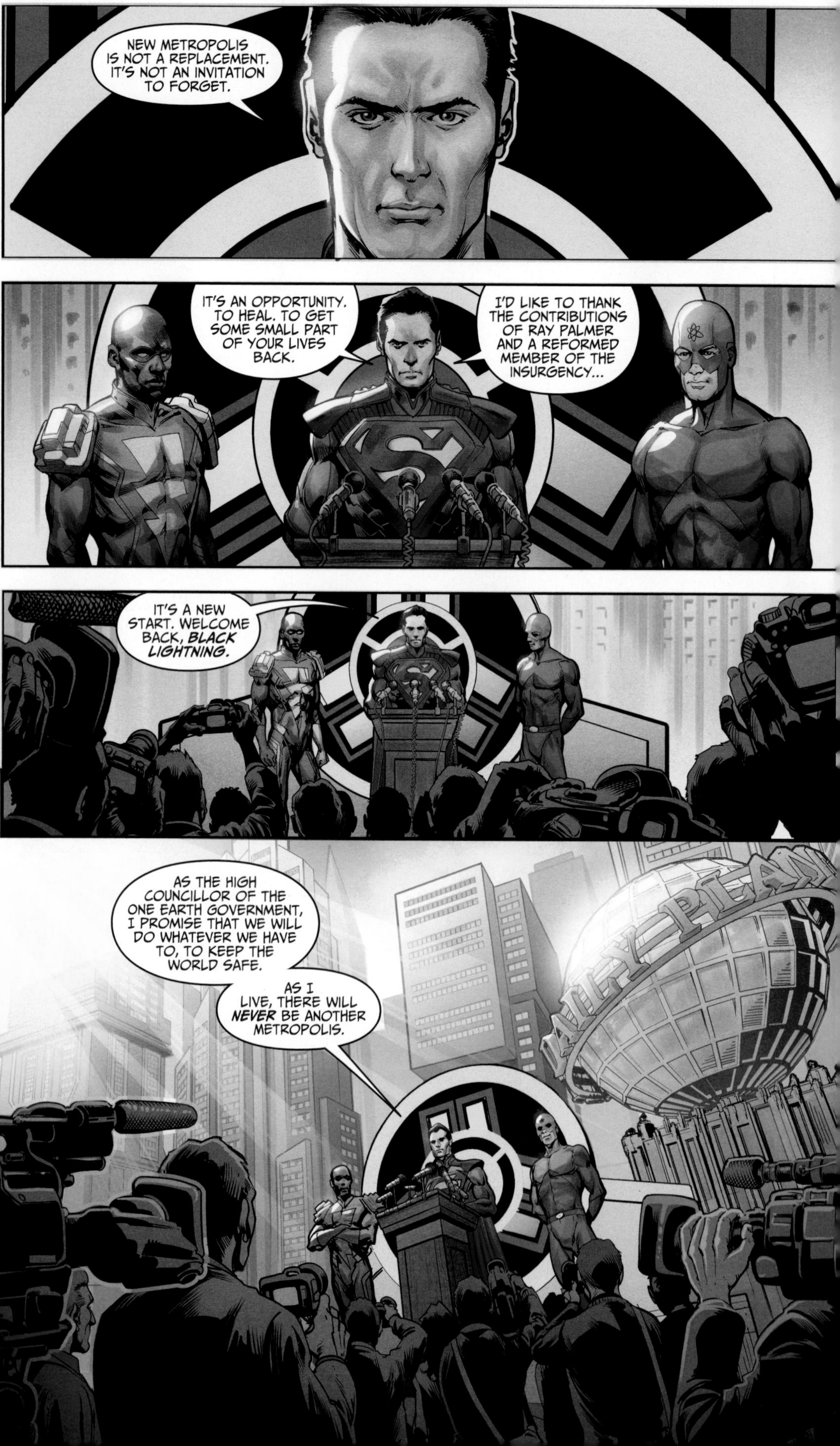

NEW METROPOLIS IS NOT A REPLACEMENT. IT'S NOT AN INVITATION TO FORGET.
IT'S AN OPPORTUNITY. TO HEAL. TO GET SOME SMALL PART OF YOUR LIVES BACK.
I'D LIKE TO THANK THE CONTRIBUTIONS OF RAY PALMER AND A REFORMED MEMBER OF THE INSURGENCY...
IT'S A NEW START. WELCOME BACK, *BLACK LIGHTNING.*
AS THE HIGH COUNCILLOR OF THE ONE EARTH GOVERNMENT, I PROMISE THAT WE WILL DO WHATEVER WE HAVE TO, TO KEEP THE WORLD SAFE.
AS I LIVE, THERE WILL *NEVER* BE ANOTHER METROPOLIS.

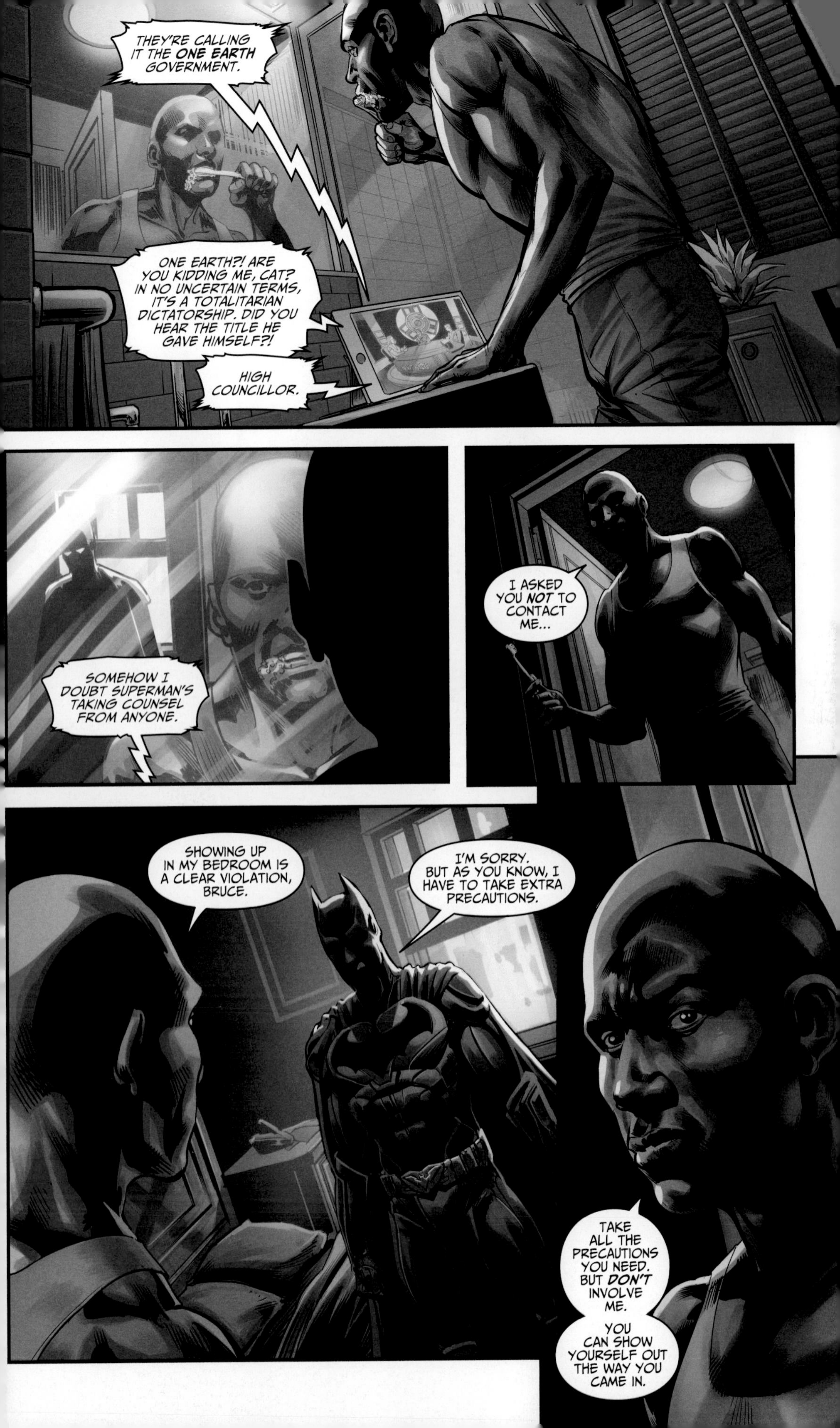
THEY'RE CALLING IT THE ONE EARTH GOVERNMENT.
ONE EARTH?! ARE YOU KIDDING ME, CAT? IN NO UNCERTAIN TERMS, IT'S A TOTALITARIAN DICTATORSHIP. DID YOU HEAR THE TITLE HE GAVE HIMSELF?!
HIGH COUNCILLOR.
SOMEHOW I DOUBT SUPERMAN'S TAKING COUNSEL FROM ANYONE.
I ASKED YOU NOT TO CONTACT ME...
SHOWING UP IN MY BEDROOM IS A CLEAR VIOLATION, BRUCE.
I'M SORRY. BUT AS YOU KNOW, I HAVE TO TAKE EXTRA PRECAUTIONS.
TAKE ALL THE PRECAUTIONS YOU NEED. BUT DON'T INVOLVE ME.
YOU CAN SHOW YOURSELF OUT THE WAY YOU CAME IN.

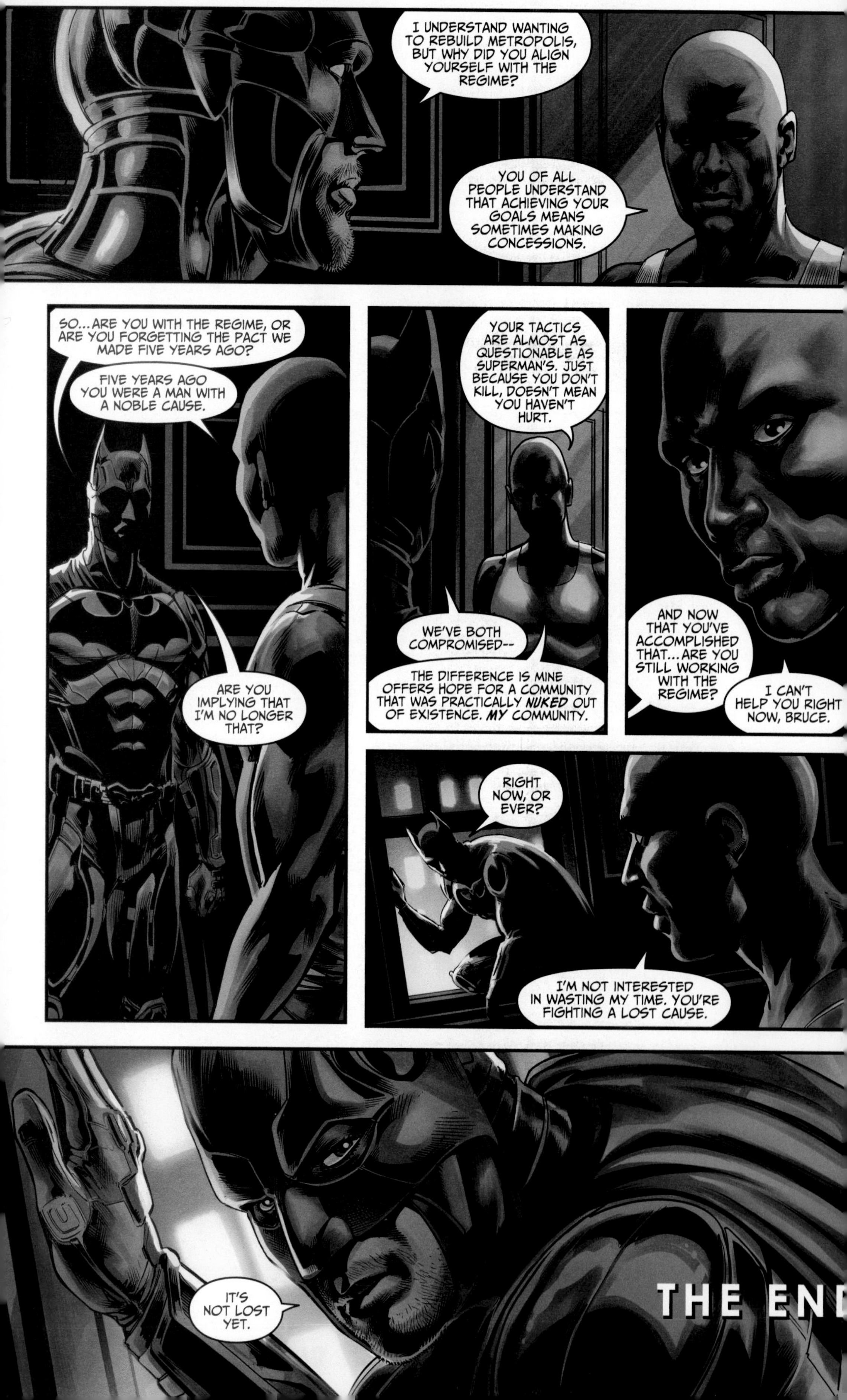
I UNDERSTAND WANTING TO REBUILD METROPOLIS, BUT WHY DID YOU ALIGN YOURSELF WITH THE REGIME?
YOU OF ALL PEOPLE UNDERSTAND THAT ACHIEVING YOUR GOALS MEANS SOMETIMES MAKING CONCESSIONS.
SO...ARE YOU WITH THE REGIME, OR ARE YOU FORGETTING THE PACT WE MADE FIVE YEARS AGO?
FIVE YEARS AGO YOU WERE A MAN WITH A NOBLE CAUSE.
ARE YOU IMPLYING THAT I'M NO LONGER THAT?
YOUR TACTICS ARE ALMOST AS QUESTIONABLE AS SUPERMAN'S. JUST BECAUSE YOU DON'T KILL, DOESN'T MEAN YOU HAVEN'T HURT.
WE'VE BOTH COMPROMISED--
THE DIFFERENCE IS MINE OFFERS HOPE FOR A COMMUNITY THAT WAS PRACTICALLY NUKED OUT OF EXISTENCE. MY COMMUNITY.
AND NOW THAT YOU'VE ACCOMPLISHED THAT...ARE YOU STILL WORKING WITH THE REGIME?
I CAN'T HELP YOU RIGHT NOW, BRUCE.
RIGHT NOW, OR EVER?
I'M NOT INTERESTED IN WASTING MY TIME. YOU'RE FIGHTING A LOST CAUSE.
IT'S NOT LOST YET.
THE END

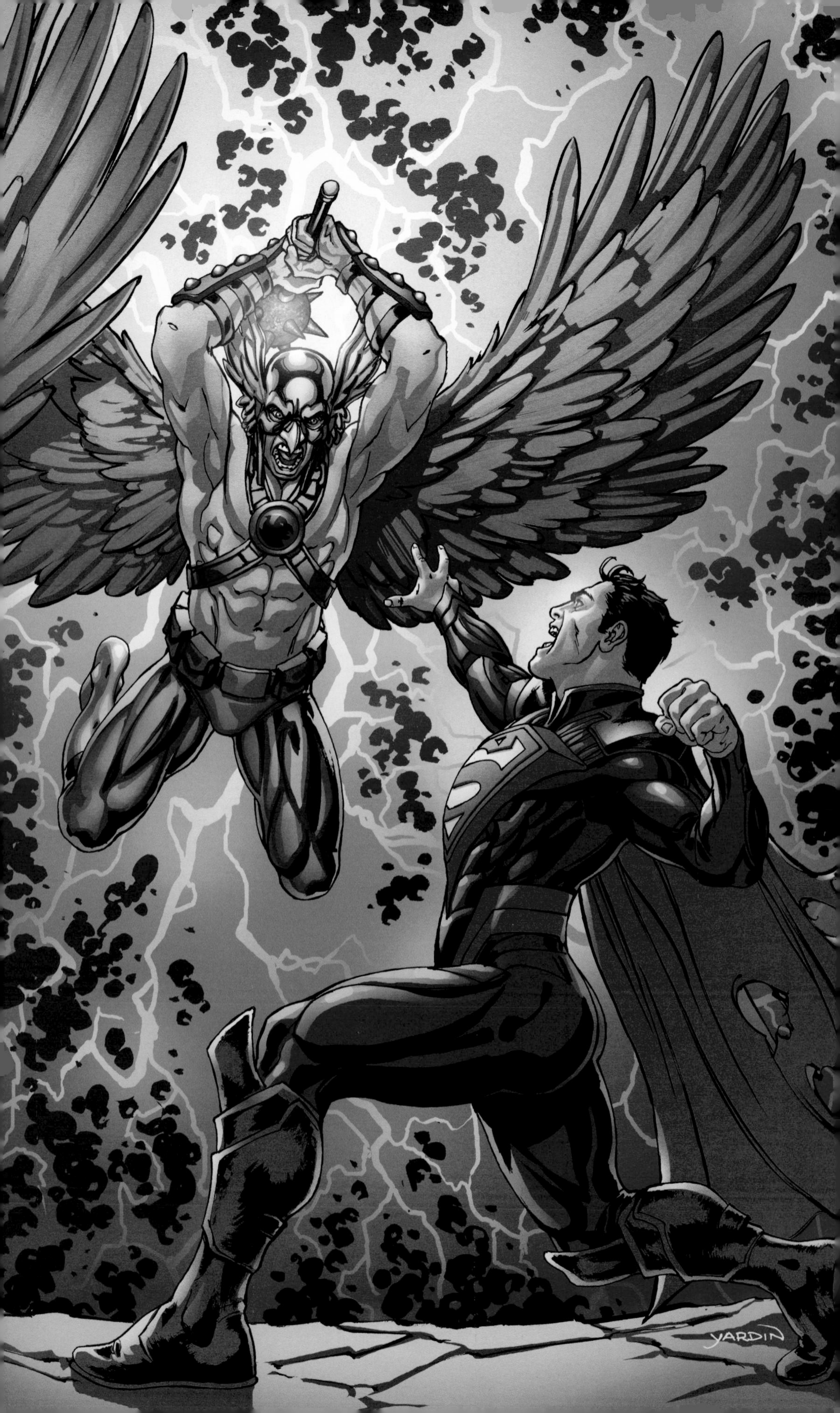
YARDIN

"Thrones" **Xermanico** Artist **Rex Lokus** Colorist

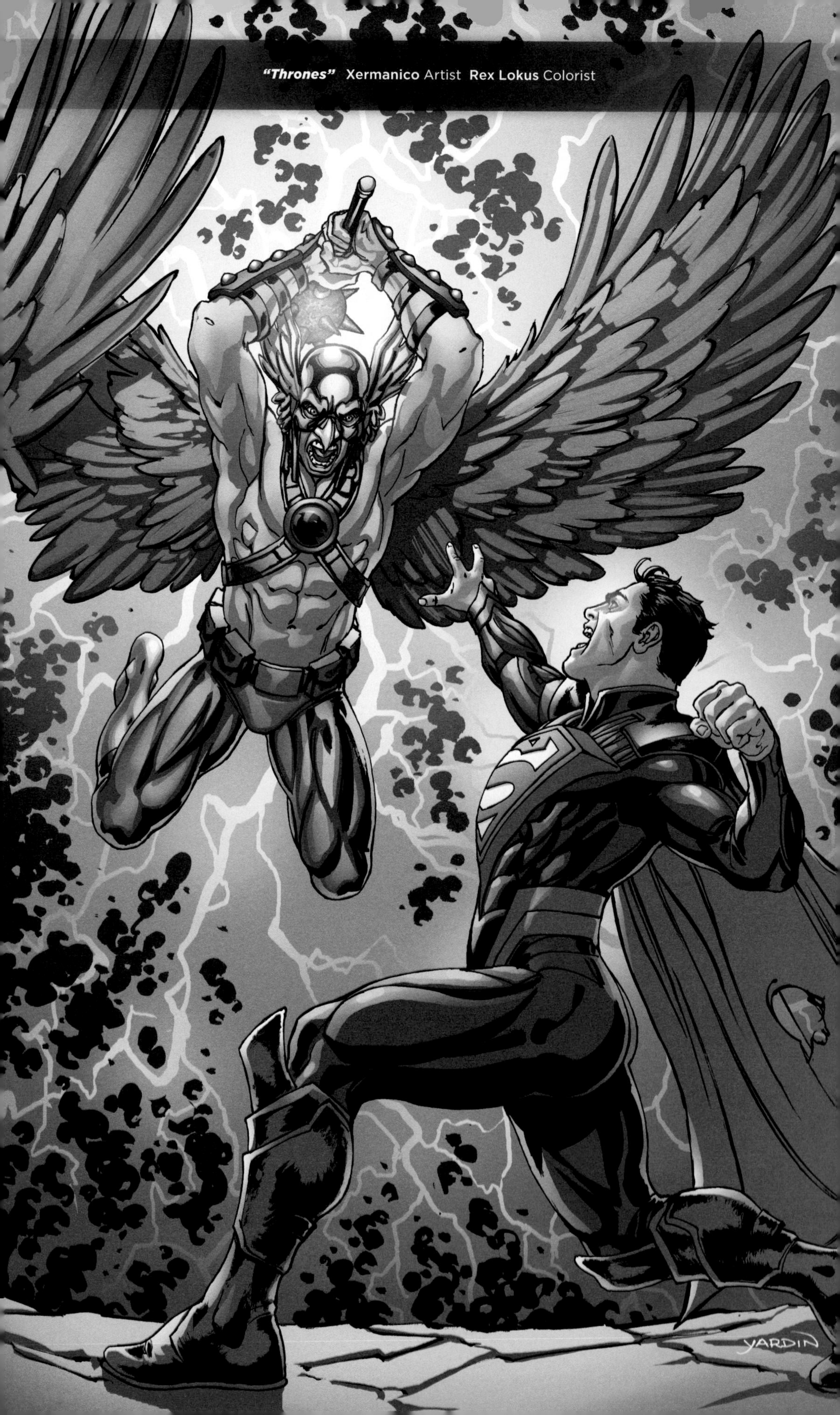
YARDIN

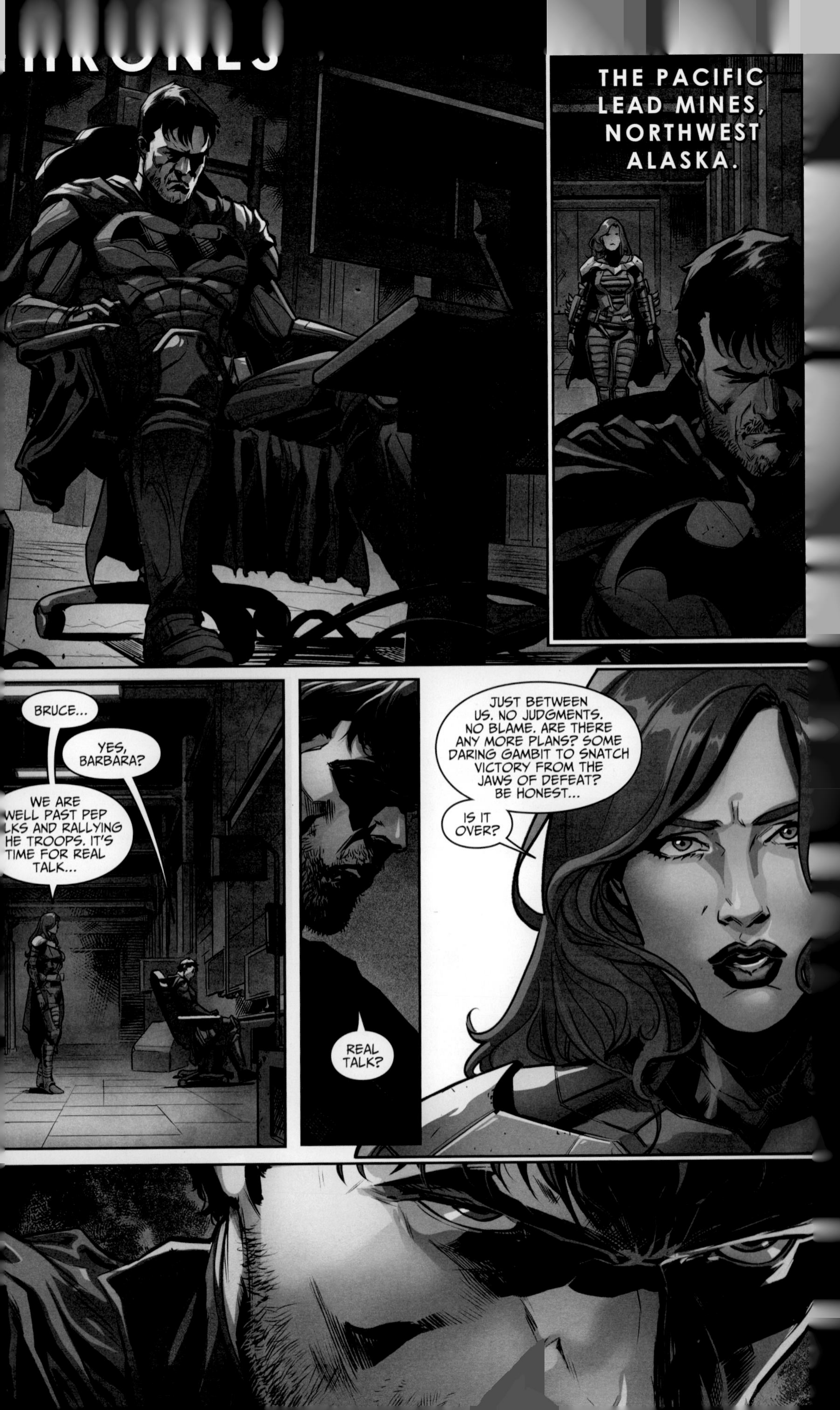
THE PACIFIC LEAD MINES, NORTHWEST ALASKA.
BRUCE...
YES, BARBARA?
WE ARE WELL PAST PEP LKS AND RALLYING HE TROOPS. IT'S TIME FOR REAL TALK...
REAL TALK?
JUST BETWEEN US. NO JUDGMENTS. NO BLAME. ARE THERE ANY MORE PLANS? SOME DARING GAMBIT TO SNATCH VICTORY FROM THE JAWS OF DEFEAT? BE HONEST...
IS IT OVER?

BARBARA...

IT'S NOT OVER.

GOOD.

BATMAN...

I NEED TO SEND A SECURE TRANSMISSION.

WHERE?

BEYOND SECTOR 2814.

THAT'S GOING TO BE HARD TO DO WITH CYBORG MONITORING EVERY TRANSMISSION, BROADCAST AND SATELLITE ON THE PLANET.

HARD, BUT NOT IMPOSSIBLE?

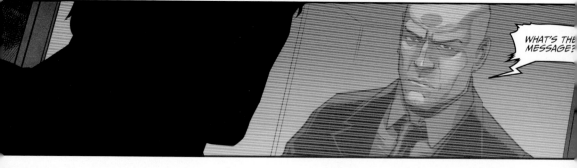

WHAT'S THE MESSAGE?

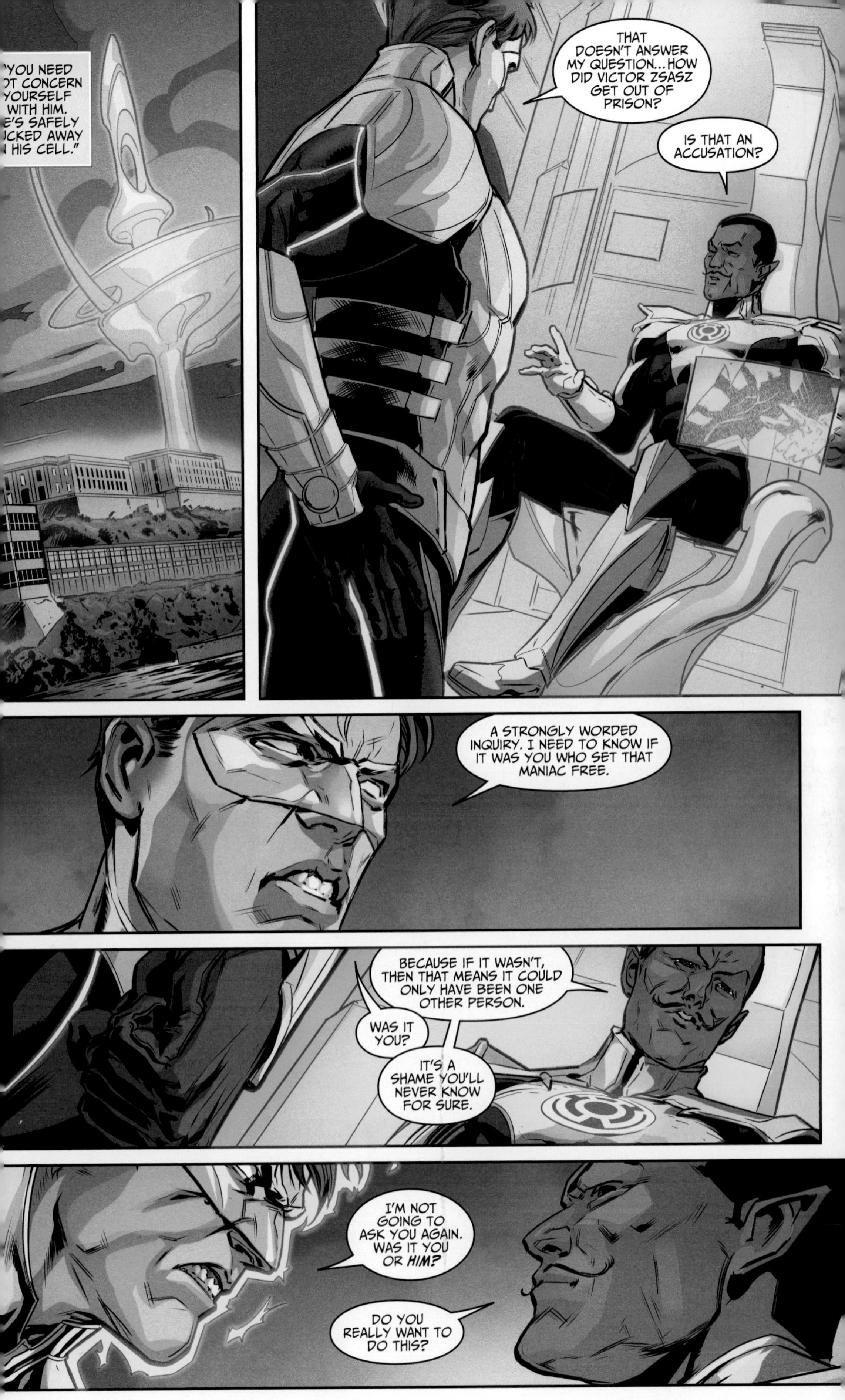
"YOU NEED
OT CONCERN
YOURSELF
WITH HIM.
E'S SAFELY
UCKED AWAY
N HIS CELL."
THAT DOESN'T ANSWER MY QUESTION...HOW DID VICTOR ZSASZ GET OUT OF PRISON?
IS THAT AN ACCUSATION?
A STRONGLY WORDED INQUIRY. I NEED TO KNOW IF IT WAS YOU WHO SET THAT MANIAC FREE.
BECAUSE IF IT WASN'T, THEN THAT MEANS IT COULD ONLY HAVE BEEN ONE OTHER PERSON.
WAS IT YOU?
IT'S A SHAME YOU'LL NEVER KNOW FOR SURE.
I'M NOT GOING TO ASK YOU AGAIN. WAS IT YOU OR *HIM?*
DO YOU REALLY WANT TO DO THIS?

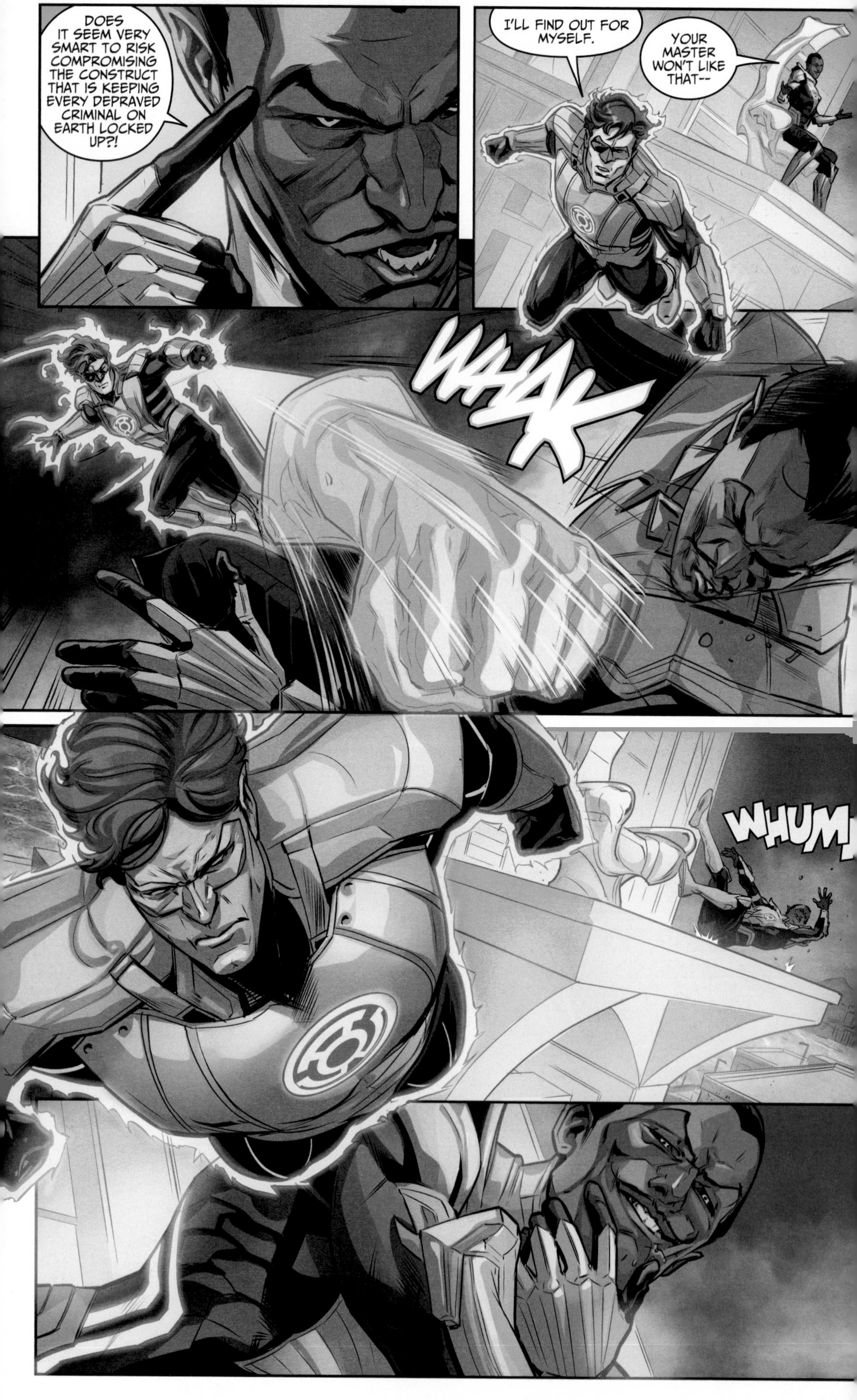
DOES IT SEEM VERY SMART TO RISK COMPROMISING THE CONSTRUCT THAT IS KEEPING EVERY DEPRAVED CRIMINAL ON EARTH LOCKED UP?!
I'LL FIND OUT FOR MYSELF.
YOUR MASTER WON'T LIKE THAT--
WAAK
WHUM

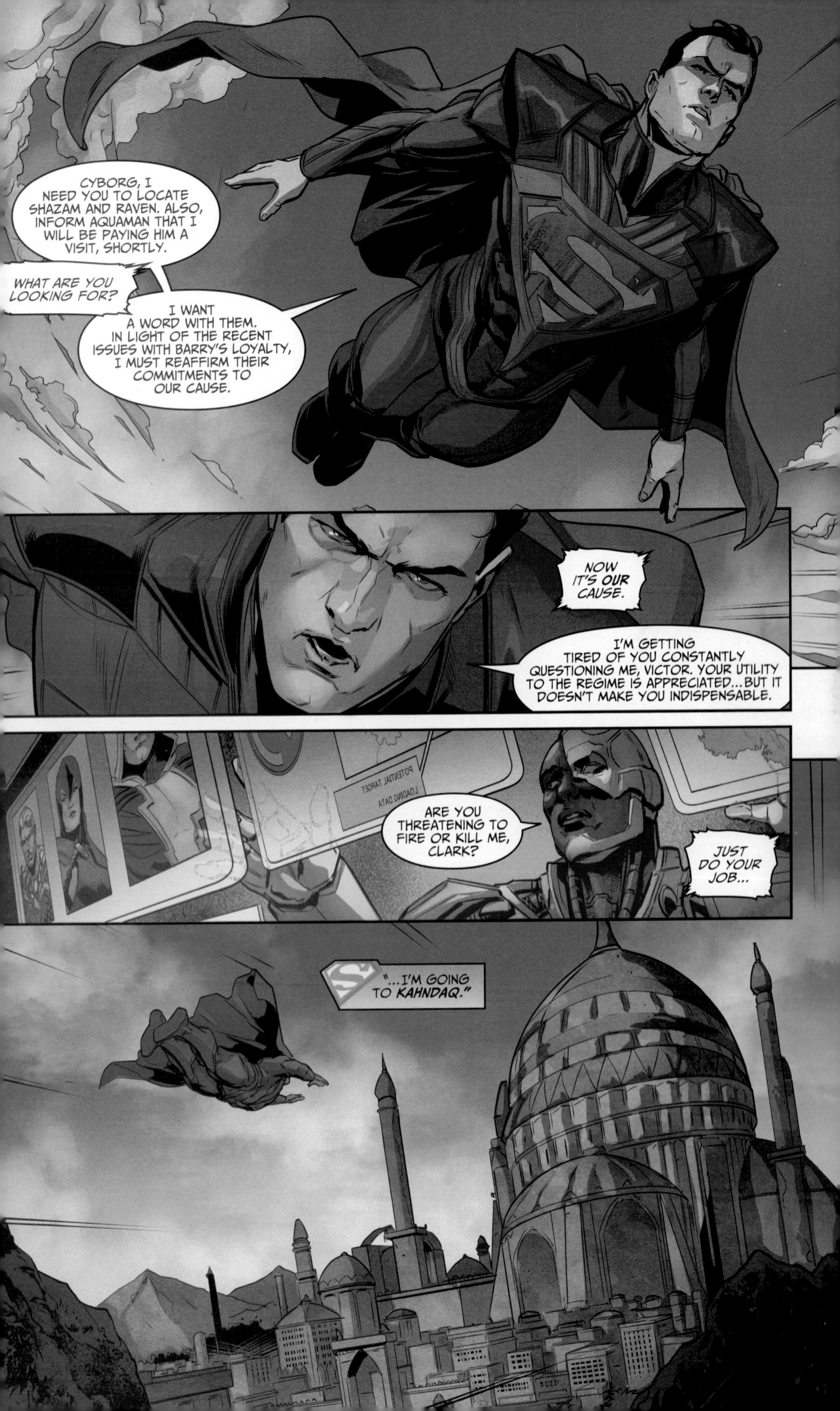
CYBORG, I NEED YOU TO LOCATE SHAZAM AND RAVEN. ALSO, INFORM AQUAMAN THAT I WILL BE PAYING HIM A VISIT, SHORTLY.
WHAT ARE YOU LOOKING FOR?
I WANT A WORD WITH THEM. IN LIGHT OF THE RECENT ISSUES WITH BARRY'S LOYALTY, I MUST REAFFIRM THEIR COMMITMENTS TO OUR CAUSE.
NOW IT'S **OUR** CAUSE.
I'M GETTING TIRED OF YOU CONSTANTLY QUESTIONING ME, VICTOR. YOUR UTILITY TO THE REGIME IS APPRECIATED...BUT IT DOESN'T MAKE YOU INDISPENSABLE.
ARE YOU THREATENING TO FIRE OR KILL ME, CLARK?
JUST DO YOUR JOB...
"...I'M GOING TO ***KAHNDAQ.***"

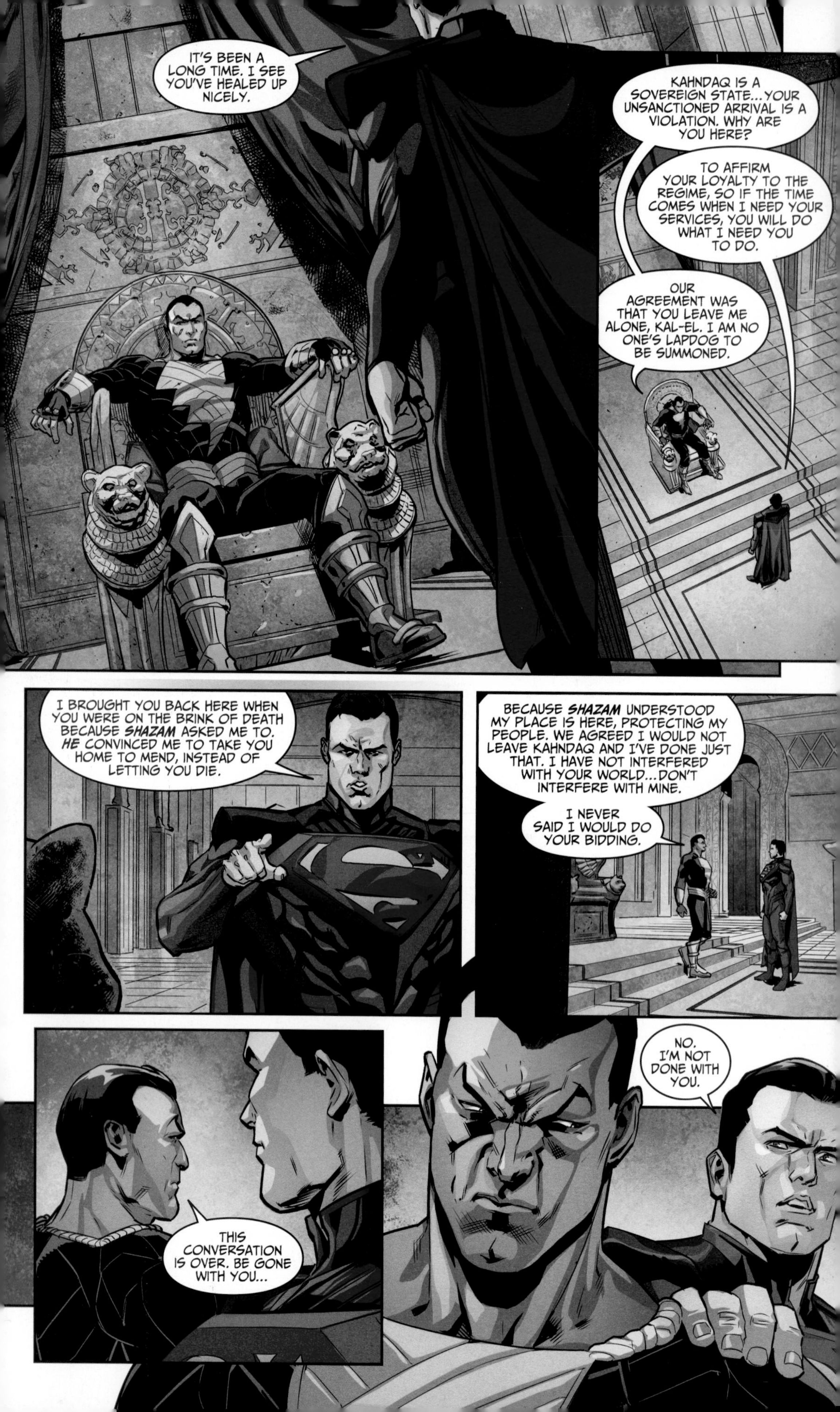
IT'S BEEN A LONG TIME. I SEE YOU'VE HEALED UP NICELY.
KAHNDAQ IS A SOVEREIGN STATE... YOUR UNSANCTIONED ARRIVAL IS A VIOLATION. WHY ARE YOU HERE?
TO AFFIRM YOUR LOYALTY TO THE REGIME, SO IF THE TIME COMES WHEN I NEED YOUR SERVICES, YOU WILL DO WHAT I NEED YOU TO DO.
OUR AGREEMENT WAS THAT YOU LEAVE ME ALONE, KAL-EL. I AM NO ONE'S LAPDOG TO BE SUMMONED.
I BROUGHT YOU BACK HERE WHEN YOU WERE ON THE BRINK OF DEATH BECAUSE SHAZAM ASKED ME TO. HE CONVINCED ME TO TAKE YOU HOME TO MEND, INSTEAD OF LETTING YOU DIE.
BECAUSE SHAZAM UNDERSTOOD MY PLACE IS HERE, PROTECTING MY PEOPLE. WE AGREED I WOULD NOT LEAVE KAHNDAQ AND I'VE DONE JUST THAT. I HAVE NOT INTERFERED WITH YOUR WORLD...DON'T INTERFERE WITH MINE.
I NEVER SAID I WOULD DO YOUR BIDDING.
THIS CONVERSATION IS OVER. BE GONE WITH YOU...
NO. I'M NOT DONE WITH YOU.

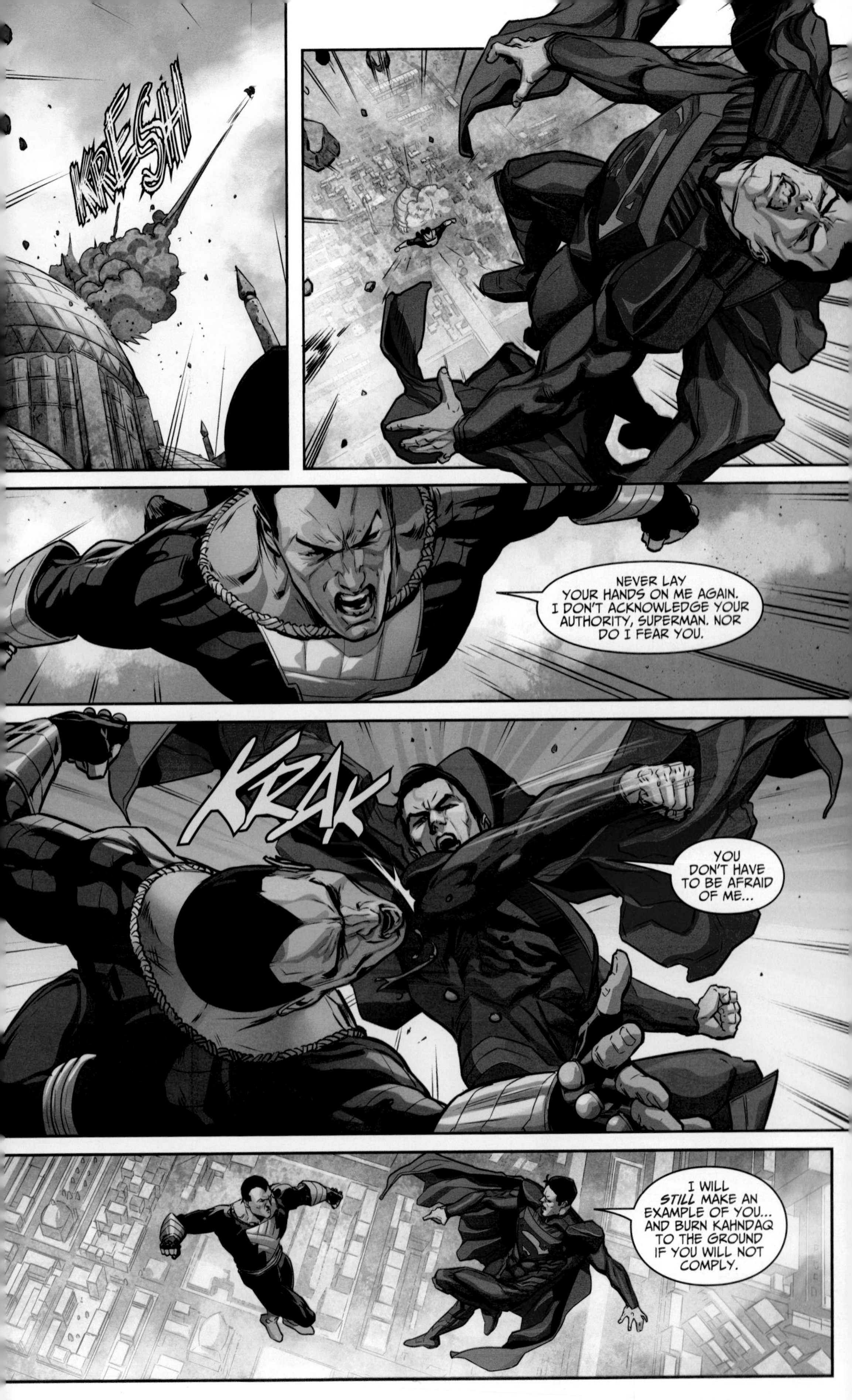
KRESH
NEVER LAY YOUR HANDS ON ME AGAIN. I DON'T ACKNOWLEDGE YOUR AUTHORITY, SUPERMAN. NOR DO I FEAR YOU.
KRAK
YOU DON'T HAVE TO BE AFRAID OF ME...
I WILL *STILL* MAKE AN EXAMPLE OF YOU... AND BURN KAHNDAQ TO THE GROUND IF YOU WILL NOT COMPLY.

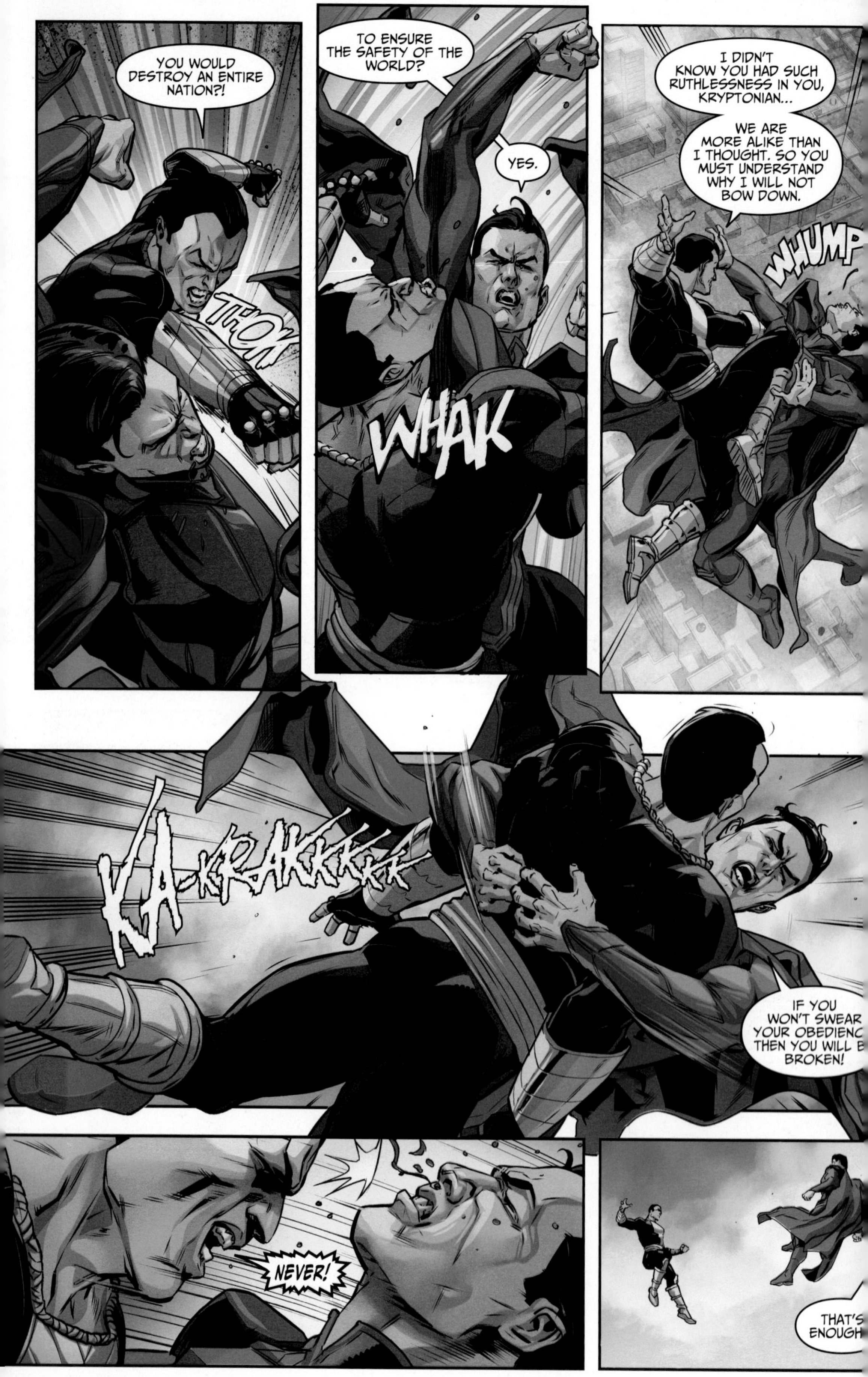

YOU WOULD DESTROY AN ENTIRE NATION?!
THOK
TO ENSURE THE SAFETY OF THE WORLD?
YES.
WHAK
I DIDN'T KNOW YOU HAD SUCH RUTHLESSNESS IN YOU, KRYPTONIAN...
WE ARE MORE ALIKE THAN I THOUGHT. SO YOU MUST UNDERSTAND WHY I WILL NOT BOW DOWN.
WHUMP
KA-KRAKKKKK
IF YOU WON'T SWEAR YOUR OBEDIENC
THEN YOU WILL B
BROKEN!
NEVER!
THAT'S ENOUGH

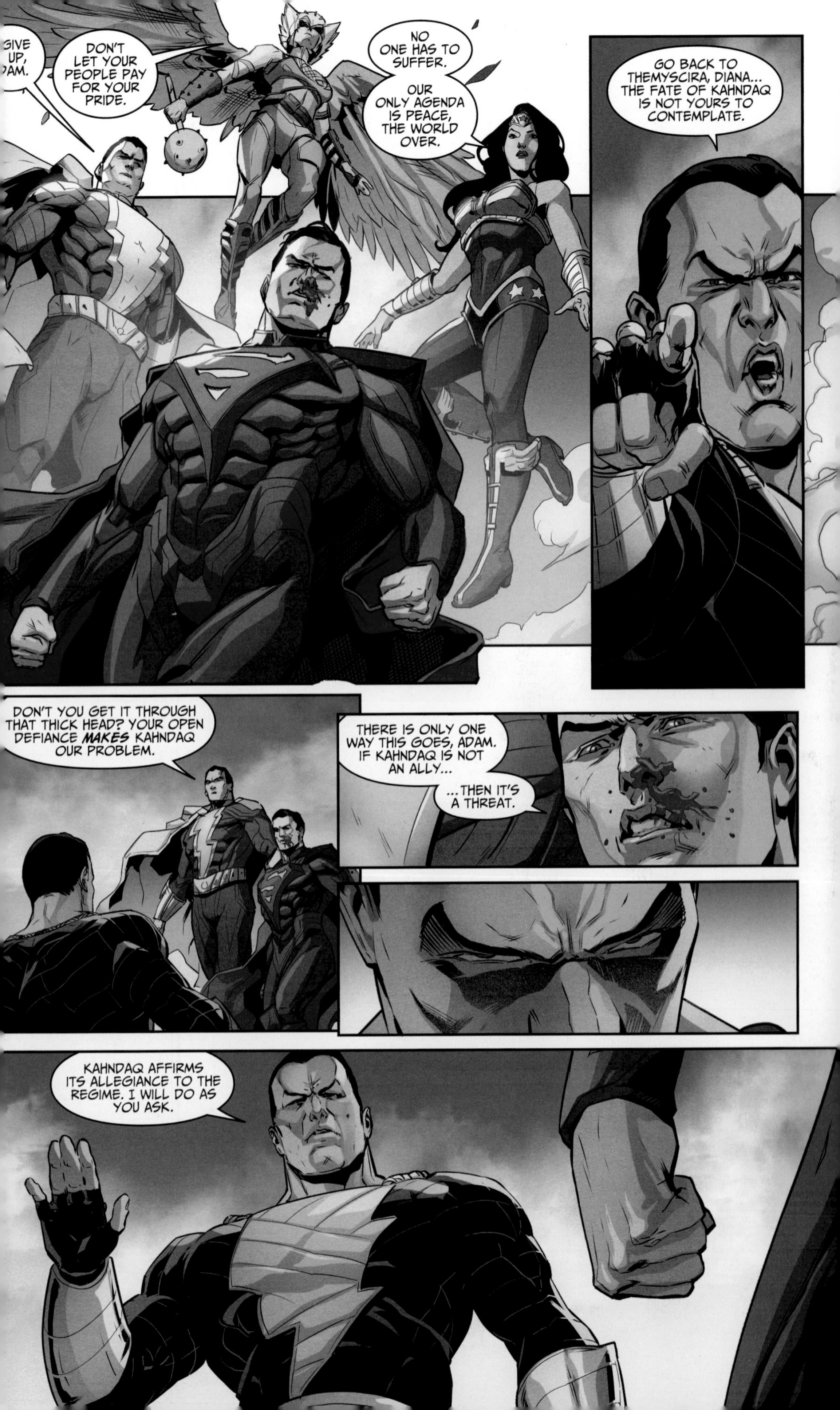

GIVE UP, ADAM.
DON'T LET YOUR PEOPLE PAY FOR YOUR PRIDE.
NO ONE HAS TO SUFFER.
OUR ONLY AGENDA IS PEACE, THE WORLD OVER.
GO BACK TO THEMYSCIRA, DIANA... THE FATE OF KAHNDAQ IS NOT YOURS TO CONTEMPLATE.
DON'T YOU GET IT THROUGH THAT THICK HEAD? YOUR OPEN DEFIANCE *MAKES* KAHNDAQ OUR PROBLEM.
THERE IS ONLY ONE WAY THIS GOES, ADAM. IF KAHNDAQ IS NOT AN ALLY...
...THEN IT'S A THREAT.
KAHNDAQ AFFIRMS ITS ALLEGIANCE TO THE REGIME. I WILL DO AS YOU ASK.

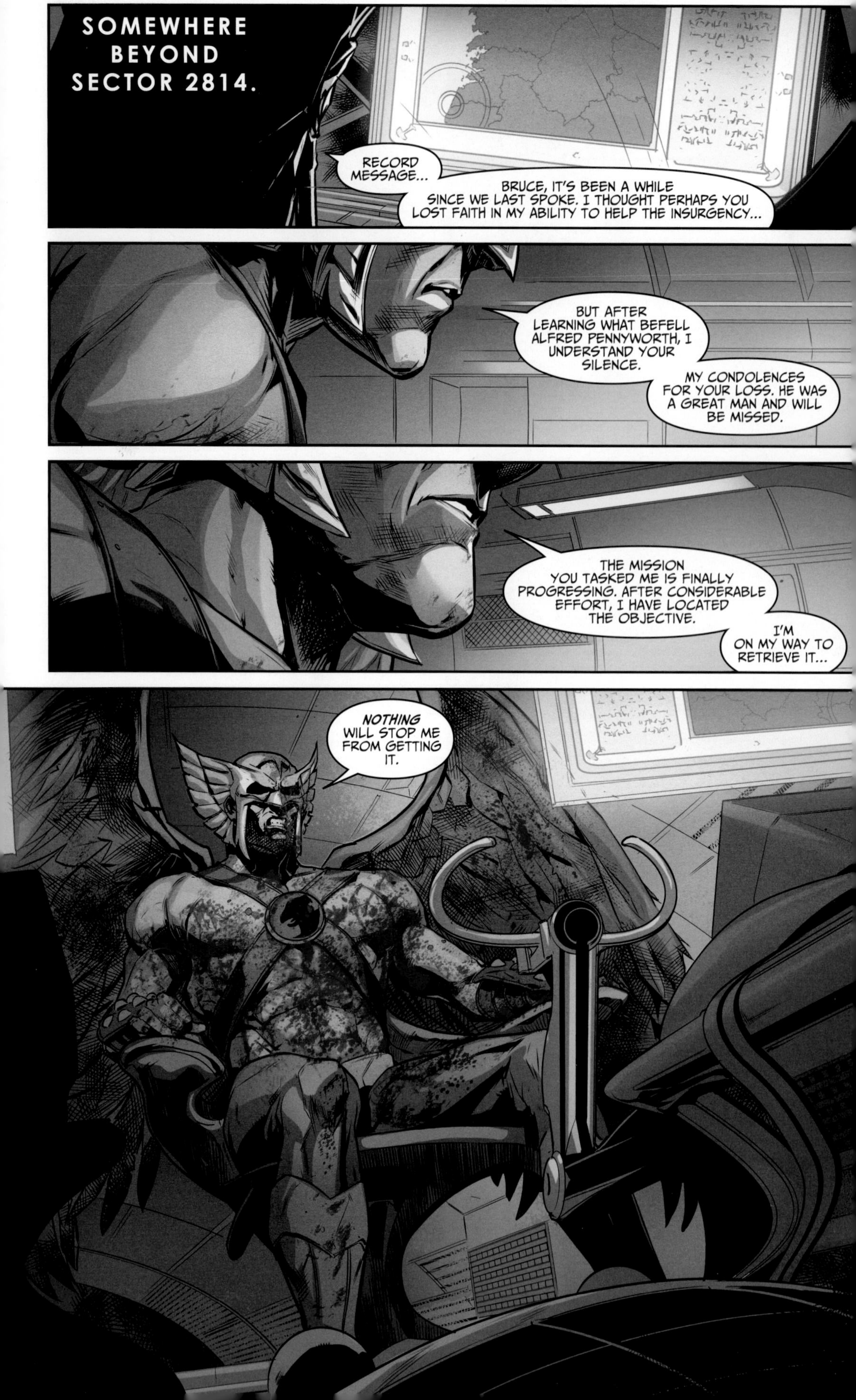

SOMEWHERE BEYOND SECTOR 2814.
RECORD MESSAGE...
BRUCE, IT'S BEEN A WHILE SINCE WE LAST SPOKE. I THOUGHT PERHAPS YOU LOST FAITH IN MY ABILITY TO HELP THE INSURGENCY...
BUT AFTER LEARNING WHAT BEFELL ALFRED PENNYWORTH, I UNDERSTAND YOUR SILENCE.
MY CONDOLENCES FOR YOUR LOSS. HE WAS A GREAT MAN AND WILL BE MISSED.
THE MISSION YOU TASKED ME IS FINALLY PROGRESSING. AFTER CONSIDERABLE EFFORT, I HAVE LOCATED THE OBJECTIVE.
I'M ON MY WAY TO RETRIEVE IT...
NOTHING WILL STOP ME FROM GETTING IT.

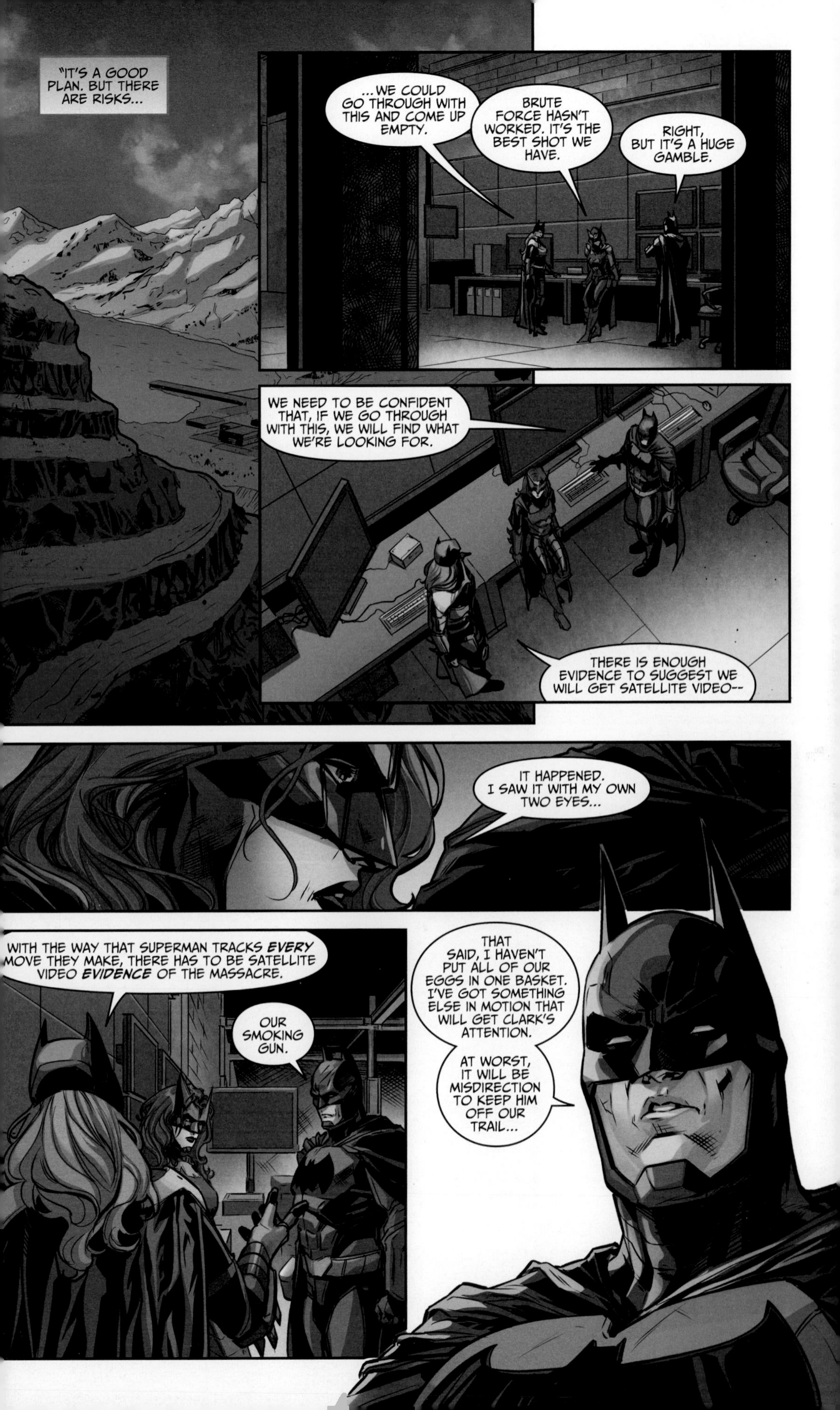
"IT'S A GOOD PLAN. BUT THERE ARE RISKS...
...WE COULD GO THROUGH WITH THIS AND COME UP EMPTY.
BRUTE FORCE HASN'T WORKED. IT'S THE BEST SHOT WE HAVE.
RIGHT, BUT IT'S A HUGE GAMBLE.
WE NEED TO BE CONFIDENT THAT, IF WE GO THROUGH WITH THIS, WE WILL FIND WHAT WE'RE LOOKING FOR.
THERE IS ENOUGH EVIDENCE TO SUGGEST WE WILL GET SATELLITE VIDEO--
IT HAPPENED. I SAW IT WITH MY OWN TWO EYES...
WITH THE WAY THAT SUPERMAN TRACKS *EVERY* MOVE THEY MAKE, THERE HAS TO BE SATELLITE VIDEO *EVIDENCE* OF THE MASSACRE.
OUR SMOKING GUN.
THAT SAID, I HAVEN'T PUT ALL OF OUR EGGS IN ONE BASKET. I'VE GOT SOMETHING ELSE IN MOTION THAT WILL GET CLARK'S ATTENTION.
AT WORST, IT WILL BE MISDIRECTION TO KEEP HIM OFF OUR TRAIL...

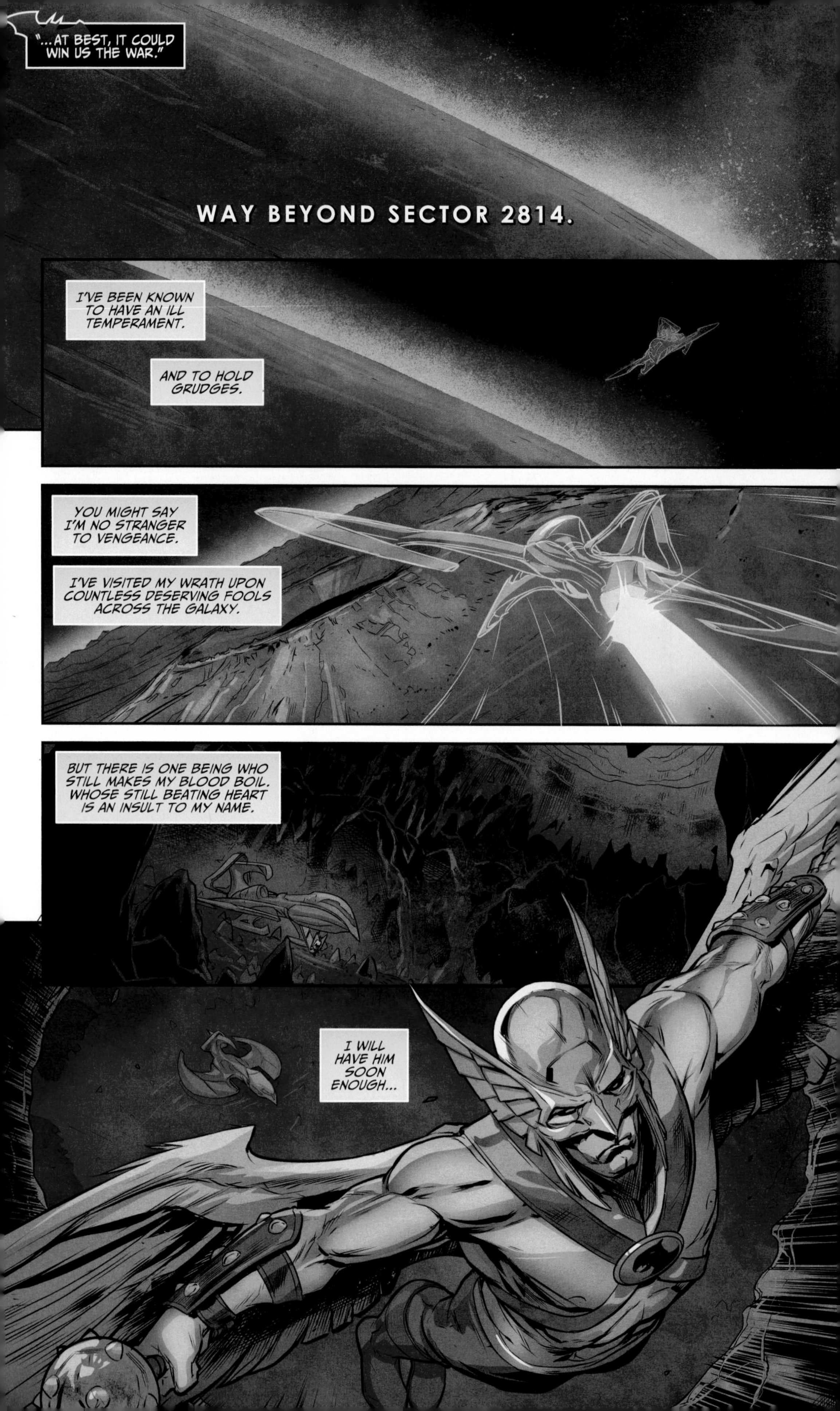
"...AT BEST, IT COULD WIN US THE WAR."
WAY BEYOND SECTOR 2814.
I'VE BEEN KNOWN TO HAVE AN ILL TEMPERAMENT.
AND TO HOLD GRUDGES.
YOU MIGHT SAY I'M NO STRANGER TO VENGEANCE.
I'VE VISITED MY WRATH UPON COUNTLESS DESERVING FOOLS ACROSS THE GALAXY.
BUT THERE IS ONE BEING WHO STILL MAKES MY BLOOD BOIL. WHOSE STILL BEATING HEART IS AN INSULT TO MY NAME.
I WILL HAVE HIM SOON ENOUGH...

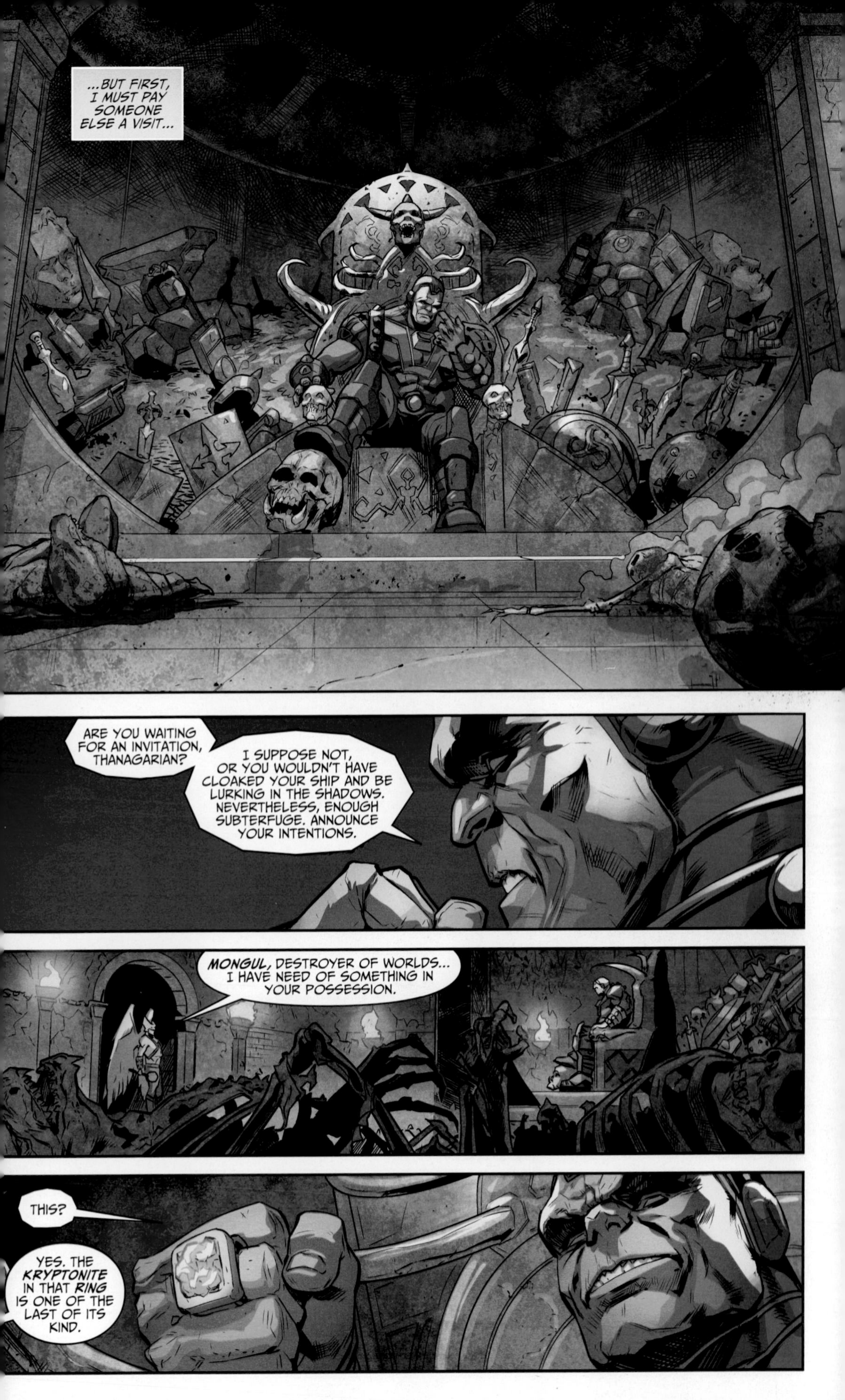
...BUT FIRST, I MUST PAY SOMEONE ELSE A VISIT...
ARE YOU WAITING FOR AN INVITATION, THANAGARIAN?
I SUPPOSE NOT, OR YOU WOULDN'T HAVE CLOAKED YOUR SHIP AND BE LURKING IN THE SHADOWS. NEVERTHELESS, ENOUGH SUBTERFUGE. ANNOUNCE YOUR INTENTIONS.
MONGUL, DESTROYER OF WORLDS... I HAVE NEED OF SOMETHING IN YOUR POSSESSION.
THIS?
YES. THE KRYPTONITE IN THAT RING IS ONE OF THE LAST OF ITS KIND.

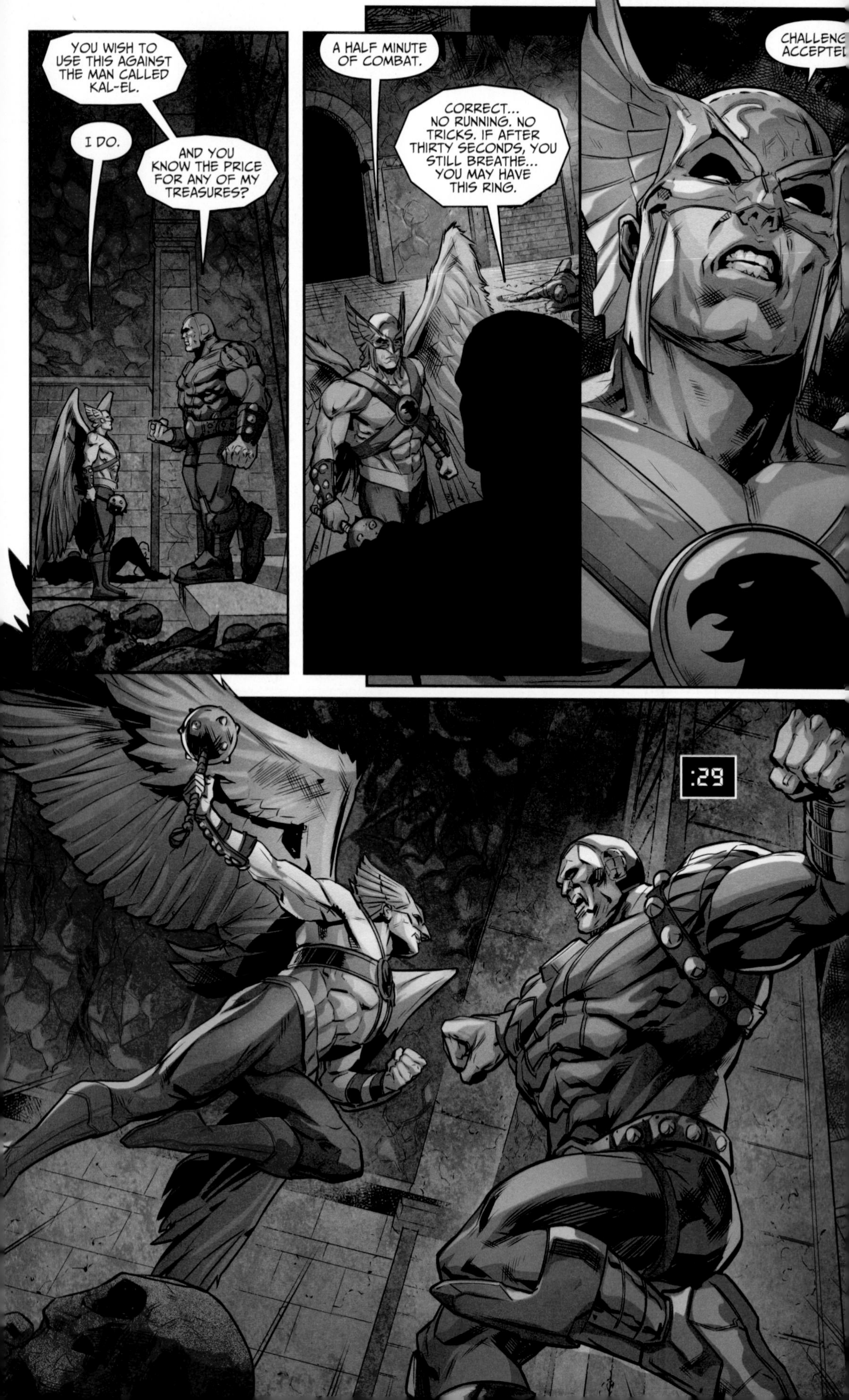
YOU WISH TO USE THIS AGAINST THE MAN CALLED KAL-EL.
I DO.
AND YOU KNOW THE PRICE FOR ANY OF MY TREASURES?
A HALF MINUTE OF COMBAT.
CORRECT... NO RUNNING. NO TRICKS. IF AFTER THIRTY SECONDS, YOU STILL BREATHE... YOU MAY HAVE THIS RING.
CHALLENG ACCEPTEI
:29

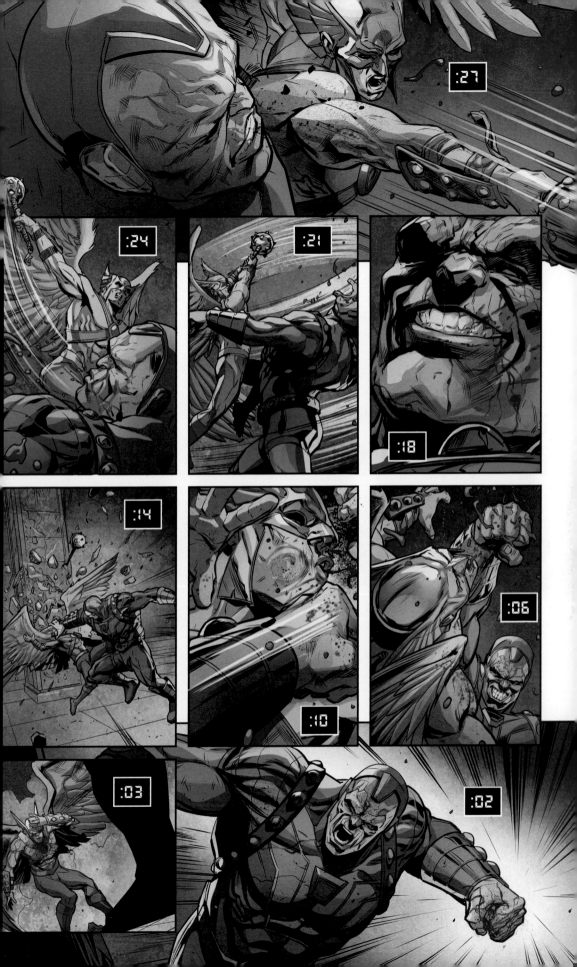

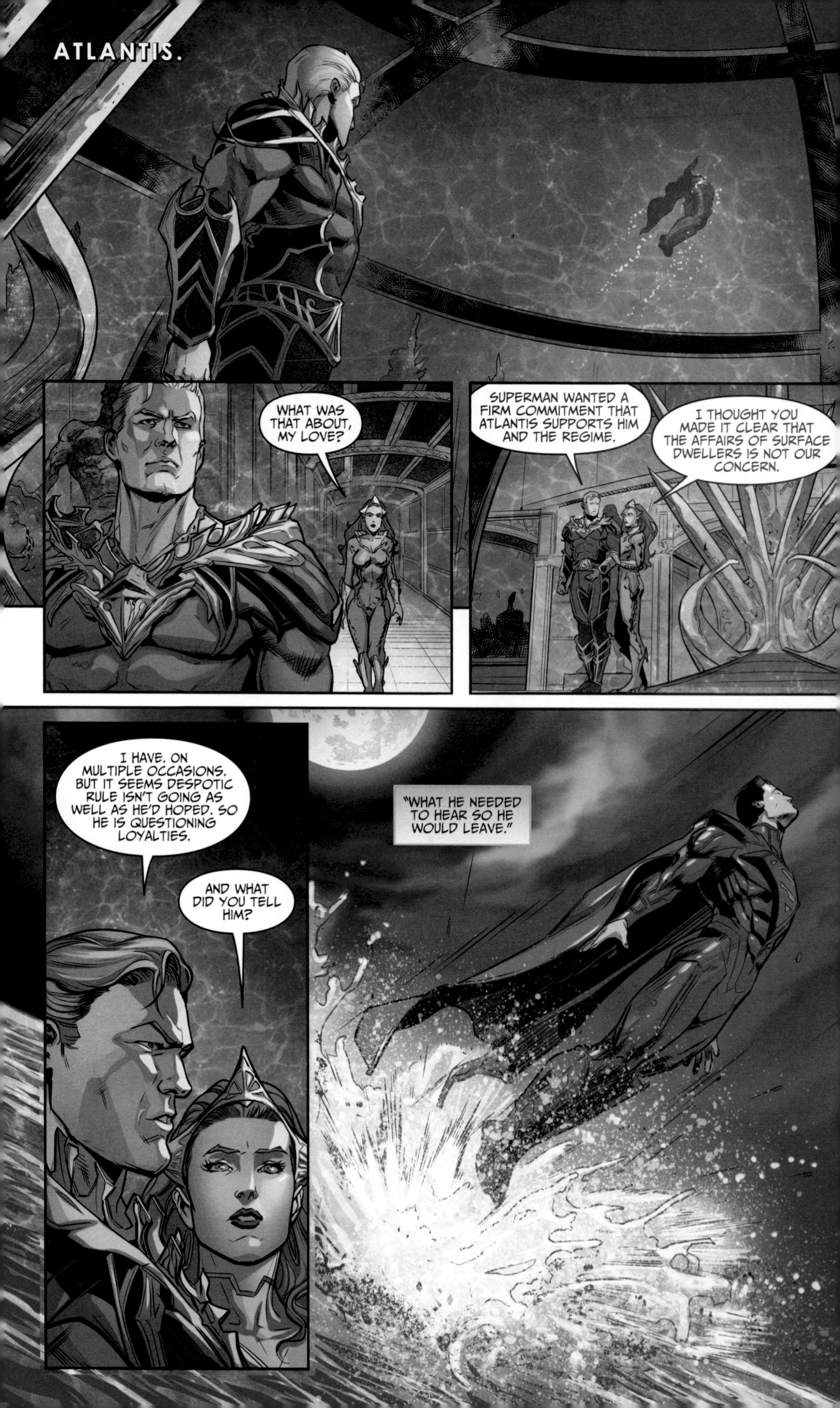
ATLANTIS.
WHAT WAS THAT ABOUT, MY LOVE?
SUPERMAN WANTED A FIRM COMMITMENT THAT ATLANTIS SUPPORTS HIM AND THE REGIME.
I THOUGHT YOU MADE IT CLEAR THAT THE AFFAIRS OF SURFACE DWELLERS IS NOT OUR CONCERN.
I HAVE. ON MULTIPLE OCCASIONS. BUT IT SEEMS DESPOTIC RULE ISN'T GOING AS WELL AS HE'D HOPED. SO HE IS QUESTIONING LOYALTIES.
AND WHAT DID YOU TELL HIM?
"WHAT HE NEEDED TO HEAR SO HE WOULD LEAVE."

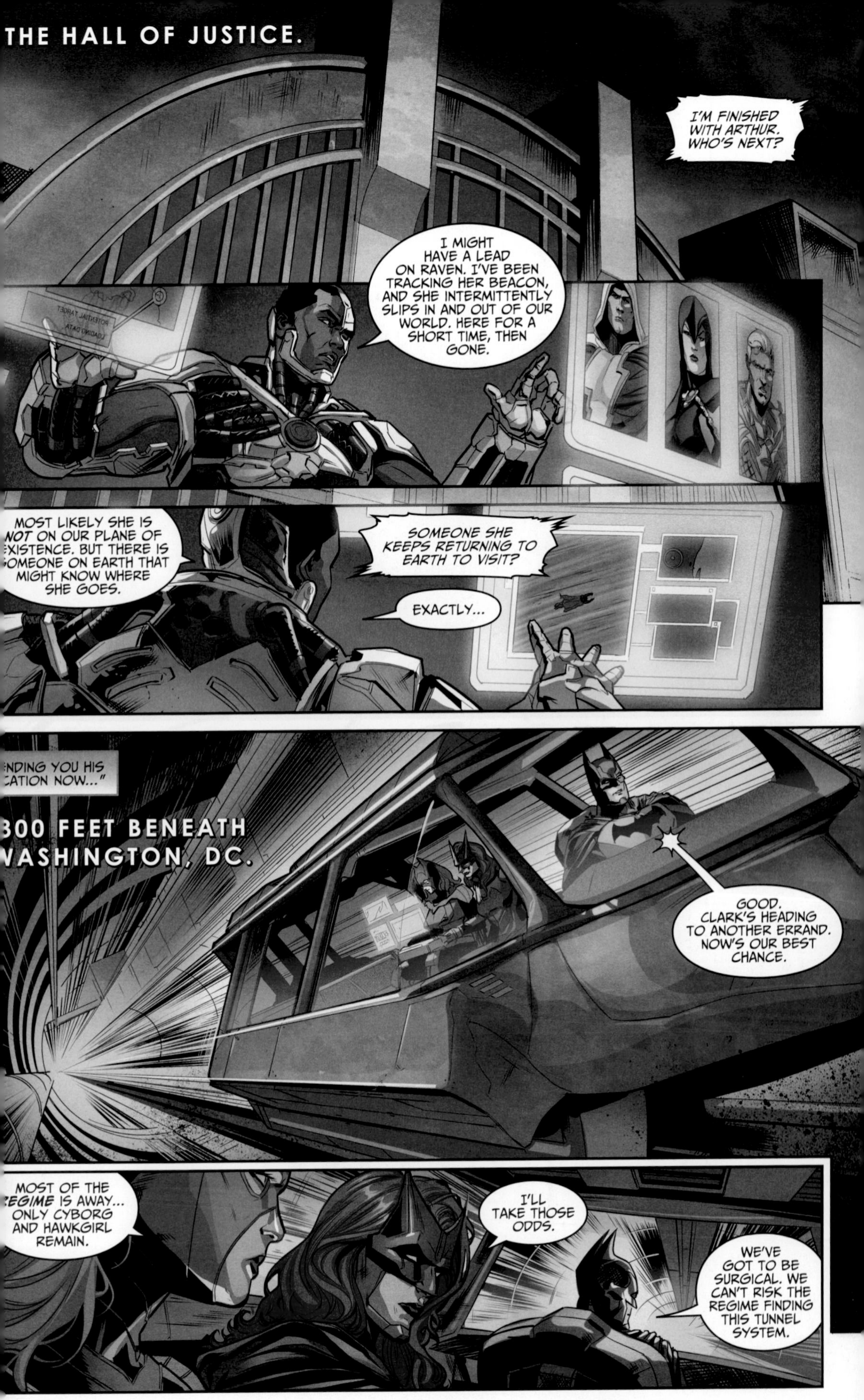
THE HALL OF JUSTICE.
I'M FINISHED WITH ARTHUR. WHO'S NEXT?
I MIGHT HAVE A LEAD ON RAVEN. I'VE BEEN TRACKING HER BEACON, AND SHE INTERMITTENTLY SLIPS IN AND OUT OF OUR WORLD. HERE FOR A SHORT TIME, THEN GONE.
MOST LIKELY SHE IS NOT ON OUR PLANE OF EXISTENCE. BUT THERE IS SOMEONE ON EARTH THAT MIGHT KNOW WHERE SHE GOES.
SOMEONE SHE KEEPS RETURNING TO EARTH TO VISIT?
EXACTLY...
NDING YOU HIS CATION NOW..."
300 FEET BENEATH WASHINGTON, DC.
GOOD. CLARK'S HEADING TO ANOTHER ERRAND. NOW'S OUR BEST CHANCE.
MOST OF THE REGIME IS AWAY... ONLY CYBORG AND HAWKGIRL REMAIN.
I'LL TAKE THOSE ODDS.
WE'VE GOT TO BE SURGICAL. WE CAN'T RISK THE REGIME FINDING THIS TUNNEL SYSTEM.

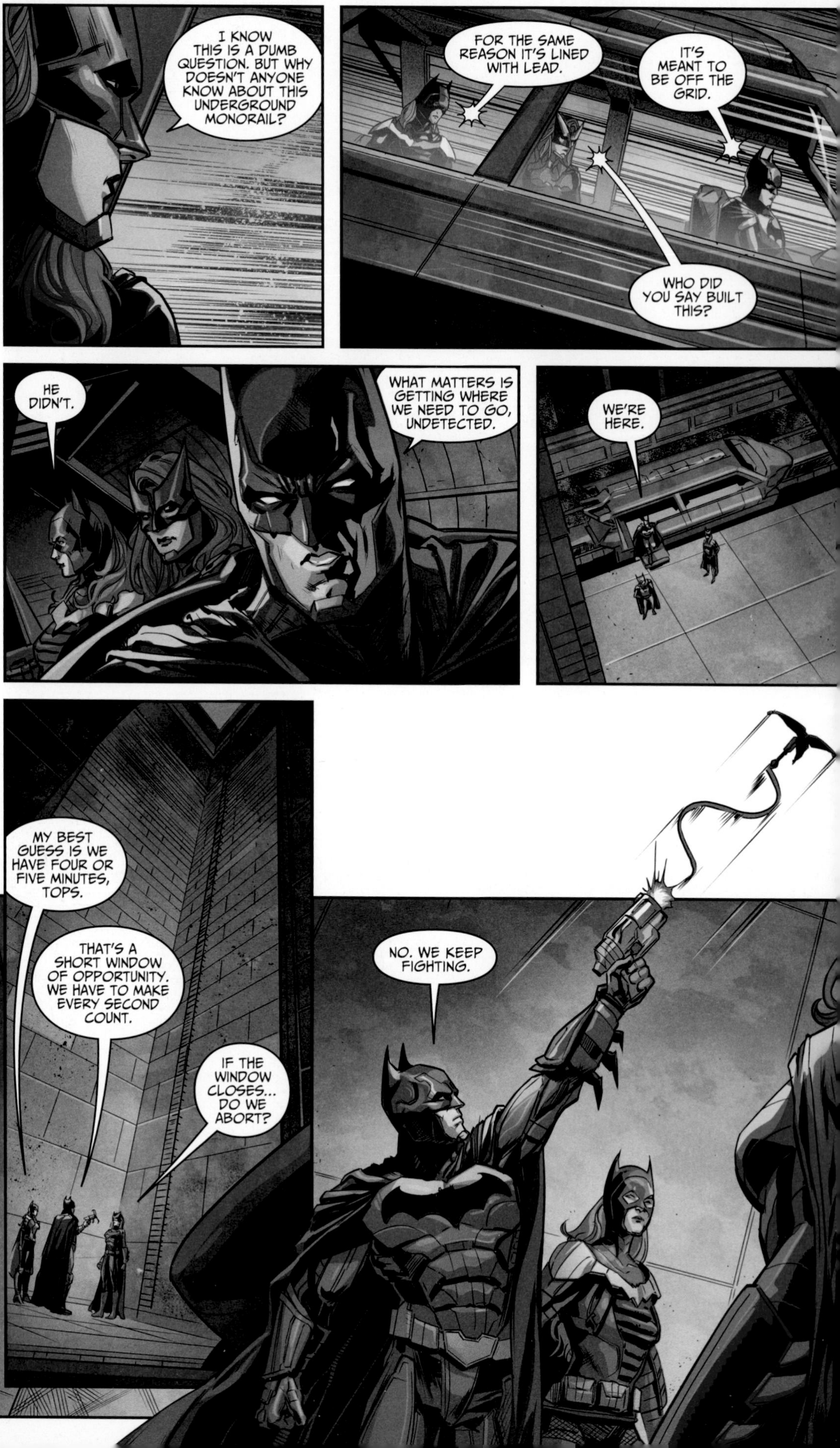
I KNOW THIS IS A DUMB QUESTION. BUT WHY DOESN'T ANYONE KNOW ABOUT THIS UNDERGROUND MONORAIL?
FOR THE SAME REASON IT'S LINED WITH LEAD.
IT'S MEANT TO BE OFF THE GRID.
WHO DID YOU SAY BUILT THIS?
HE DIDN'T.
WHAT MATTERS IS GETTING WHERE WE NEED TO GO, UNDETECTED.
WE'RE HERE.
MY BEST GUESS IS WE HAVE FOUR OR FIVE MINUTES, TOPS.
THAT'S A SHORT WINDOW OF OPPORTUNITY. WE HAVE TO MAKE EVERY SECOND COUNT.
IF THE WINDOW CLOSES... DO WE ABORT?
NO. WE KEEP FIGHTING.

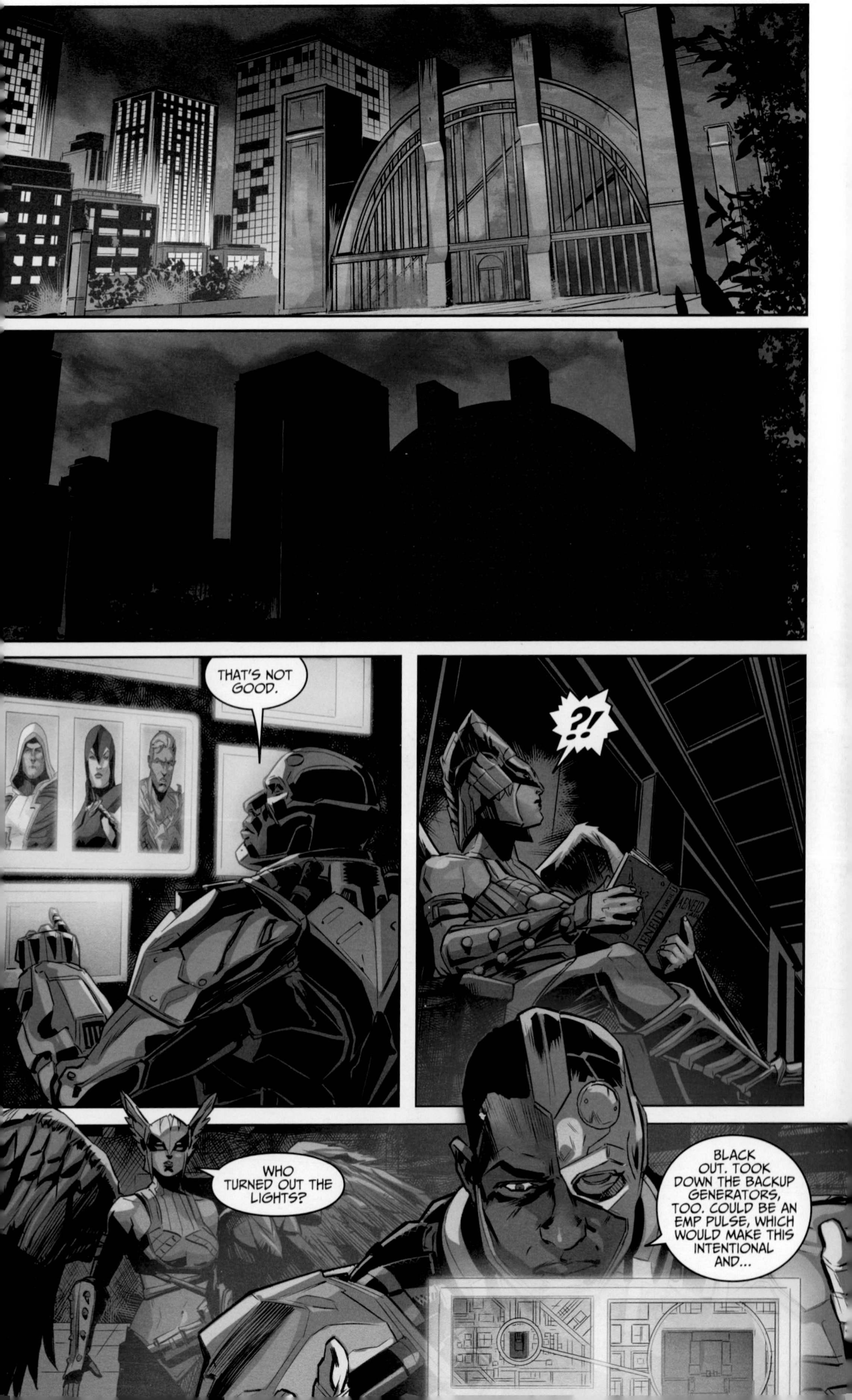
THAT'S NOT GOOD.
?!
WHO TURNED OUT THE LIGHTS?
BLACK OUT. TOOK DOWN THE BACKUP GENERATORS, TOO. COULD BE AN EMP PULSE, WHICH WOULD MAKE THIS INTENTIONAL AND...

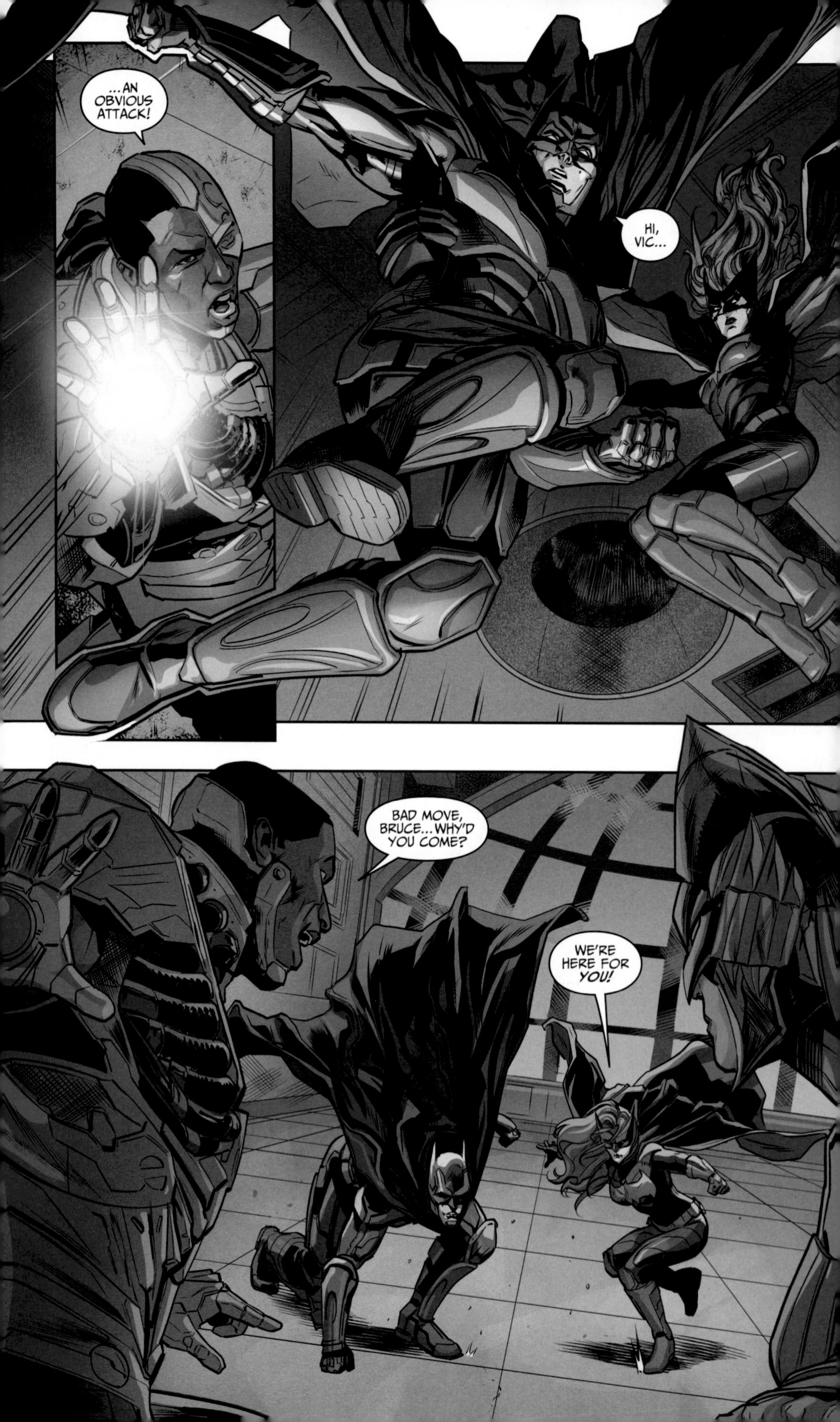
...AN OBVIOUS ATTACK!
HI, VIC...
BAD MOVE, BRUCE...WHY'D YOU COME?
WE'RE HERE FOR YOU!

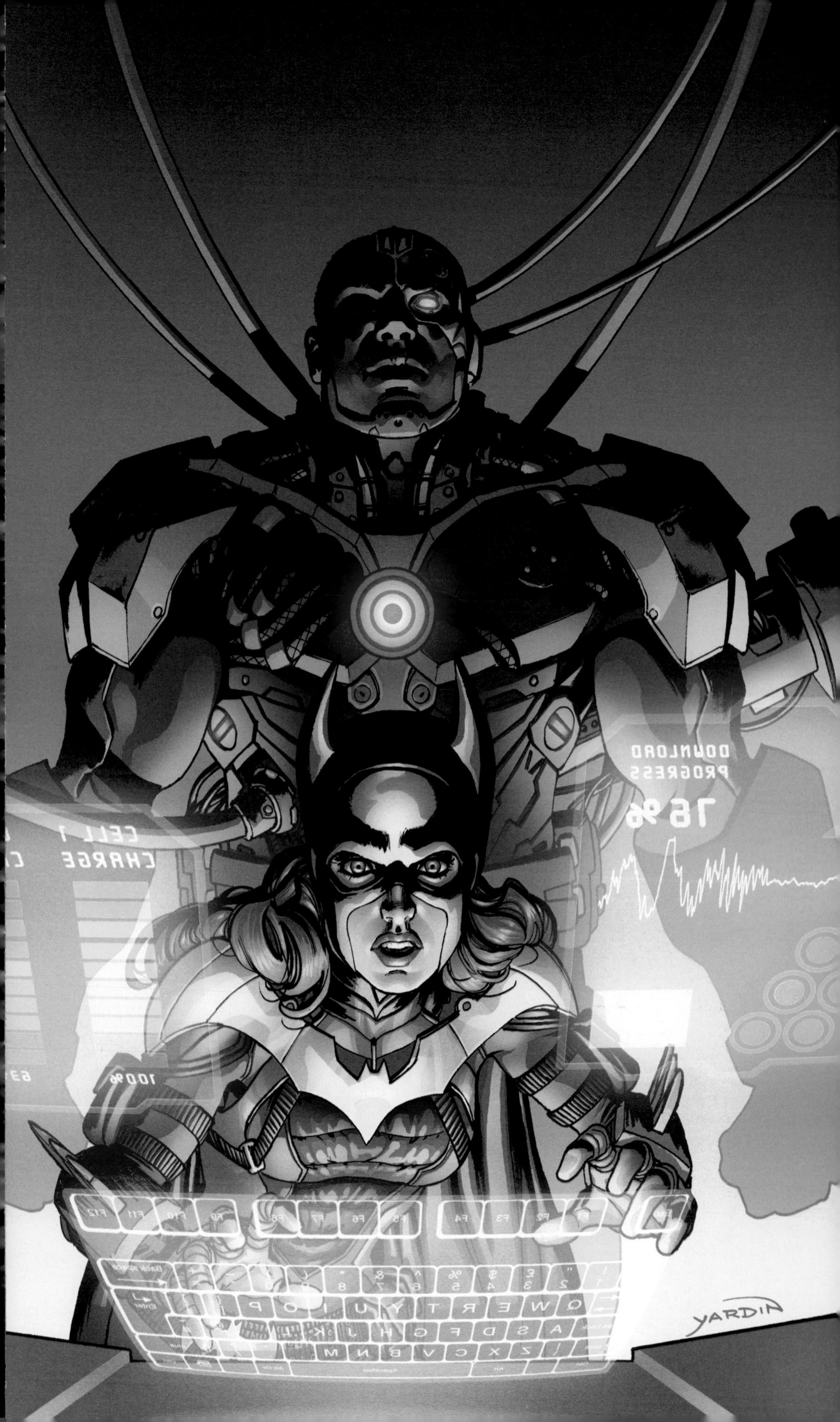
DOWNLOAD PROGRESS
16%
CELL 1
CHARGE
100%
YARDIN

"Surgical Strike" **Marco Santucci** Artist **Rex Lokus** Colorist

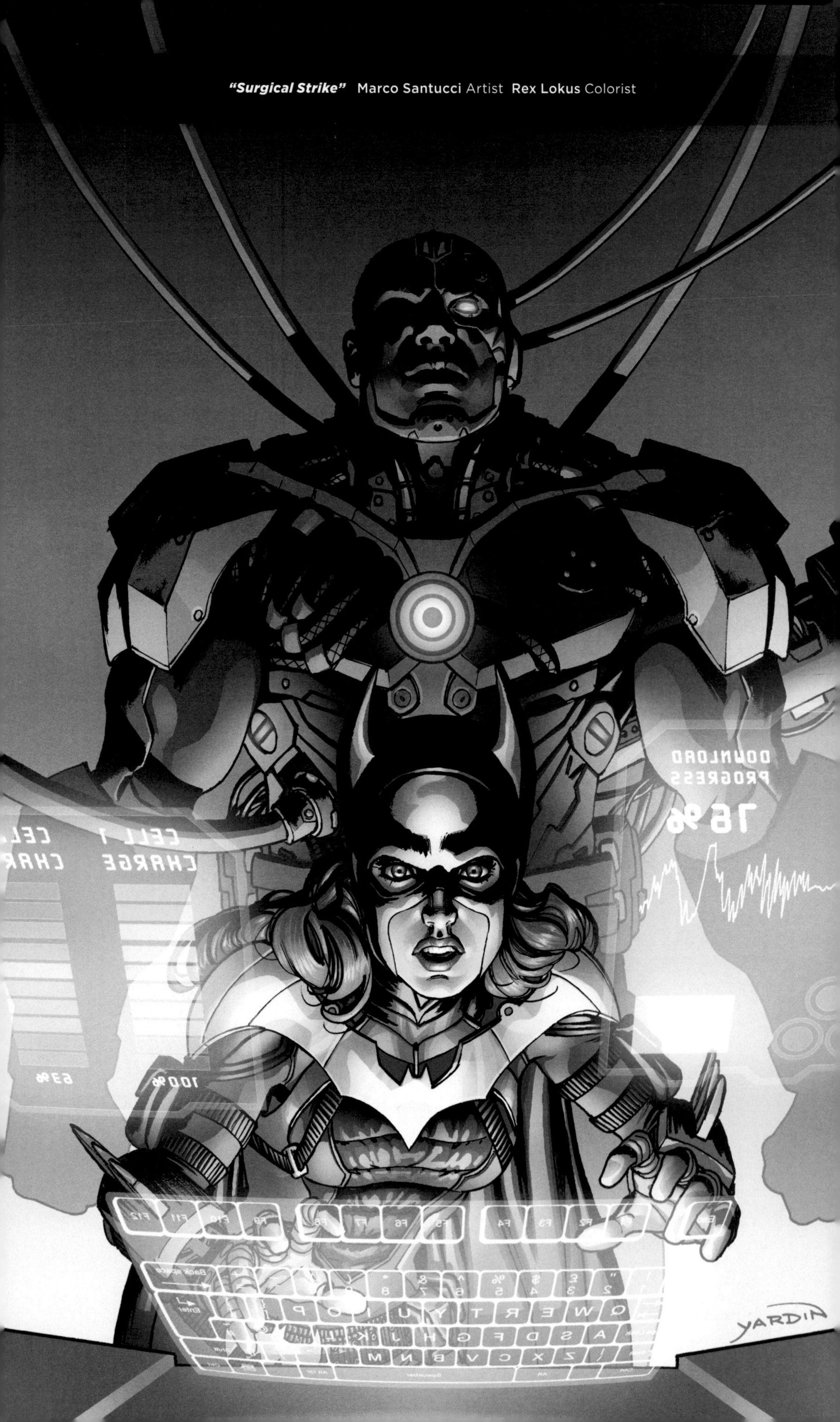

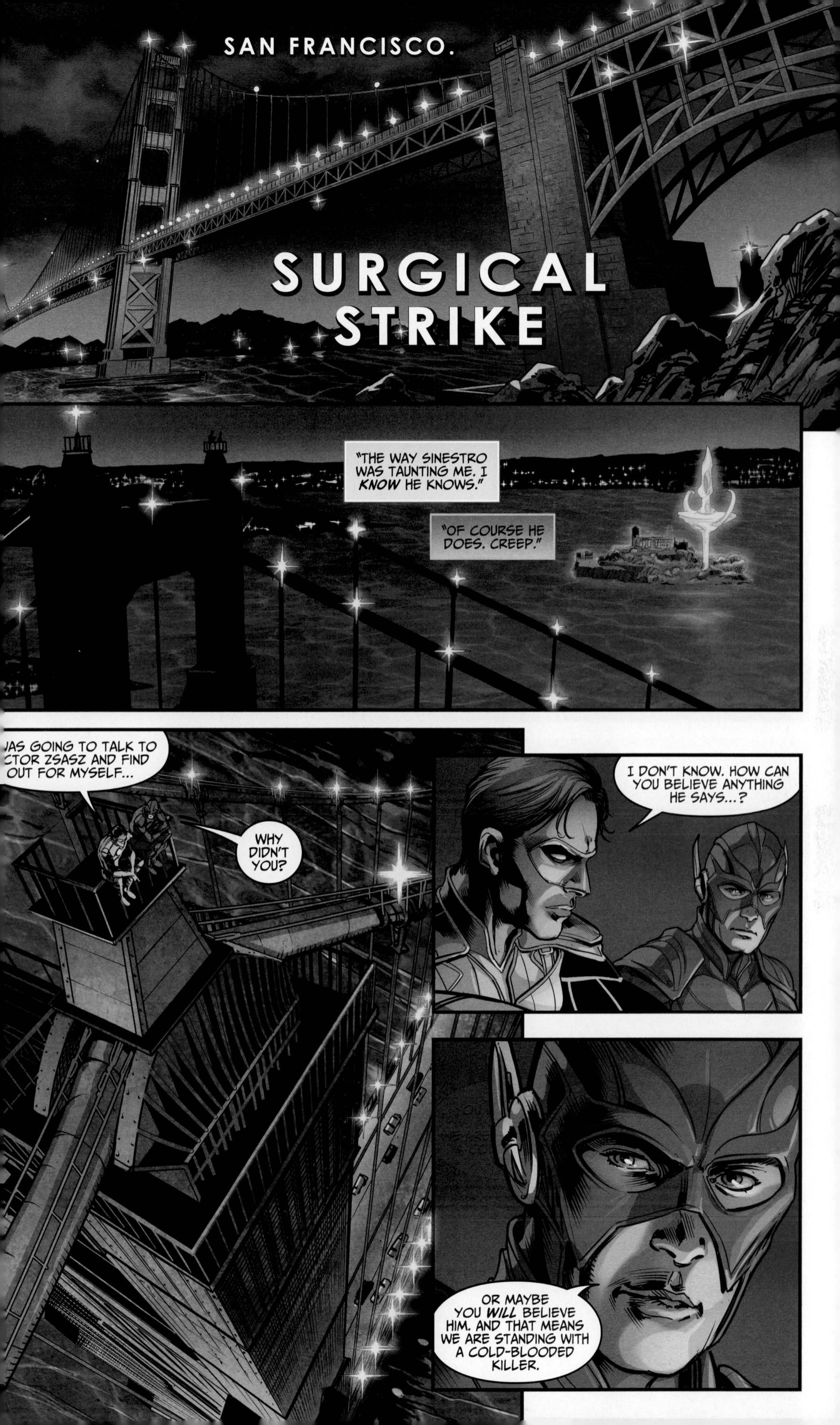
SAN FRANCISCO.
SURGICAL STRIKE
"THE WAY SINESTRO WAS TAUNTING ME. I KNOW HE KNOWS."
"OF COURSE HE DOES. CREEP."
WAS GOING TO TALK TO CTOR ZSASZ AND FIND OUT FOR MYSELF...
WHY DIDN'T YOU?
I DON'T KNOW. HOW CAN YOU BELIEVE ANYTHING HE SAYS...?
OR MAYBE YOU WILL BELIEVE HIM. AND THAT MEANS WE ARE STANDING WITH A COLD-BLOODED KILLER.

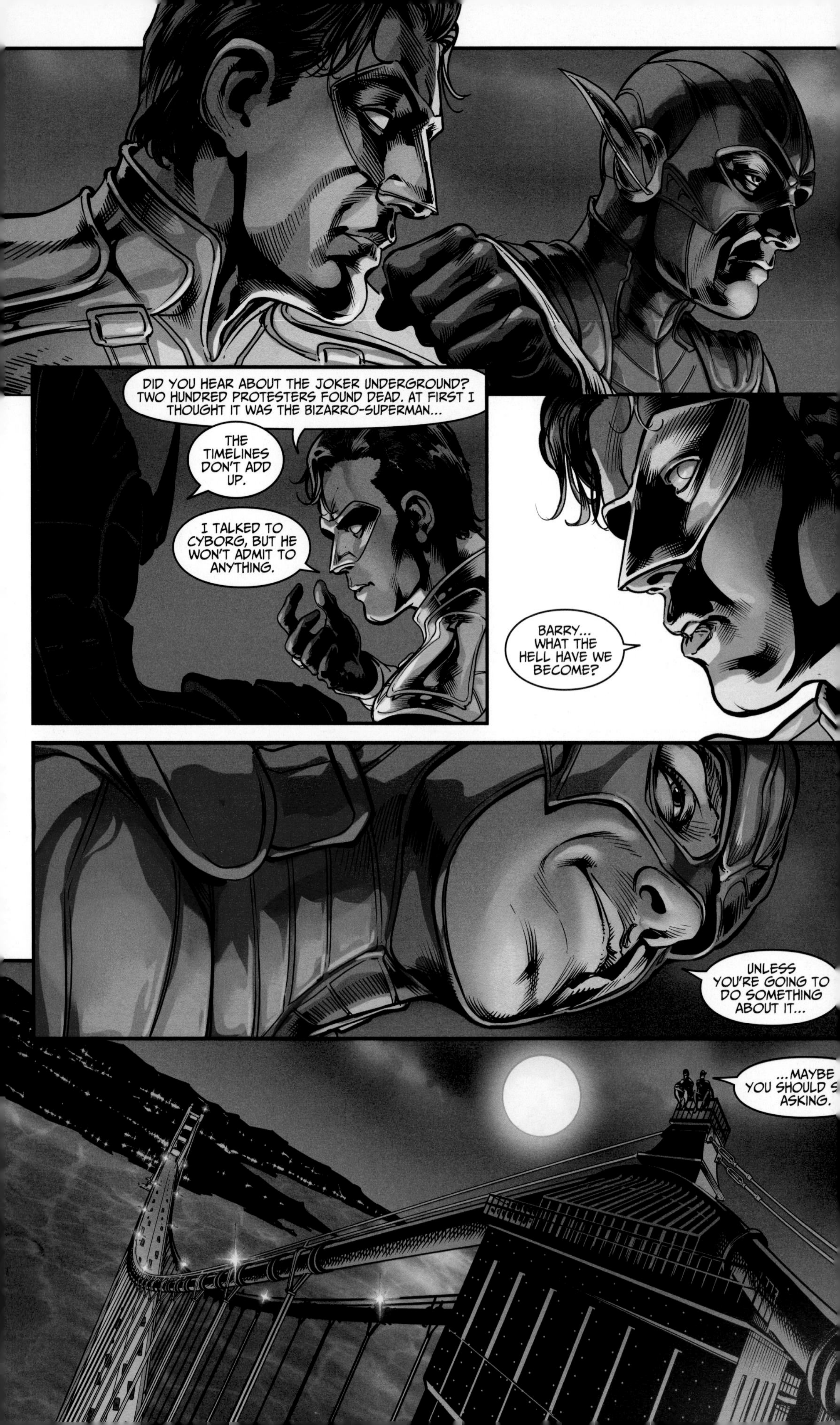
DID YOU HEAR ABOUT THE JOKER UNDERGROUND? TWO HUNDRED PROTESTERS FOUND DEAD. AT FIRST I THOUGHT IT WAS THE BIZARRO-SUPERMAN...
THE TIMELINES DON'T ADD UP.
I TALKED TO CYBORG, BUT HE WON'T ADMIT TO ANYTHING.
BARRY... WHAT THE HELL HAVE WE BECOME?
UNLESS YOU'RE GOING TO DO SOMETHING ABOUT IT...
...MAYBE YOU SHOULD
ASKING.

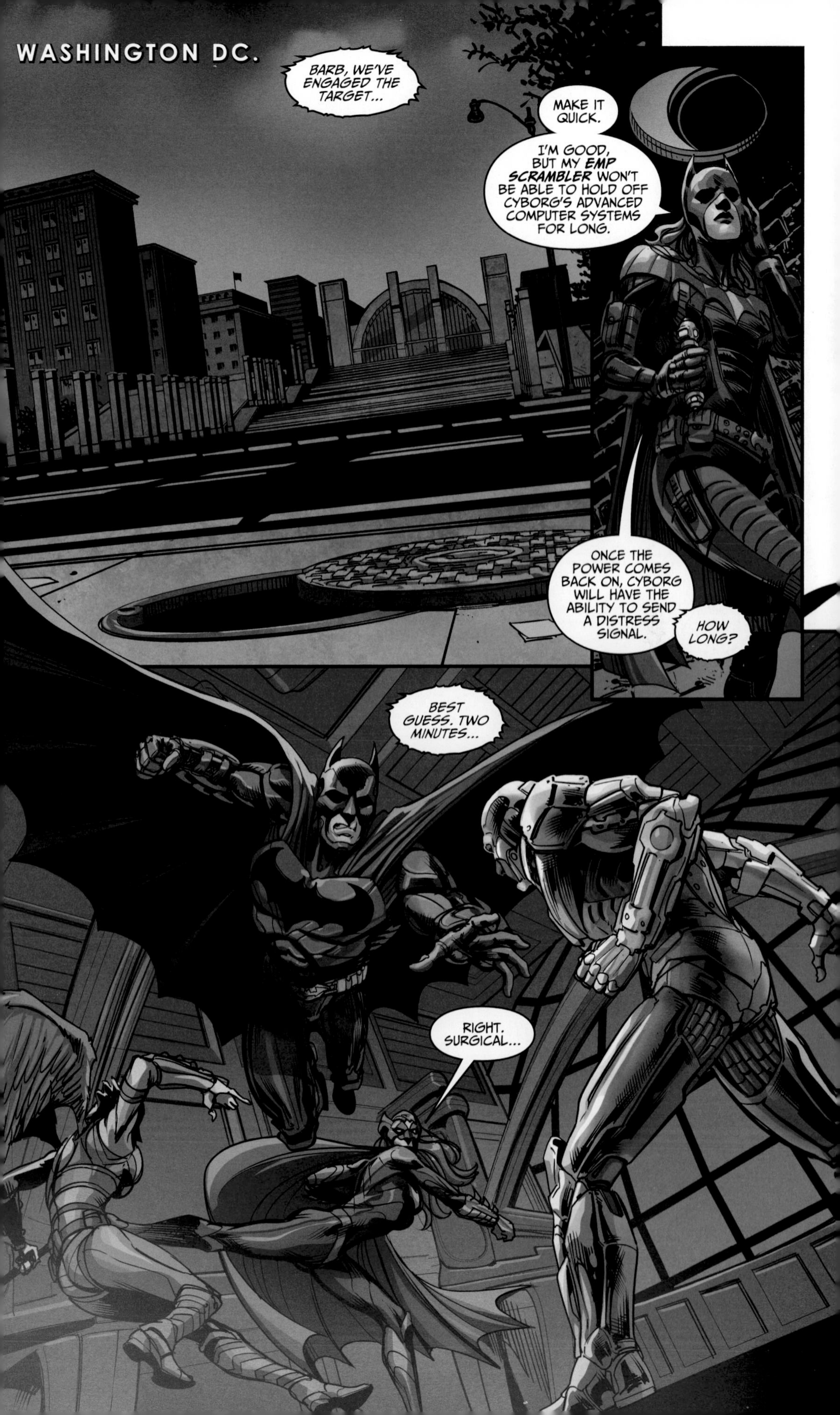

WASHINGTON DC.
BARB, WE'VE ENGAGED THE TARGET...
MAKE IT QUICK.
I'M GOOD, BUT MY EMP SCRAMBLER WON'T BE ABLE TO HOLD OFF CYBORG'S ADVANCED COMPUTER SYSTEMS FOR LONG.
ONCE THE POWER COMES BACK ON, CYBORG WILL HAVE THE ABILITY TO SEND A DISTRESS SIGNAL.
HOW LONG?
BEST GUESS. TWO MINUTES...
RIGHT. SURGICAL...

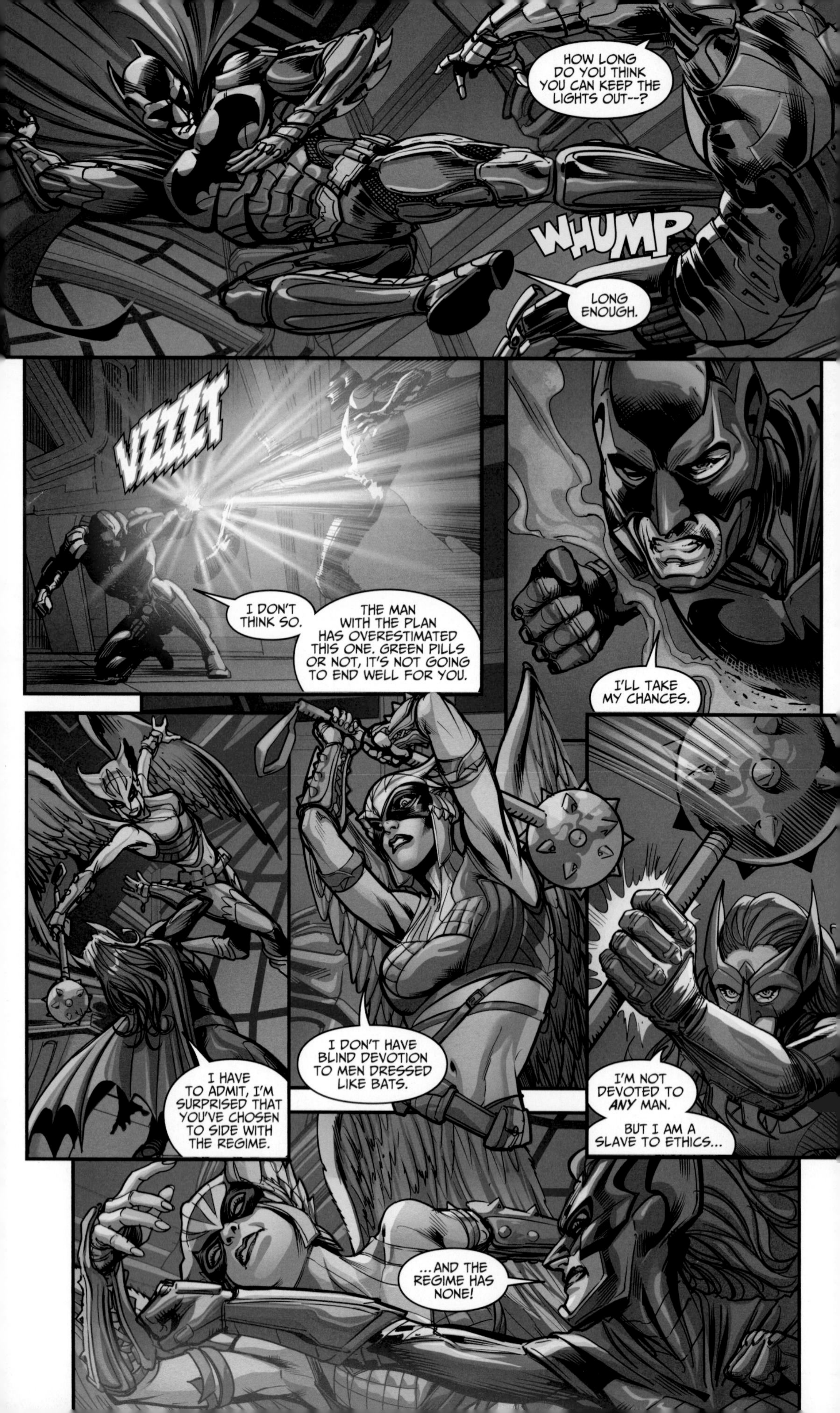
HOW LONG DO YOU THINK YOU CAN KEEP THE LIGHTS OUT--?
WHUMP
LONG ENOUGH.
VZZZT
I DON'T THINK SO.
THE MAN WITH THE PLAN HAS OVERESTIMATED THIS ONE. GREEN PILLS OR NOT, IT'S NOT GOING TO END WELL FOR YOU.
I'LL TAKE MY CHANCES.
I HAVE TO ADMIT, I'M SURPRISED THAT YOU'VE CHOSEN TO SIDE WITH THE REGIME.
I DON'T HAVE BLIND DEVOTION TO MEN DRESSED LIKE BATS.
I'M NOT DEVOTED TO *ANY* MAN.
BUT I AM A SLAVE TO ETHICS...
...AND THE REGIME HAS NONE!

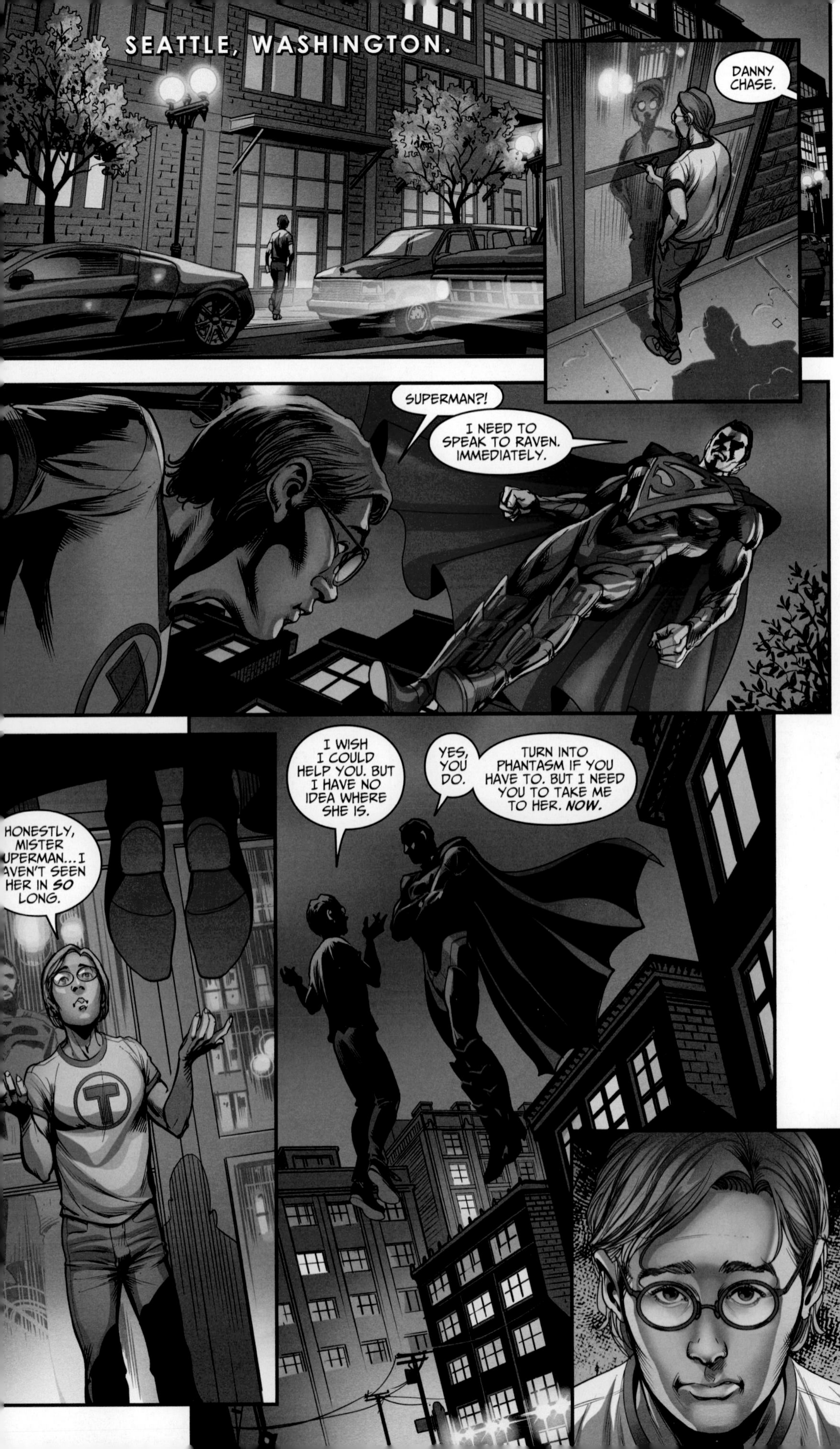
SEATTLE, WASHINGTON.
DANNY CHASE.
SUPERMAN?!
I NEED TO SPEAK TO RAVEN. IMMEDIATELY.
HONESTLY, MISTER SUPERMAN... I HAVEN'T SEEN HER IN *SO* LONG.
I WISH I COULD HELP YOU. BUT I HAVE NO IDEA WHERE SHE IS.
YES, YOU DO.
TURN INTO PHANTASM IF YOU HAVE TO. BUT I NEED YOU TO TAKE ME TO HER. *NOW.*

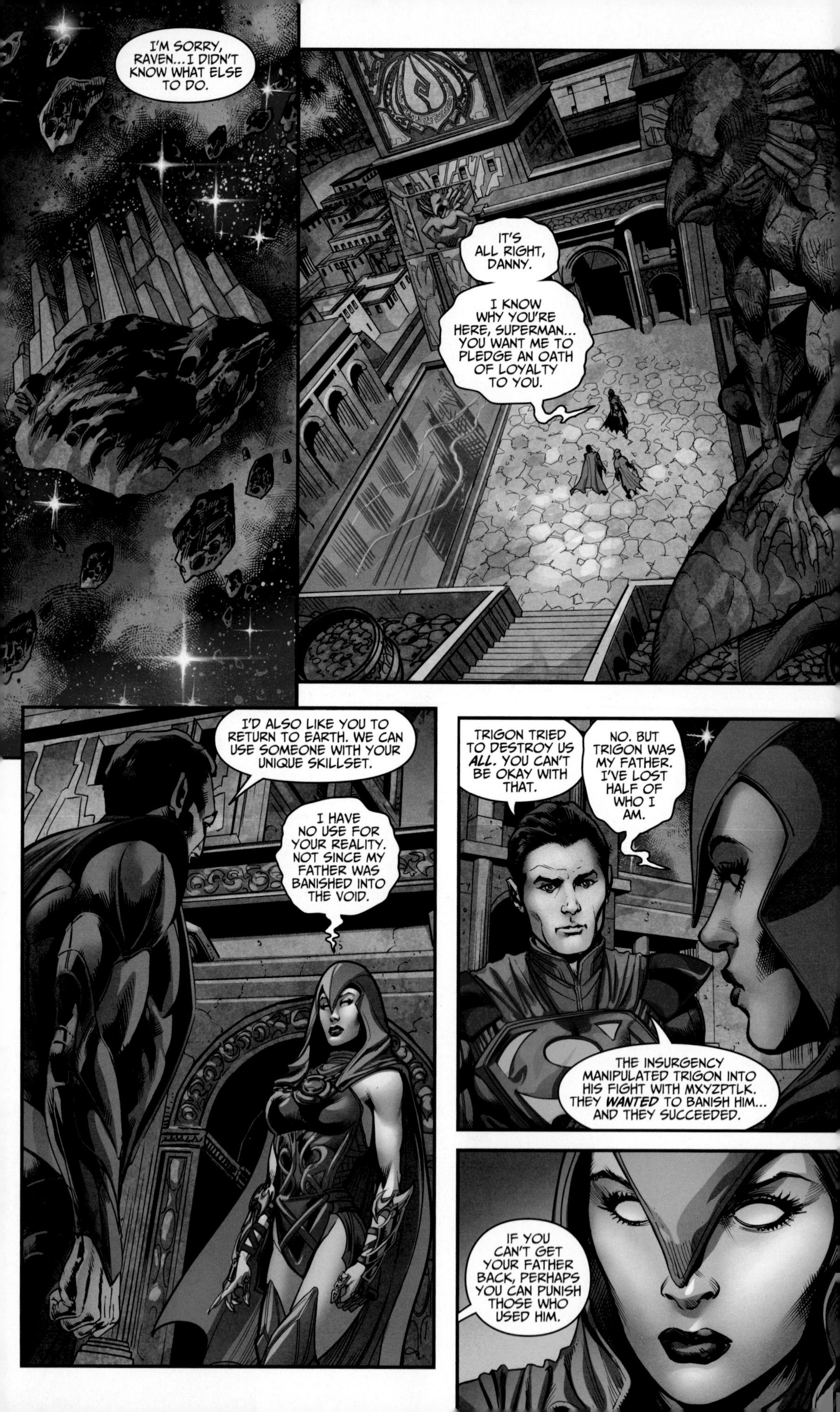
I'M SORRY, RAVEN... I DIDN'T KNOW WHAT ELSE TO DO.
IT'S ALL RIGHT, DANNY.
I KNOW WHY YOU'RE HERE, SUPERMAN... YOU WANT ME TO PLEDGE AN OATH OF LOYALTY TO YOU.
I'D ALSO LIKE YOU TO RETURN TO EARTH. WE CAN USE SOMEONE WITH YOUR UNIQUE SKILLSET.
I HAVE NO USE FOR YOUR REALITY. NOT SINCE MY FATHER WAS BANISHED INTO THE VOID.
TRIGON TRIED TO DESTROY US ALL. YOU CAN'T BE OKAY WITH THAT.
NO. BUT TRIGON WAS MY FATHER. I'VE LOST HALF OF WHO I AM.
THE INSURGENCY MANIPULATED TRIGON INTO HIS FIGHT WITH MXYZPTLK. THEY WANTED TO BANISH HIM... AND THEY SUCCEEDED.
IF YOU CAN'T GET YOUR FATHER BACK, PERHAPS YOU CAN PUNISH THOSE WHO USED HIM.

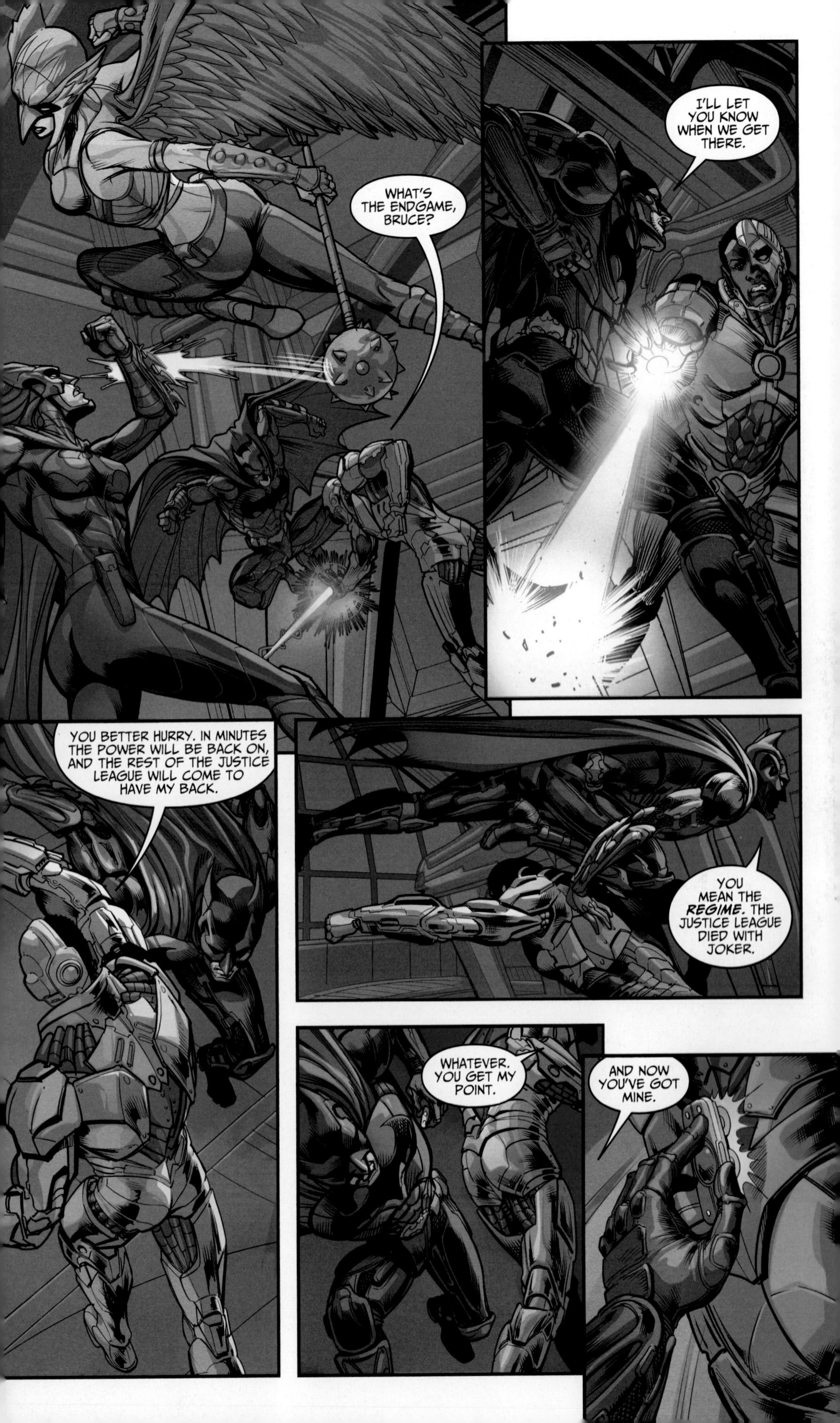
WHAT'S THE ENDGAME, BRUCE?
I'LL LET YOU KNOW WHEN WE GET THERE.
YOU BETTER HURRY. IN MINUTES THE POWER WILL BE BACK ON, AND THE REST OF THE JUSTICE LEAGUE WILL COME TO HAVE MY BACK.
YOU MEAN THE *REGIME*. THE JUSTICE LEAGUE DIED WITH JOKER.
WHATEVER. YOU GET MY POINT.
AND NOW YOU'VE GOT MINE.

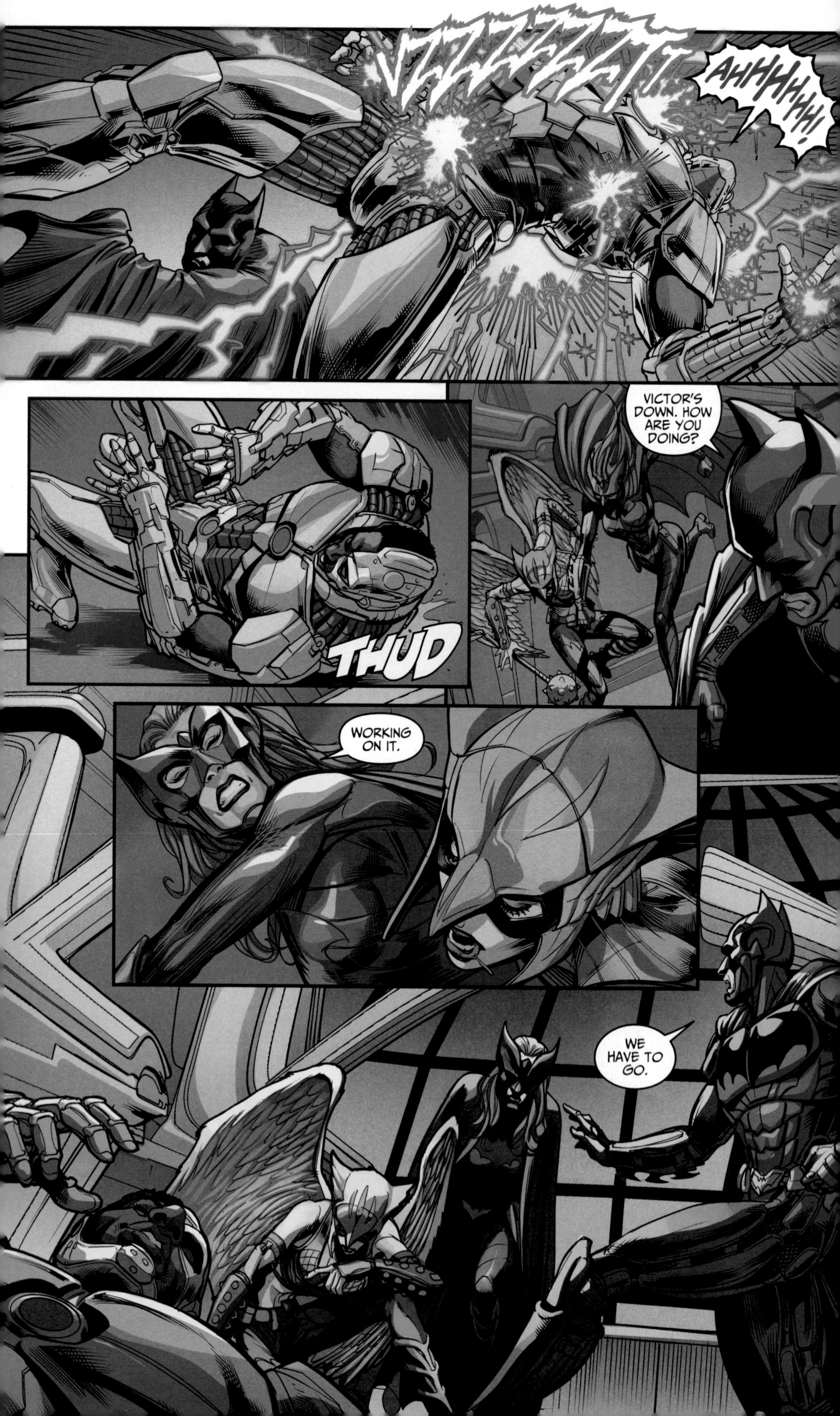
ZZZZAAT!
AHHHHHH!
THUD
VICTOR'S DOWN. HOW ARE YOU DOING?
WORKING ON IT.
WE HAVE TO GO.

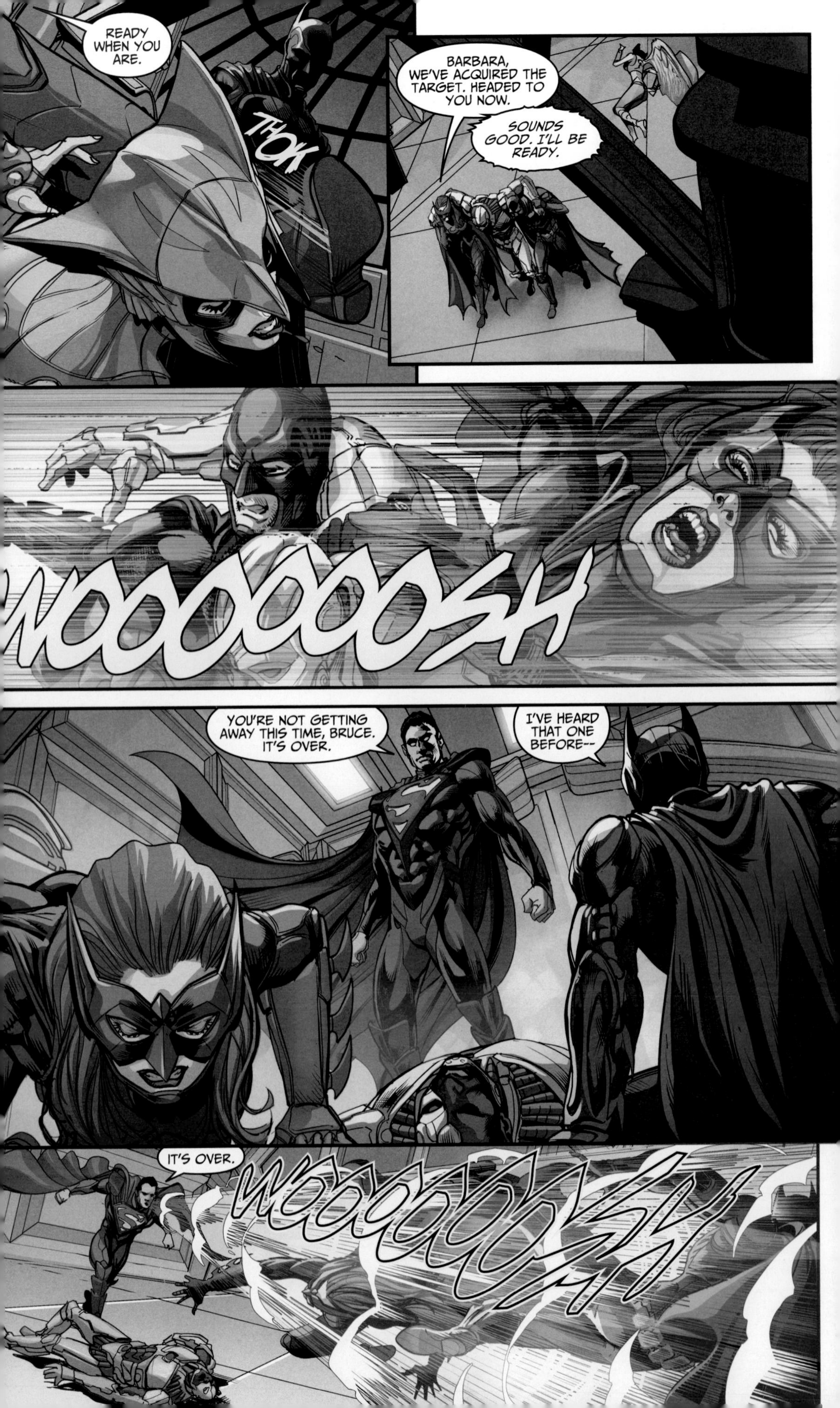
READY WHEN YOU ARE.
THOK
BARBARA, WE'VE ACQUIRED THE TARGET. HEADED TO YOU NOW.
SOUNDS GOOD. I'LL BE READY.
WOOOOOOSH
YOU'RE NOT GETTING AWAY THIS TIME, BRUCE. IT'S OVER.
I'VE HEARD THAT ONE BEFORE--
IT'S OVER.
WOOOOOOSH

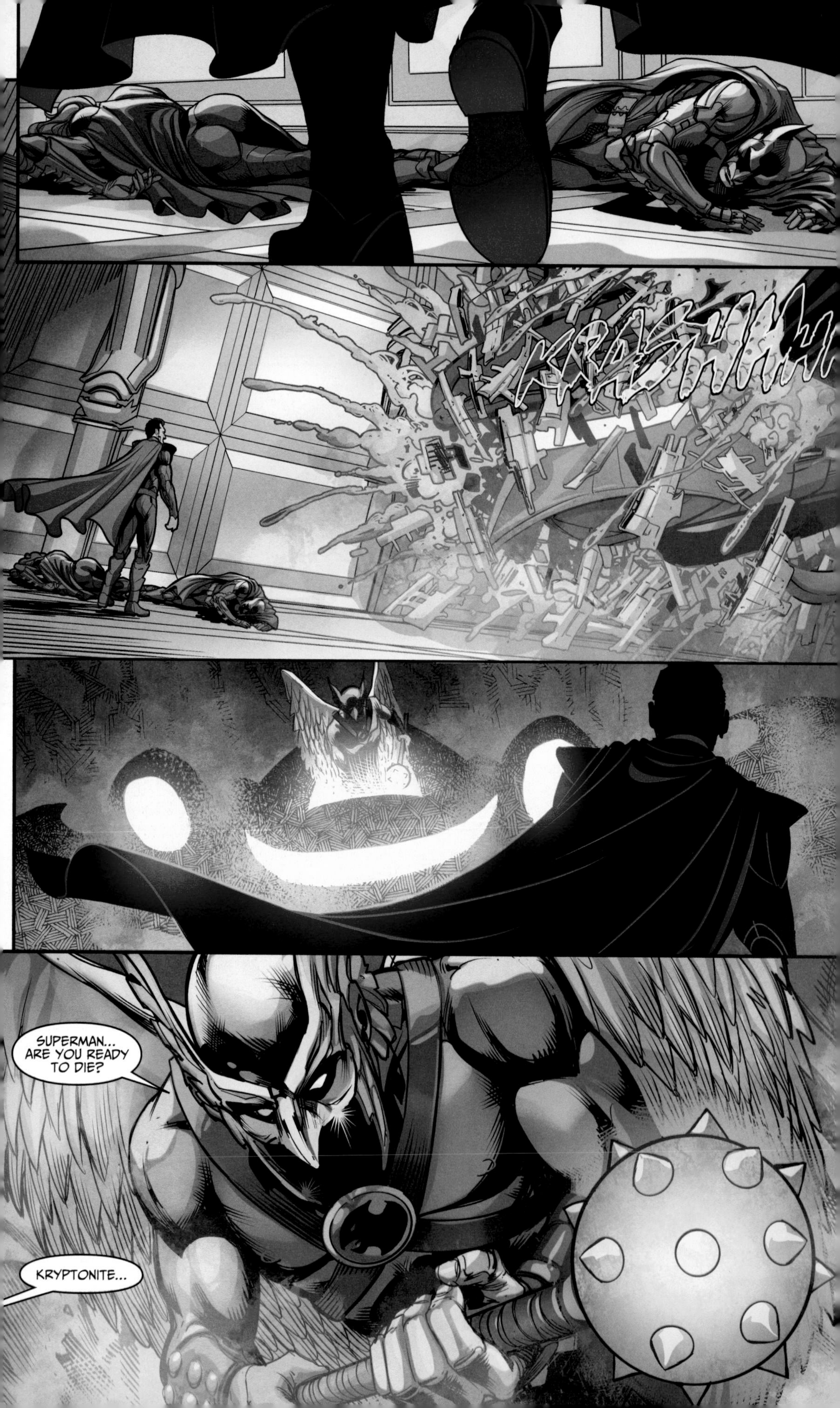
KRASHHH
SUPERMAN... ARE YOU READY TO DIE?
KRYPTONITE...

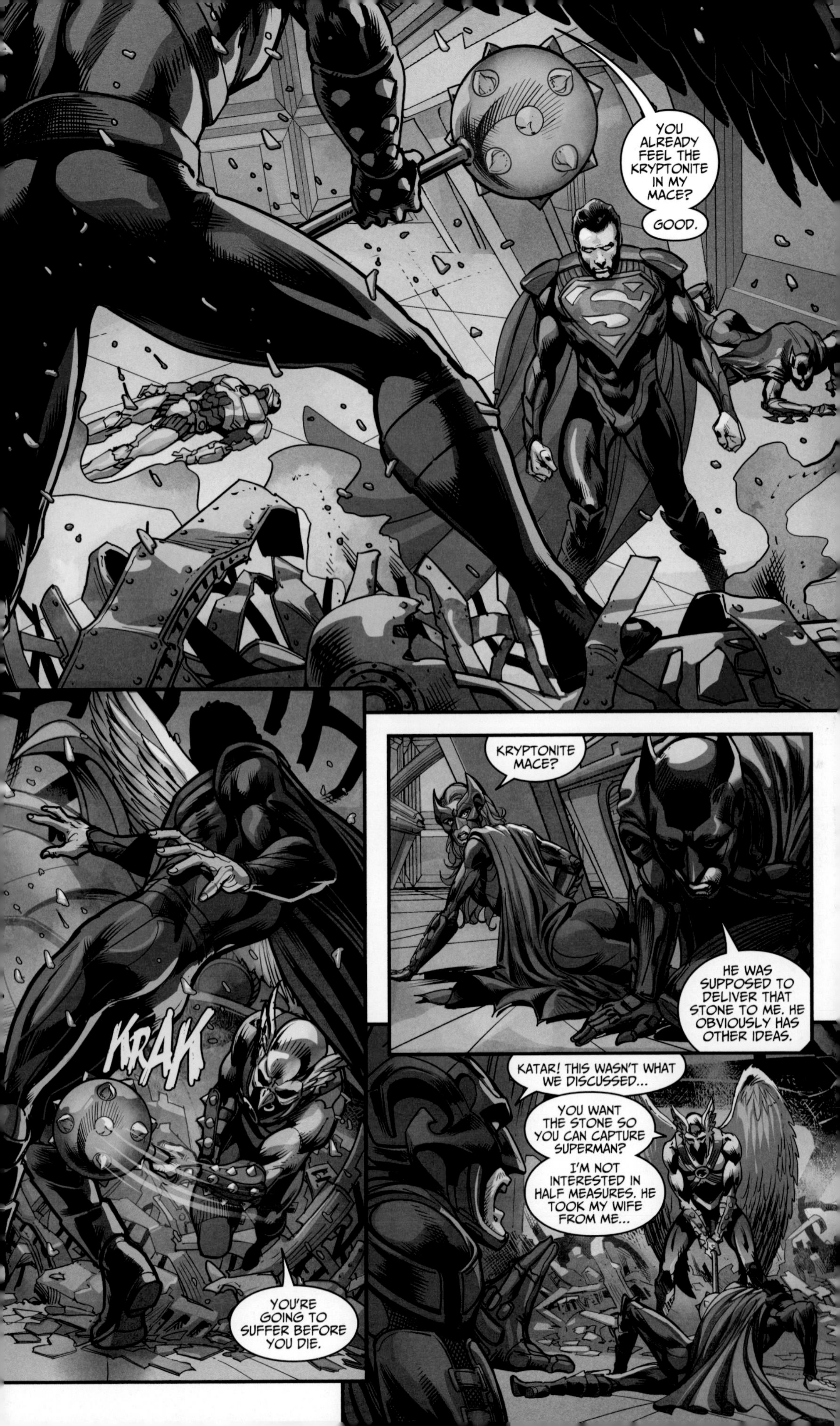
YOU ALREADY FEEL THE KRYPTONITE IN MY MACE?
GOOD.
KRAK
YOU'RE GOING TO SUFFER BEFORE YOU DIE.
KRYPTONITE MACE?
HE WAS SUPPOSED TO DELIVER THAT STONE TO ME. HE OBVIOUSLY HAS OTHER IDEAS.
KATAR! THIS WASN'T WHAT WE DISCUSSED...
YOU WANT THE STONE SO YOU CAN CAPTURE SUPERMAN?
I'M NOT INTERESTED IN HALF MEASURES. HE TOOK MY WIFE FROM ME...

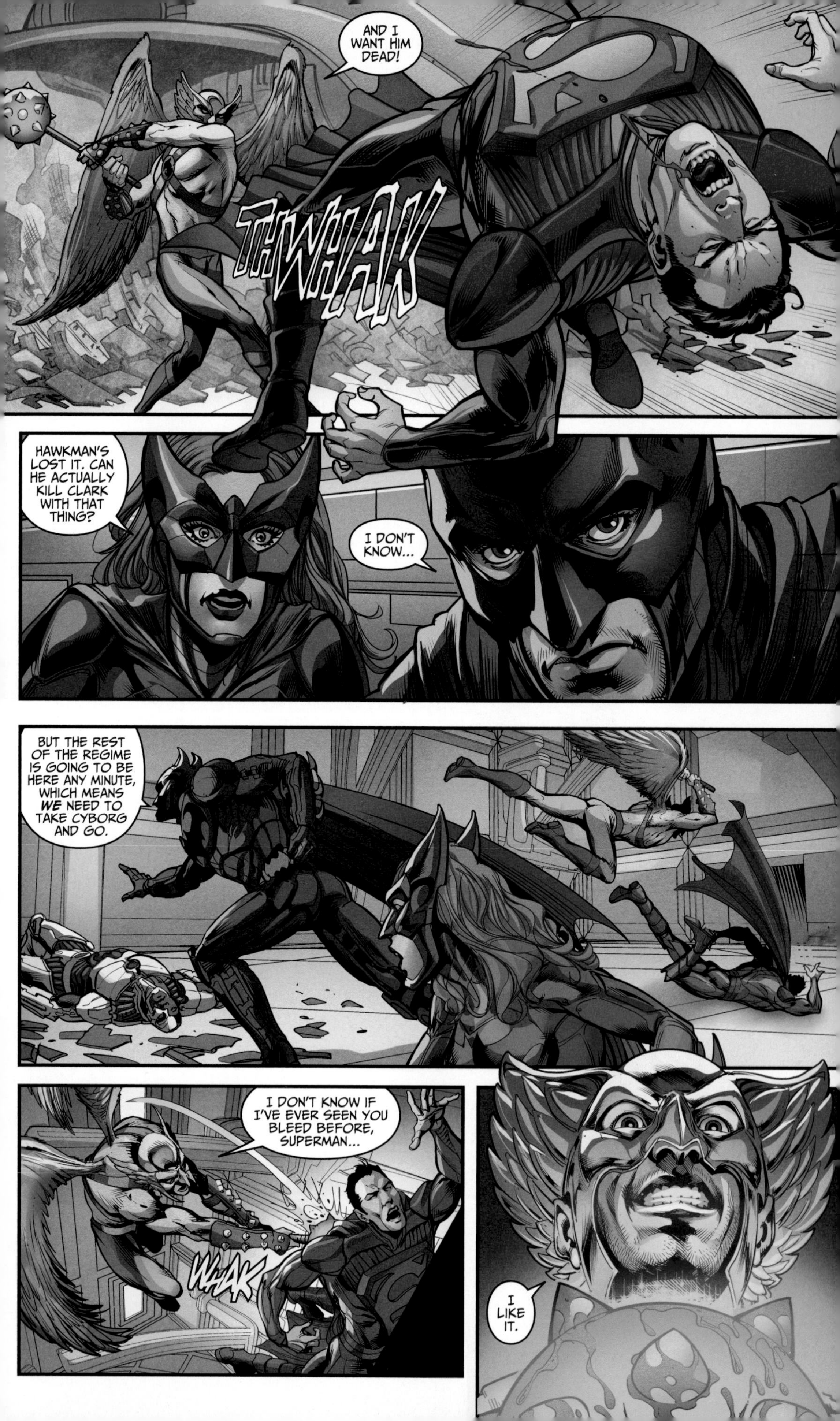
AND I WANT HIM DEAD!
THWAAK
HAWKMAN'S LOST IT. CAN HE ACTUALLY KILL CLARK WITH THAT THING?
I DON'T KNOW...
BUT THE REST OF THE REGIME IS GOING TO BE HERE ANY MINUTE, WHICH MEANS *WE* NEED TO TAKE CYBORG AND GO.
I DON'T KNOW IF I'VE EVER SEEN YOU BLEED BEFORE, SUPERMAN...
WHAK
I LIKE IT.

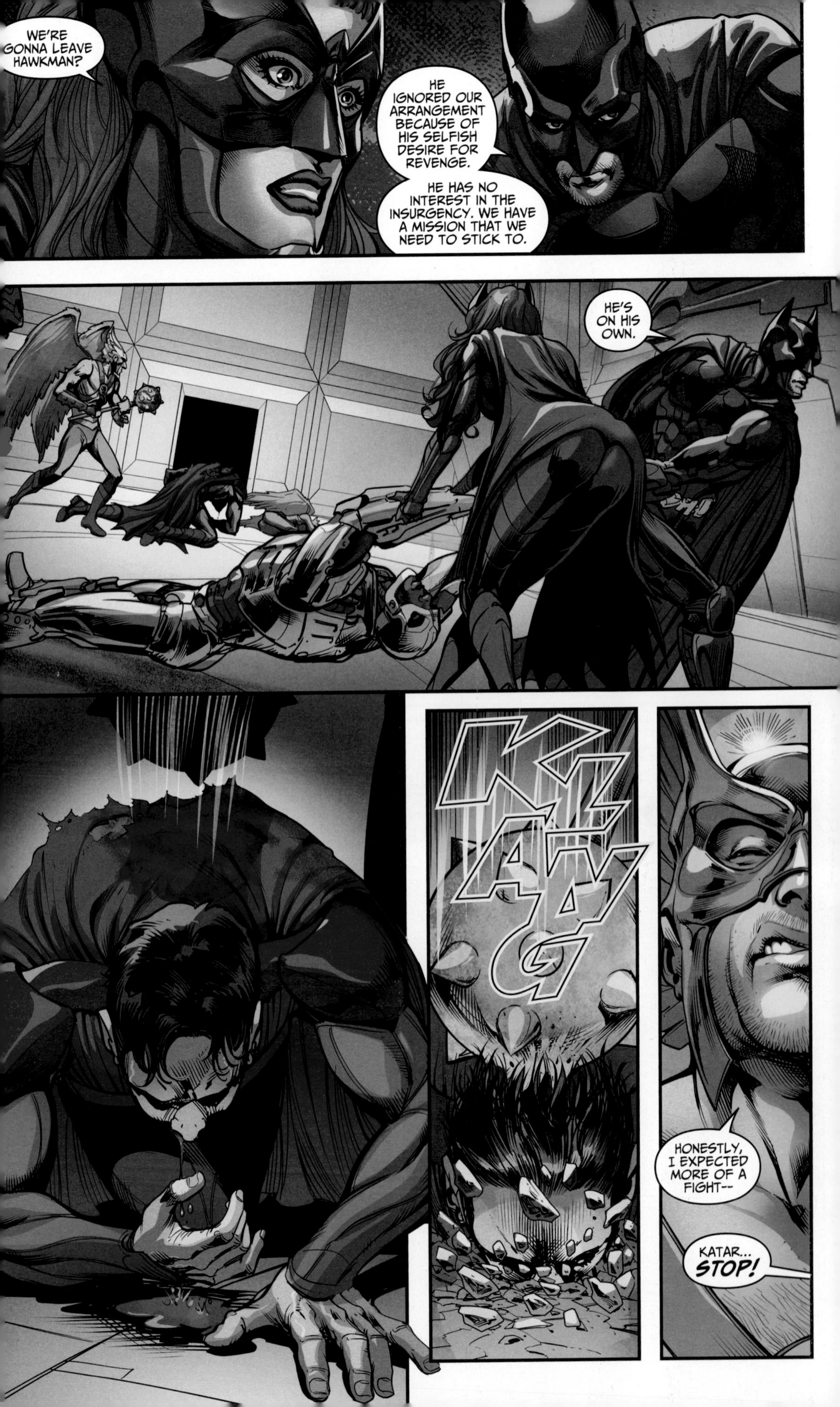
WE'RE GONNA LEAVE HAWKMAN?
HE IGNORED OUR ARRANGEMENT BECAUSE OF HIS SELFISH DESIRE FOR REVENGE.
HE HAS NO INTEREST IN THE INSURGENCY. WE HAVE A MISSION THAT WE NEED TO STICK TO.
HE'S ON HIS OWN.
KLAGG
HONESTLY, I EXPECTED MORE OF A FIGHT--
KATAR... STOP!

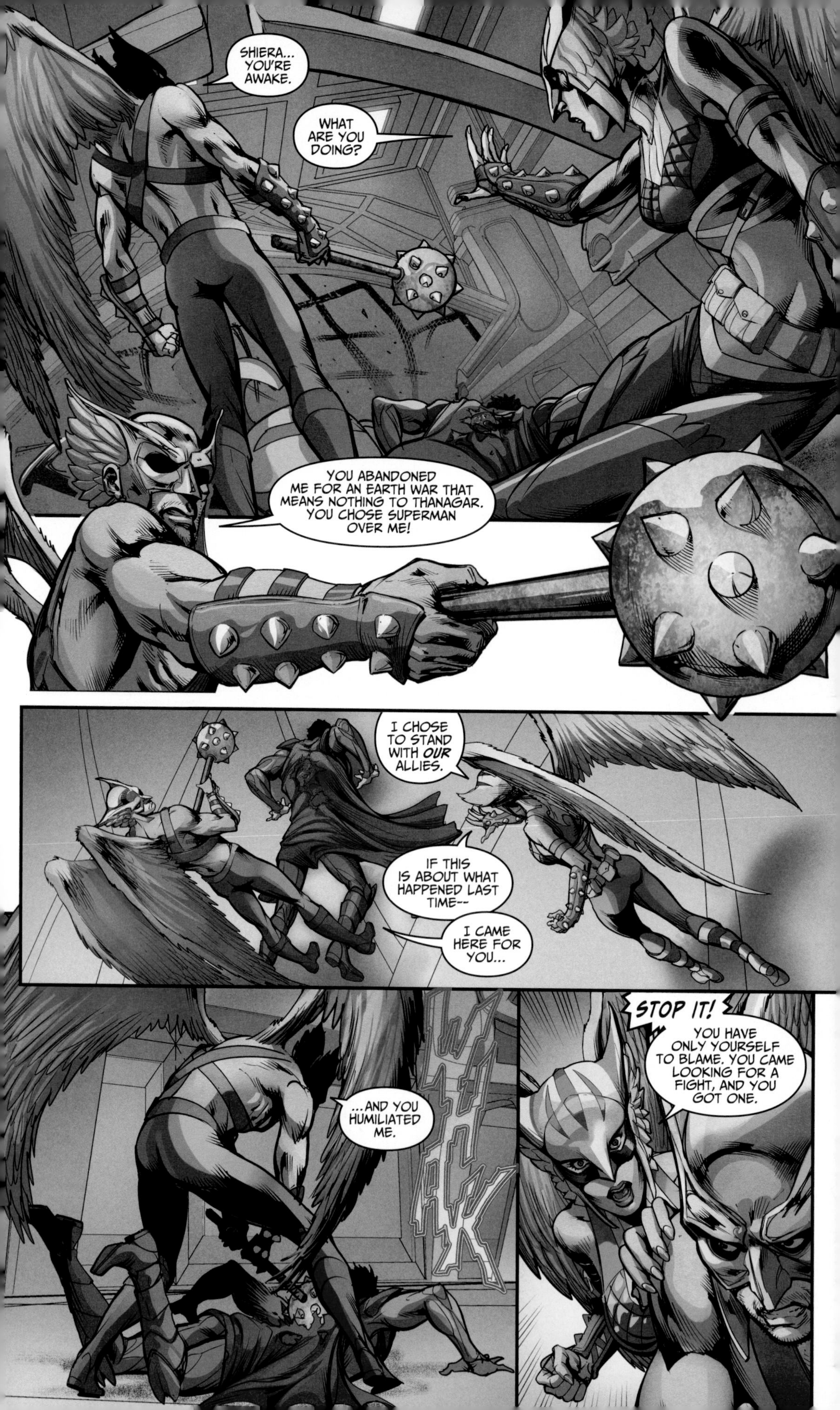

SHIERA... YOU'RE AWAKE.
WHAT ARE YOU DOING?
YOU ABANDONED ME FOR AN EARTH WAR THAT MEANS NOTHING TO THANAGAR. YOU CHOSE SUPERMAN OVER ME!
I CHOSE TO STAND WITH OUR ALLIES.
IF THIS IS ABOUT WHAT HAPPENED LAST TIME--
I CAME HERE FOR YOU...
...AND YOU HUMILIATED ME.
WHACK
STOP IT!
YOU HAVE ONLY YOURSELF TO BLAME. YOU CAME LOOKING FOR A FIGHT, AND YOU GOT ONE.

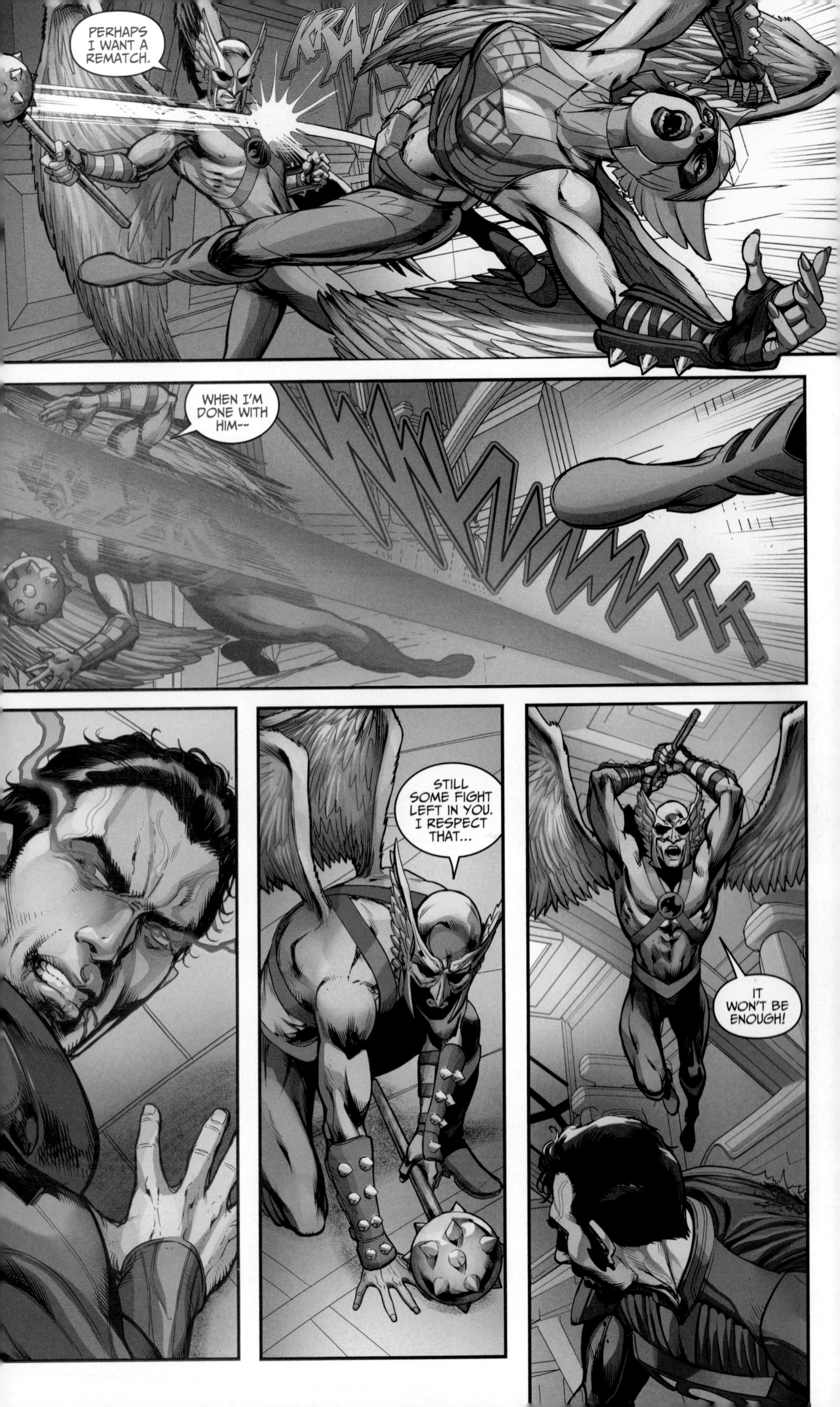
PERHAPS I WANT A REMATCH.
KRAK
WHEN I'M DONE WITH HIM--
WHAMTT
STILL SOME FIGHT LEFT IN YOU. I RESPECT THAT...
IT WON'T BE ENOUGH!

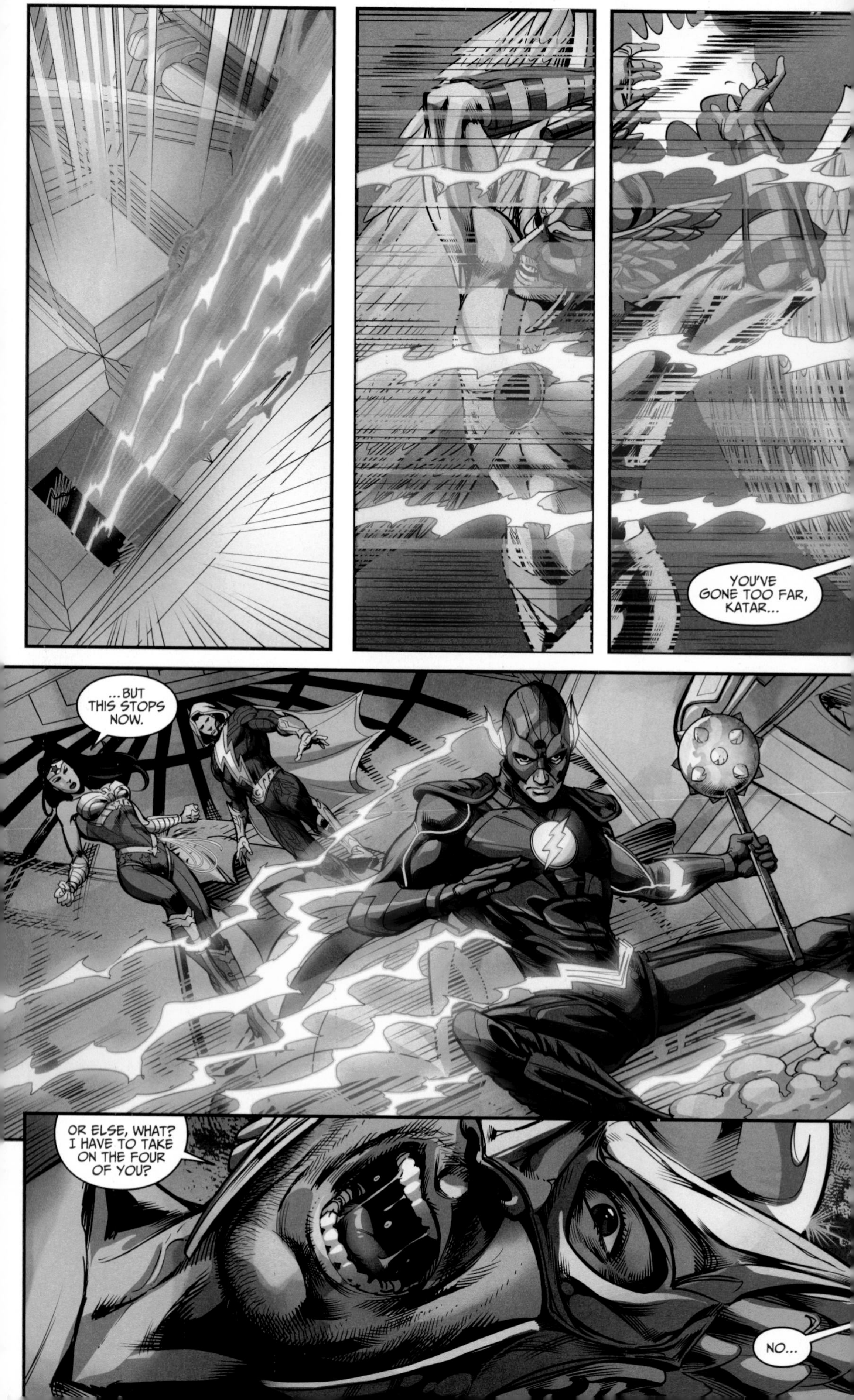
YOU'VE GONE TOO FAR, KATAR...
...BUT THIS STOPS NOW.
OR ELSE, WHAT? I HAVE TO TAKE ON THE FOUR OF YOU?
NO...

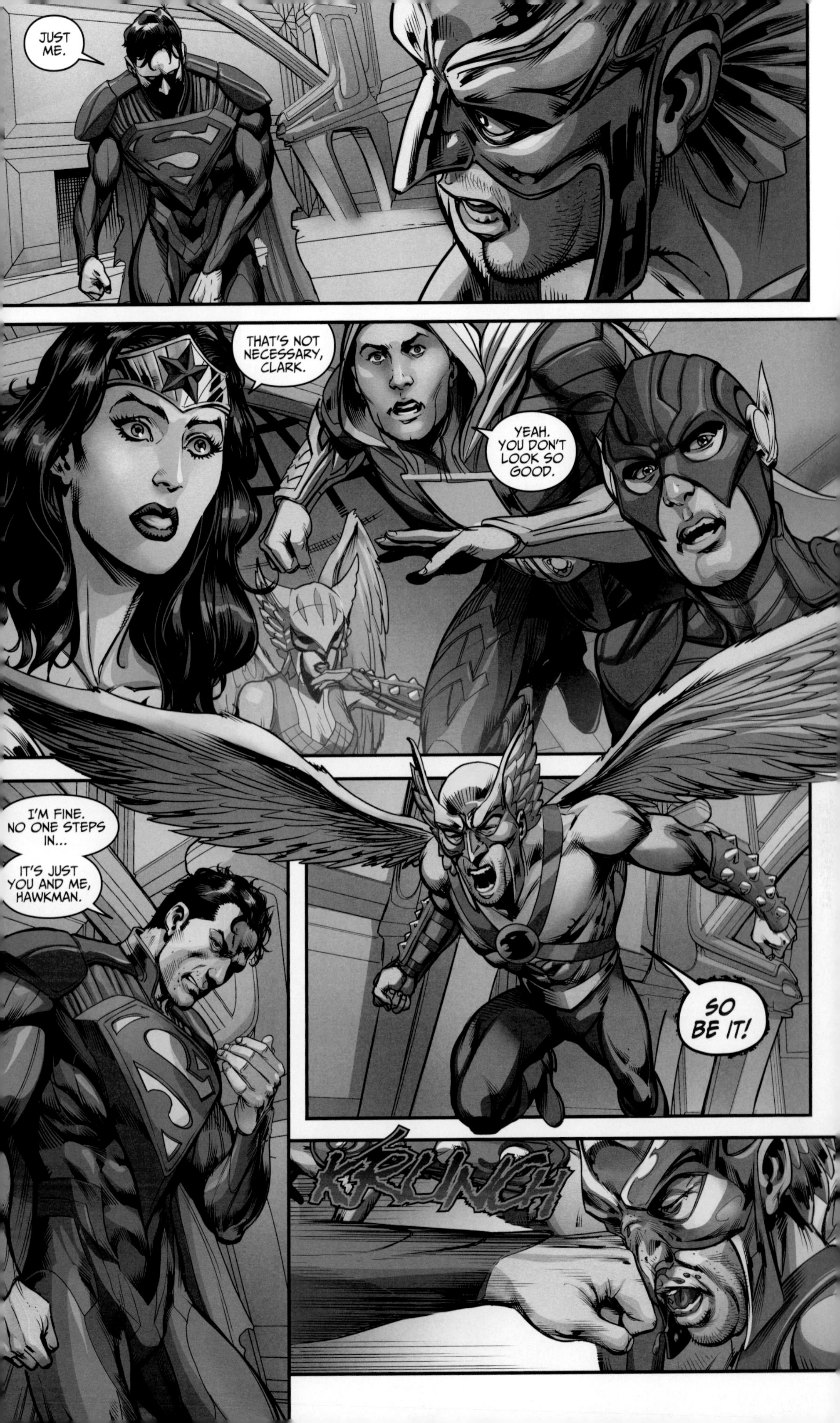
JUST ME.
THAT'S NOT NECESSARY, CLARK.
YEAH. YOU DON'T LOOK SO GOOD.
I'M FINE. NO ONE STEPS IN...
IT'S JUST YOU AND ME, HAWKMAN.
SO BE IT!
KRUNCH

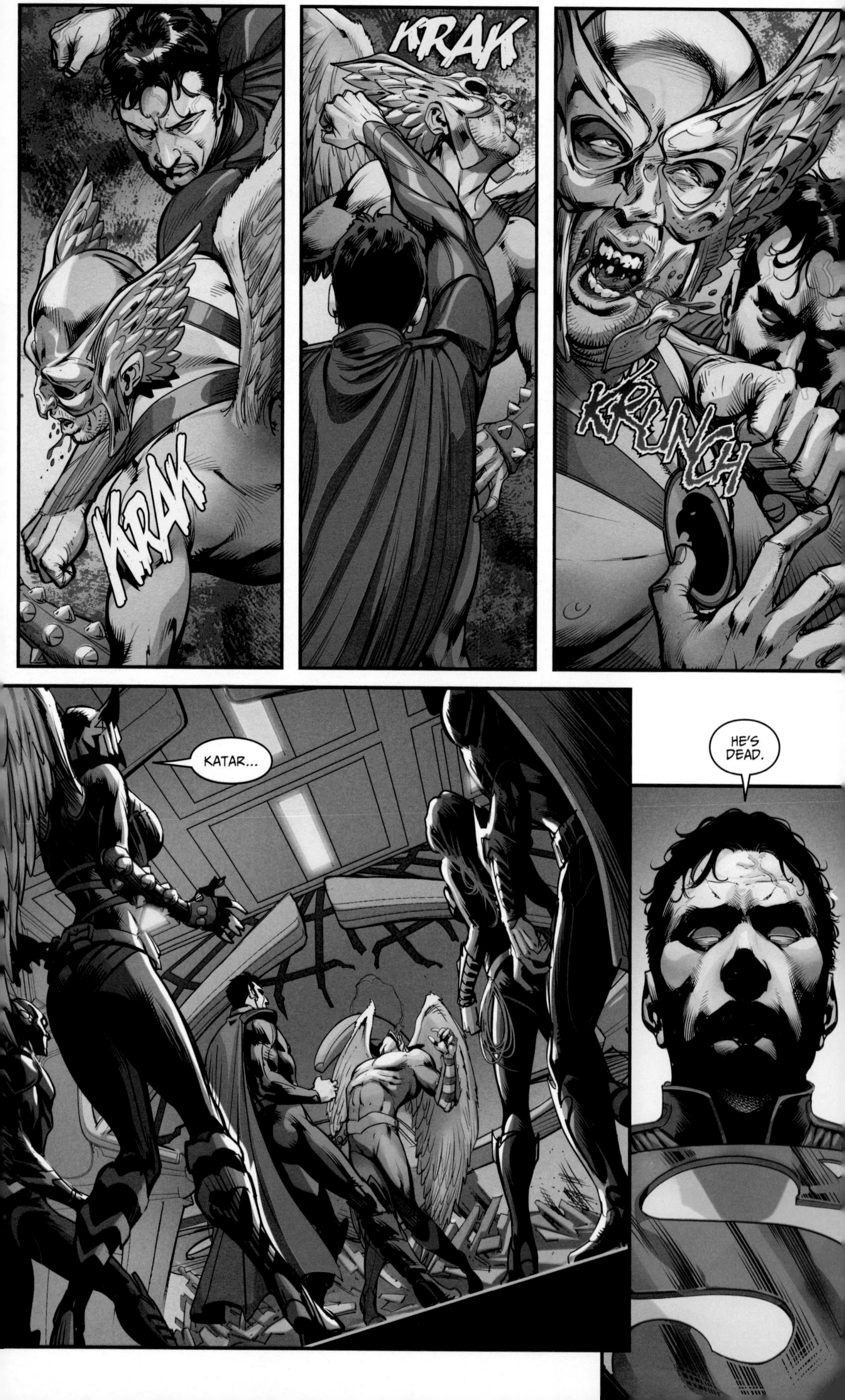
KRAK
KRAK
KRUNCH
KATAR...
HE'S DEAD.

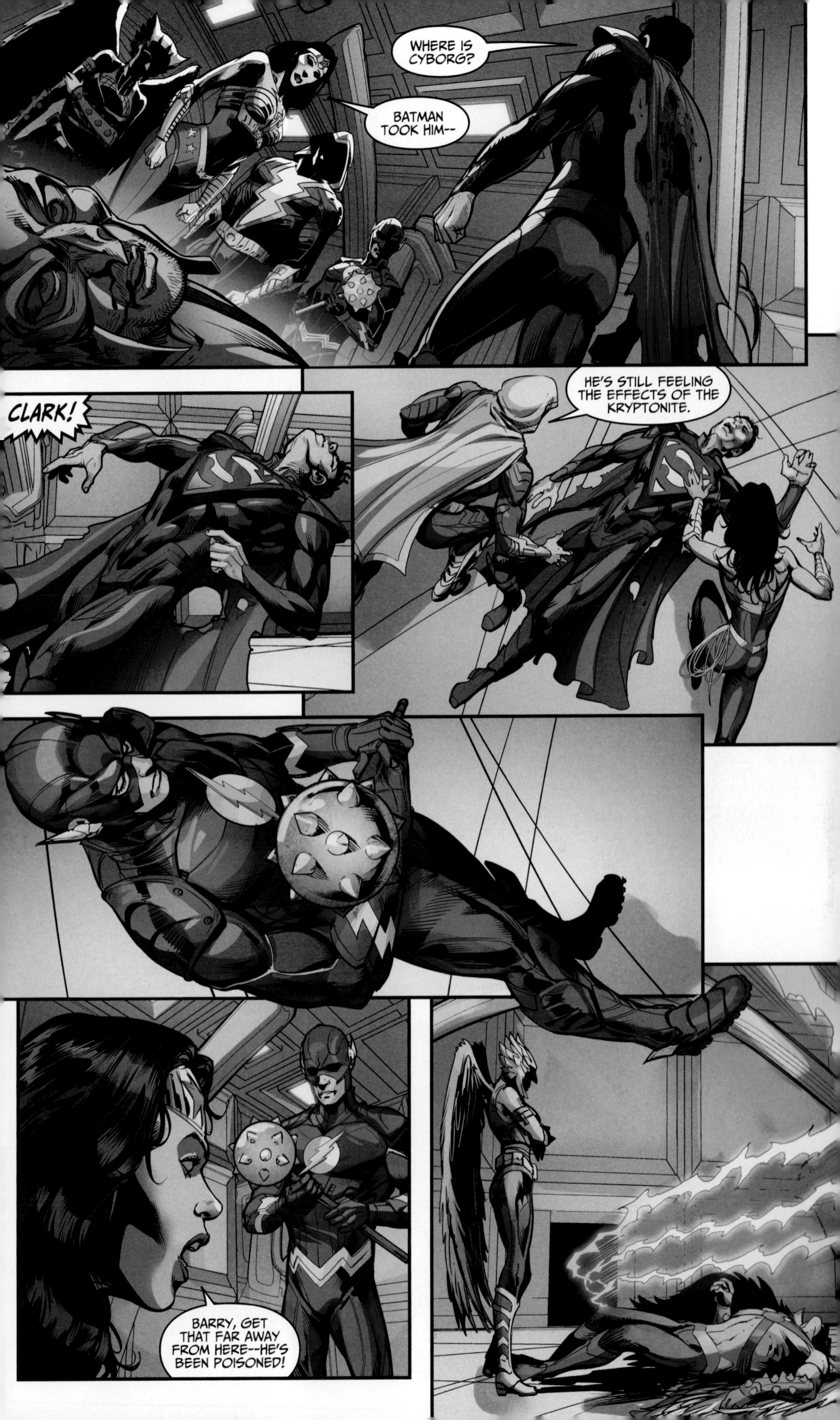
WHERE IS CYBORG?
BATMAN TOOK HIM--
CLARK!
HE'S STILL FEELING THE EFFECTS OF THE KRYPTONITE.
BARRY, GET THAT FAR AWAY FROM HERE--HE'S BEEN POISONED!

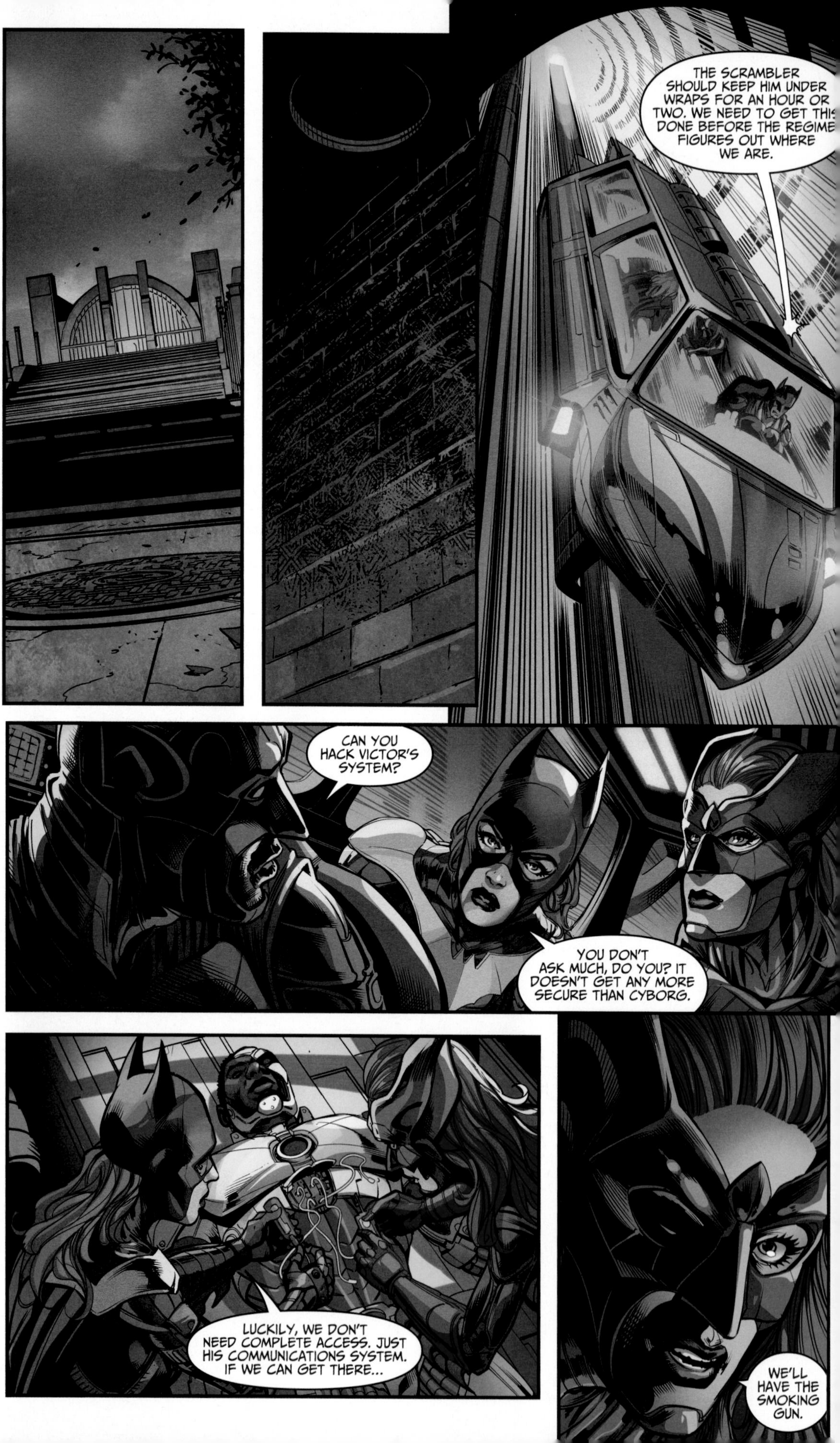
THE SCRAMBLER SHOULD KEEP HIM UNDER WRAPS FOR AN HOUR OR TWO. WE NEED TO GET THIS DONE BEFORE THE REGIME FIGURES OUT WHERE WE ARE.
CAN YOU HACK VICTOR'S SYSTEM?
YOU DON'T ASK MUCH, DO YOU? IT DOESN'T GET ANY MORE SECURE THAN CYBORG.
LUCKILY, WE DON'T NEED COMPLETE ACCESS. JUST HIS COMMUNICATIONS SYSTEM. IF WE CAN GET THERE...
WE'LL HAVE THE SMOKING GUN.

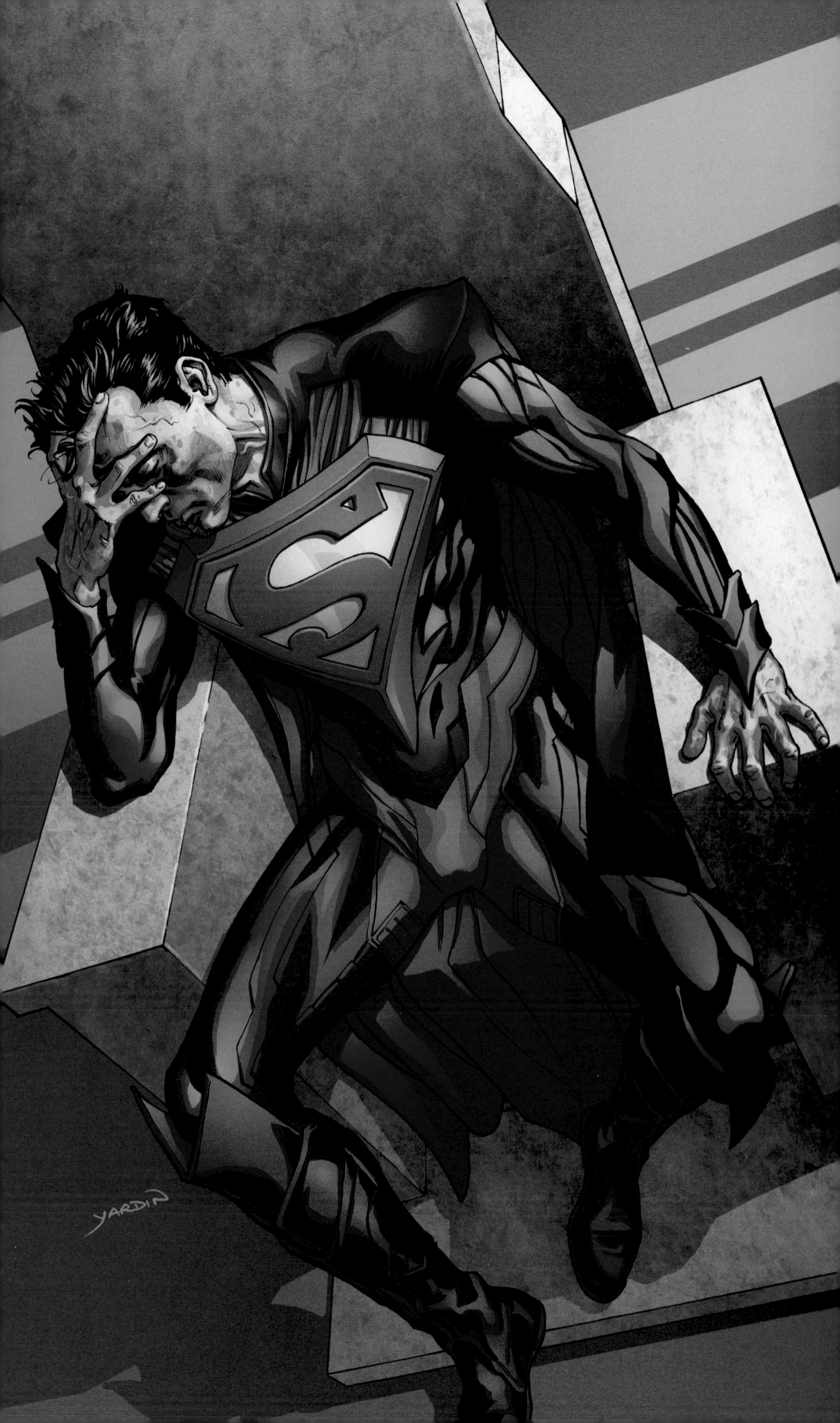
YARDIN

"The Smoking Gun" **Tom Derenick** Artist **Rex Lokus** Colorist

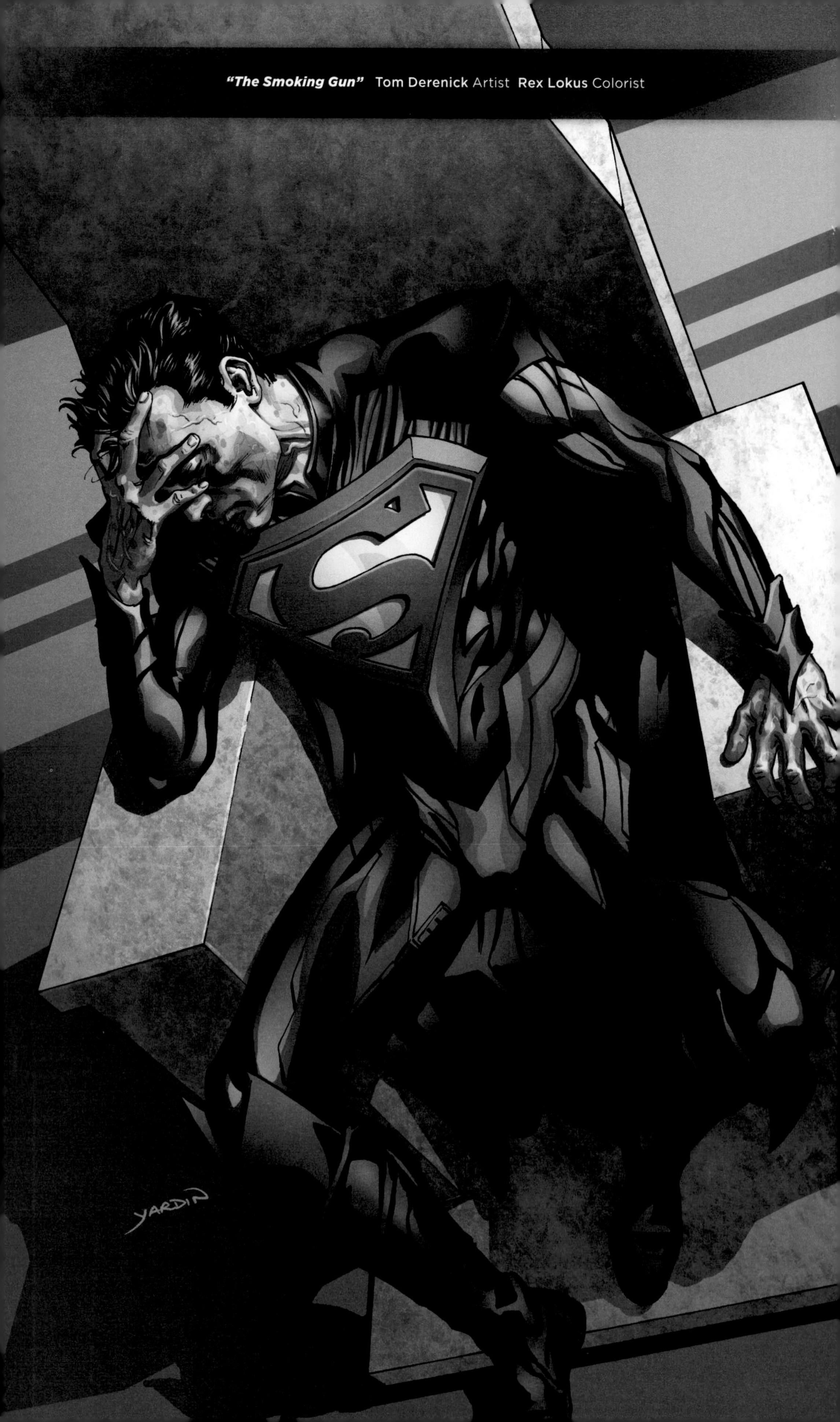
YARDIN

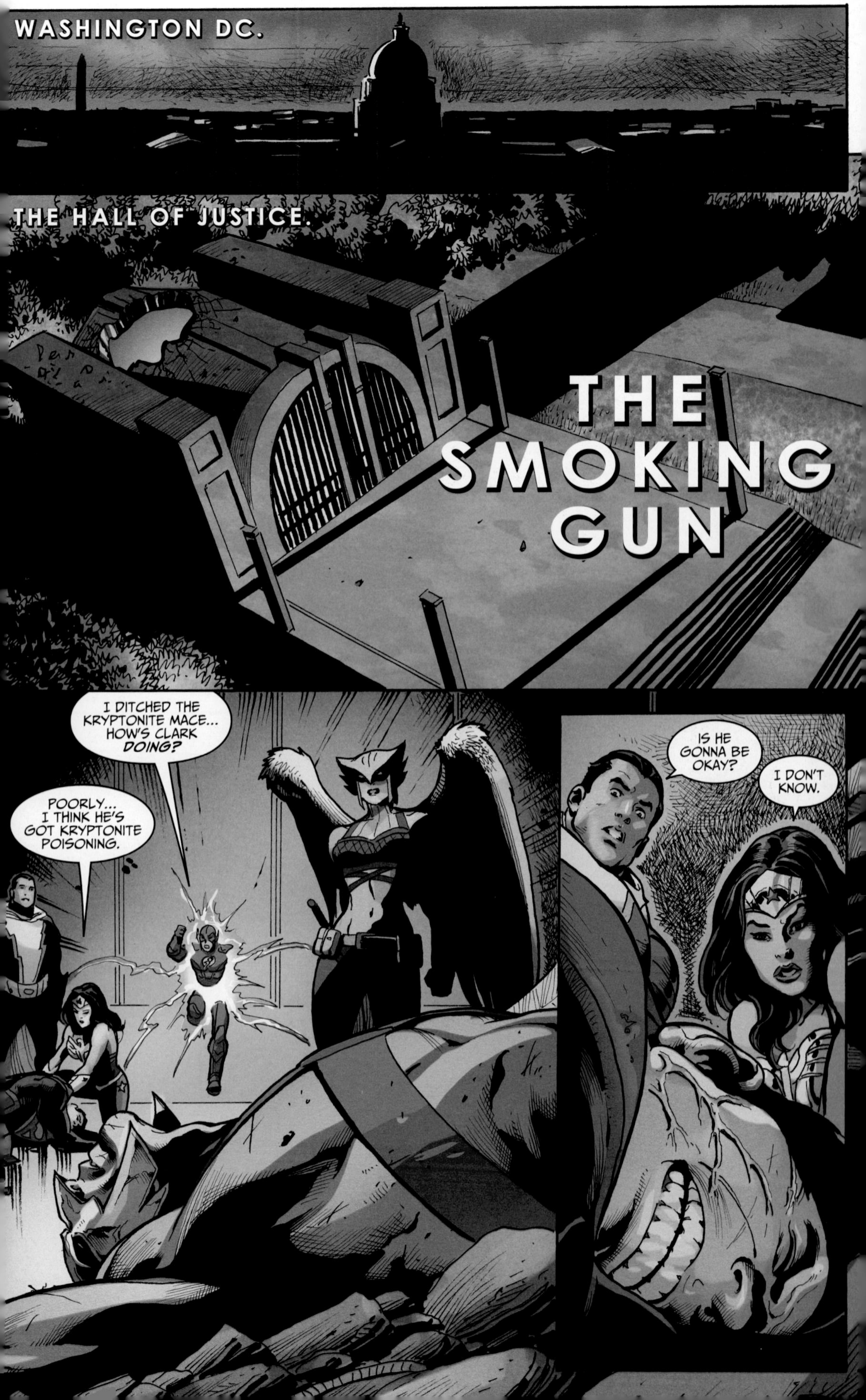
WASHINGTON DC.
THE HALL OF JUSTICE.
THE SMOKING GUN
I DITCHED THE KRYPTONITE MACE... HOW'S CLARK DOING?
POORLY... I THINK HE'S GOT KRYPTONITE POISONING.
IS HE GONNA BE OKAY?
I DON'T KNOW.

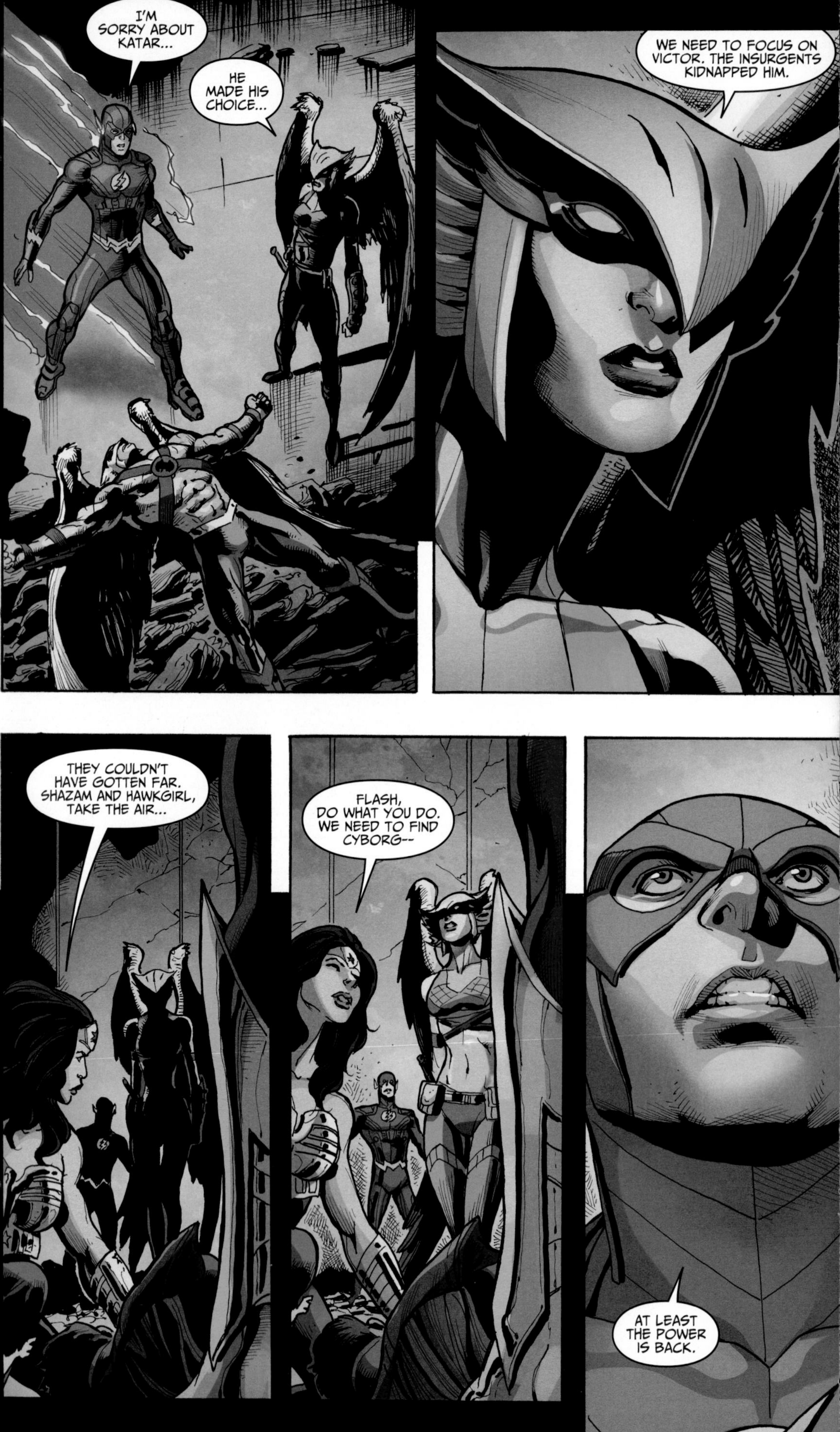

I'M SORRY ABOUT KATAR...
HE MADE HIS CHOICE...
WE NEED TO FOCUS ON VICTOR. THE INSURGENTS KIDNAPPED HIM.
THEY COULDN'T HAVE GOTTEN FAR. SHAZAM AND HAWKGIRL, TAKE THE AIR...
FLASH, DO WHAT YOU DO. WE NEED TO FIND CYBORG--
AT LEAST THE POWER IS BACK.

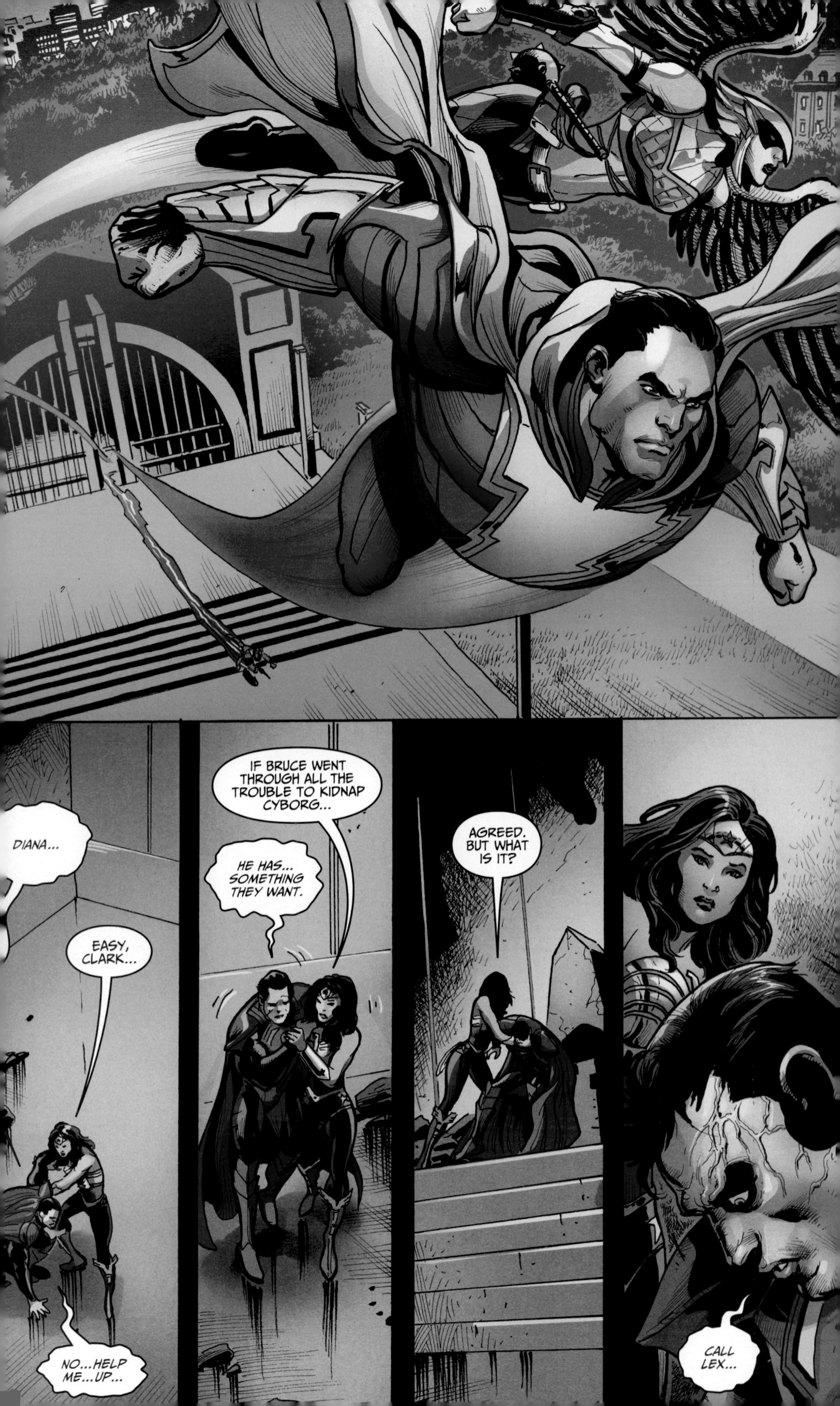
DIANA...
EASY, CLARK...
NO...HELP ME...UP...
IF BRUCE WENT THROUGH ALL THE TROUBLE TO KIDNAP CYBORG...
HE HAS... SOMETHING THEY WANT.
AGREED. BUT WHAT IS IT?
CALL LEX...

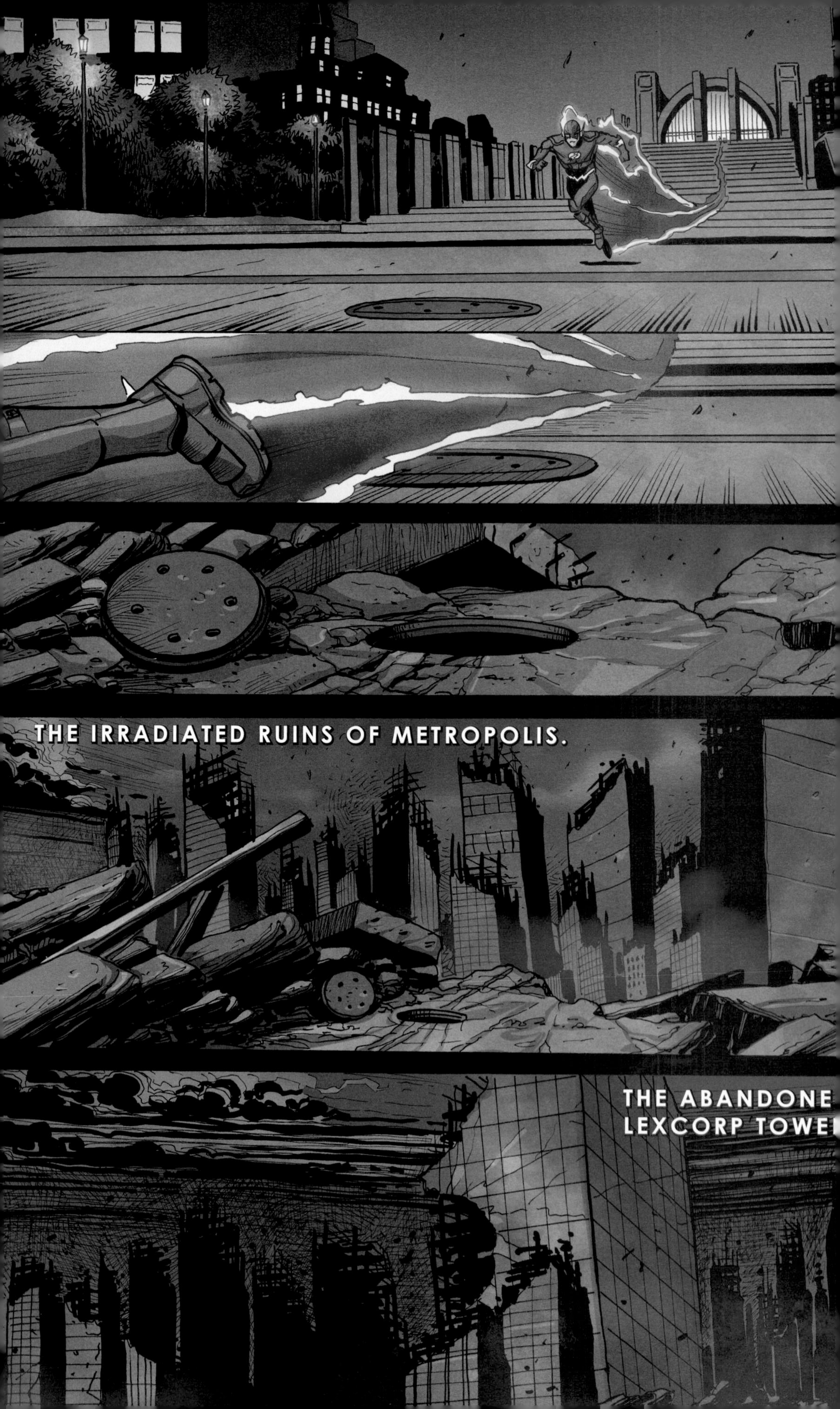
THE IRRADIATED RUINS OF METROPOLIS.
THE ABANDONE
LEXCORP TOWE

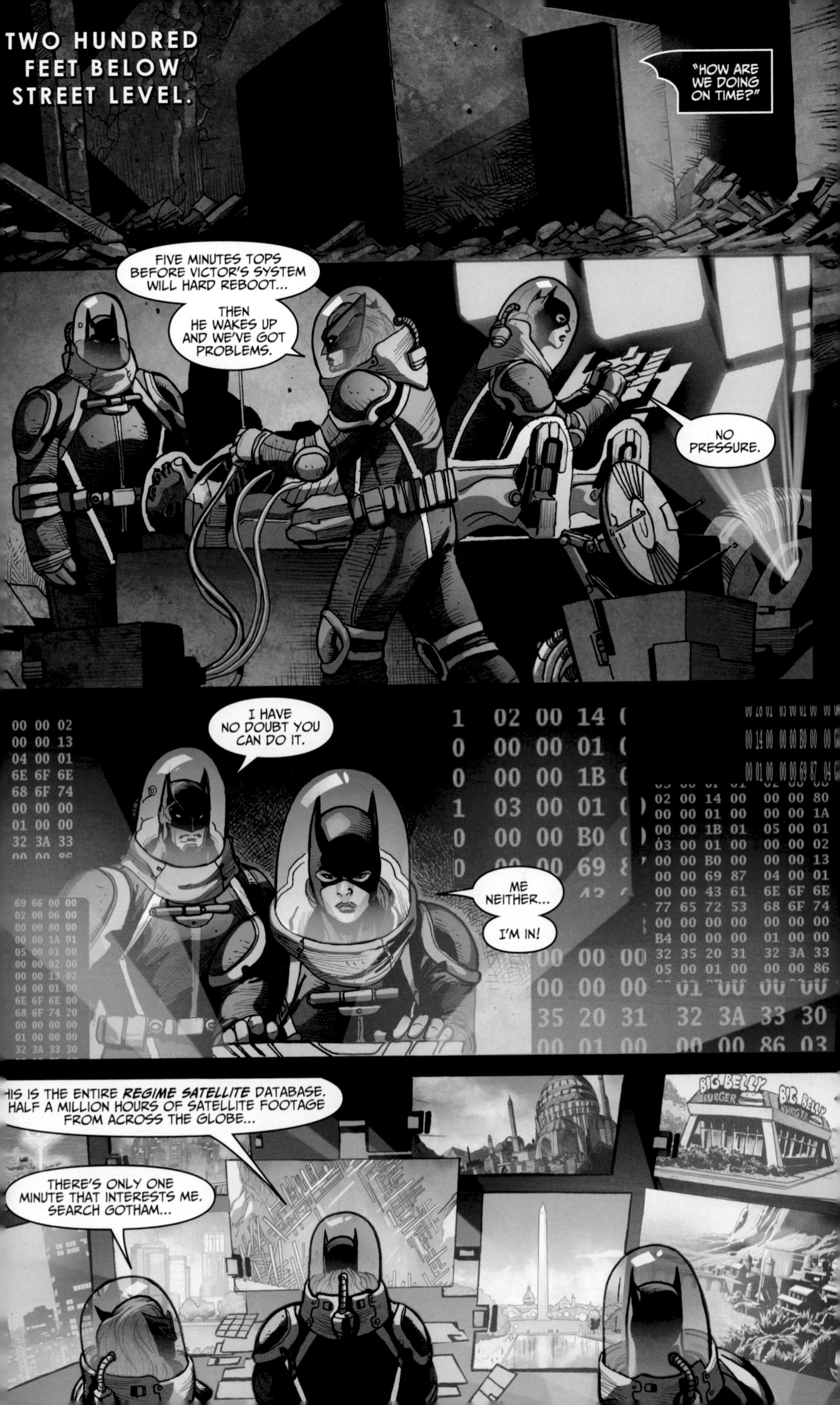

TWO HUNDRED FEET BELOW STREET LEVEL.
"HOW ARE WE DOING ON TIME?"
FIVE MINUTES TOPS BEFORE VICTOR'S SYSTEM WILL HARD REBOOT...
THEN HE WAKES UP AND WE'VE GOT PROBLEMS.
NO PRESSURE.
I HAVE NO DOUBT YOU CAN DO IT.
ME NEITHER...
I'M IN!
HIS IS THE ENTIRE *REGIME SATELLITE* DATABASE. HALF A MILLION HOURS OF SATELLITE FOOTAGE FROM ACROSS THE GLOBE...
THERE'S ONLY ONE MINUTE THAT INTERESTS ME. SEARCH GOTHAM...
BIG BELLY BURGER

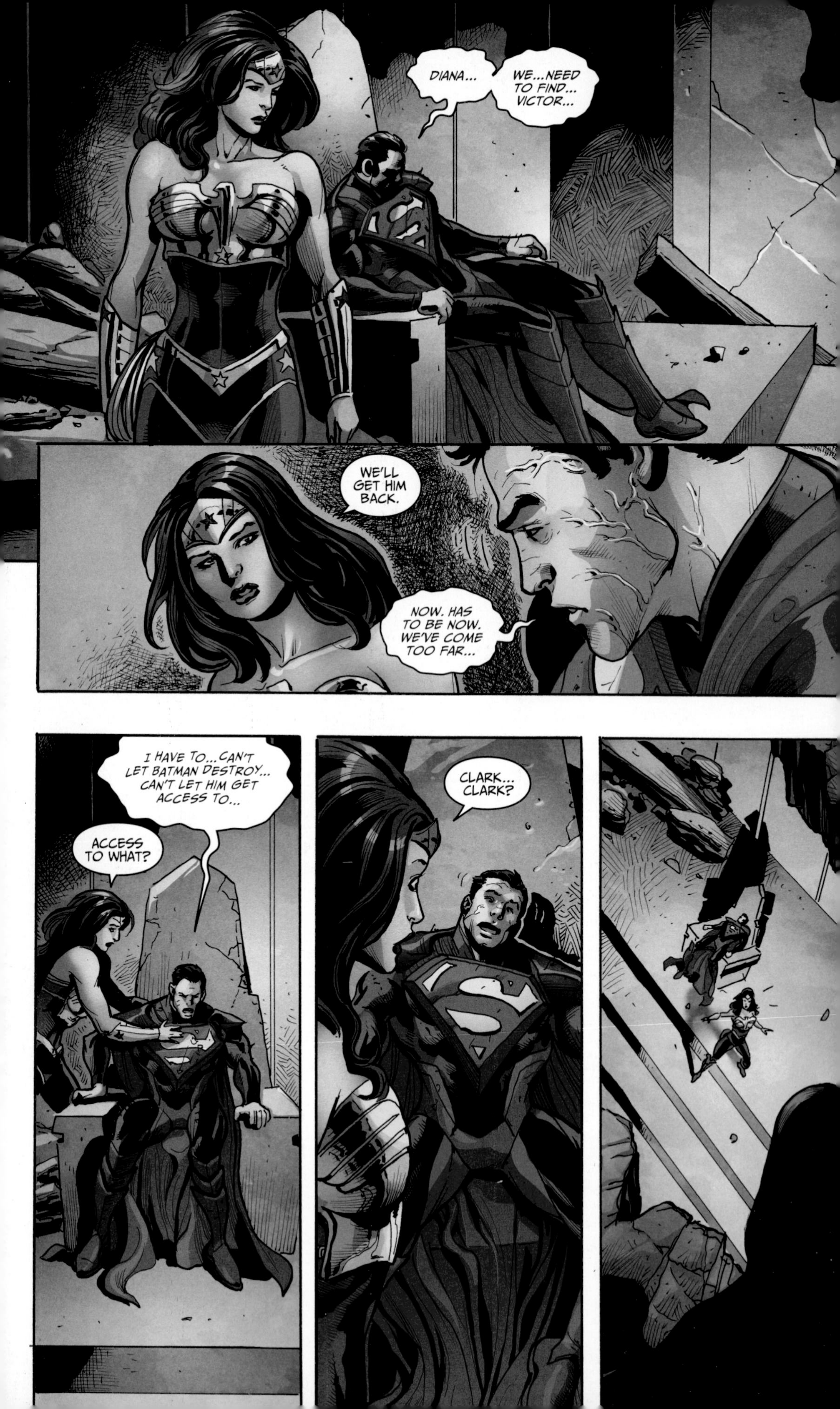
DIANA...
WE...NEED TO FIND... VICTOR...
WE'LL GET HIM BACK.
NOW. HAS TO BE NOW. WE'VE COME TOO FAR...
I HAVE TO...CAN'T LET BATMAN DESTROY... CAN'T LET HIM GET ACCESS TO...
ACCESS TO WHAT?
CLARK... CLARK?

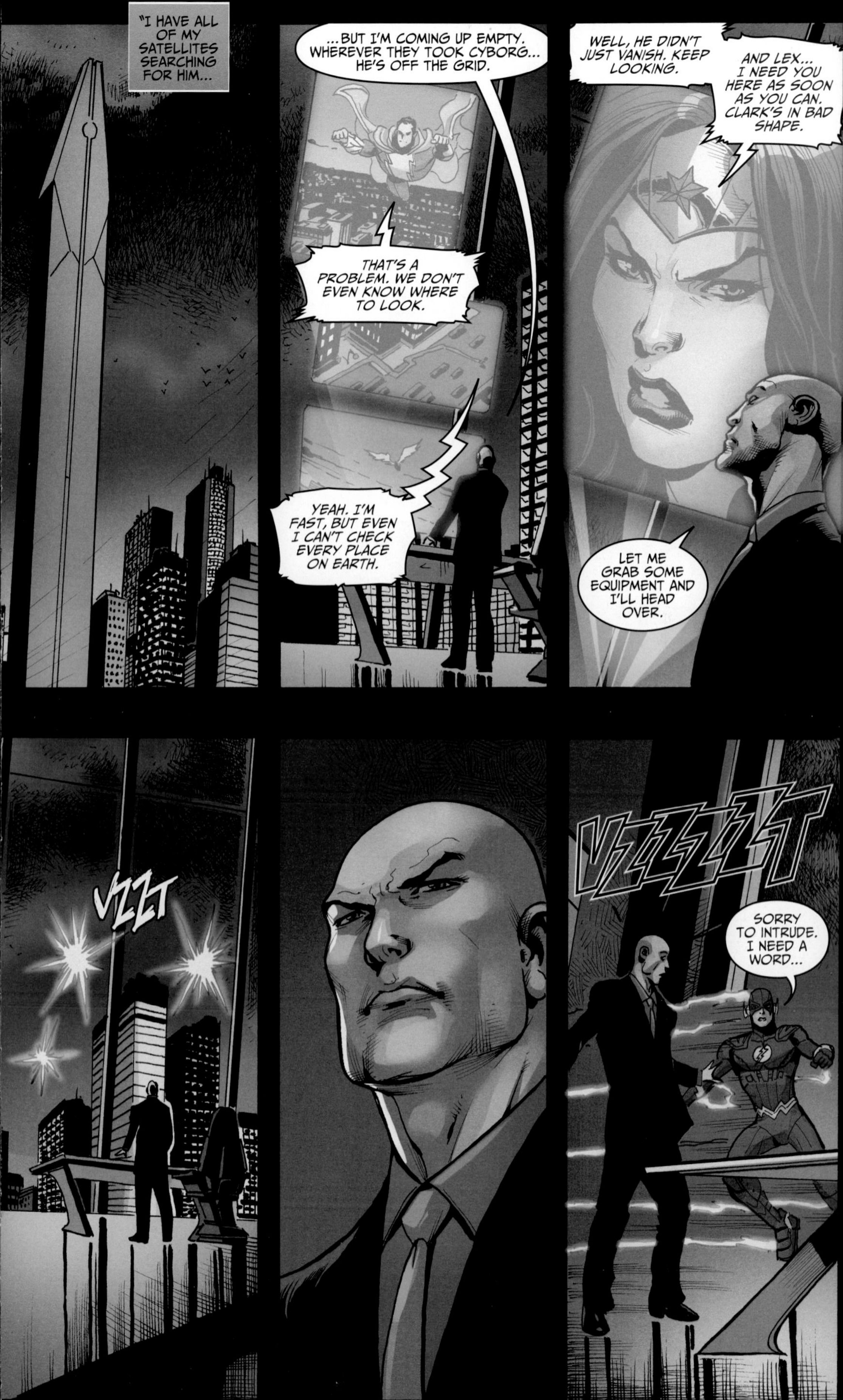
"I HAVE ALL OF MY SATELLITES SEARCHING FOR HIM...
...BUT I'M COMING UP EMPTY. WHEREVER THEY TOOK CYBORG... HE'S OFF THE GRID.
THAT'S A PROBLEM. WE DON'T EVEN KNOW WHERE TO LOOK.
YEAH. I'M FAST, BUT EVEN I CAN'T CHECK EVERY PLACE ON EARTH.
WELL, HE DIDN'T JUST VANISH. KEEP LOOKING.
AND LEX... I NEED YOU HERE AS SOON AS YOU CAN. CLARK'S IN BAD SHAPE.
LET ME GRAB SOME EQUIPMENT AND I'LL HEAD OVER.
VZZT
VZZZZZT
SORRY TO INTRUDE. I NEED A WORD...

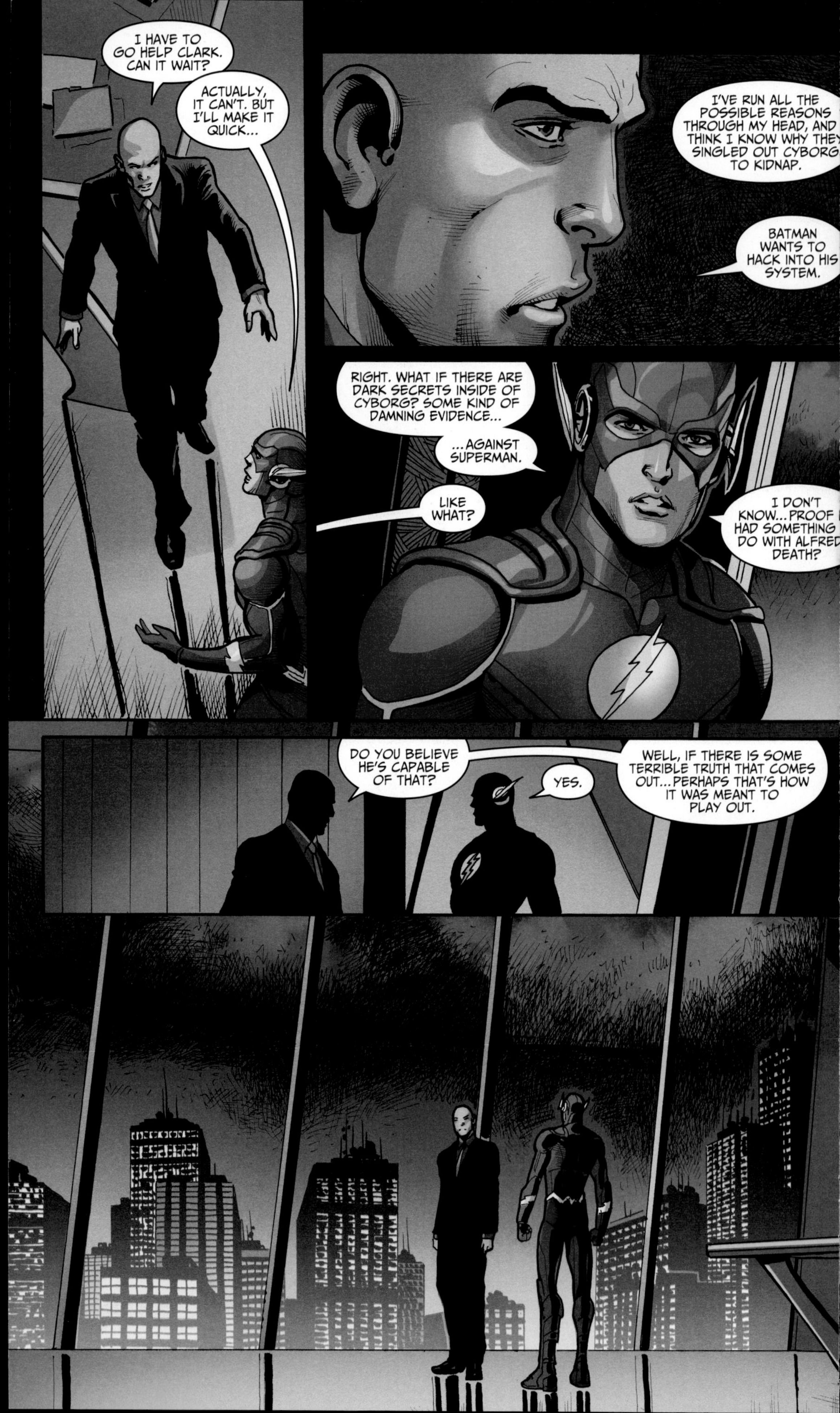
I HAVE TO GO HELP CLARK. CAN IT WAIT?
ACTUALLY, IT CAN'T. BUT I'LL MAKE IT QUICK...
I'VE RUN ALL THE POSSIBLE REASONS THROUGH MY HEAD, AND THINK I KNOW WHY THEY SINGLED OUT CYBORG TO KIDNAP.
BATMAN WANTS TO HACK INTO HIS SYSTEM.
RIGHT. WHAT IF THERE ARE DARK SECRETS INSIDE OF CYBORG? SOME KIND OF DAMNING EVIDENCE...
...AGAINST SUPERMAN.
LIKE WHAT?
I DON'T KNOW...PROOF HAD SOMETHING DO WITH ALFRED DEATH?
DO YOU BELIEVE HE'S CAPABLE OF THAT?
YES.
WELL, IF THERE IS SOME TERRIBLE TRUTH THAT COMES OUT...PERHAPS THAT'S HOW IT WAS MEANT TO PLAY OUT.

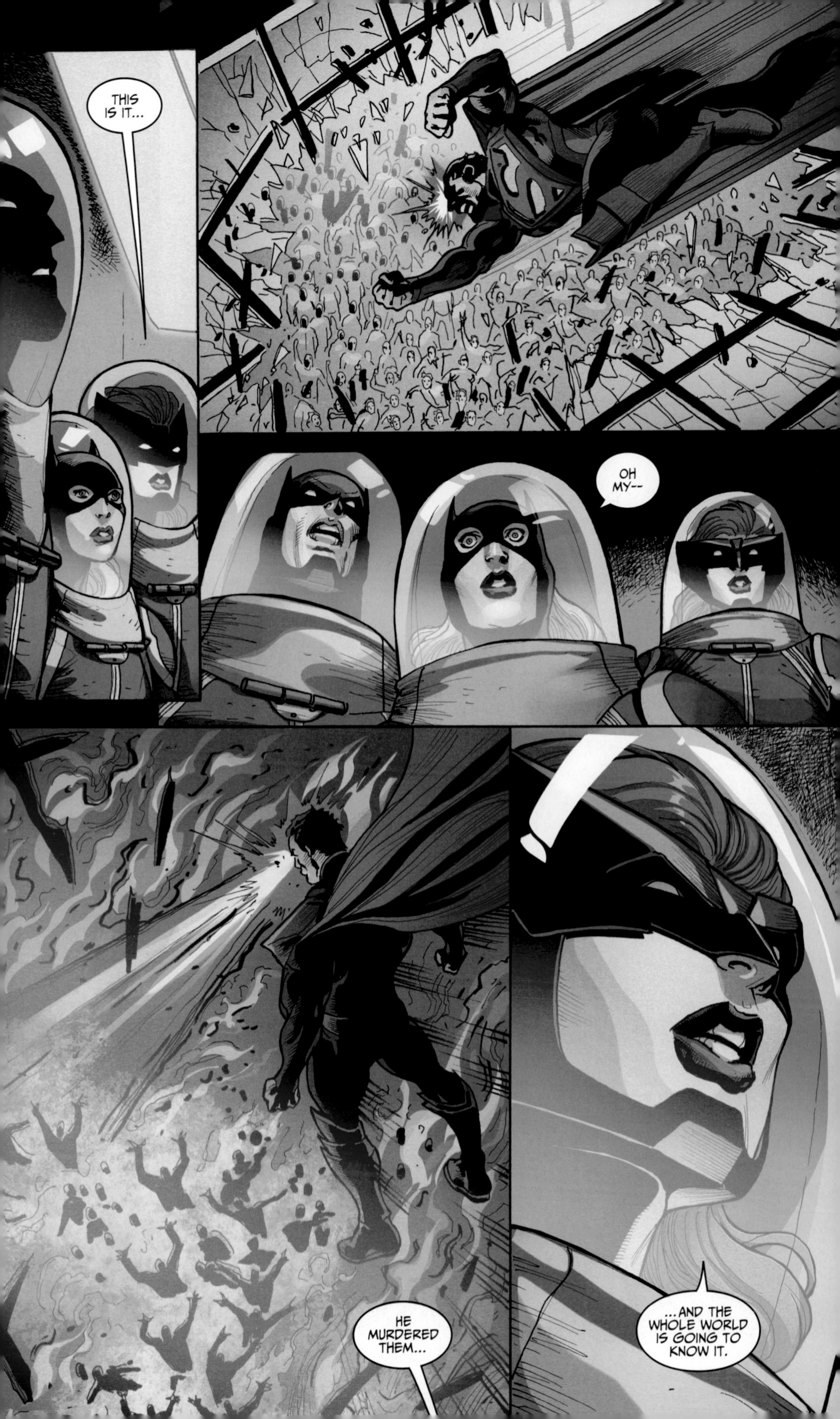
THIS IS IT...
OH MY--
HE MURDERED THEM...
...AND THE WHOLE WORLD IS GOING TO KNOW IT.

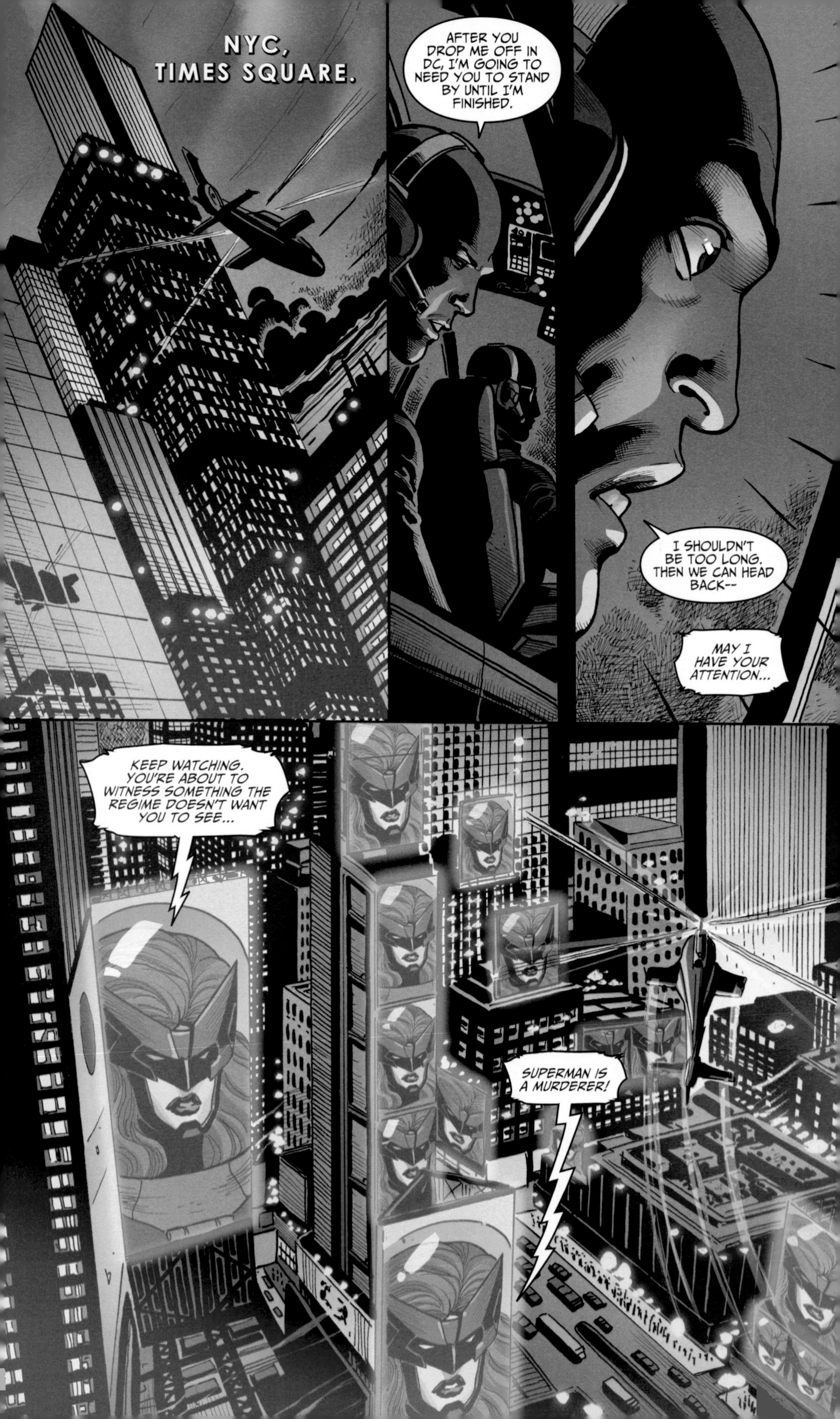
NYC, TIMES SQUARE.
AFTER YOU DROP ME OFF IN DC, I'M GOING TO NEED YOU TO STAND BY UNTIL I'M FINISHED.
I SHOULDN'T BE TOO LONG. THEN WE CAN HEAD BACK--
MAY I HAVE YOUR ATTENTION...
KEEP WATCHING. YOU'RE ABOUT TO WITNESS SOMETHING THE REGIME DOESN'T WANT YOU TO SEE...
SUPERMAN IS A MURDERER!

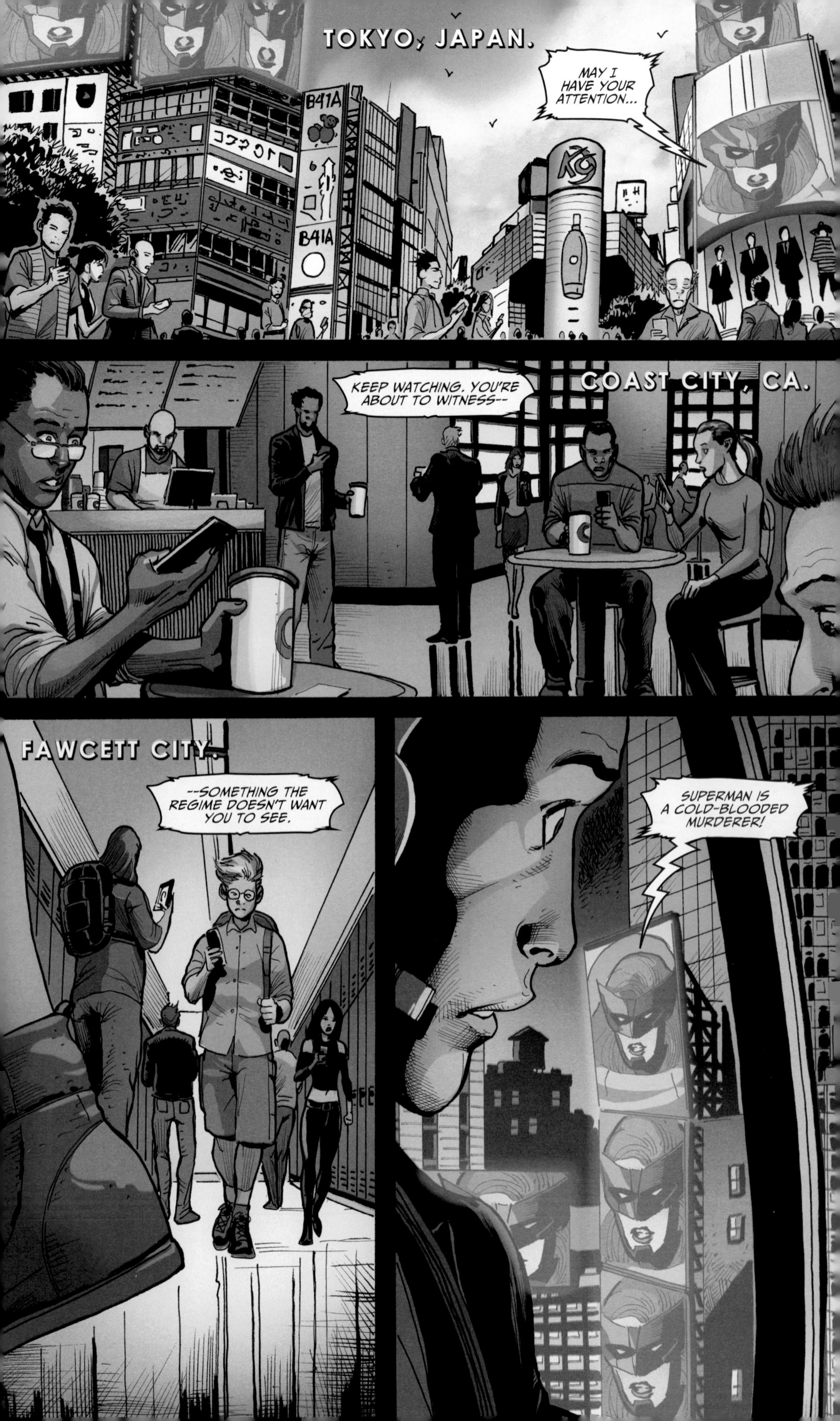
TOKYO, JAPAN.
MAY I HAVE YOUR ATTENTION...
COAST CITY, CA.
KEEP WATCHING. YOU'RE ABOUT TO WITNESS--
FAWCETT CITY.
--SOMETHING THE REGIME DOESN'T WANT YOU TO SEE.
SUPERMAN IS A COLD-BLOODED MURDERER!

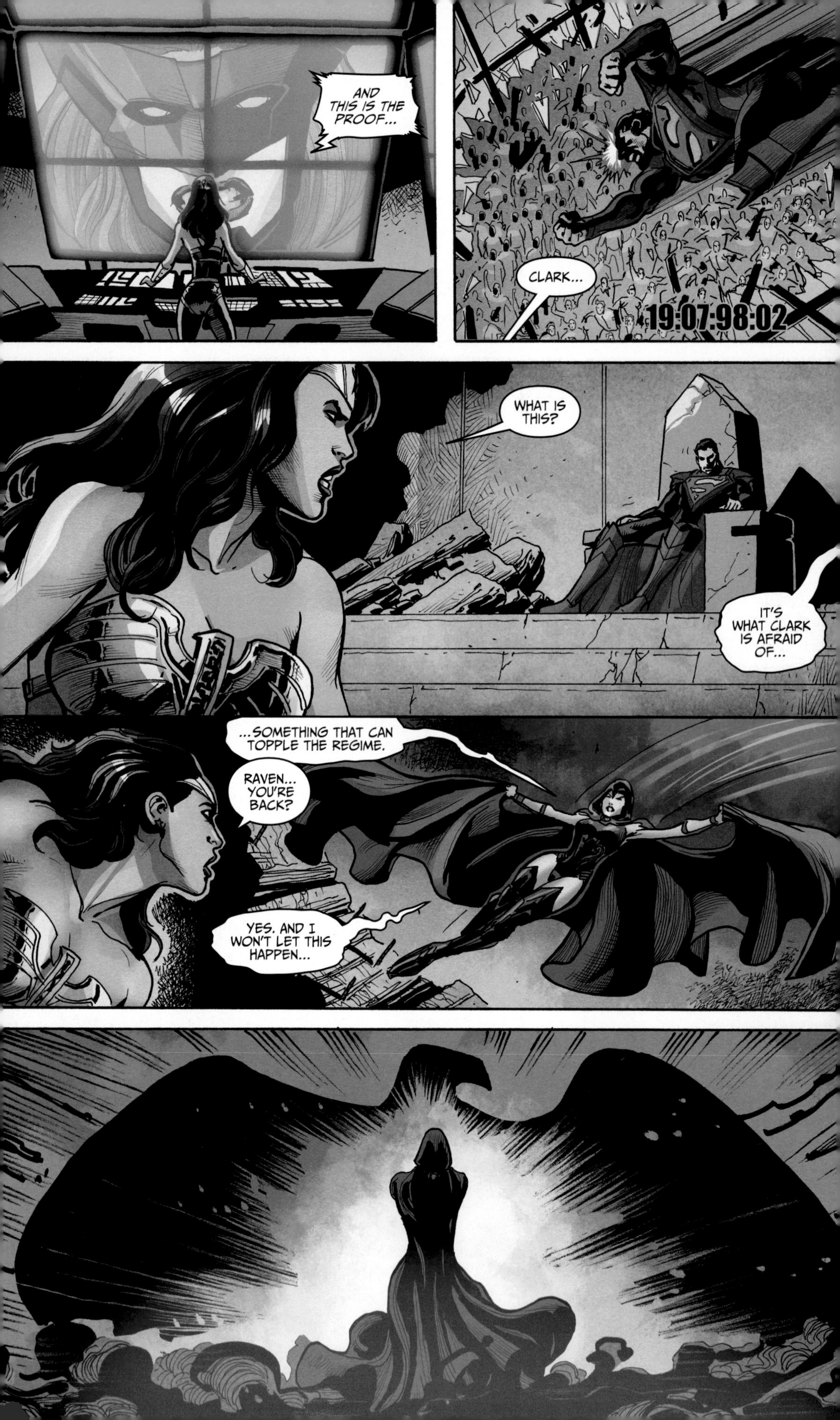
AND THIS IS THE PROOF...
CLARK...
19:07:98:02
WHAT IS THIS?
IT'S WHAT CLARK IS AFRAID OF...
...SOMETHING THAT CAN TOPPLE THE REGIME.
RAVEN... YOU'RE BACK?
YES. AND I WON'T LET THIS HAPPEN...

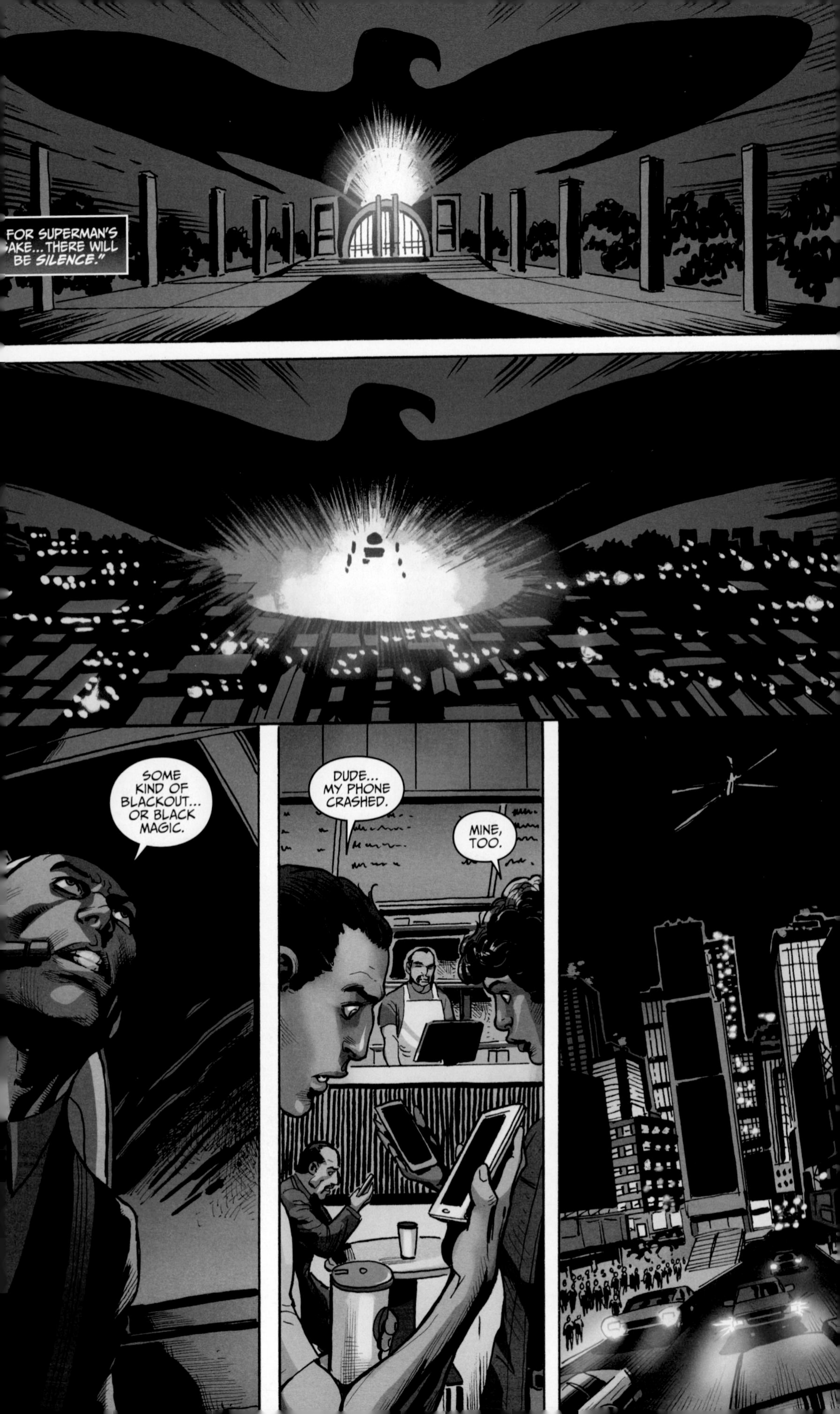
FOR SUPERMAN'S SAKE...THERE WILL BE *SILENCE*."
SOME KIND OF BLACKOUT... OR BLACK MAGIC.
DUDE... MY PHONE CRASHED.
MINE, TOO.

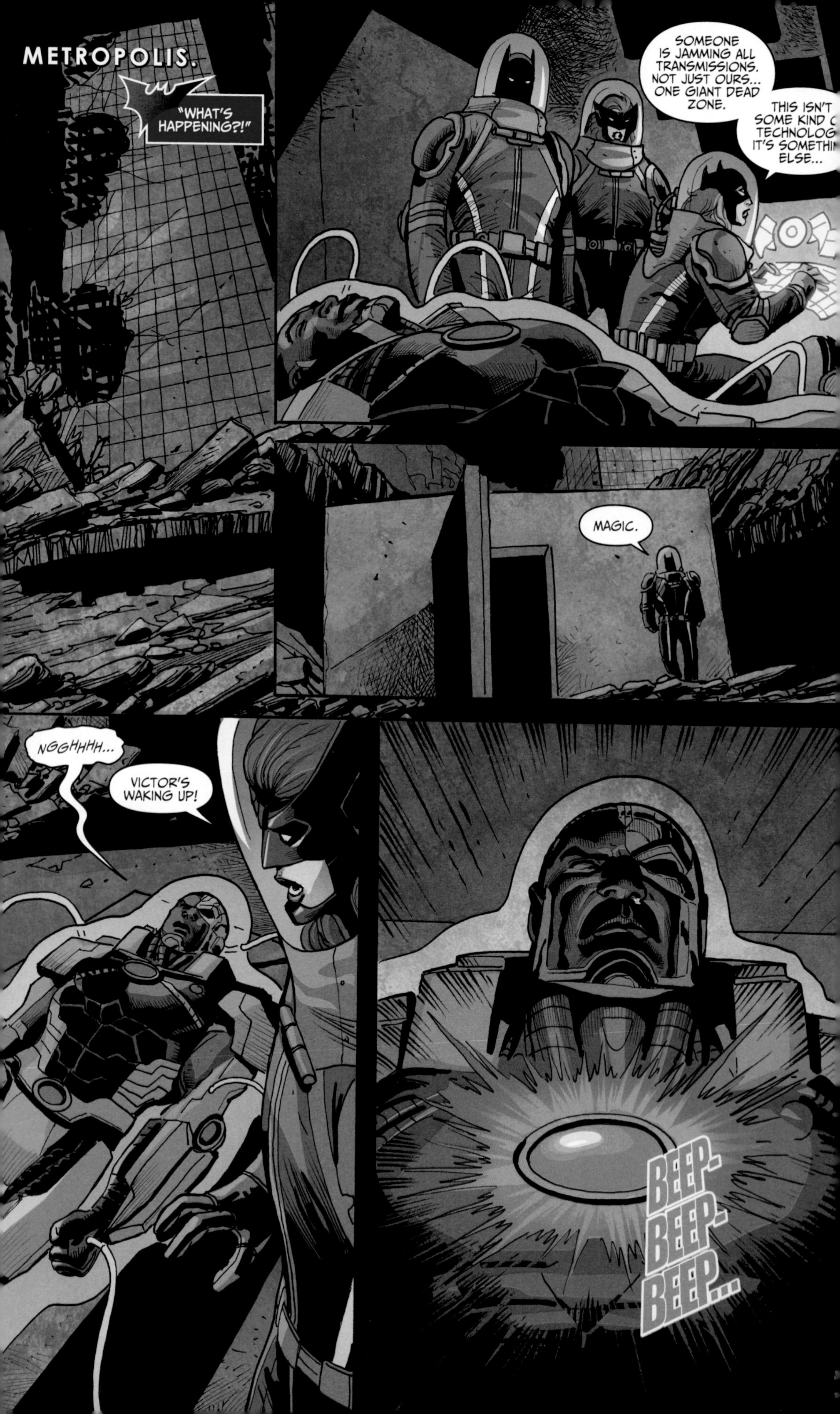
METROPOLIS.
"WHAT'S HAPPENING?!"
SOMEONE IS JAMMING ALL TRANSMISSIONS. NOT JUST OURS... ONE GIANT DEAD ZONE.
THIS ISN'T SOME KIND O TECHNOLOG IT'S SOMETHIN ELSE...
MAGIC.
NGGHHHH...
VICTOR'S WAKING UP!
BEEP-BEEP-BEEP...

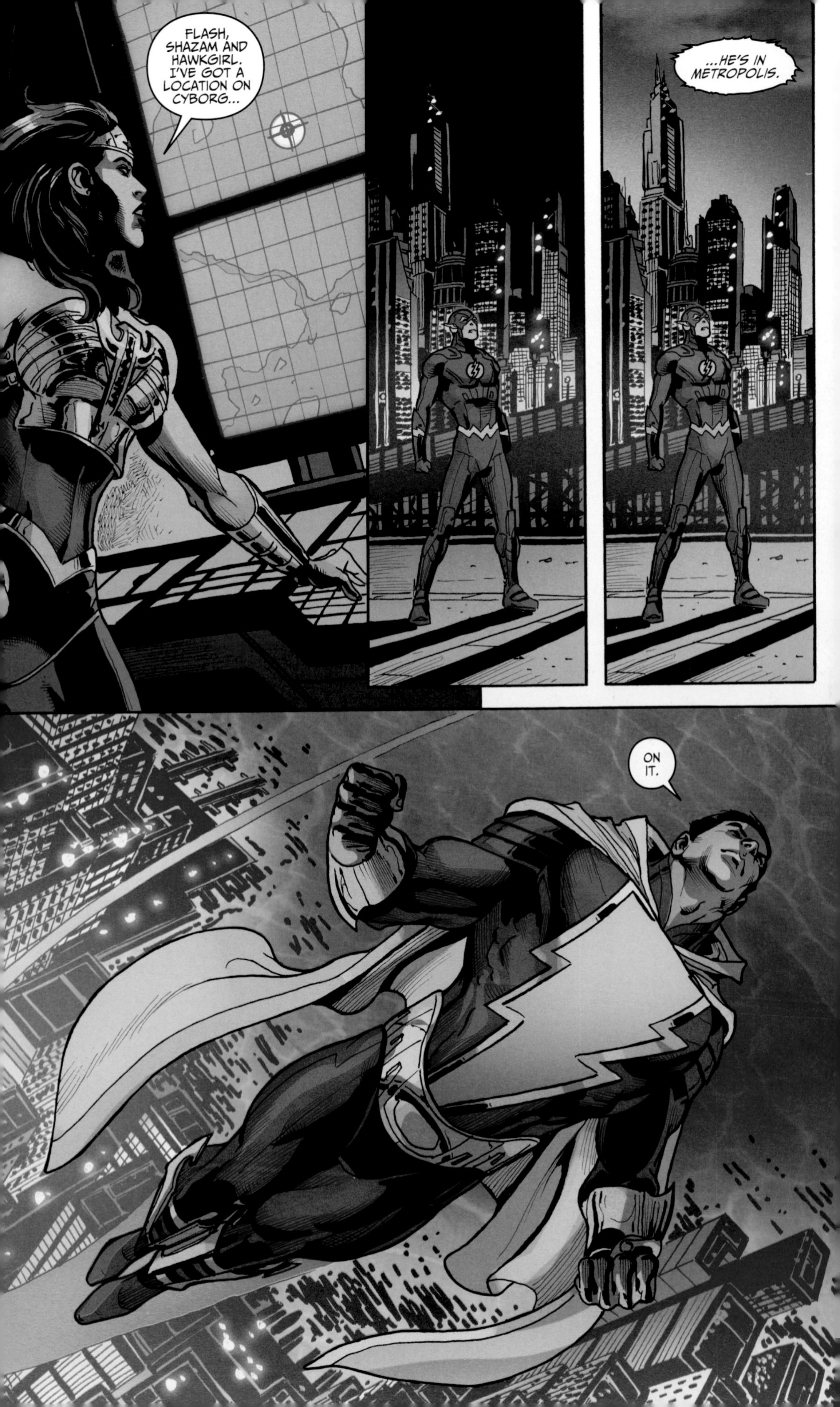
FLASH, SHAZAM AND HAWKGIRL. I'VE GOT A LOCATION ON CYBORG...
...HE'S IN METROPOLIS.
ON IT.

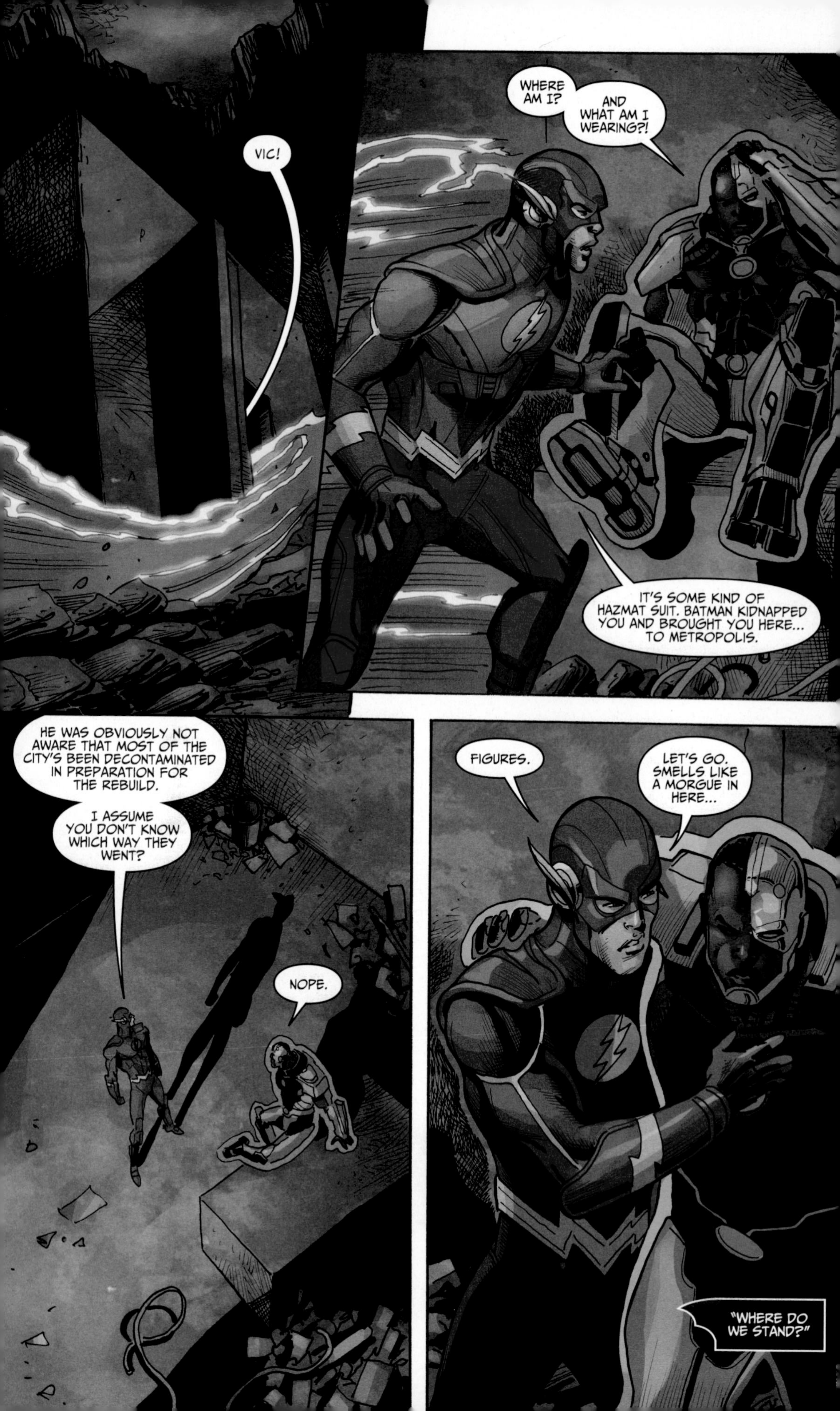
VIC!
WHERE AM I?
AND WHAT AM I WEARING?!
IT'S SOME KIND OF HAZMAT SUIT. BATMAN KIDNAPPED YOU AND BROUGHT YOU HERE... TO METROPOLIS.
HE WAS OBVIOUSLY NOT AWARE THAT MOST OF THE CITY'S BEEN DECONTAMINATED IN PREPARATION FOR THE REBUILD.
I ASSUME YOU DON'T KNOW WHICH WAY THEY WENT?
NOPE.
FIGURES.
LET'S GO. SMELLS LIKE A MORGUE IN HERE...
"WHERE DO WE STAND?"

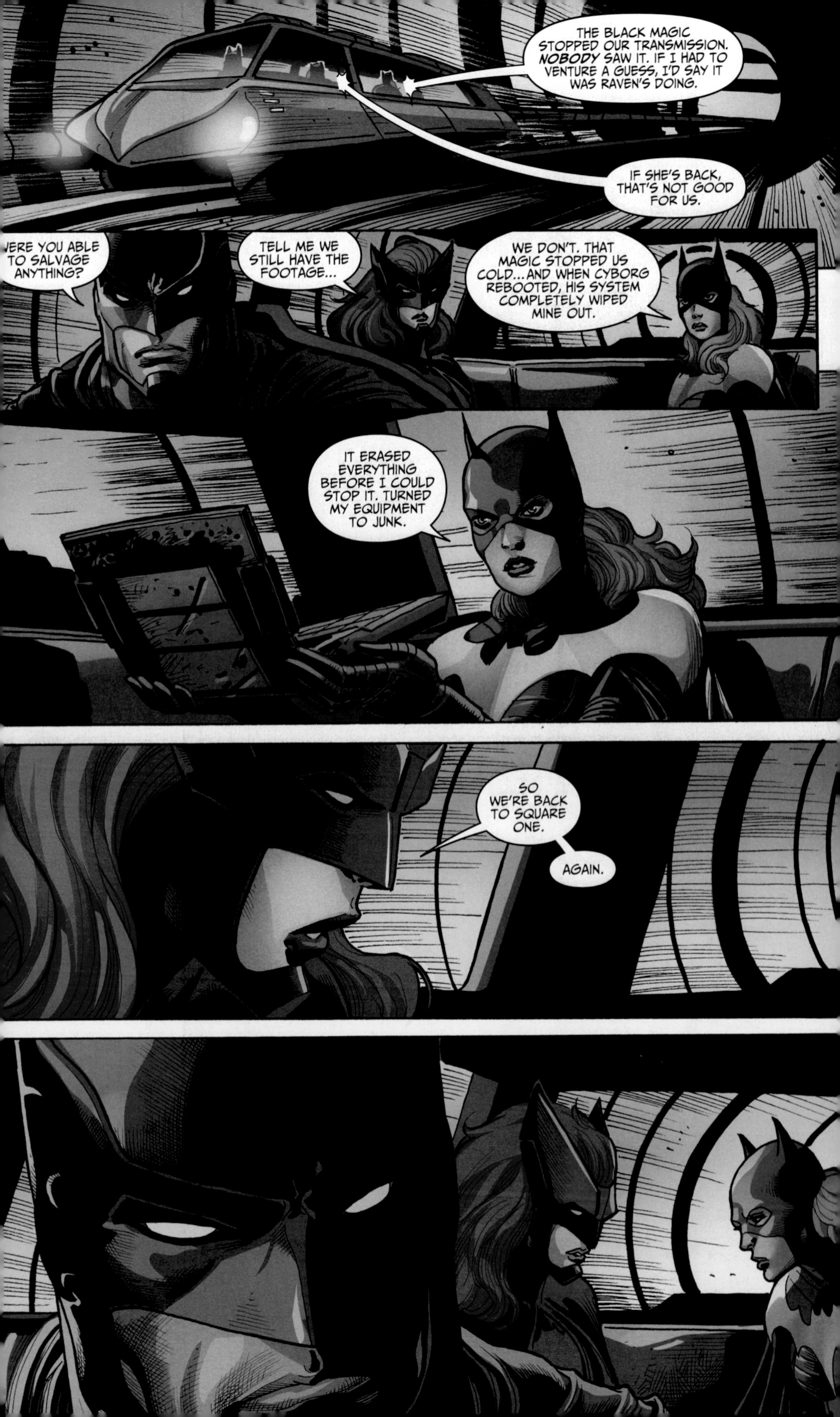
THE BLACK MAGIC STOPPED OUR TRANSMISSION. NOBODY SAW IT. IF I HAD TO VENTURE A GUESS, I'D SAY IT WAS RAVEN'S DOING.
IF SHE'S BACK, THAT'S NOT GOOD FOR US.
WERE YOU ABLE TO SALVAGE ANYTHING?
TELL ME WE STILL HAVE THE FOOTAGE...
WE DON'T. THAT MAGIC STOPPED US COLD...AND WHEN CYBORG REBOOTED, HIS SYSTEM COMPLETELY WIPED MINE OUT.
IT ERASED EVERYTHING BEFORE I COULD STOP IT. TURNED MY EQUIPMENT TO JUNK.
SO WE'RE BACK TO SQUARE ONE.
AGAIN.

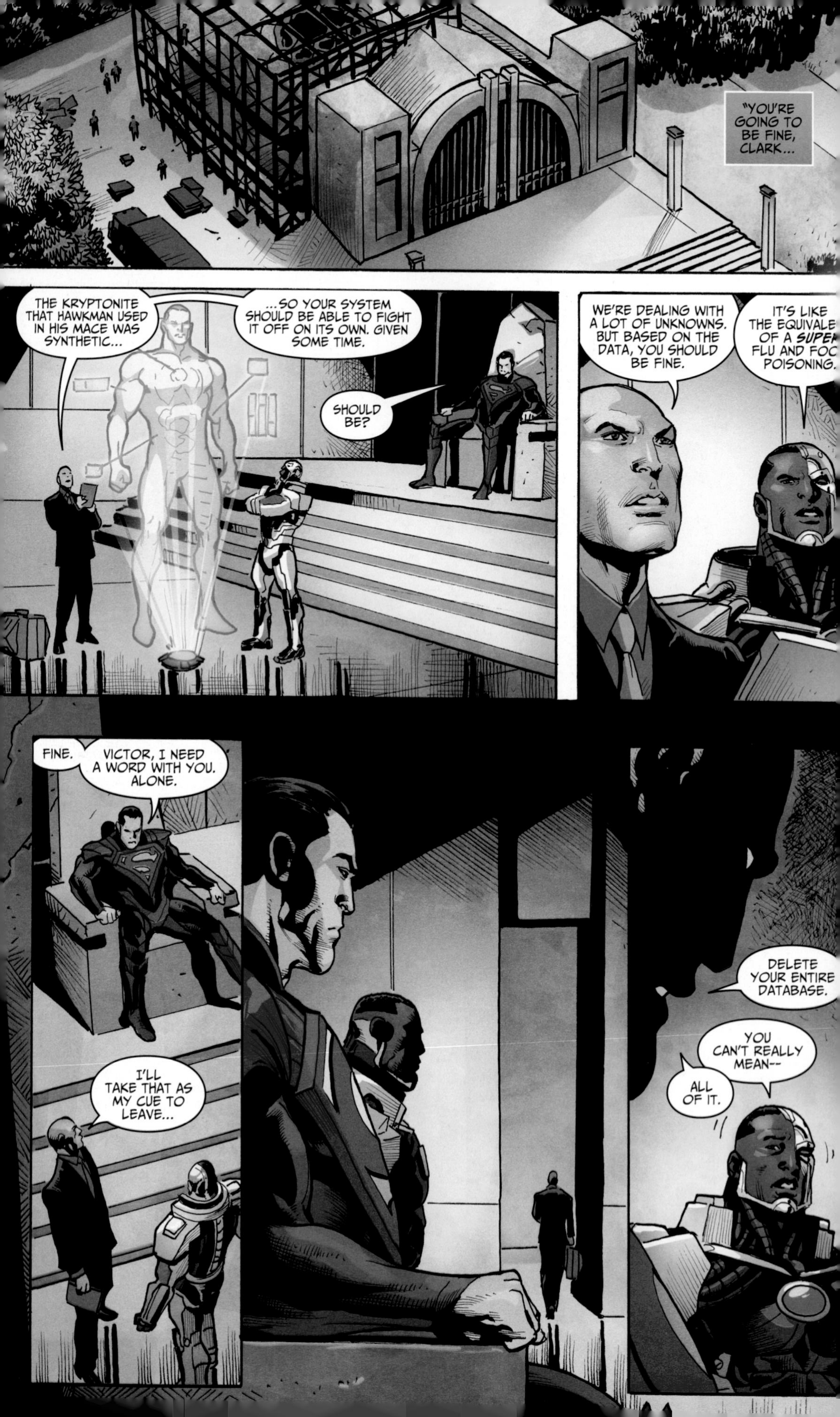
"YOU'RE GOING TO BE FINE, CLARK...
THE KRYPTONITE THAT HAWKMAN USED IN HIS MACE WAS SYNTHETIC...
...SO YOUR SYSTEM SHOULD BE ABLE TO FIGHT IT OFF ON ITS OWN. GIVEN SOME TIME.
SHOULD BE?
WE'RE DEALING WITH A LOT OF UNKNOWNS. BUT BASED ON THE DATA, YOU SHOULD BE FINE.
IT'S LIKE THE EQUIVALE OF A SUPEI FLU AND FOC POISONING.
FINE.
VICTOR, I NEED A WORD WITH YOU. ALONE.
I'LL TAKE THAT AS MY CUE TO LEAVE...
DELETE YOUR ENTIRE DATABASE.
YOU CAN'T REALLY MEAN--
ALL OF IT.

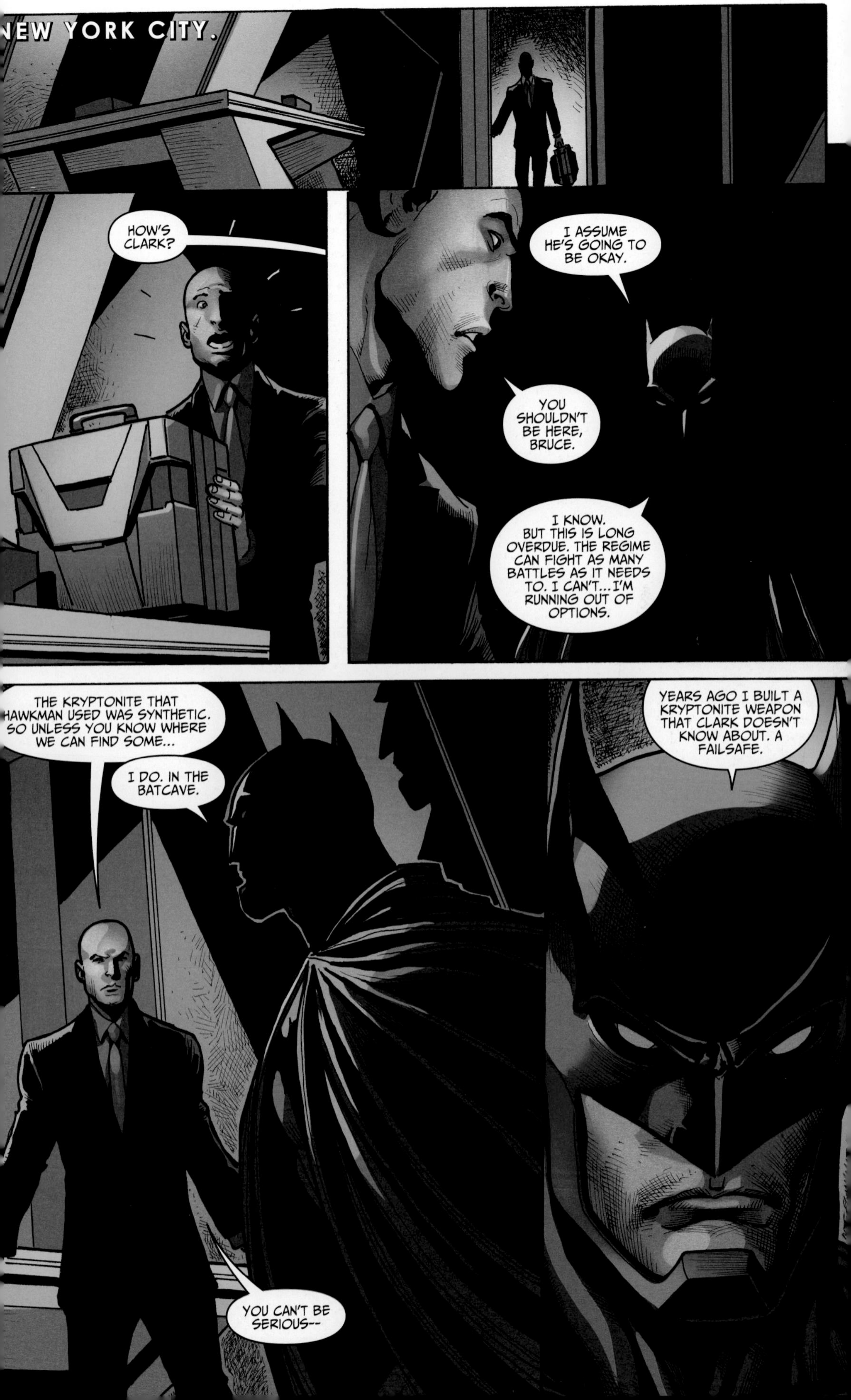
NEW YORK CITY.
HOW'S CLARK?
I ASSUME HE'S GOING TO BE OKAY.
YOU SHOULDN'T BE HERE, BRUCE.
I KNOW. BUT THIS IS LONG OVERDUE. THE REGIME CAN FIGHT AS MANY BATTLES AS IT NEEDS TO. I CAN'T...I'M RUNNING OUT OF OPTIONS.
THE KRYPTONITE THAT HAWKMAN USED WAS SYNTHETIC. SO UNLESS YOU KNOW WHERE WE CAN FIND SOME...
I DO. IN THE BATCAVE.
YEARS AGO I BUILT A KRYPTONITE WEAPON THAT CLARK DOESN'T KNOW ABOUT. A FAILSAFE.
YOU CAN'T BE SERIOUS--

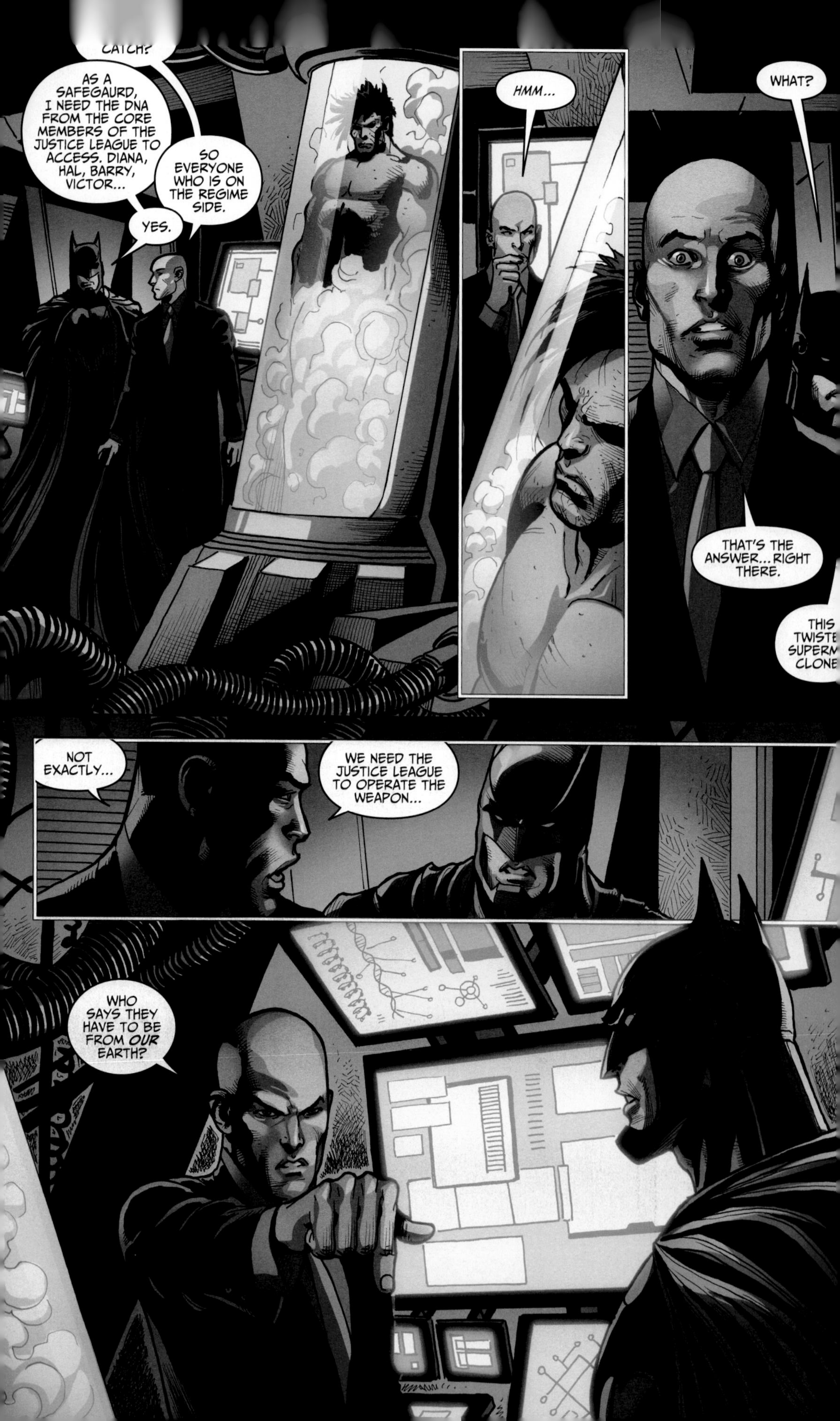

CATCH?
AS A SAFEGAURD, I NEED THE DNA FROM THE CORE MEMBERS OF THE JUSTICE LEAGUE TO ACCESS. DIANA, HAL, BARRY, VICTOR...
SO EVERYONE WHO IS ON THE REGIME SIDE.
YES.
HMM...
WHAT?
THAT'S THE ANSWER... RIGHT THERE.
THIS TWISTE SUPERM CLONE
NOT EXACTLY...
WE NEED THE JUSTICE LEAGUE TO OPERATE THE WEAPON...
WHO SAYS THEY HAVE TO BE FROM *OUR* EARTH?

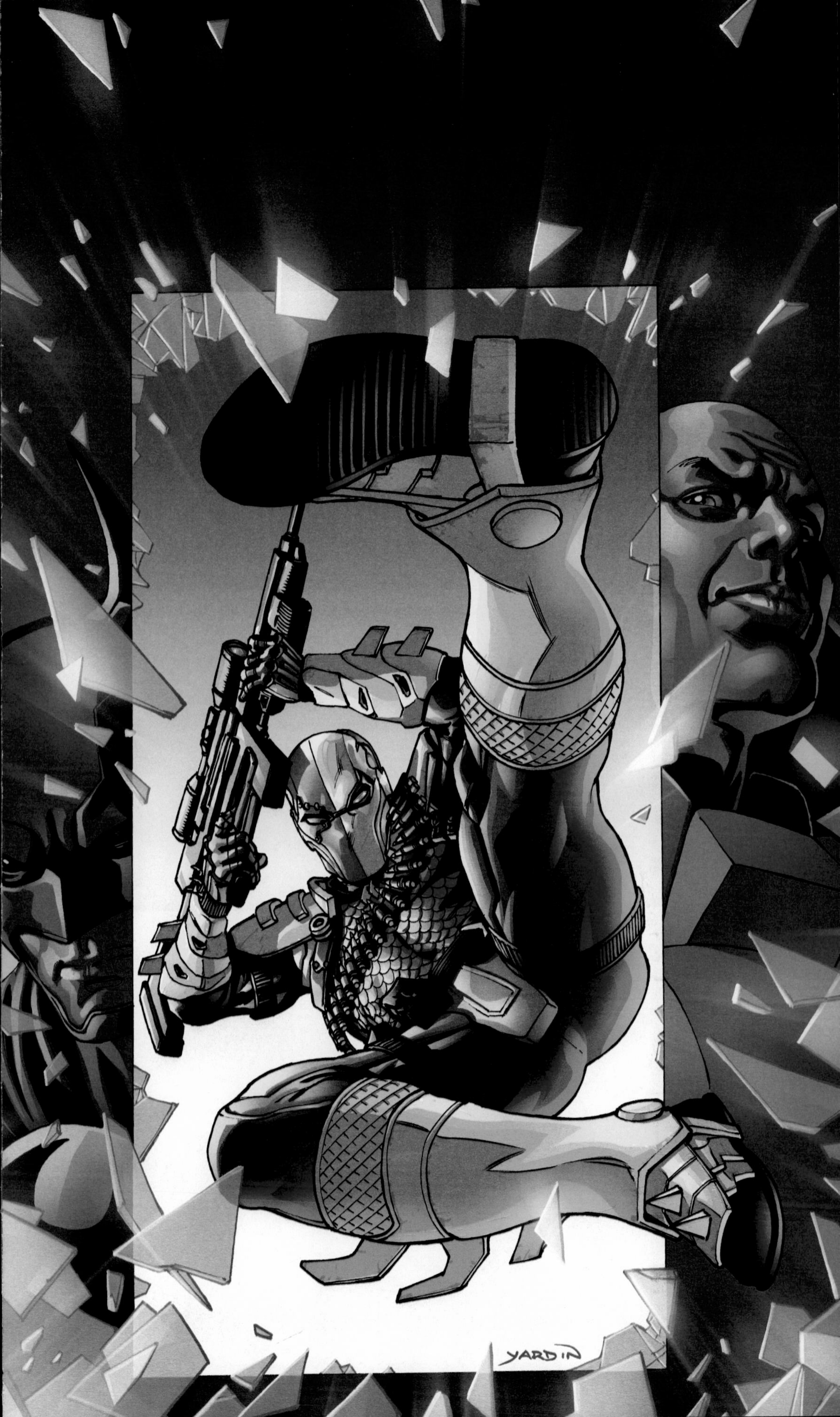
YARDIN

"The Plan" **Mike S. Miller** Artist **J. Nanjan** Colorist

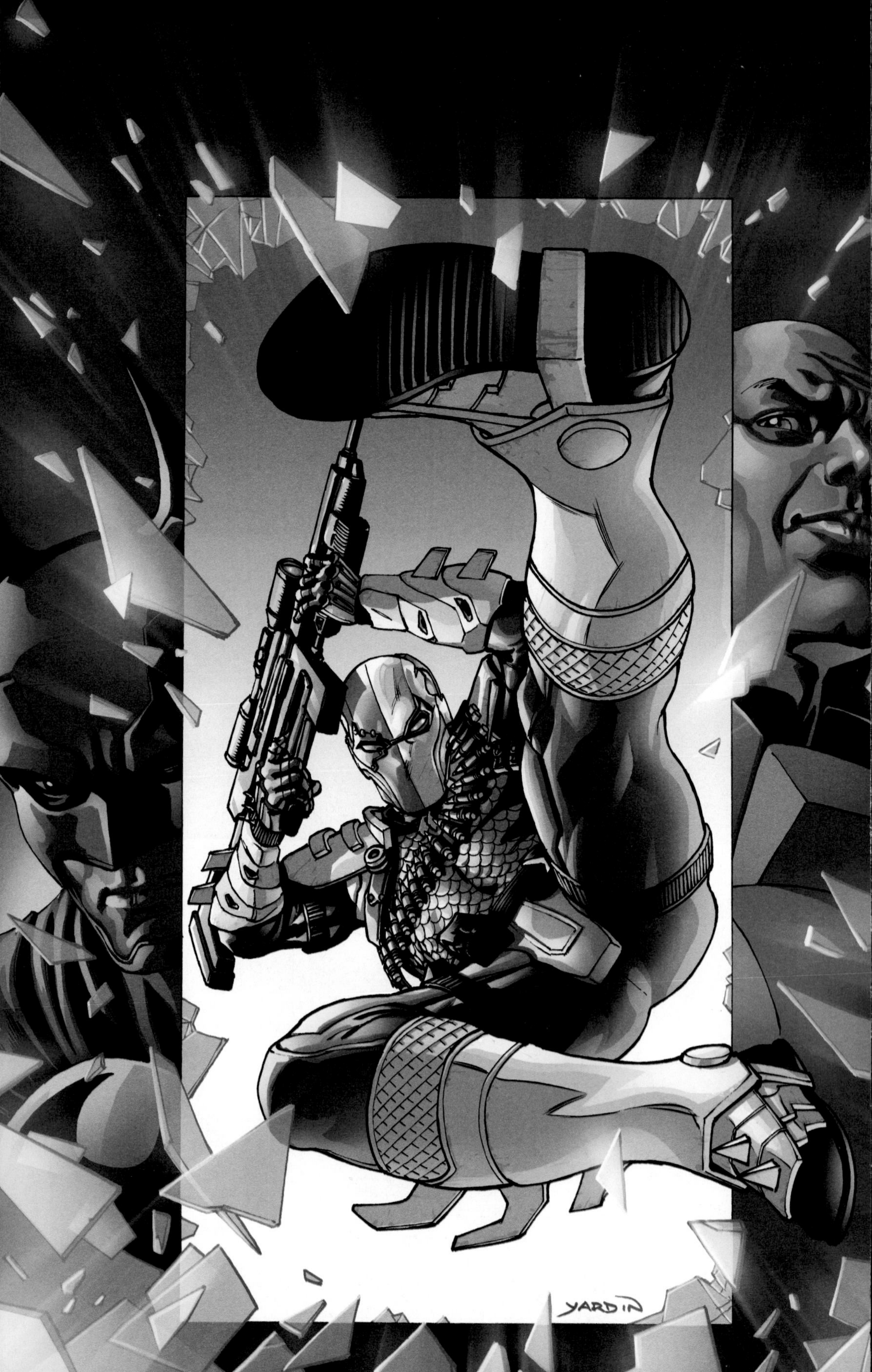
YARDIN

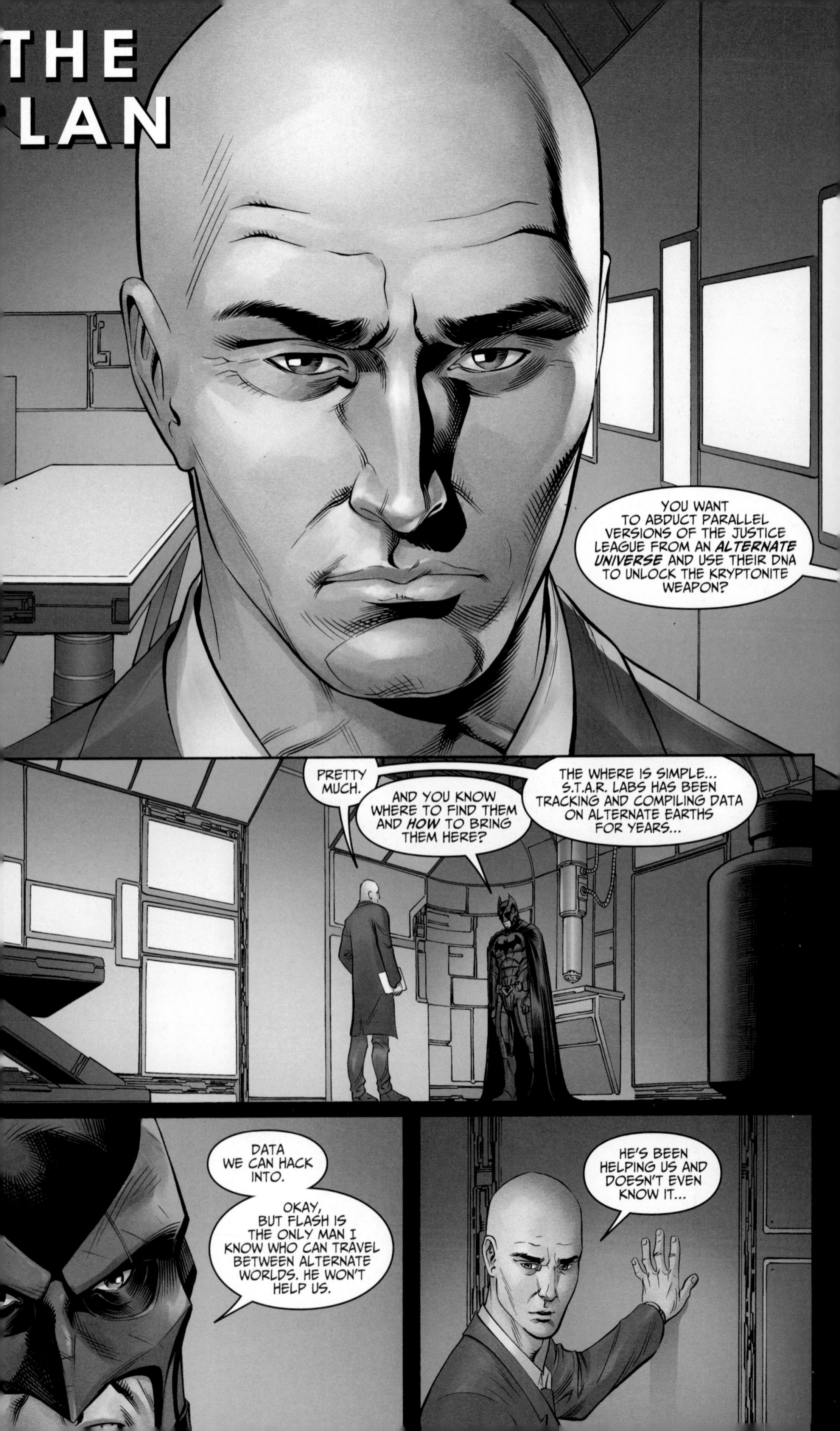
THE
LAN
YOU WANT TO ABDUCT PARALLEL VERSIONS OF THE JUSTICE LEAGUE FROM AN *ALTERNATE UNIVERSE* AND USE THEIR DNA TO UNLOCK THE KRYPTONITE WEAPON?
PRETTY MUCH.
AND YOU KNOW WHERE TO FIND THEM AND *HOW* TO BRING THEM HERE?
THE WHERE IS SIMPLE... S.T.A.R. LABS HAS BEEN TRACKING AND COMPILING DATA ON ALTERNATE EARTHS FOR YEARS...
DATA WE CAN HACK INTO.
OKAY, BUT FLASH IS THE ONLY MAN I KNOW WHO CAN TRAVEL BETWEEN ALTERNATE WORLDS. HE WON'T HELP US.
HE'S BEEN HELPING US AND DOESN'T EVEN KNOW IT...

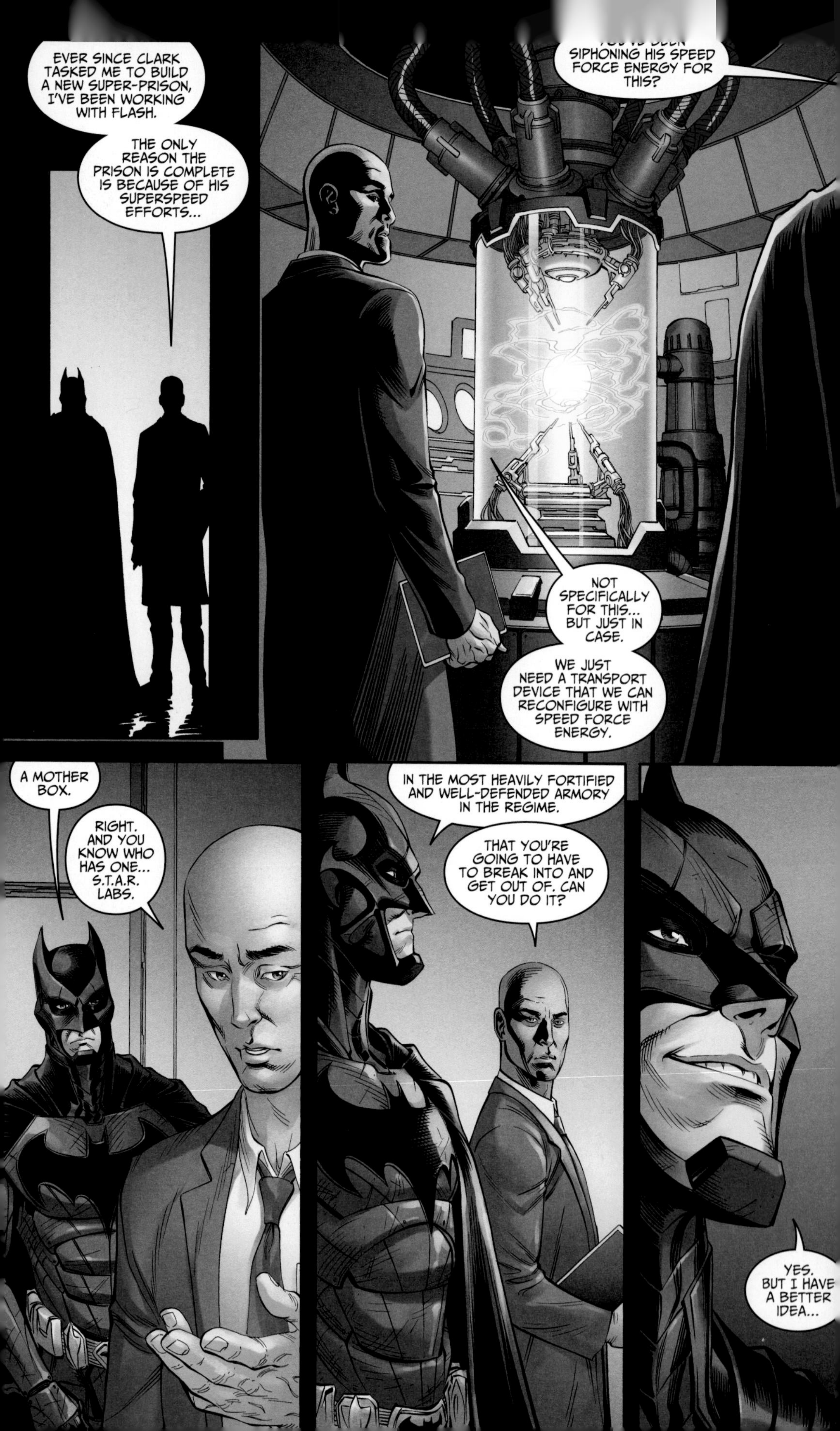
EVER SINCE CLARK TASKED ME TO BUILD A NEW SUPER-PRISON, I'VE BEEN WORKING WITH FLASH.
THE ONLY REASON THE PRISON IS COMPLETE IS BECAUSE OF HIS SUPERSPEED EFFORTS...
SIPHONING HIS SPEED FORCE ENERGY FOR THIS?
NOT SPECIFICALLY FOR THIS... BUT JUST IN CASE.
WE JUST NEED A TRANSPORT DEVICE THAT WE CAN RECONFIGURE WITH SPEED FORCE ENERGY.
A MOTHER BOX.
RIGHT. AND YOU KNOW WHO HAS ONE... S.T.A.R. LABS.
IN THE MOST HEAVILY FORTIFIED AND WELL-DEFENDED ARMORY IN THE REGIME.
THAT YOU'RE GOING TO HAVE TO BREAK INTO AND GET OUT OF. CAN YOU DO IT?
YES. BUT I HAVE A BETTER IDEA...

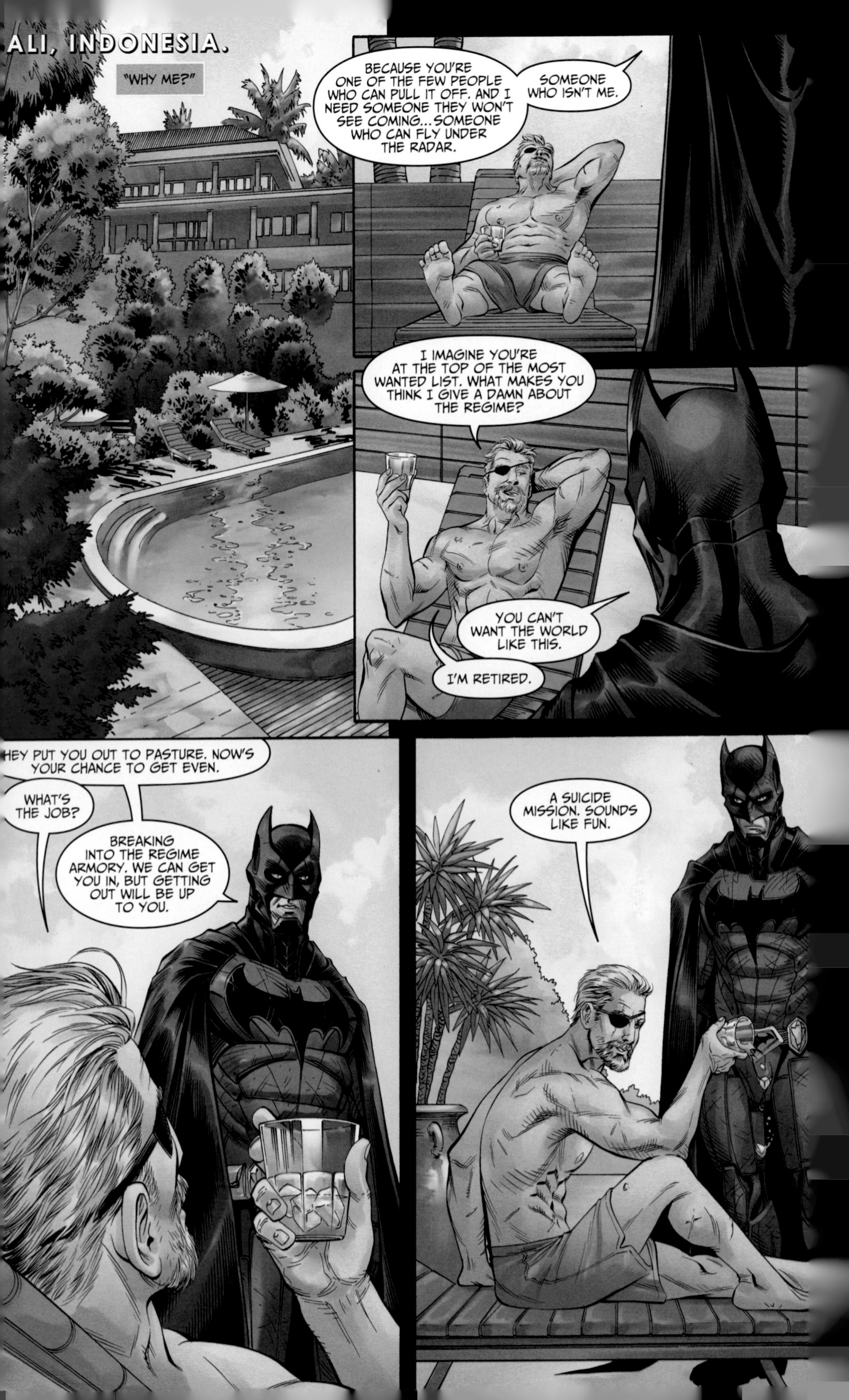
ALI, INDONESIA.
"WHY ME?"
BECAUSE YOU'RE ONE OF THE FEW PEOPLE WHO CAN PULL IT OFF. AND I NEED SOMEONE THEY WON'T SEE COMING...SOMEONE WHO CAN FLY UNDER THE RADAR.
SOMEONE WHO ISN'T ME.
I IMAGINE YOU'RE AT THE TOP OF THE MOST WANTED LIST. WHAT MAKES YOU THINK I GIVE A DAMN ABOUT THE REGIME?
YOU CAN'T WANT THE WORLD LIKE THIS.
I'M RETIRED.
HEY PUT YOU OUT TO PASTURE. NOW'S YOUR CHANCE TO GET EVEN.
WHAT'S THE JOB?
BREAKING INTO THE REGIME ARMORY. WE CAN GET YOU IN, BUT GETTING OUT WILL BE UP TO YOU.
A SUICIDE MISSION. SOUNDS LIKE FUN.

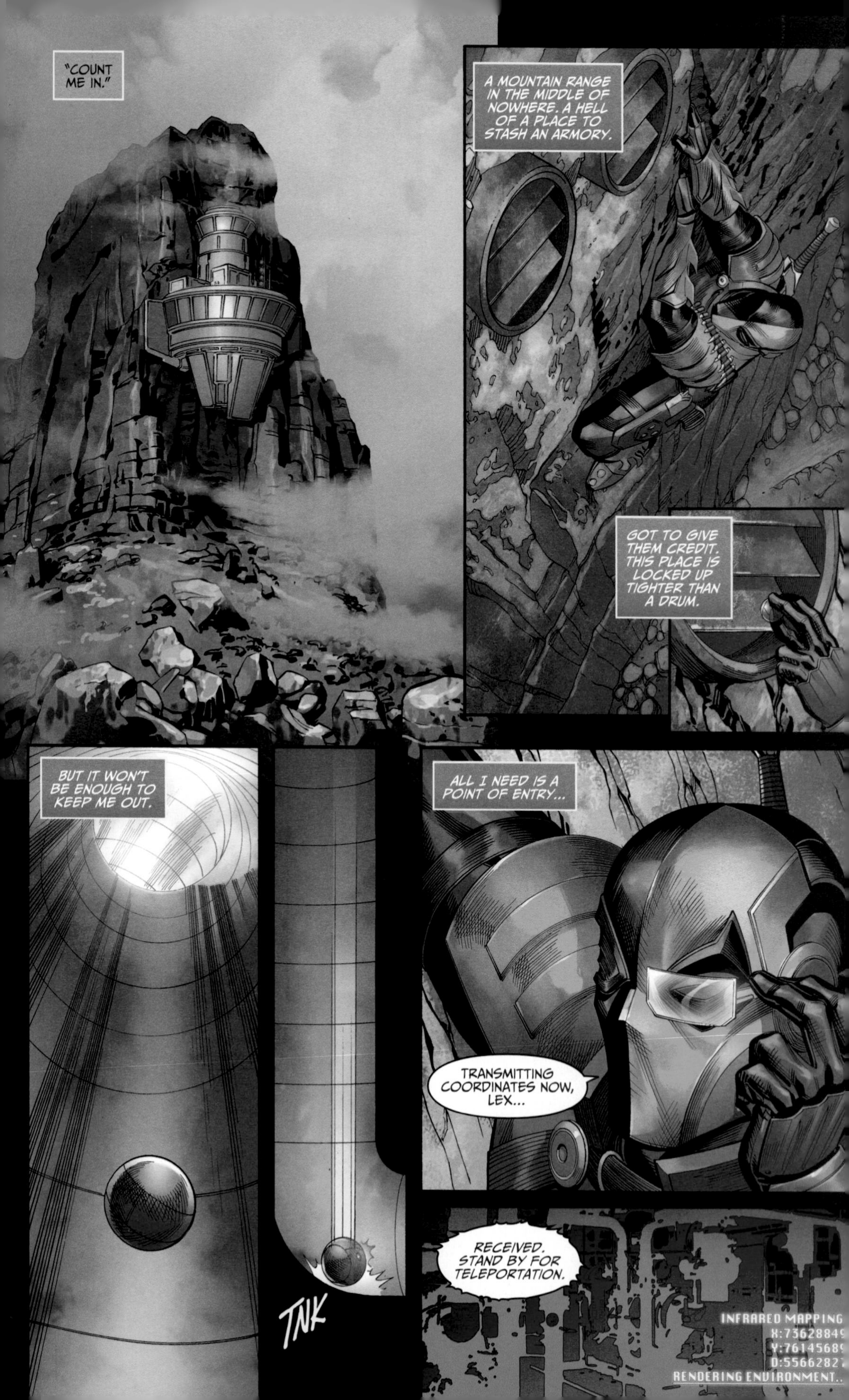
"COUNT ME IN."
A MOUNTAIN RANGE IN THE MIDDLE OF NOWHERE. A HELL OF A PLACE TO STASH AN ARMORY.
GOT TO GIVE THEM CREDIT. THIS PLACE IS LOCKED UP TIGHTER THAN A DRUM.
BUT IT WON'T BE ENOUGH TO KEEP ME OUT.
TNK
ALL I NEED IS A POINT OF ENTRY...
TRANSMITTING COORDINATES NOW, LEX...
RECEIVED. STAND BY FOR TELEPORTATION.
INFRARED MAPPING
X:73628849
Y:76145689
D:5566282
RENDERING ENVIRONMENT..

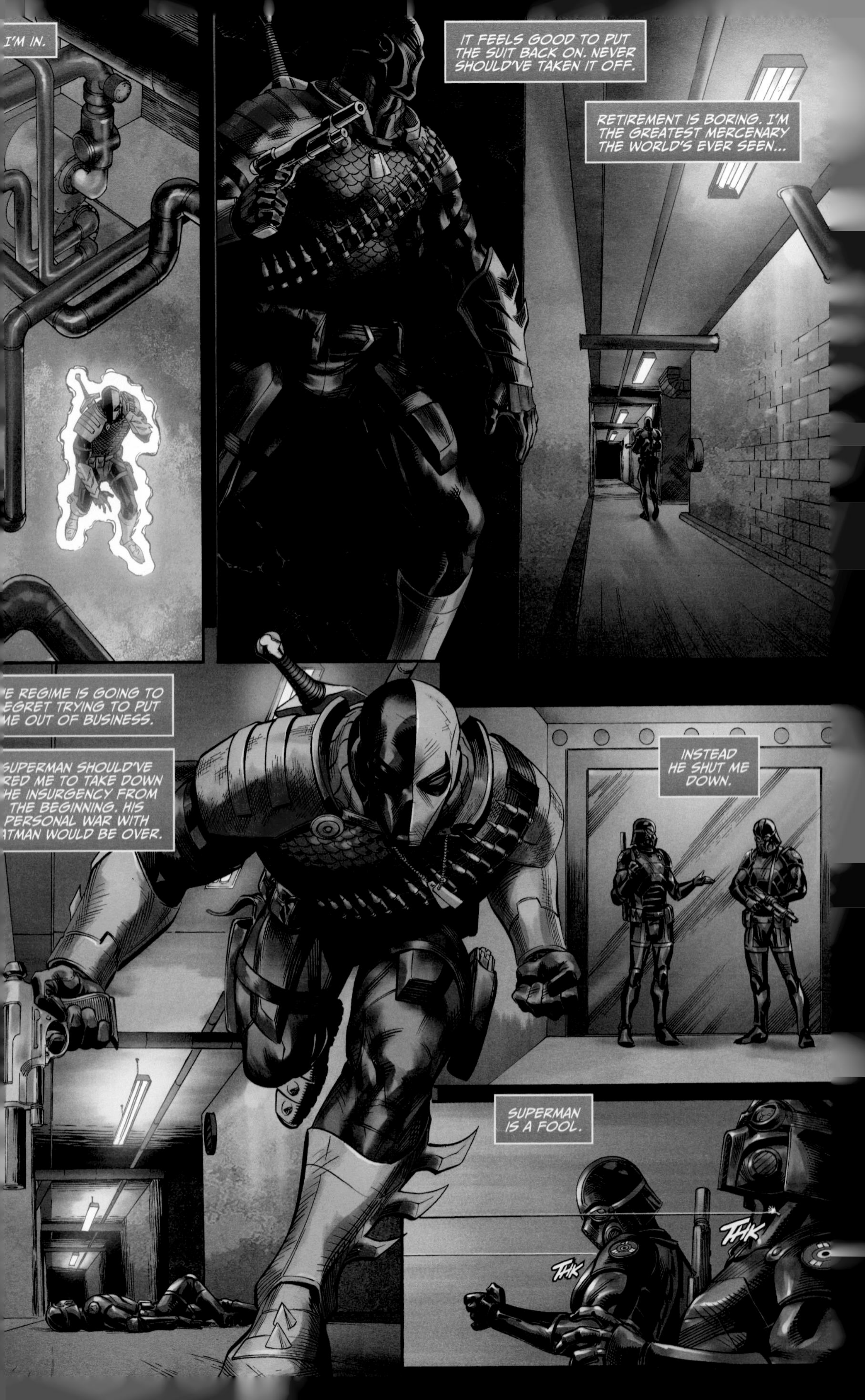

I'M IN.
IT FEELS GOOD TO PUT THE SUIT BACK ON. NEVER SHOULD'VE TAKEN IT OFF.
RETIREMENT IS BORING. I'M THE GREATEST MERCENARY THE WORLD'S EVER SEEN...
E REGIME IS GOING TO EGRET TRYING TO PUT ME OUT OF BUSINESS.
SUPERMAN SHOULD'VE RED ME TO TAKE DOWN HE INSURGENCY FROM THE BEGINNING. HIS PERSONAL WAR WITH ATMAN WOULD BE OVER.
INSTEAD HE SHUT ME DOWN.
SUPERMAN IS A FOOL.
THK
THK

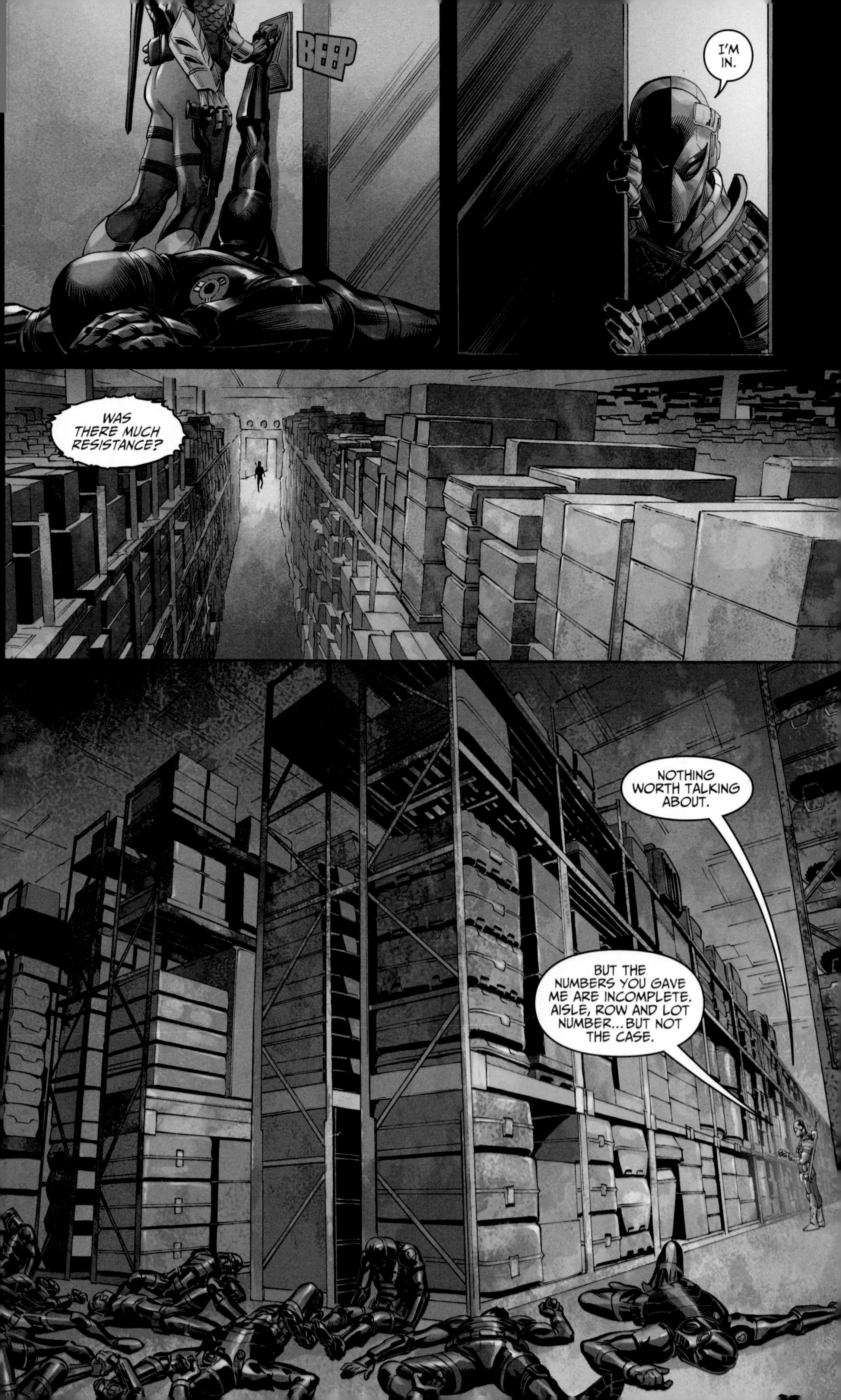
BEEP
I'M IN.
WAS THERE MUCH RESISTANCE?
NOTHING WORTH TALKING ABOUT.
BUT THE NUMBERS YOU GAVE ME ARE INCOMPLETE. AISLE, ROW AND LOT NUMBER... BUT NOT THE CASE.

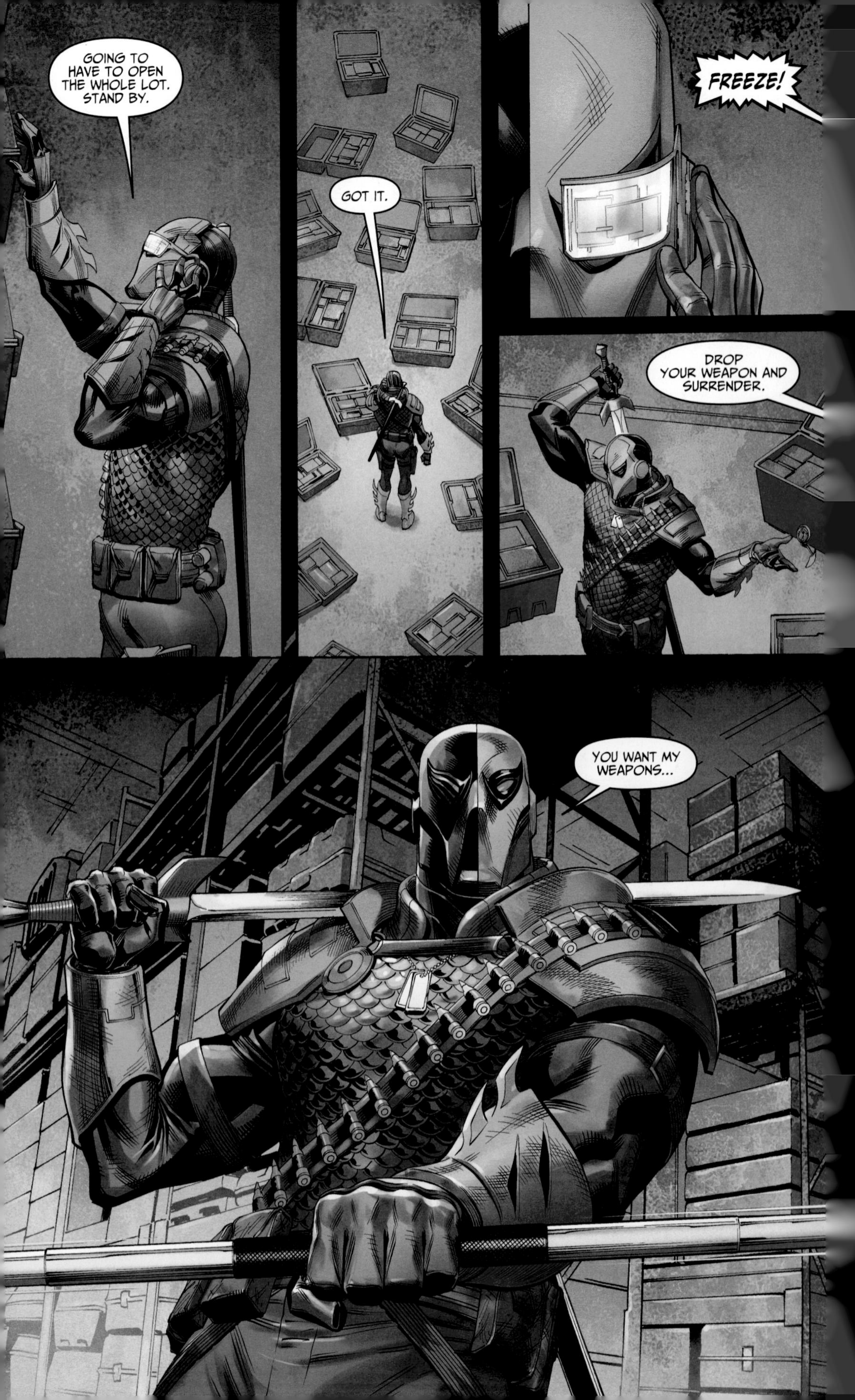

GOING TO HAVE TO OPEN THE WHOLE LOT. STAND BY.
GOT IT.
FREEZE!
DROP YOUR WEAPON AND SURRENDER.
YOU WANT MY WEAPONS...

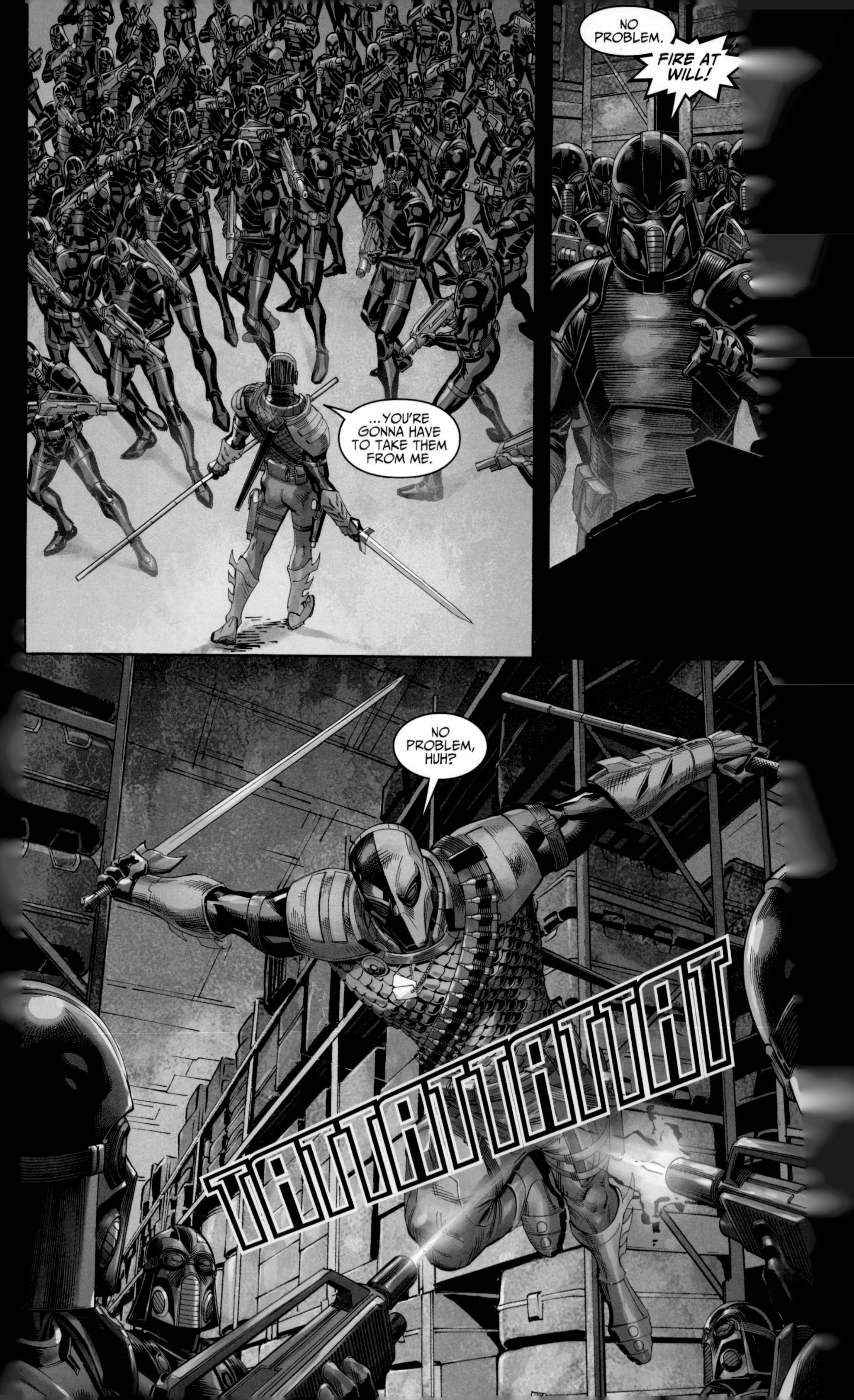
...YOU'RE GONNA HAVE TO TAKE THEM FROM ME.
NO PROBLEM.
FIRE AT WILL!
NO PROBLEM, HUH?
TATTATTATTAT

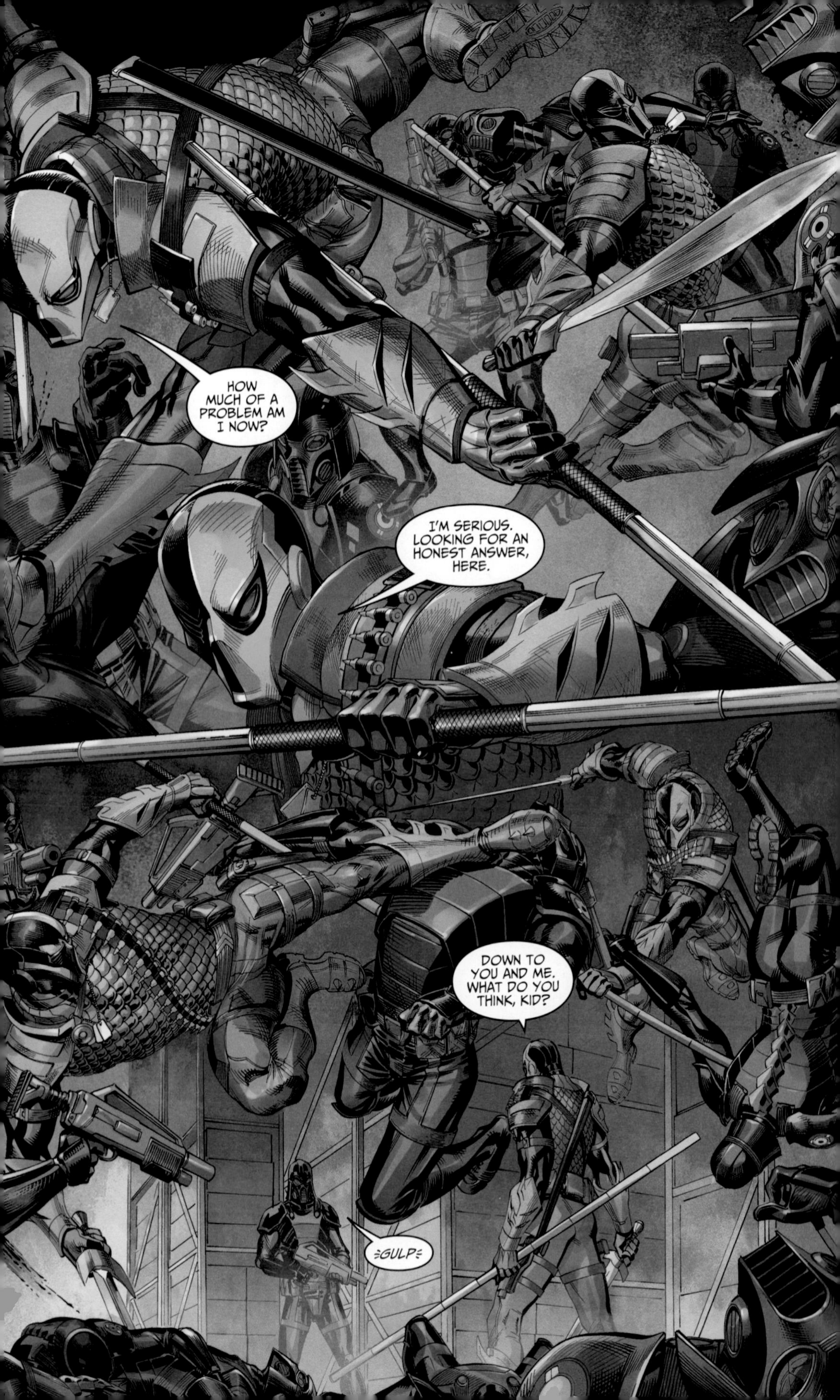
HOW MUCH OF A PROBLEM AM I NOW?
I'M SERIOUS. LOOKING FOR AN HONEST ANSWER, HERE.
DOWN TO YOU AND ME. WHAT DO YOU THINK, KID?
GULP

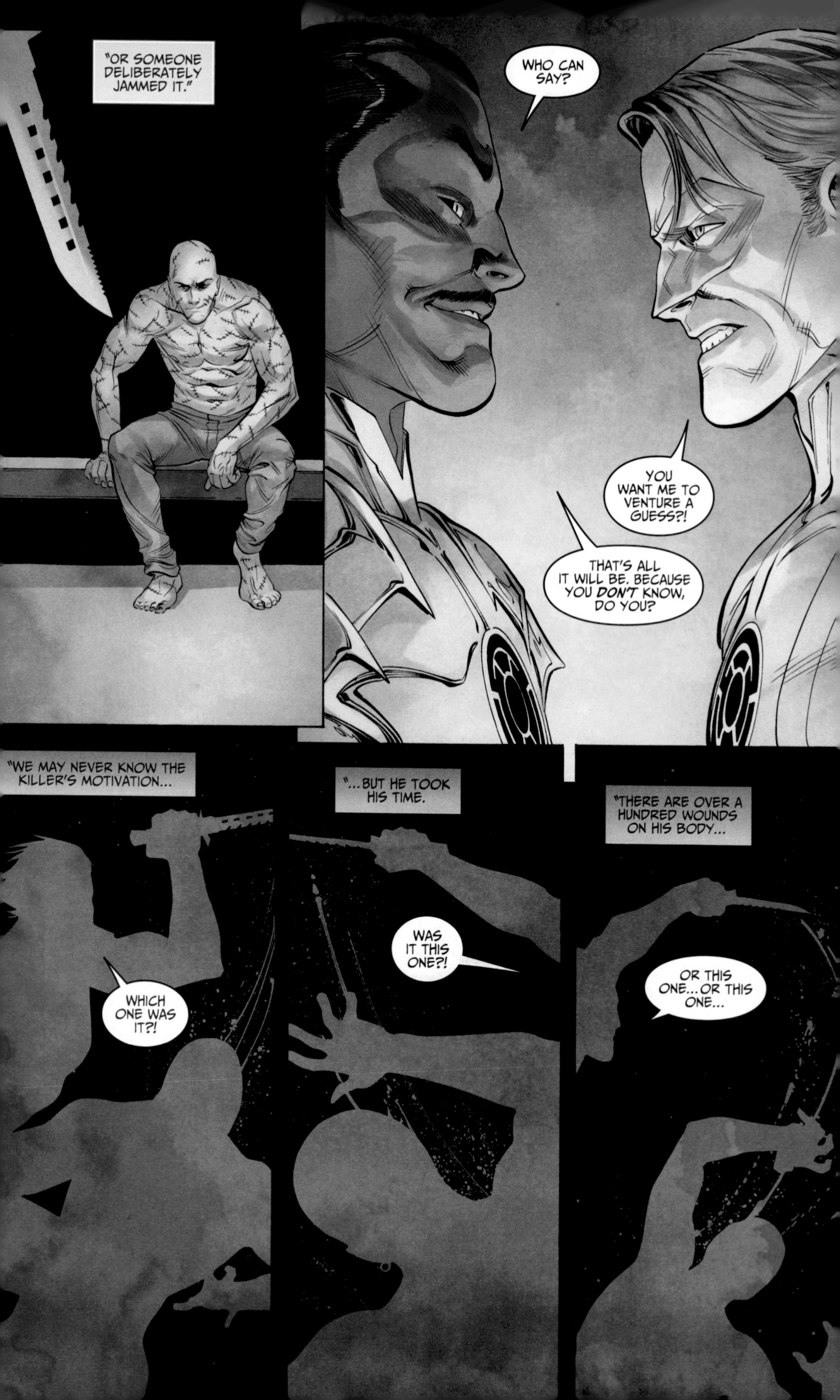
"OR SOMEONE DELIBERATELY JAMMED IT."
WHO CAN SAY?
YOU WANT ME TO VENTURE A GUESS?!
THAT'S ALL IT WILL BE. BECAUSE YOU *DON'T* KNOW, DO YOU?
"WE MAY NEVER KNOW THE KILLER'S MOTIVATION...
WHICH ONE WAS IT?!
"...BUT HE TOOK HIS TIME.
WAS IT THIS ONE?!
"THERE ARE OVER A HUNDRED WOUNDS ON HIS BODY...
OR THIS ONE...OR THIS ONE...

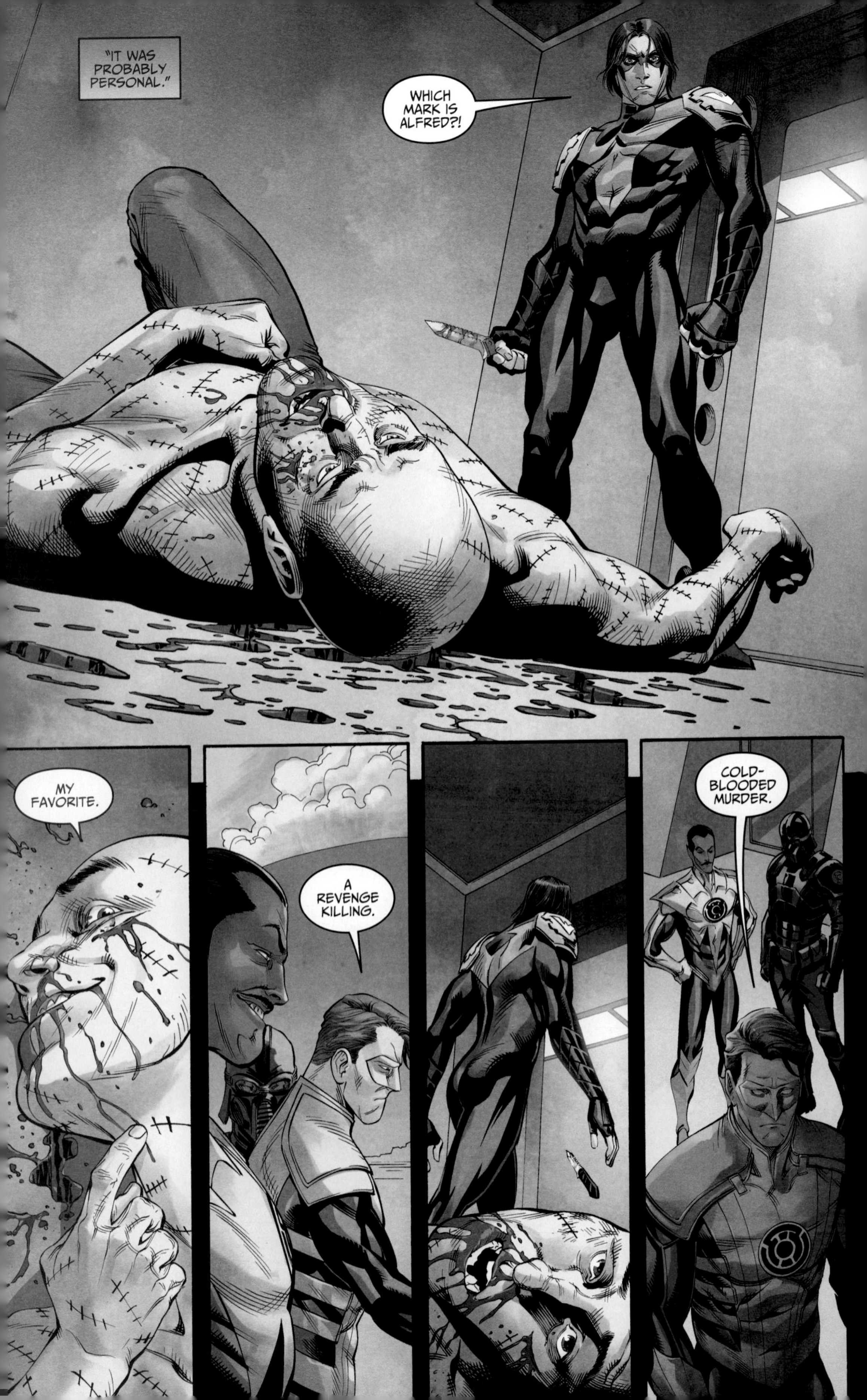
"IT WAS PROBABLY PERSONAL."
WHICH MARK IS ALFRED?!
MY FAVORITE.
A REVENGE KILLING.
COLD-BLOODED MURDER.

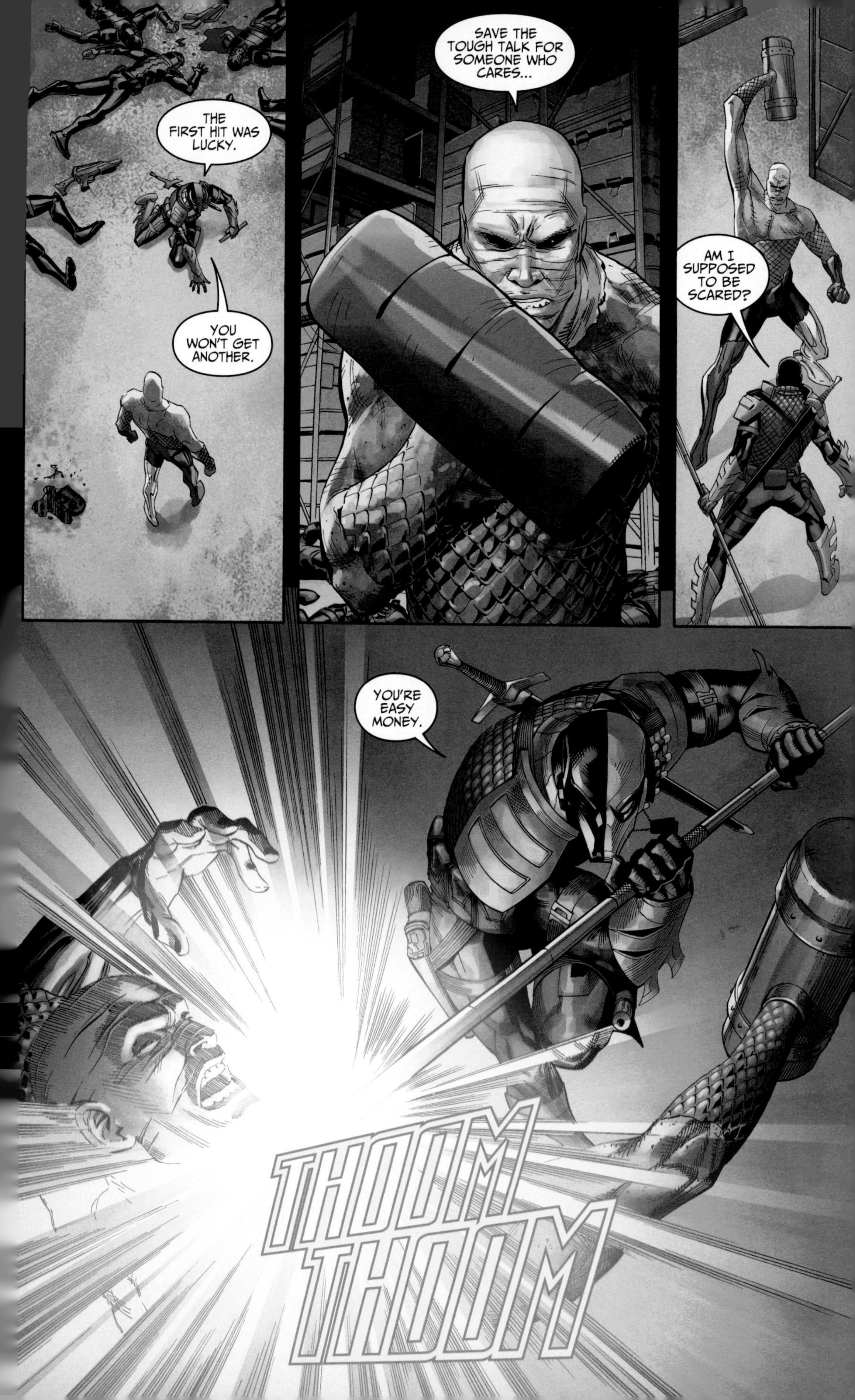
THE FIRST HIT WAS LUCKY.
YOU WON'T GET ANOTHER.
SAVE THE TOUGH TALK FOR SOMEONE WHO CARES...
AM I SUPPOSED TO BE SCARED?
YOU'RE EASY MONEY.
THOOM
THOOM

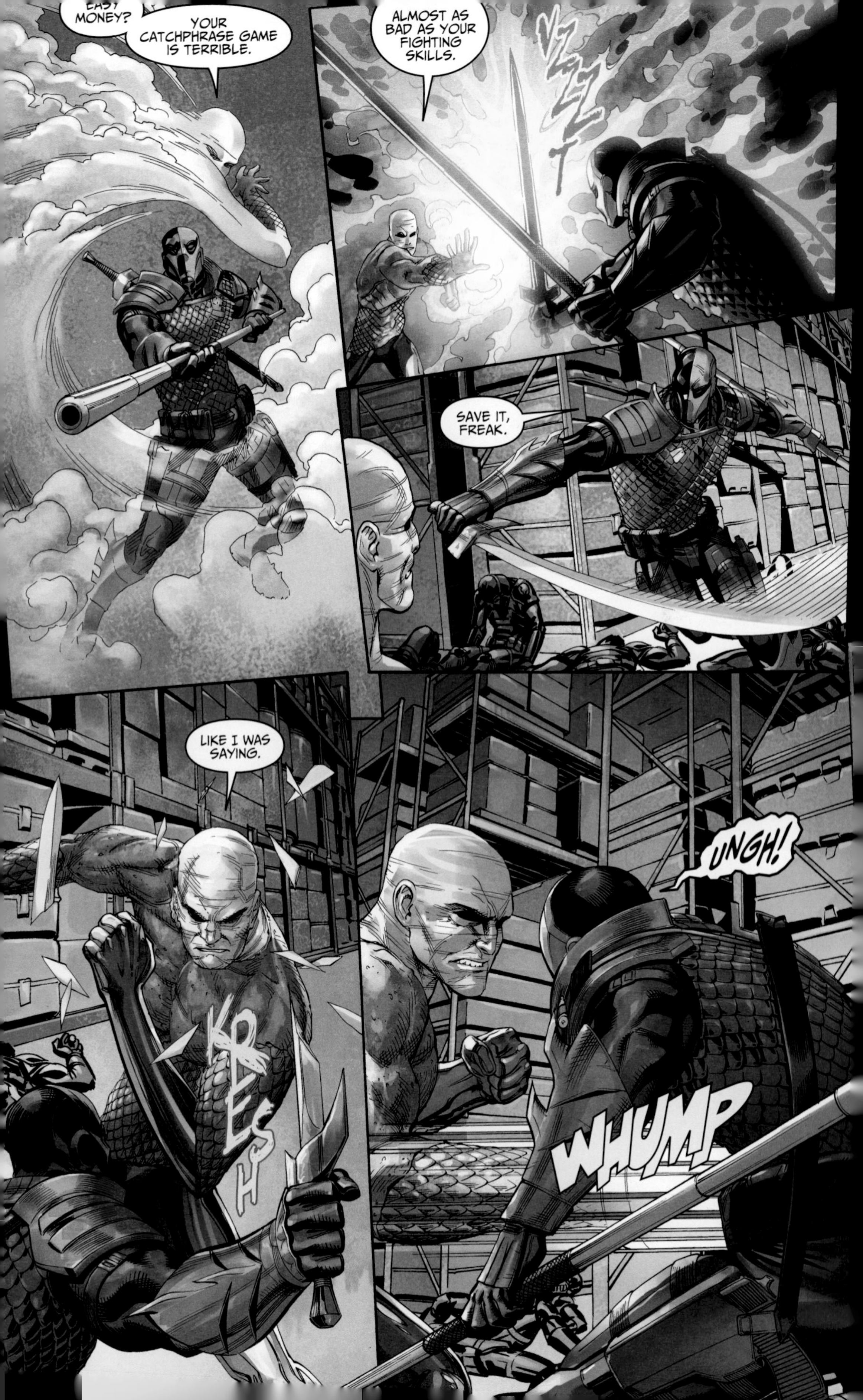
MONEY?
YOUR CATCHPHRASE GAME IS TERRIBLE.
ALMOST AS BAD AS YOUR FIGHTING SKILLS.
VZZZT
SAVE IT, FREAK.
LIKE I WAS SAYING.
UNGH!
WHUMP

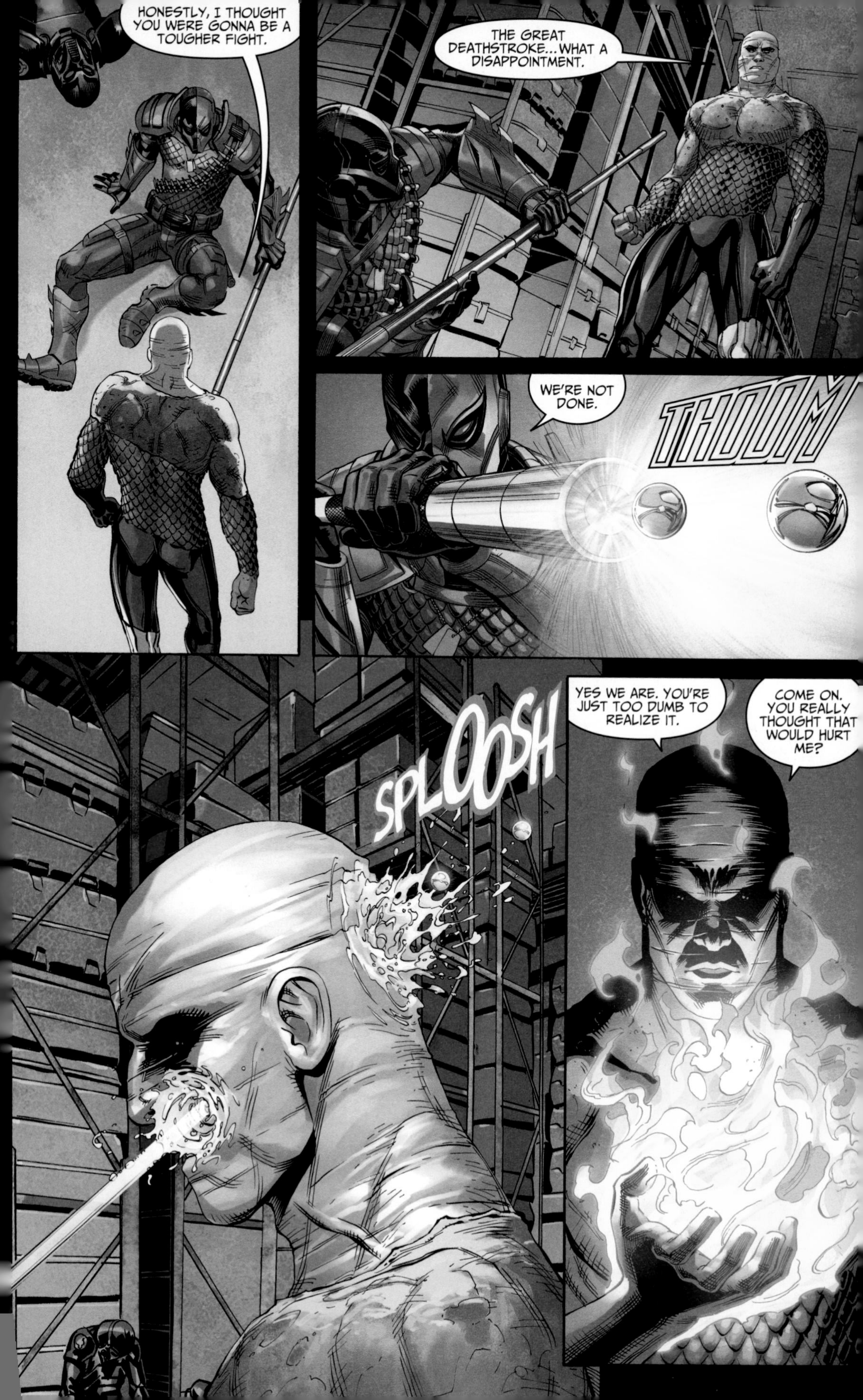
HONESTLY, I THOUGHT YOU WERE GONNA BE A TOUGHER FIGHT.
THE GREAT DEATHSTROKE...WHAT A DISAPPOINTMENT.
WE'RE NOT DONE.
THOOM
SPLOOSH
YES WE ARE. YOU'RE JUST TOO DUMB TO REALIZE IT.
COME ON. YOU REALLY THOUGHT THAT WOULD HURT ME?

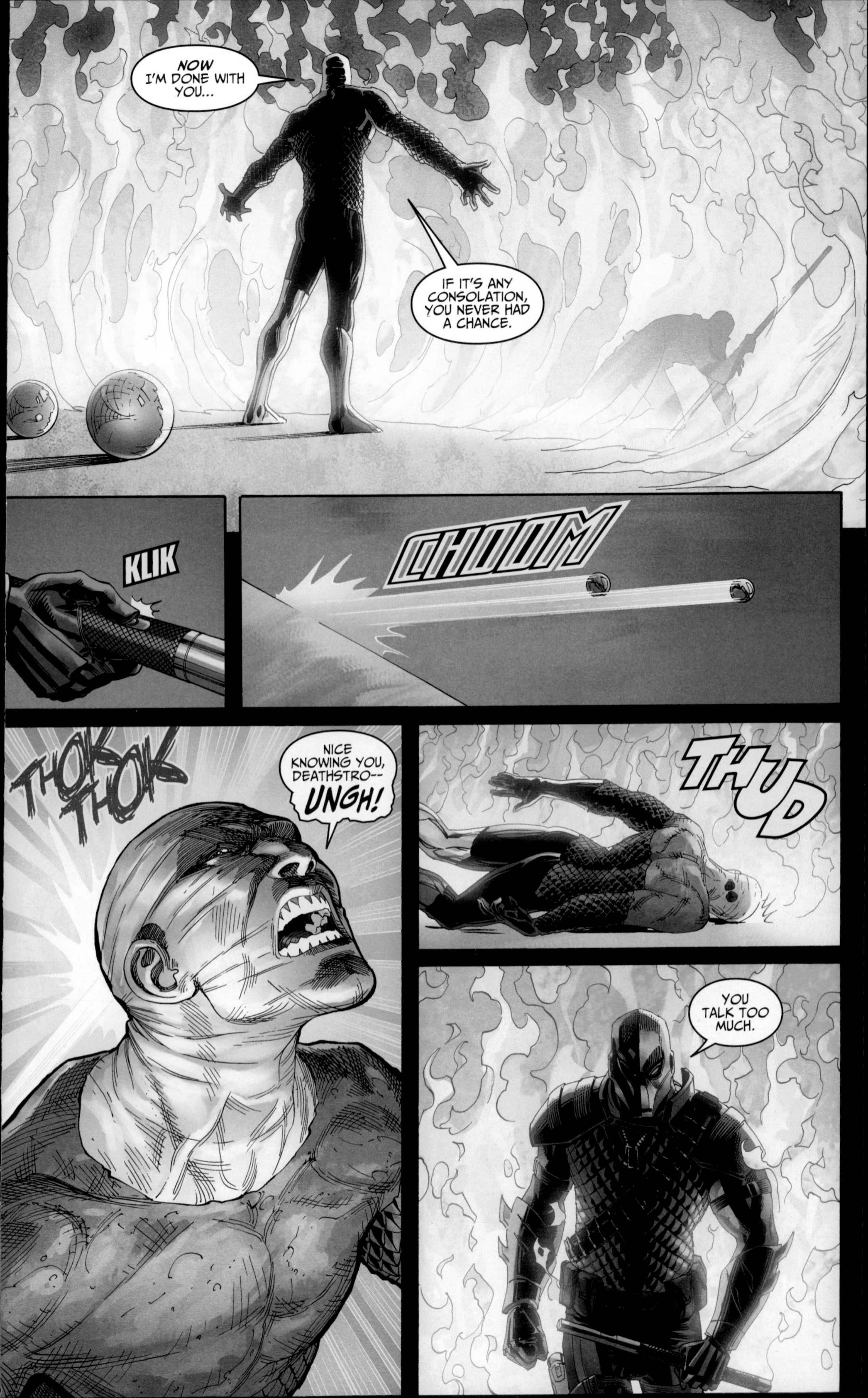
NOW I'M DONE WITH YOU...
IF IT'S ANY CONSOLATION, YOU NEVER HAD A CHANCE.
KLIK
CHOOM
THOK THOK
NICE KNOWING YOU, DEATHSTRO-- UNGH!
THUD
YOU TALK TOO MUCH.

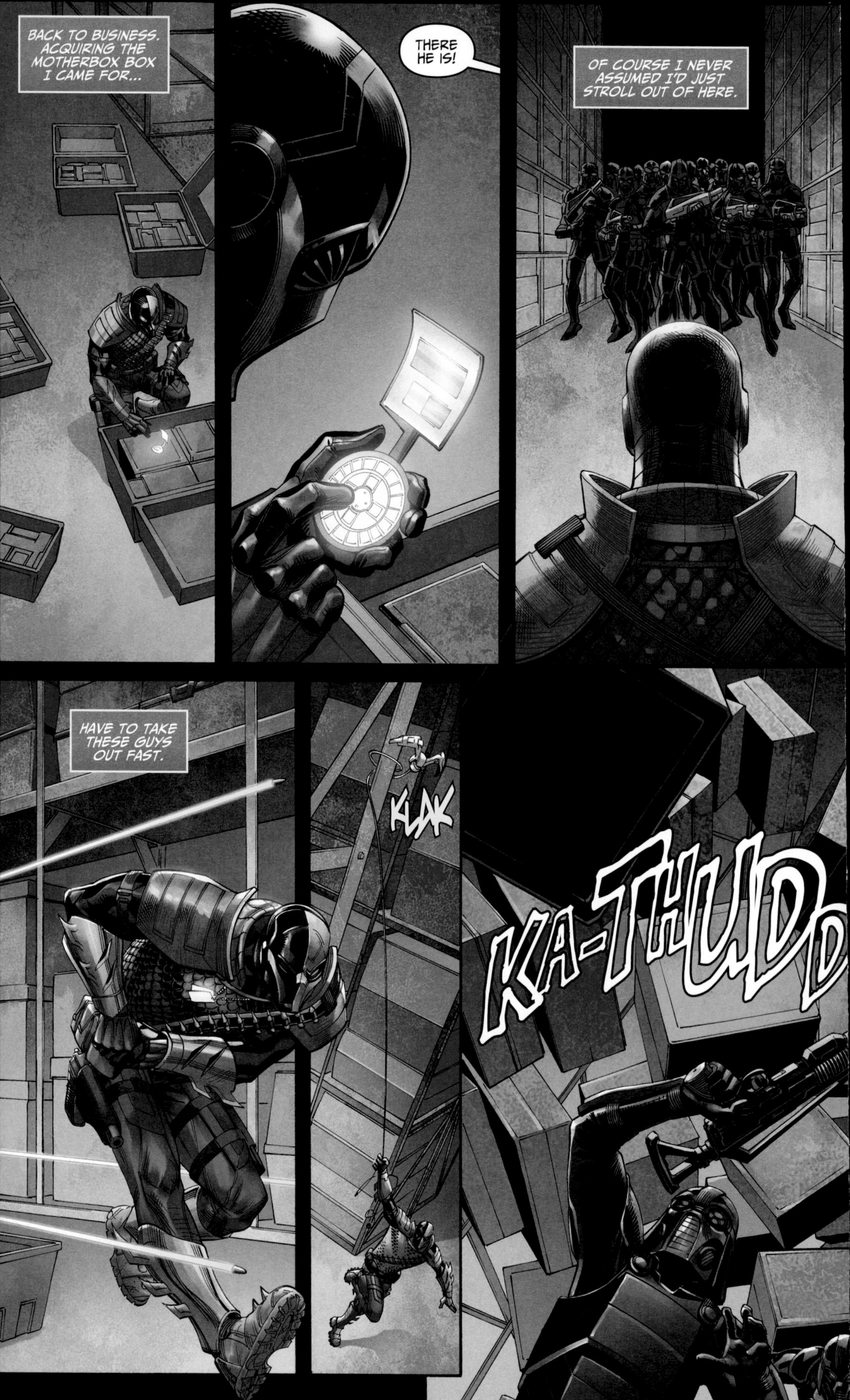

BACK TO BUSINESS. ACQUIRING THE MOTHERBOX BOX I CAME FOR...
THERE HE IS!
OF COURSE I NEVER ASSUMED I'D JUST STROLL OUT OF HERE.
HAVE TO TAKE THESE GUYS OUT FAST.
KLAK
KA-THUDD

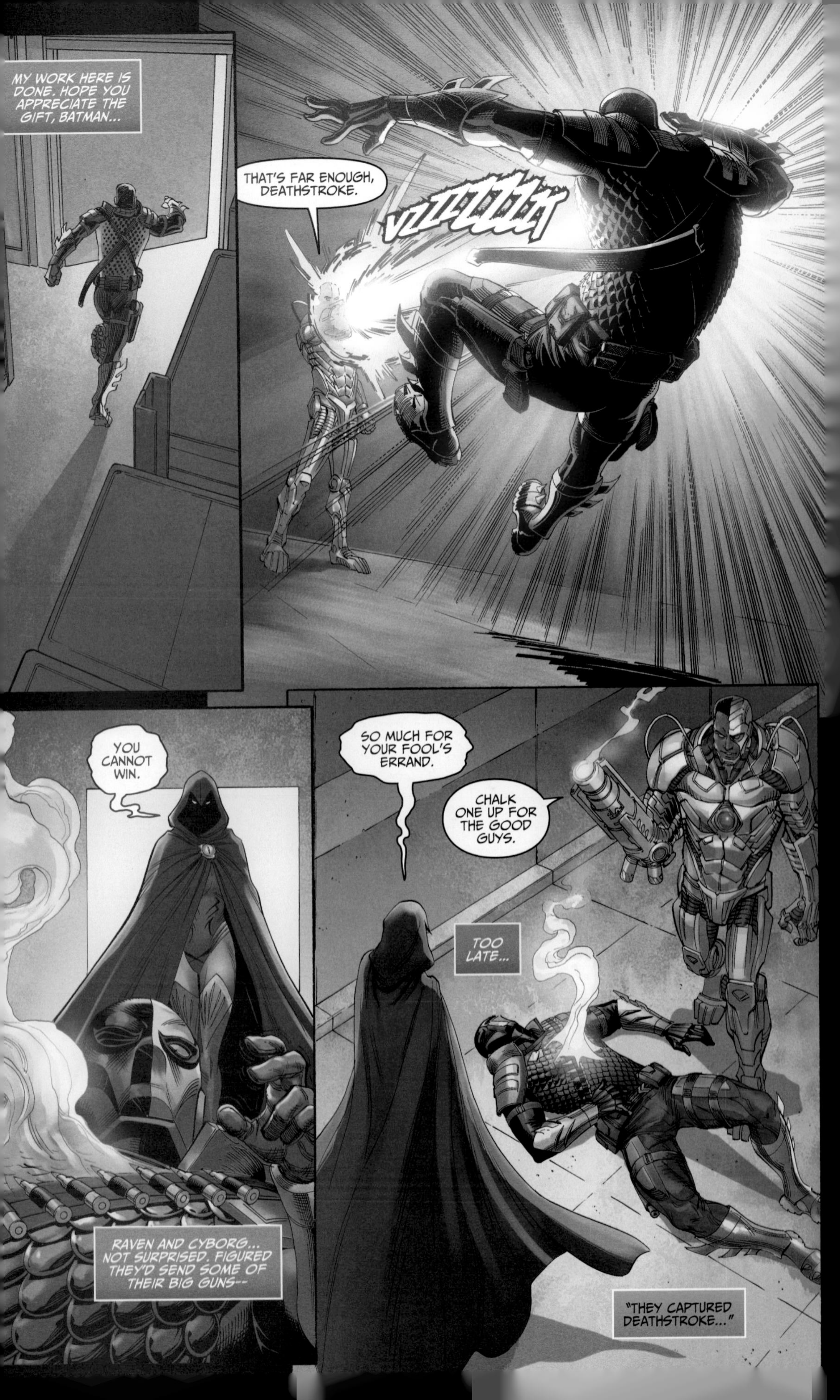
MY WORK HERE IS DONE. HOPE YOU APPRECIATE THE GIFT, BATMAN...
THAT'S FAR ENOUGH, DEATHSTROKE.
VZZZZOOOM
YOU CANNOT WIN.
RAVEN AND CYBORG... NOT SURPRISED. FIGURED THEY'D SEND SOME OF THEIR BIG GUNS--
SO MUCH FOR YOUR FOOL'S ERRAND.
CHALK ONE UP FOR THE GOOD GUYS.
TOO LATE...
"THEY CAPTURED DEATHSTROKE..."

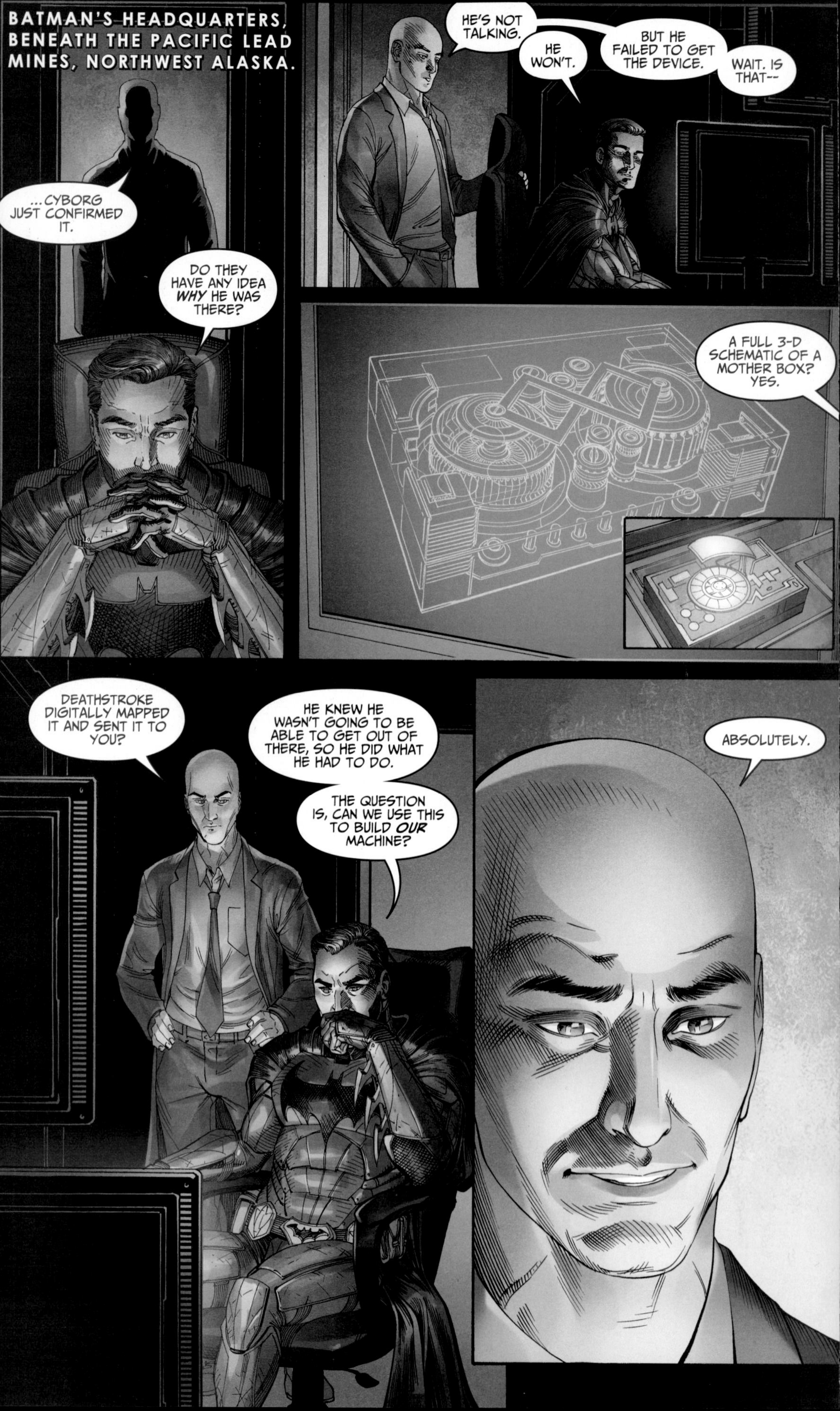
BATMAN'S HEADQUARTERS, BENEATH THE PACIFIC LEAD MINES, NORTHWEST ALASKA.
...CYBORG JUST CONFIRMED IT.
DO THEY HAVE ANY IDEA *WHY* HE WAS THERE?
HE'S NOT TALKING.
HE WON'T.
BUT HE FAILED TO GET THE DEVICE.
WAIT. IS THAT--
A FULL 3-D SCHEMATIC OF A MOTHER BOX? YES.
DEATHSTROKE DIGITALLY MAPPED IT AND SENT IT TO YOU?
HE KNEW HE WASN'T GOING TO BE ABLE TO GET OUT OF THERE, SO HE DID WHAT HE HAD TO DO.
THE QUESTION IS, CAN WE USE THIS TO BUILD *OUR* MACHINE?
ABSOLUTELY.

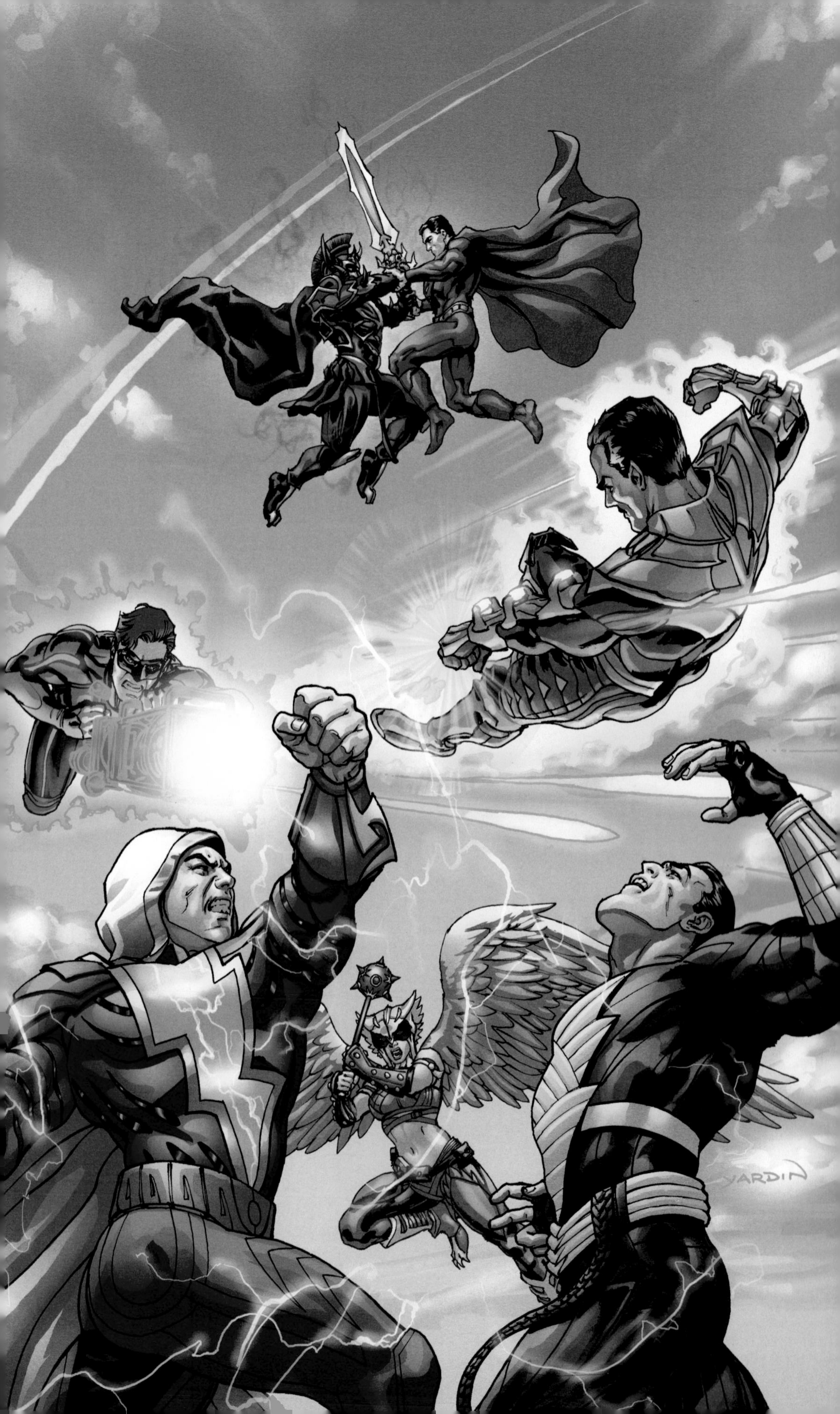
YARDIN

"A Better World" **Xermanico** Artist **Rex Lokus** Colorist
"Funsies" **Marco Santucci** Artist **Rex Lokus** Colorist

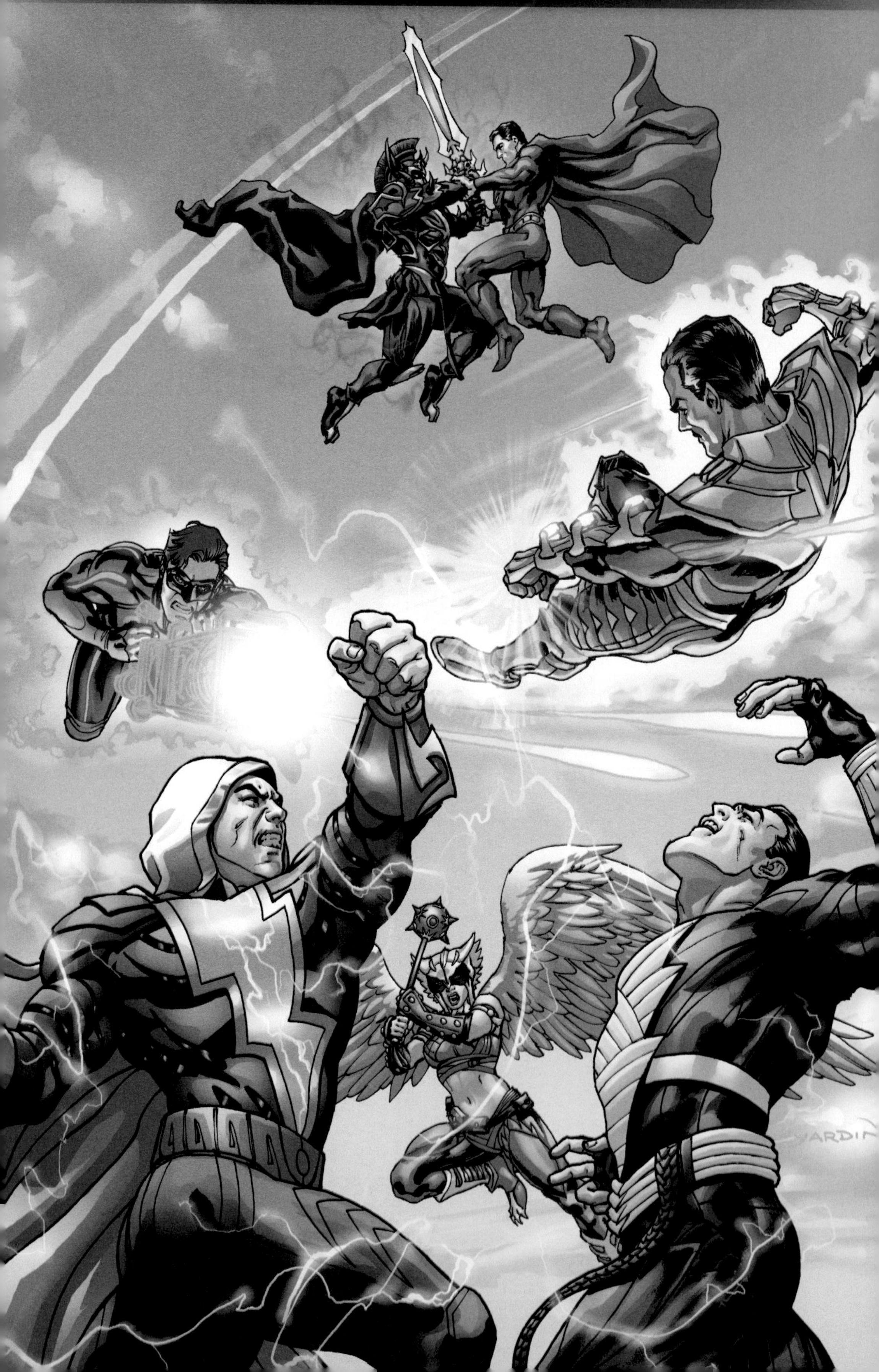

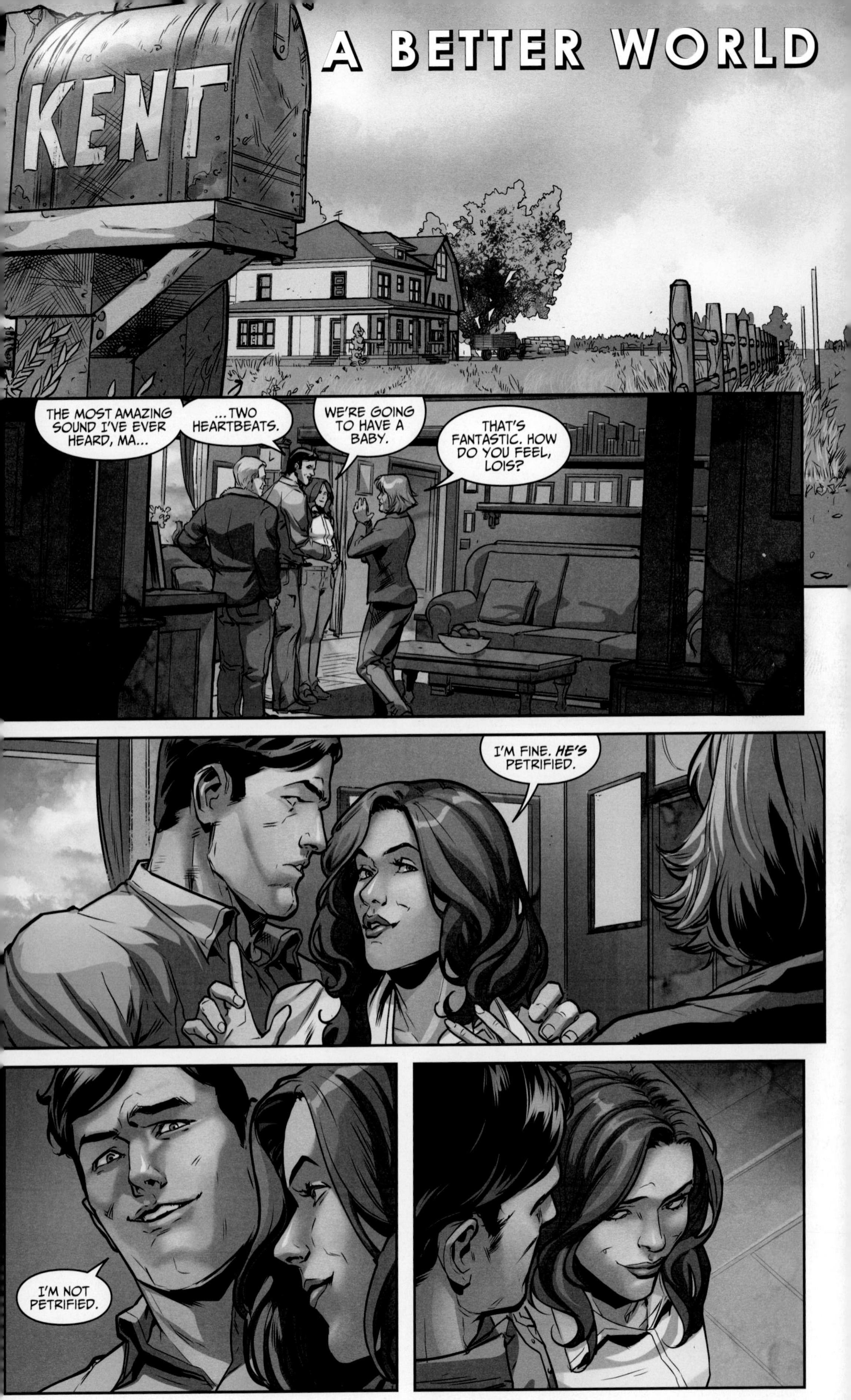
A BETTER WORLD
KENT
THE MOST AMAZING SOUND I'VE EVER HEARD, MA...
...TWO HEARTBEATS.
WE'RE GOING TO HAVE A BABY.
THAT'S FANTASTIC. HOW DO YOU FEEL, LOIS?
I'M FINE. HE'S PETRIFIED.
I'M NOT PETRIFIED.

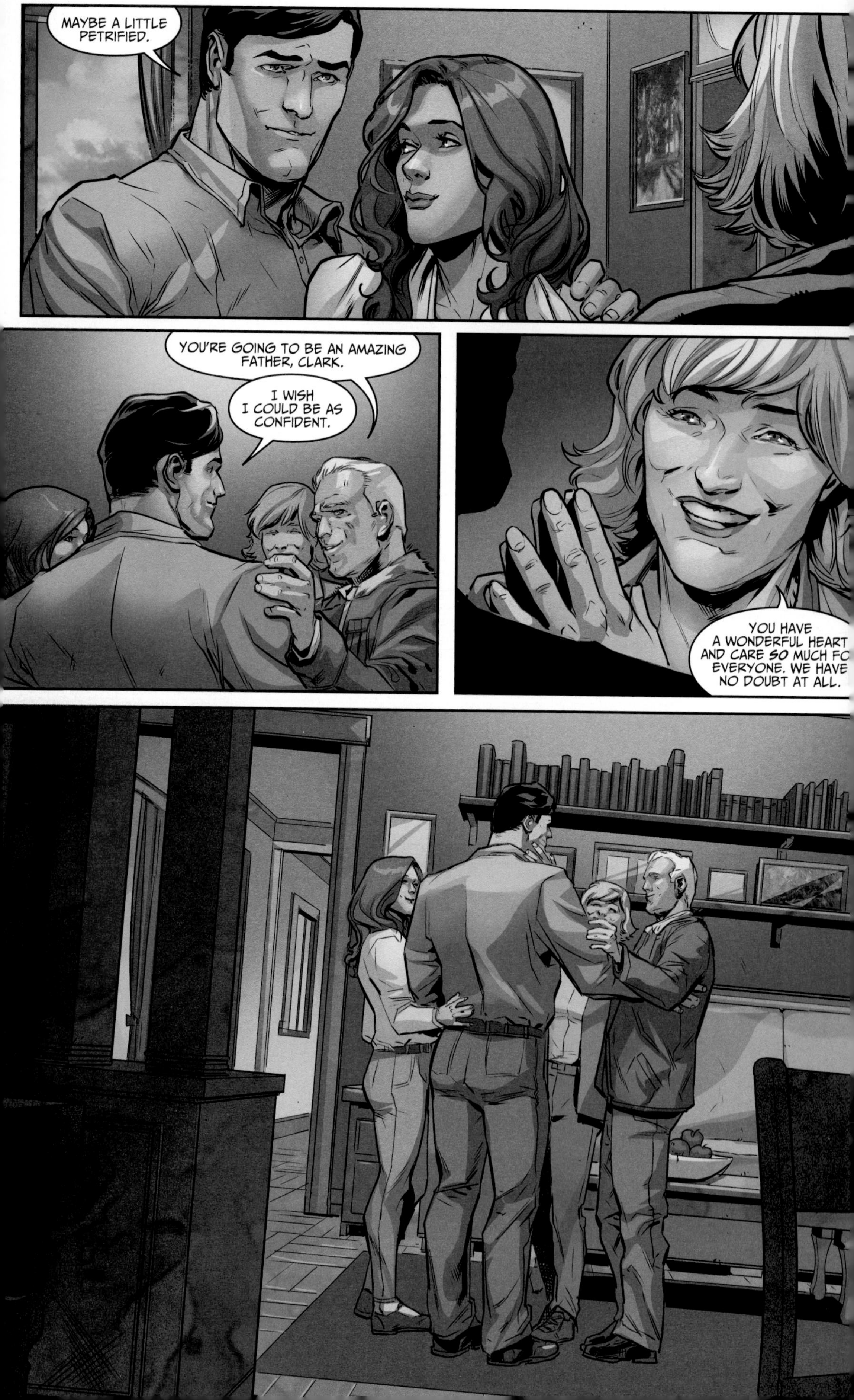
MAYBE A LITTLE PETRIFIED.
YOU'RE GOING TO BE AN AMAZING FATHER, CLARK.
I WISH I COULD BE AS CONFIDENT.
YOU HAVE A WONDERFUL HEART AND CARE SO MUCH FO EVERYONE. WE HAVE NO DOUBT AT ALL.

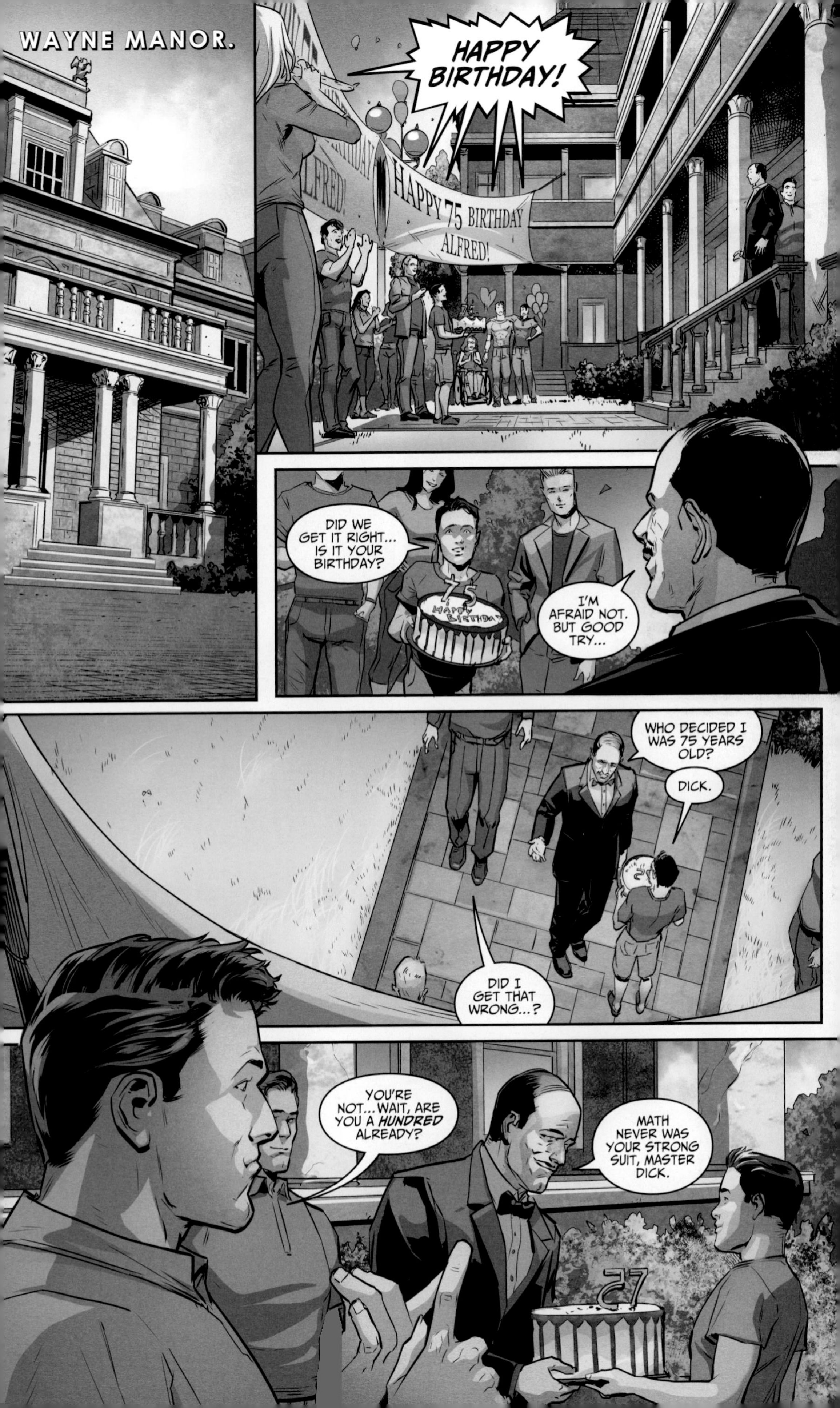
WAYNE MANOR.
HAPPY BIRTHDAY!
HAPPY 75 BIRTHDAY ALFRED!
DID WE GET IT RIGHT... IS IT YOUR BIRTHDAY?
I'M AFRAID NOT. BUT GOOD TRY...
WHO DECIDED I WAS 75 YEARS OLD?
DICK.
DID I GET THAT WRONG...?
YOU'RE NOT... WAIT, ARE YOU A *HUNDRED* ALREADY?
MATH NEVER WAS YOUR STRONG SUIT, MASTER DICK.

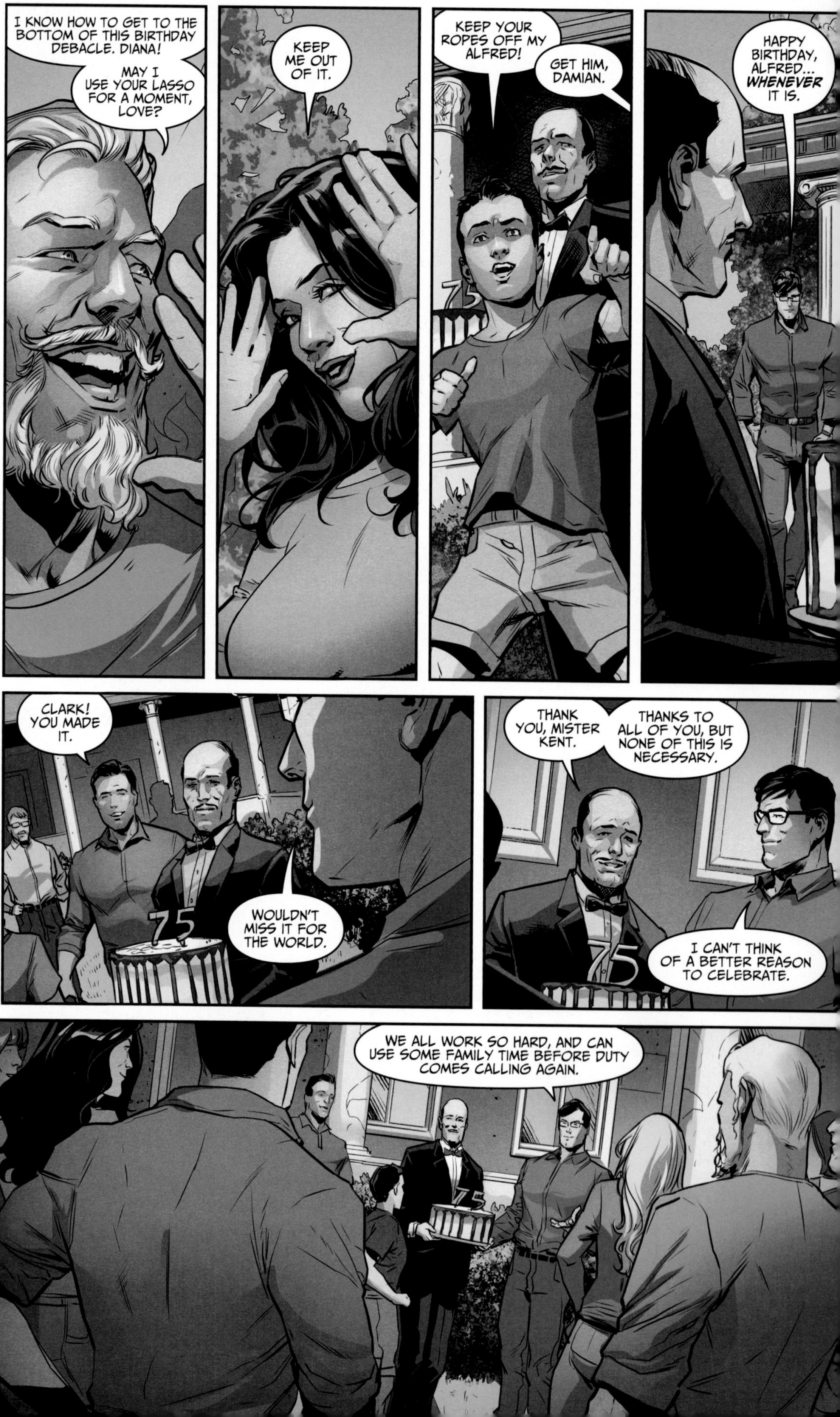
I KNOW HOW TO GET TO THE BOTTOM OF THIS BIRTHDAY DEBACLE. DIANA!
MAY I USE YOUR LASSO FOR A MOMENT, LOVE?
KEEP ME OUT OF IT.
KEEP YOUR ROPES OFF MY ALFRED!
GET HIM, DAMIAN.
HAPPY BIRTHDAY, ALFRED... *WHENEVER* IT IS.
CLARK! YOU MADE IT.
WOULDN'T MISS IT FOR THE WORLD.
THANK YOU, MISTER KENT.
THANKS TO ALL OF YOU, BUT NONE OF THIS IS NECESSARY.
I CAN'T THINK OF A BETTER REASON TO CELEBRATE.
WE ALL WORK SO HARD, AND CAN USE SOME FAMILY TIME BEFORE DUTY COMES CALLING AGAIN.

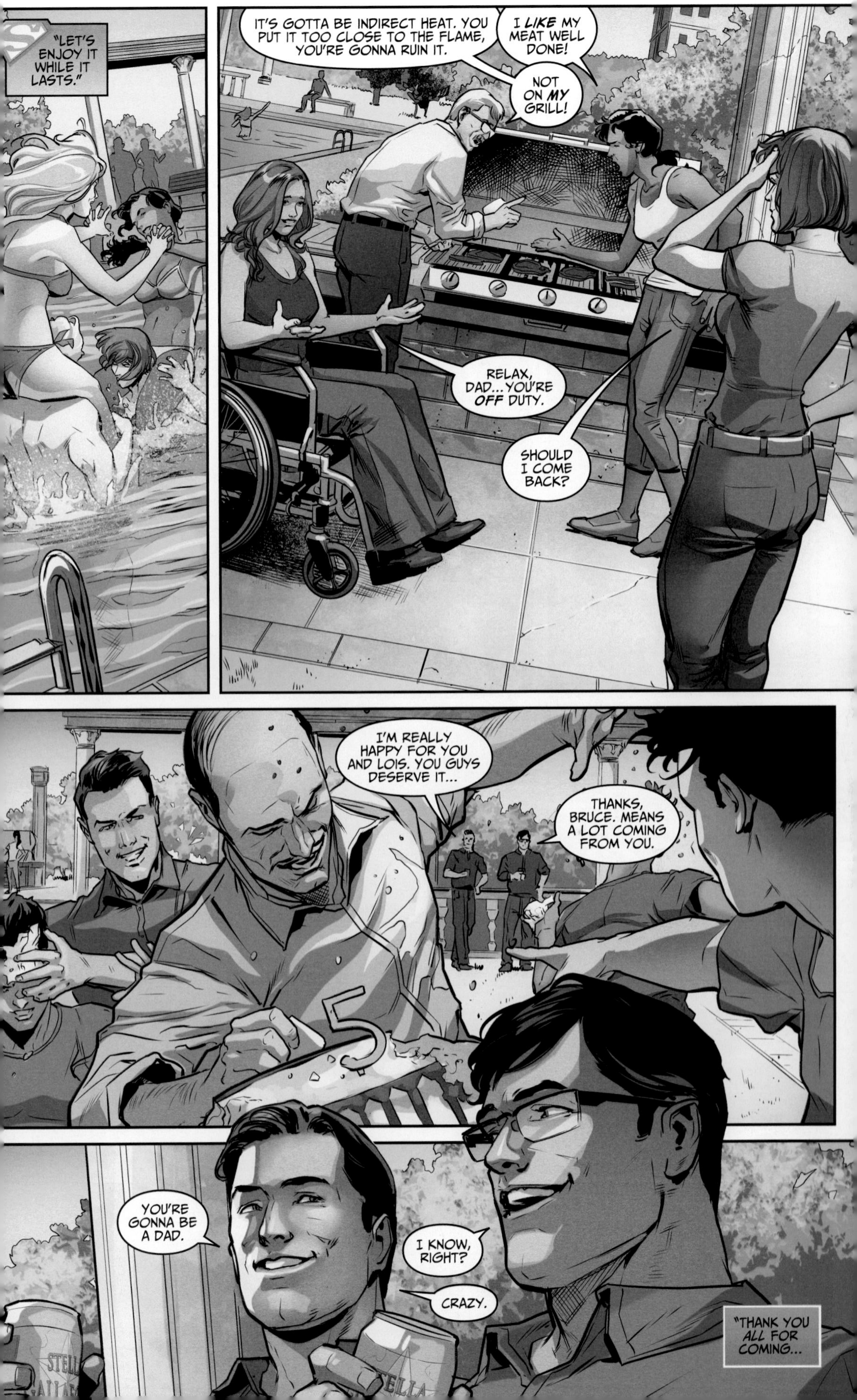
"LET'S ENJOY IT WHILE IT LASTS."
IT'S GOTTA BE INDIRECT HEAT. YOU PUT IT TOO CLOSE TO THE FLAME, YOU'RE GONNA RUIN IT.
I LIKE MY MEAT WELL DONE!
NOT ON MY GRILL!
RELAX, DAD... YOU'RE OFF DUTY.
SHOULD I COME BACK?
I'M REALLY HAPPY FOR YOU AND LOIS. YOU GUYS DESERVE IT...
THANKS, BRUCE. MEANS A LOT COMING FROM YOU.
YOU'RE GONNA BE A DAD.
I KNOW, RIGHT?
CRAZY.
"THANK YOU ALL FOR COMING...

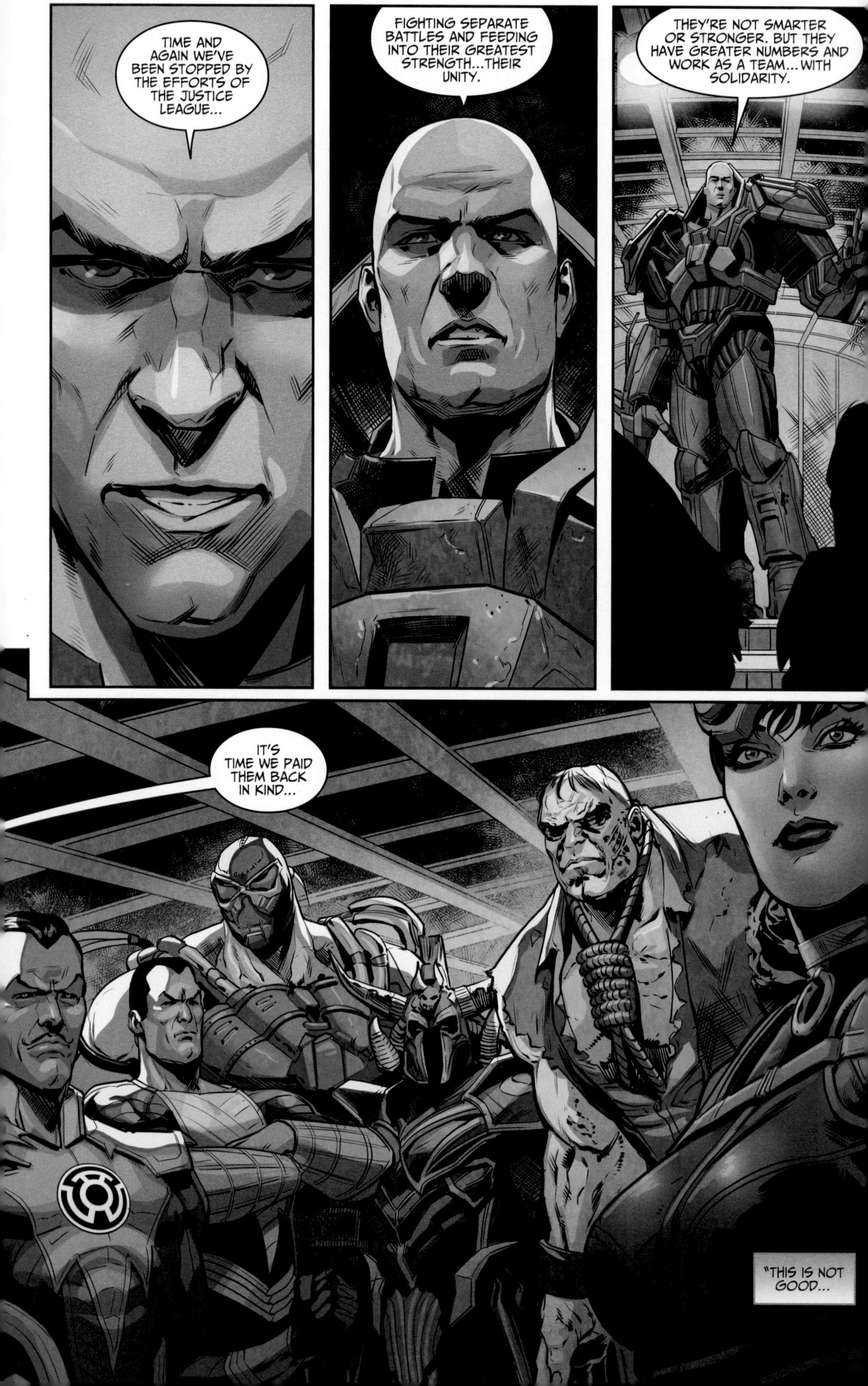
TIME AND AGAIN WE'VE BEEN STOPPED BY THE EFFORTS OF THE JUSTICE LEAGUE...
FIGHTING SEPARATE BATTLES AND FEEDING INTO THEIR GREATEST STRENGTH...THEIR UNITY.
THEY'RE NOT SMARTER OR STRONGER. BUT THEY HAVE GREATER NUMBERS AND WORK AS A TEAM...WITH SOLIDARITY.
IT'S TIME WE PAID THEM BACK IN KIND...
"THIS IS NOT GOOD...

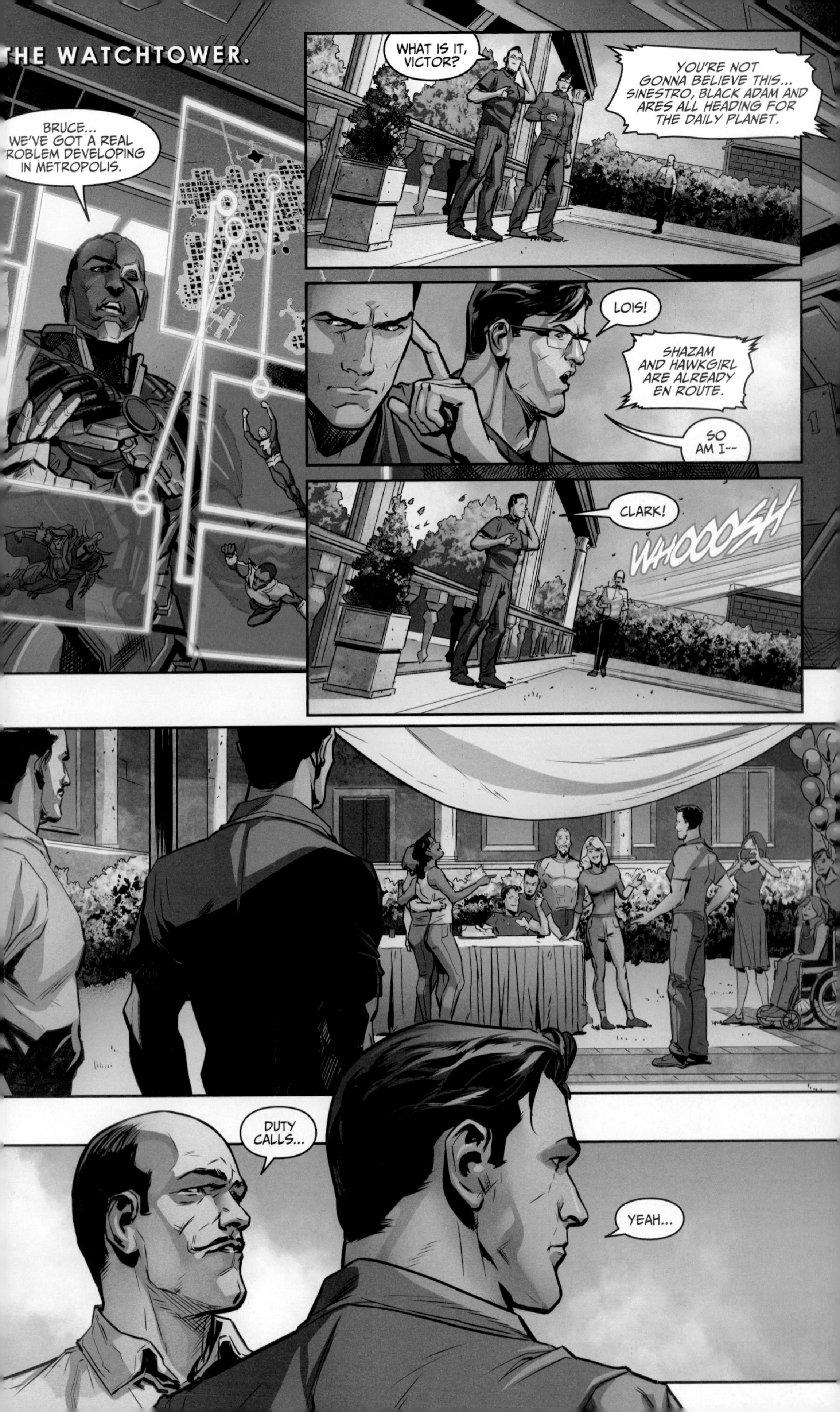
THE WATCHTOWER.
BRUCE... WE'VE GOT A REAL PROBLEM DEVELOPING IN METROPOLIS.
WHAT IS IT, VICTOR?
YOU'RE NOT GONNA BELIEVE THIS... SINESTRO, BLACK ADAM AND ARES ALL HEADING FOR THE DAILY PLANET.
LOIS!
SHAZAM AND HAWKGIRL ARE ALREADY EN ROUTE.
SO AM I--
CLARK!
WHOOOSH
DUTY CALLS...
YEAH...

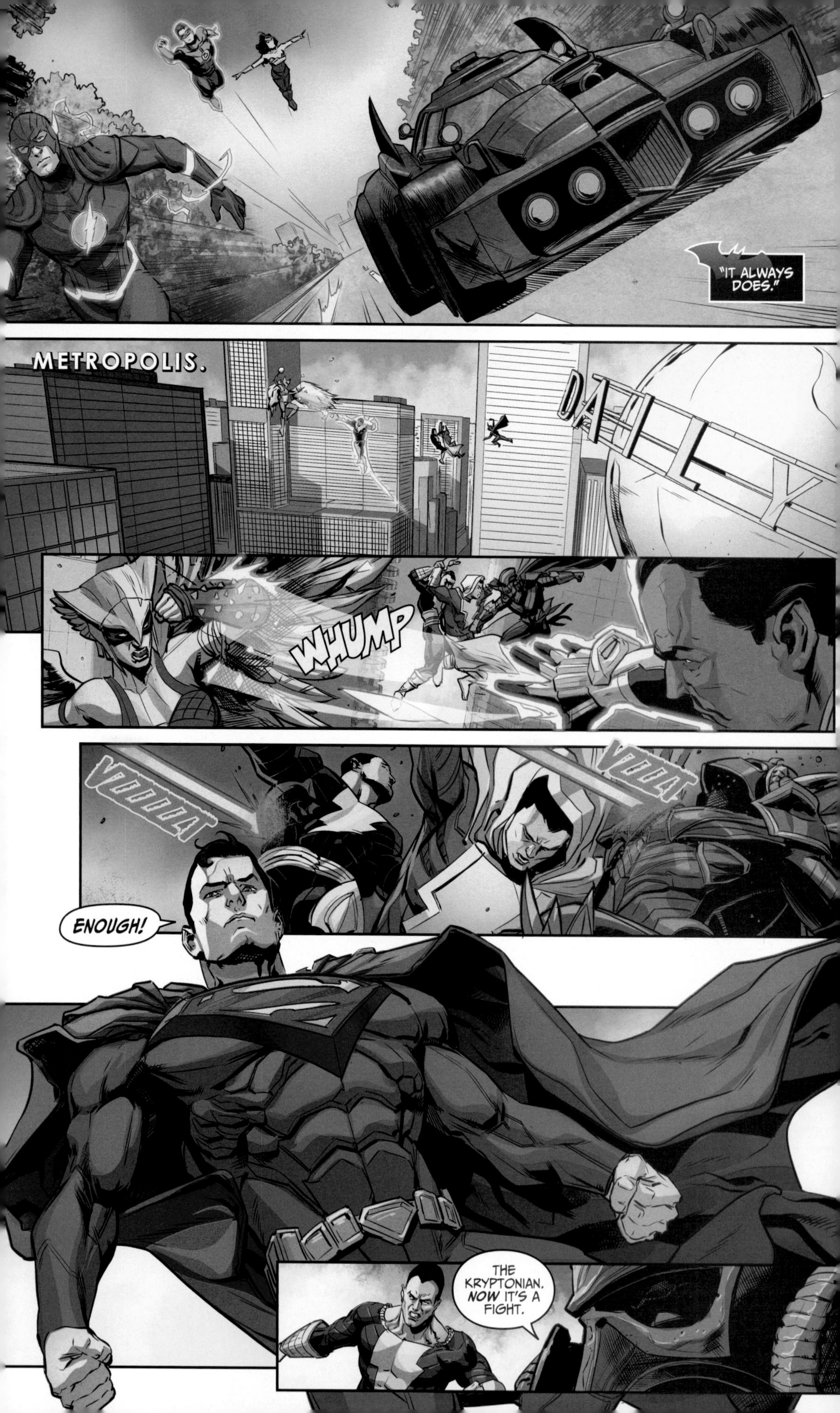
"IT ALWAYS DOES."
METROPOLIS.
WHUMP
ENOUGH!
THE KRYPTONIAN. NOW IT'S A FIGHT.

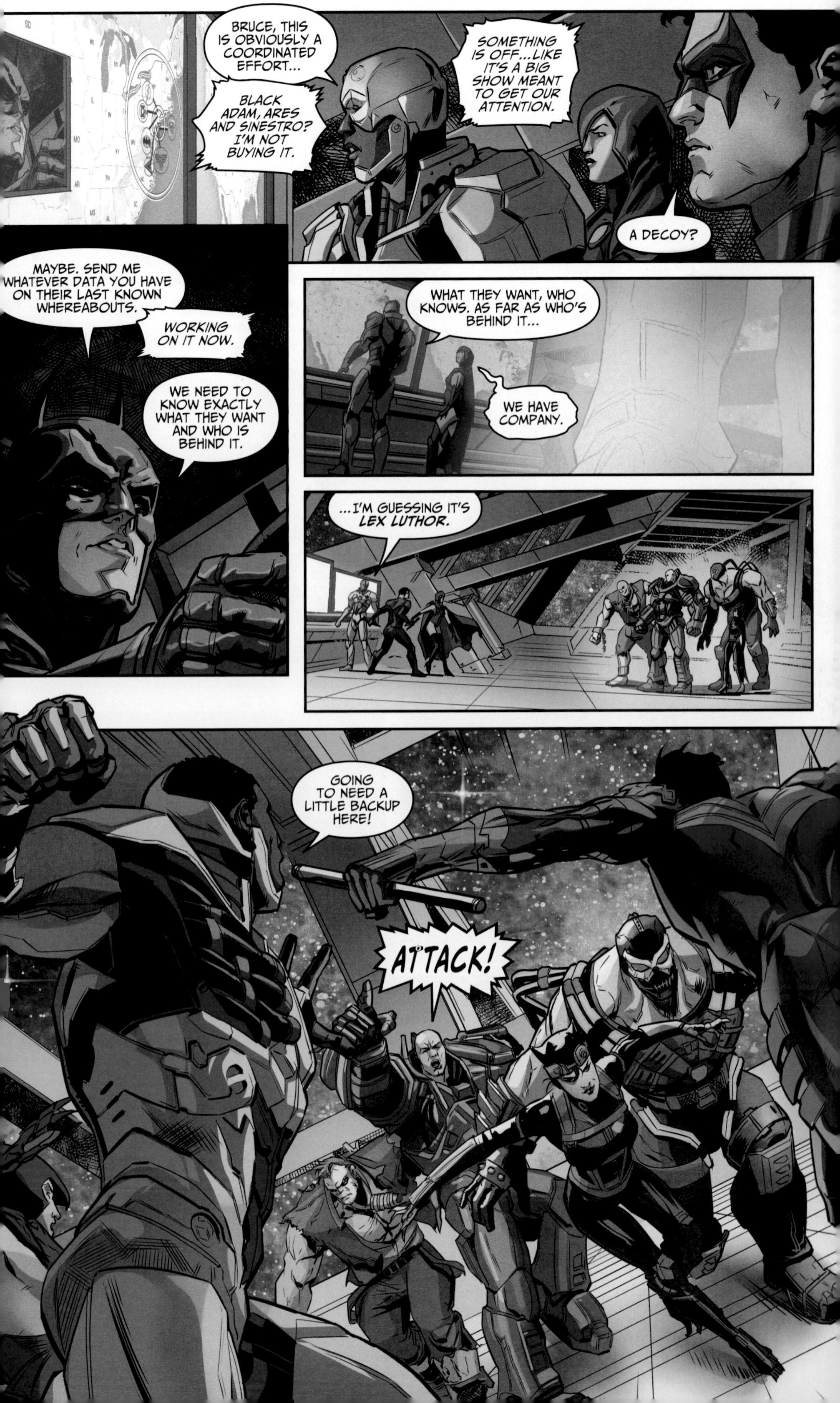
BRUCE, THIS IS OBVIOUSLY A COORDINATED EFFORT...
BLACK ADAM, ARES AND SINESTRO? I'M NOT BUYING IT.
SOMETHING IS OFF...LIKE IT'S A BIG SHOW MEANT TO GET OUR ATTENTION.
A DECOY?
MAYBE. SEND ME WHATEVER DATA YOU HAVE ON THEIR LAST KNOWN WHEREABOUTS.
WORKING ON IT NOW.
WE NEED TO KNOW EXACTLY WHAT THEY WANT AND WHO IS BEHIND IT.
WHAT THEY WANT, WHO KNOWS. AS FAR AS WHO'S BEHIND IT...
WE HAVE COMPANY.
...I'M GUESSING IT'S LEX LUTHOR.
GOING TO NEED A LITTLE BACKUP HERE!
ATTACK!

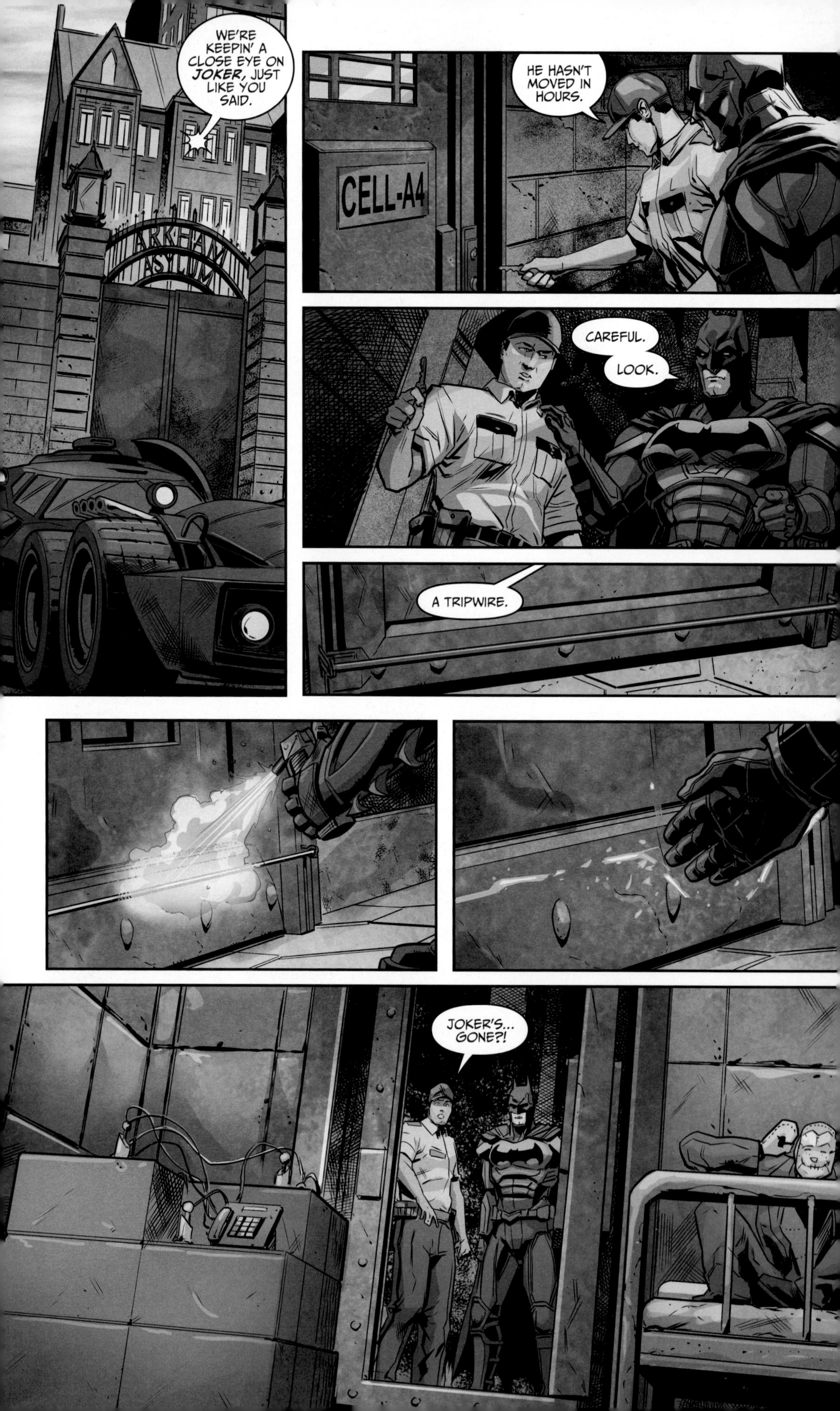
WE'RE KEEPIN' A CLOSE EYE ON JOKER, JUST LIKE YOU SAID.
ARKHAM ASYLUM
HE HASN'T MOVED IN HOURS.
CELL-A4
CAREFUL.
LOOK.
A TRIPWIRE.
JOKER'S... GONE?!

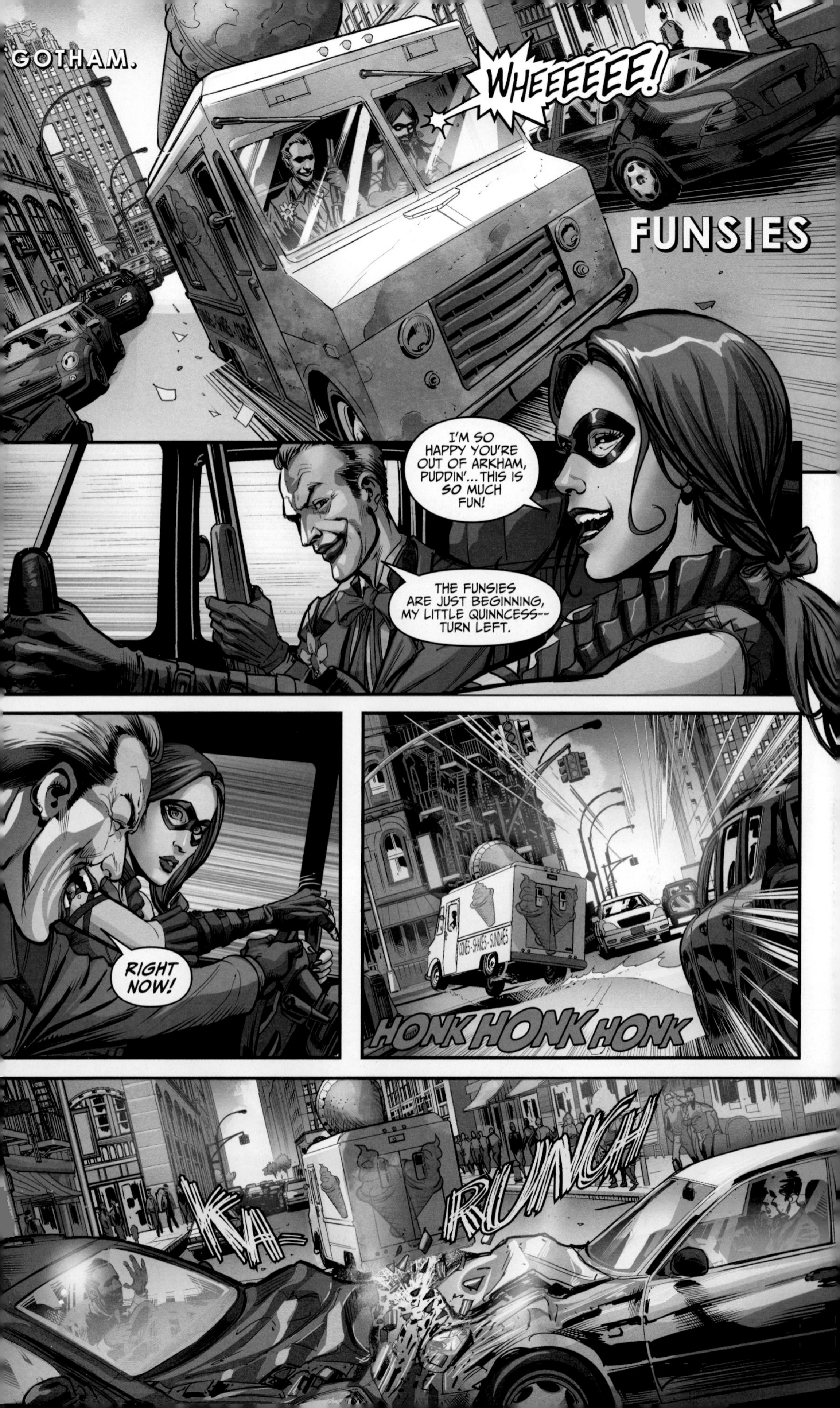
GOTHAM.
WHEEEEEEE!
FUNSIES
I'M SO HAPPY YOU'RE OUT OF ARKHAM, PUDDIN'... THIS IS SO MUCH FUN!
THE FUNSIES ARE JUST BEGINNING, MY LITTLE QUINNCESS-- TURN LEFT.
RIGHT NOW!
CONES-SHAKES-SUNDAES
HONK HONK HONK HONK
KA-RUNCH

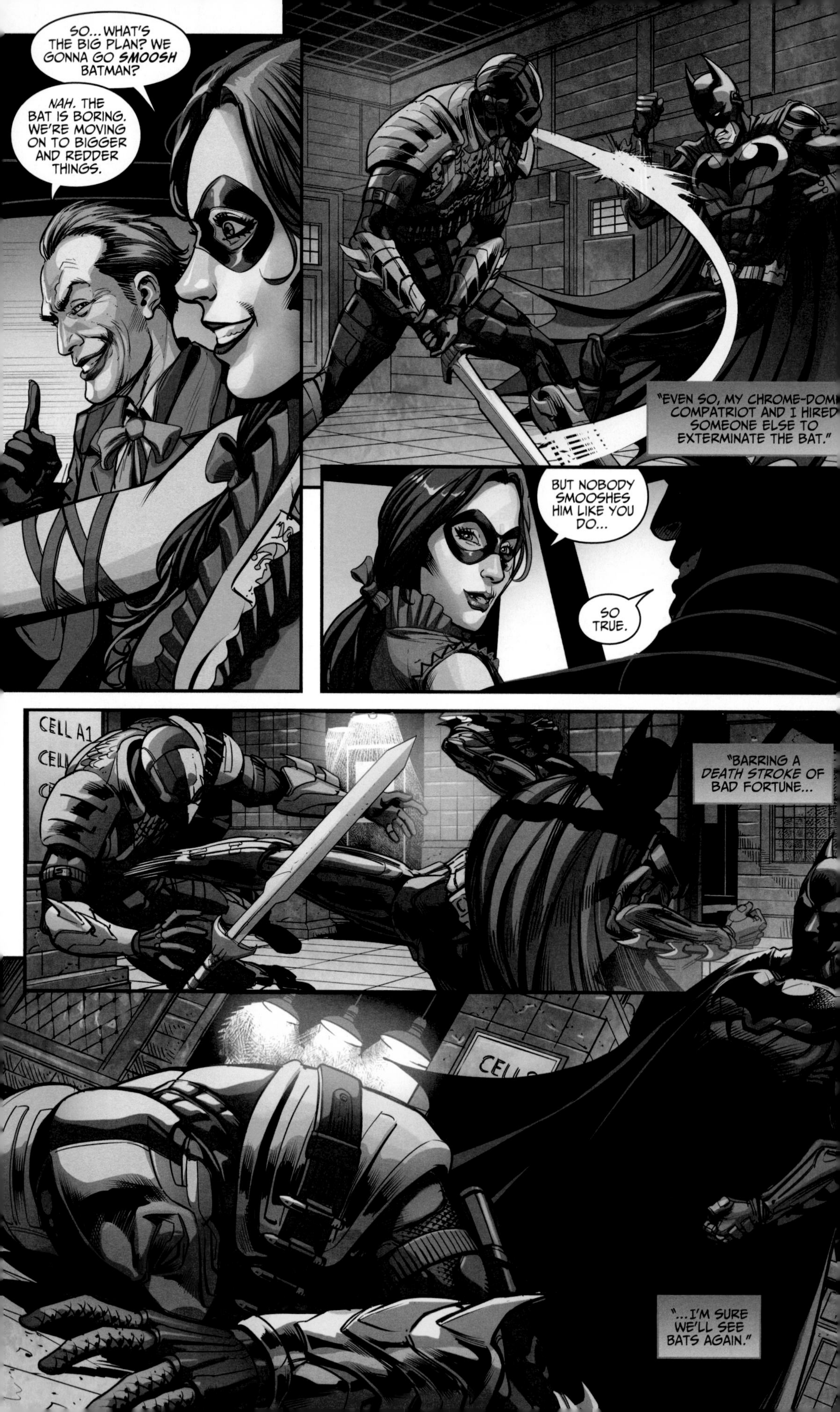
SO... WHAT'S THE BIG PLAN? WE GONNA GO SMOOSH BATMAN?
NAH. THE BAT IS BORING. WE'RE MOVING ON TO BIGGER AND REDDER THINGS.
"EVEN SO, MY CHROME-DOME COMPATRIOT AND I HIRED SOMEONE ELSE TO EXTERMINATE THE BAT."
BUT NOBODY SMOOSHES HIM LIKE YOU DO...
SO TRUE.
CELL A1
"BARRING A DEATH STROKE OF BAD FORTUNE...
"...I'M SURE WE'LL SEE BATS AGAIN."

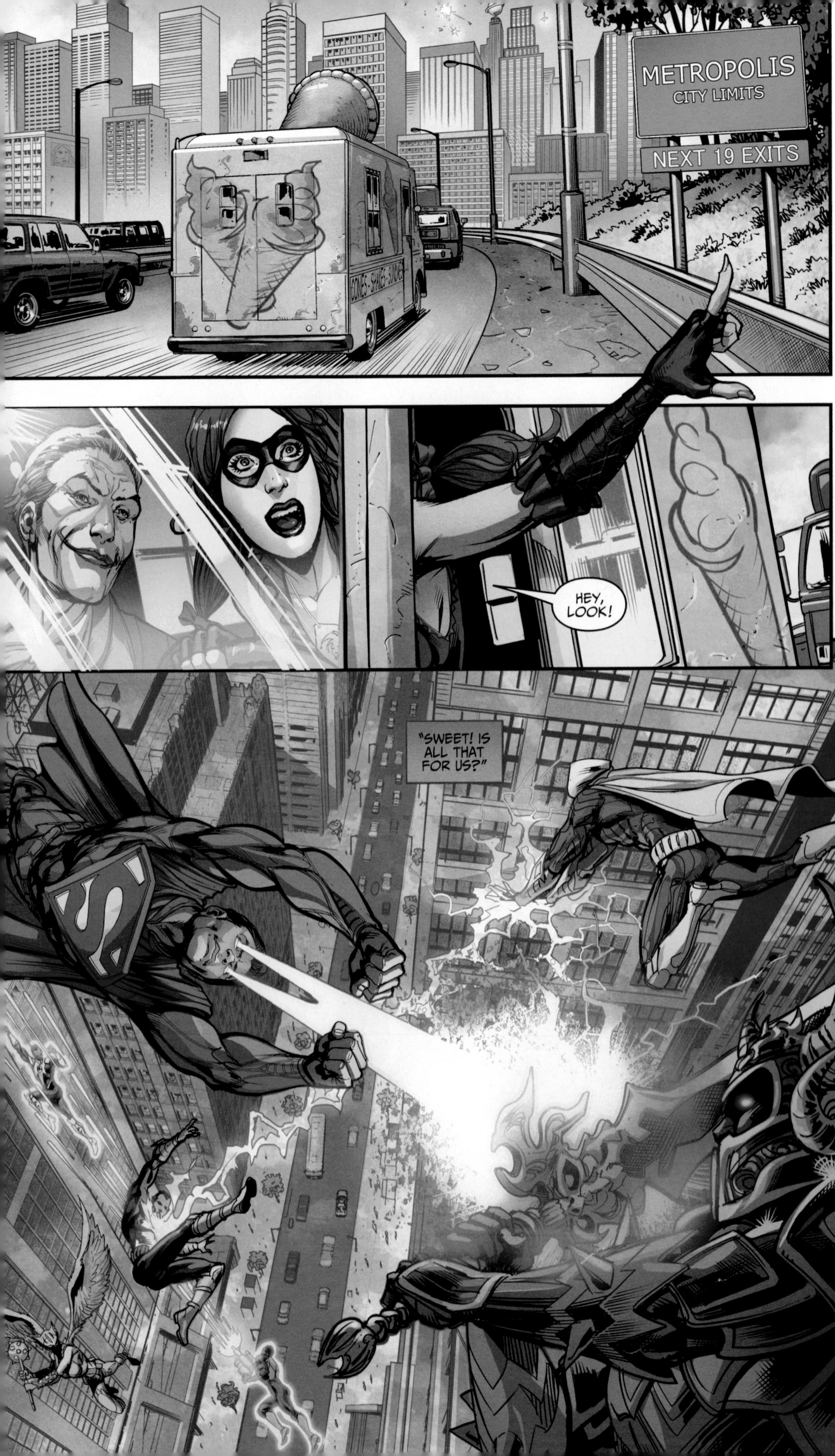

METROPOLIS
CITY LIMITS
NEXT 19 EXITS
CONES - SHAKES - SUNDAES
HEY, LOOK!
"SWEET! IS ALL THAT FOR US?"

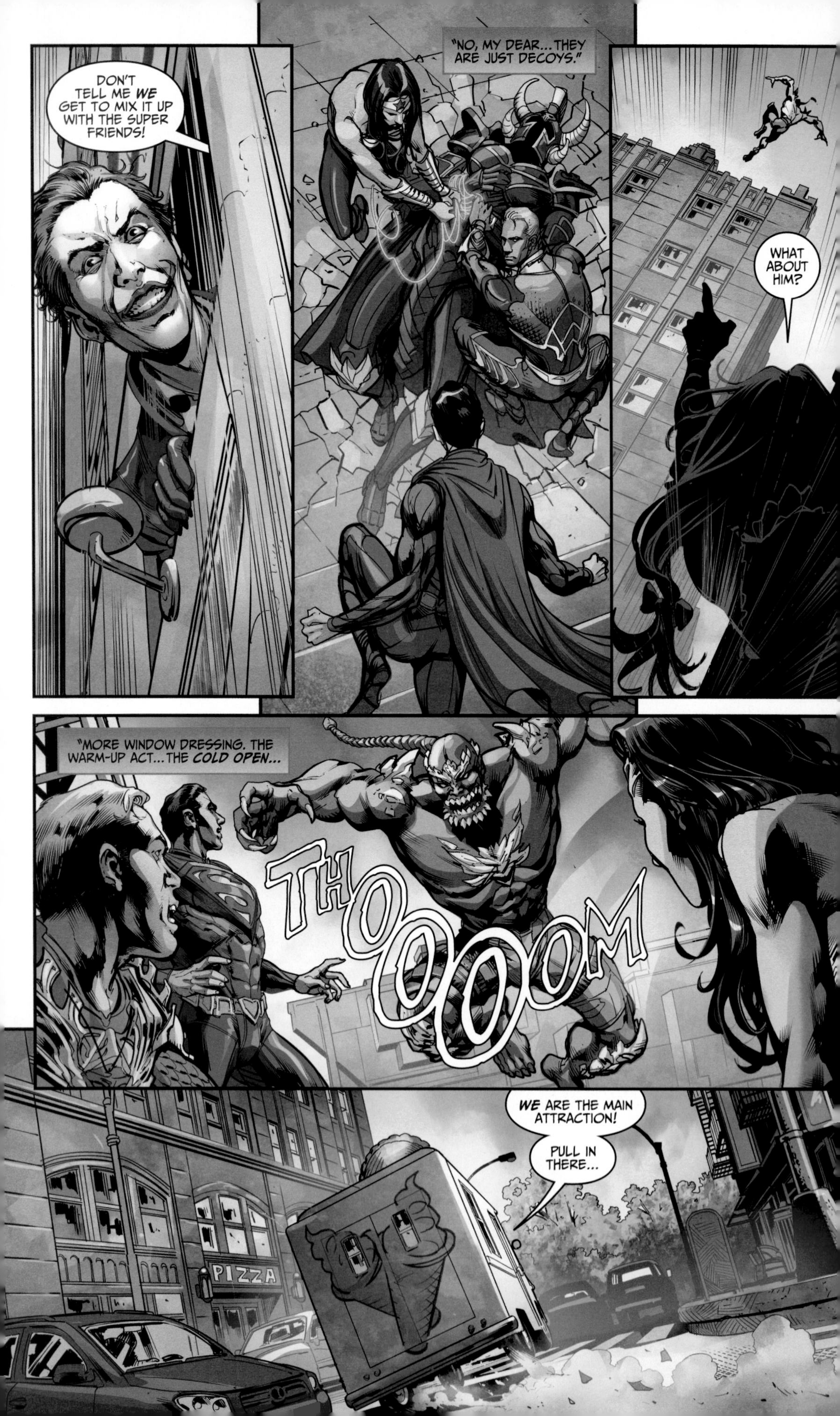
DON'T TELL ME WE GET TO MIX IT UP WITH THE SUPER FRIENDS!
"NO, MY DEAR...THEY ARE JUST DECOYS."
WHAT ABOUT HIM?
"MORE WINDOW DRESSING. THE WARM-UP ACT...THE COLD OPEN...
THOOOOOM
WE ARE THE MAIN ATTRACTION!
PULL IN THERE...
PIZZA

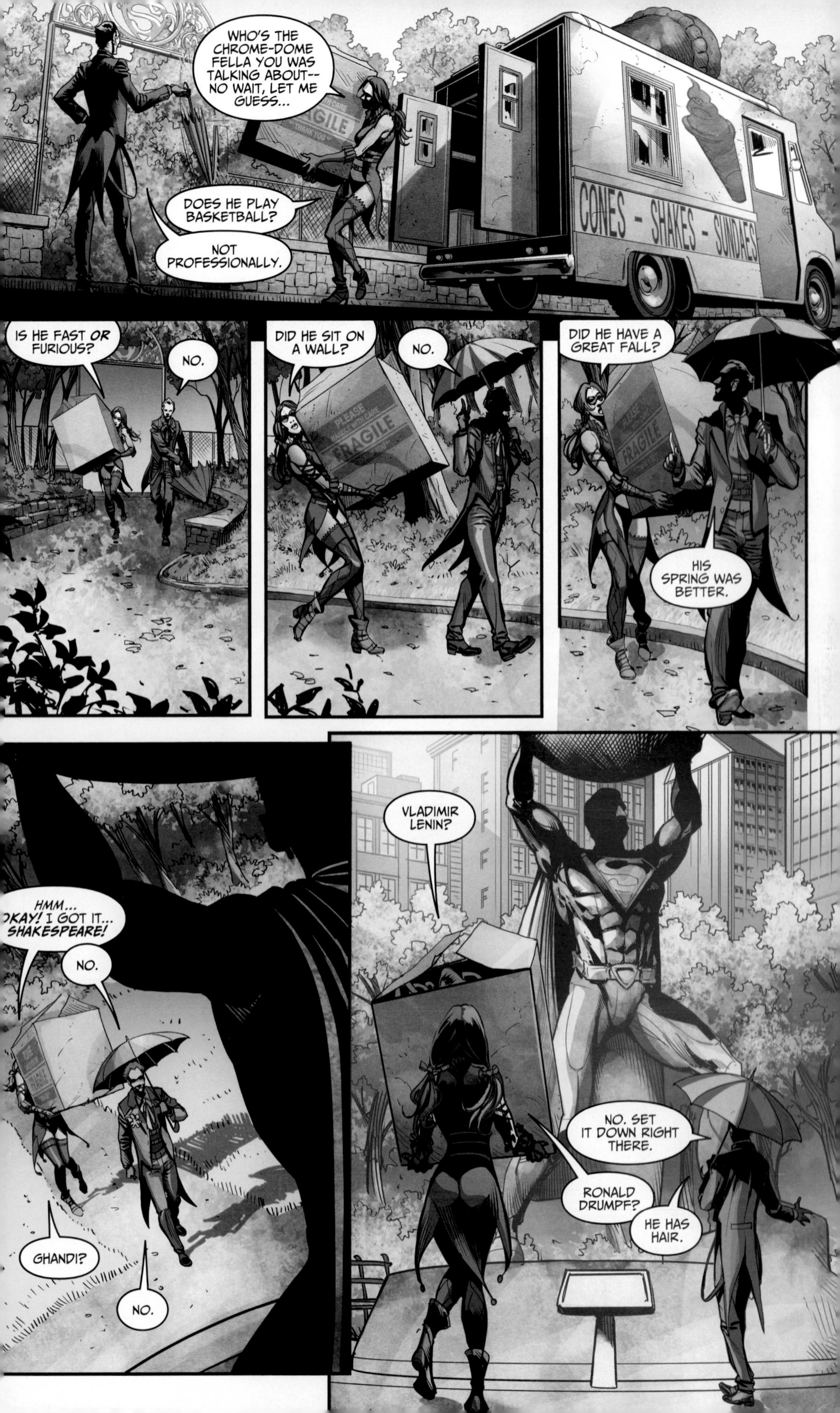
WHO'S THE CHROME-DOME FELLA YOU WAS TALKING ABOUT-- NO WAIT, LET ME GUESS...
FRAGILE
CONES - SHAKES - SUNDAES
DOES HE PLAY BASKETBALL?
NOT PROFESSIONALLY.
IS HE FAST OR FURIOUS?
NO.
DID HE SIT ON A WALL?
NO.
PLEASE HANDLE WITH CARE
FRAGILE
DID HE HAVE A GREAT FALL?
HIS SPRING WAS BETTER.
HMM... OKAY! I GOT IT... SHAKESPEARE!
NO.
GHANDI?
NO.
VLADIMIR LENIN?
NO. SET IT DOWN RIGHT THERE.
RONALD DRUMPF?
HE HAS HAIR.

BUT IT'S NOT REAL.

NO.

ELMER FUDD?

"NO, MY DIMWITTED PARAMOUR...

"...IT'S LEX LUTHOR."

TOOK ME ALMOST TWO MINUTES TO BREAK YOUR ENCRYPTION. NICE WORK.

FRAGILE

LEX LUTHOR! I KNEW IT! I WAS GONNA SAY THAT. ARE WE MEETING HIM IN THE PARK?

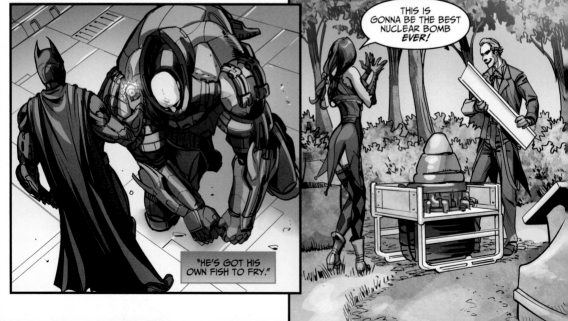

THIS IS GONNA BE THE BEST NUCLEAR BOMB *EVER!*

"HE'S GOT HIS OWN FISH TO FRY."

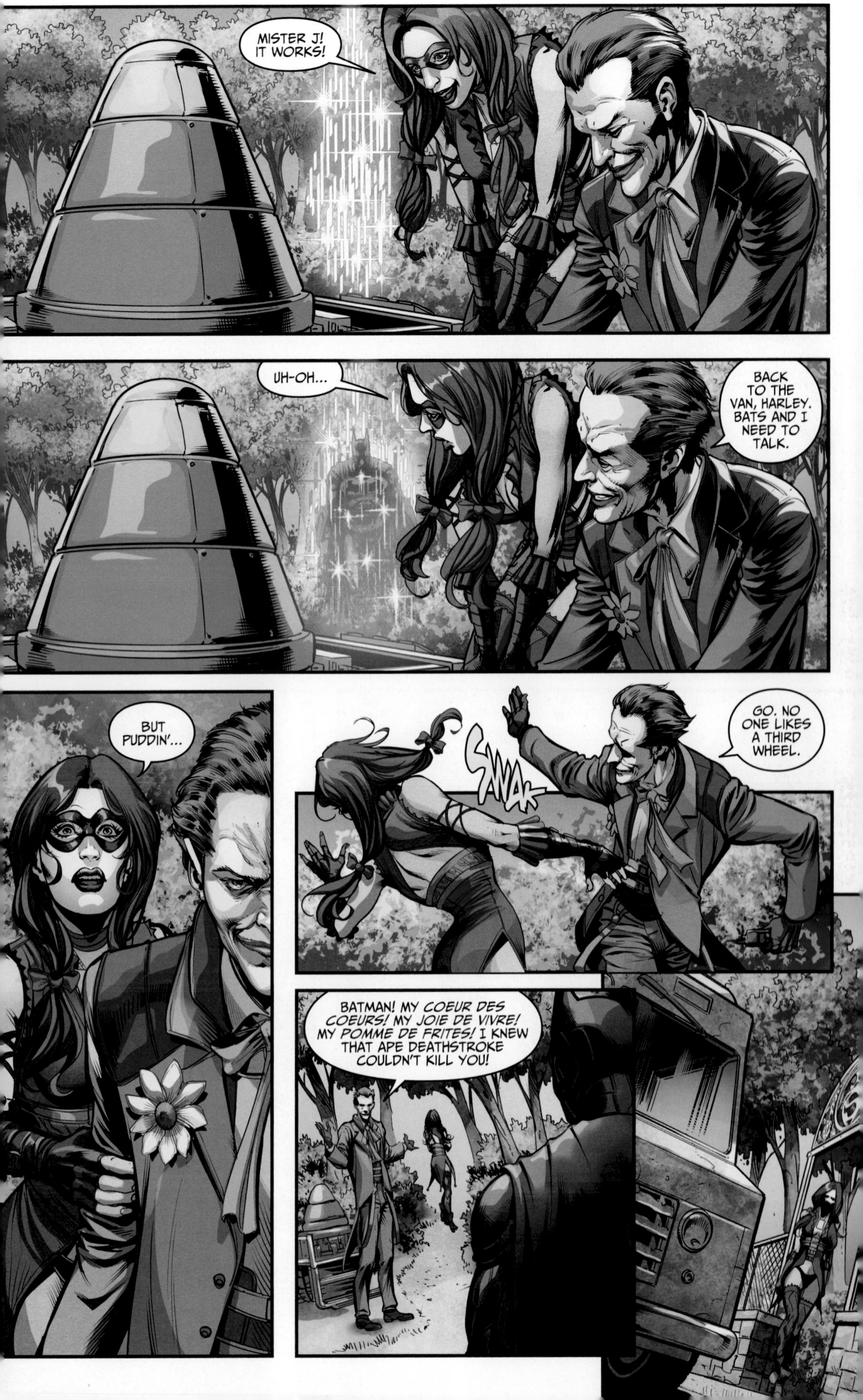
MISTER J! IT WORKS!
UH-OH...
BACK TO THE VAN, HARLEY. BATS AND I NEED TO TALK.
BUT PUDDIN'...
GO. NO ONE LIKES A THIRD WHEEL.
SNAK
BATMAN! MY *COEUR DES COEURS!* MY *JOIE DE VIVRE!* MY *POMME DE FRITES!* I KNEW THAT APE DEATHSTROKE COULDN'T KILL YOU!

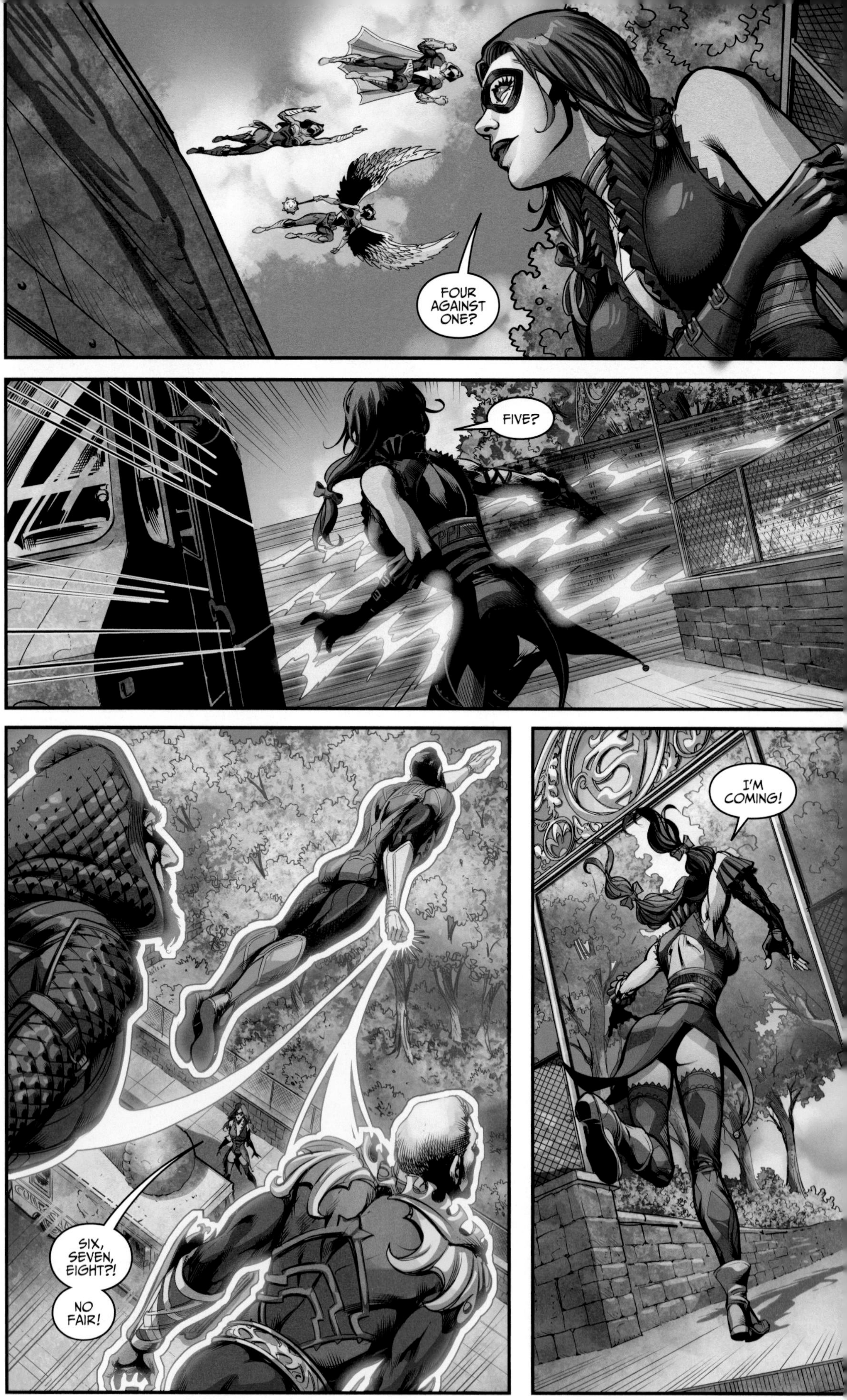
FOUR AGAINST ONE?
FIVE?
SIX, SEVEN, EIGHT?!
NO FAIR!
I'M COMING!

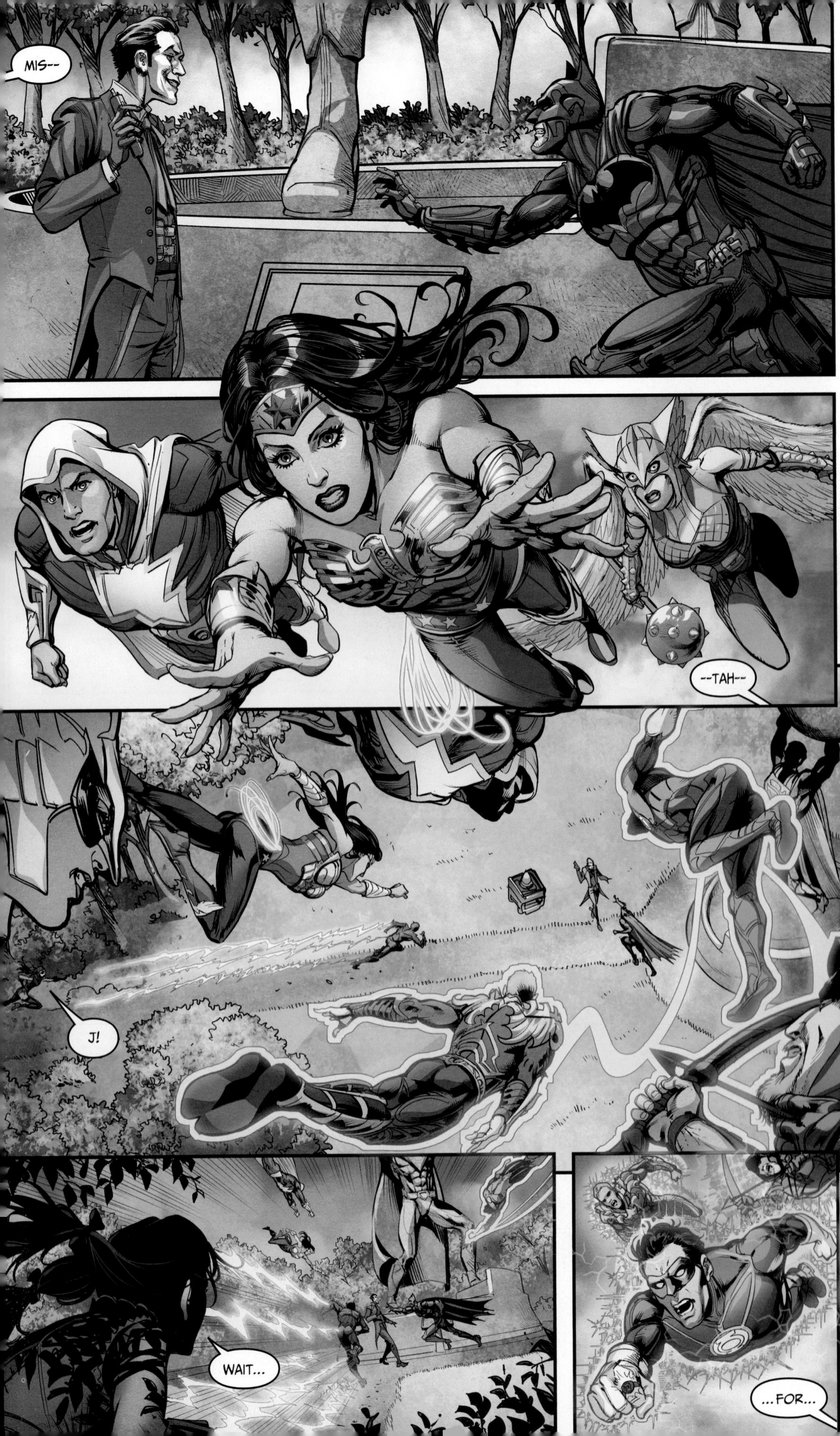
MIS--
--TAH--
J!
WAIT...
...FOR...

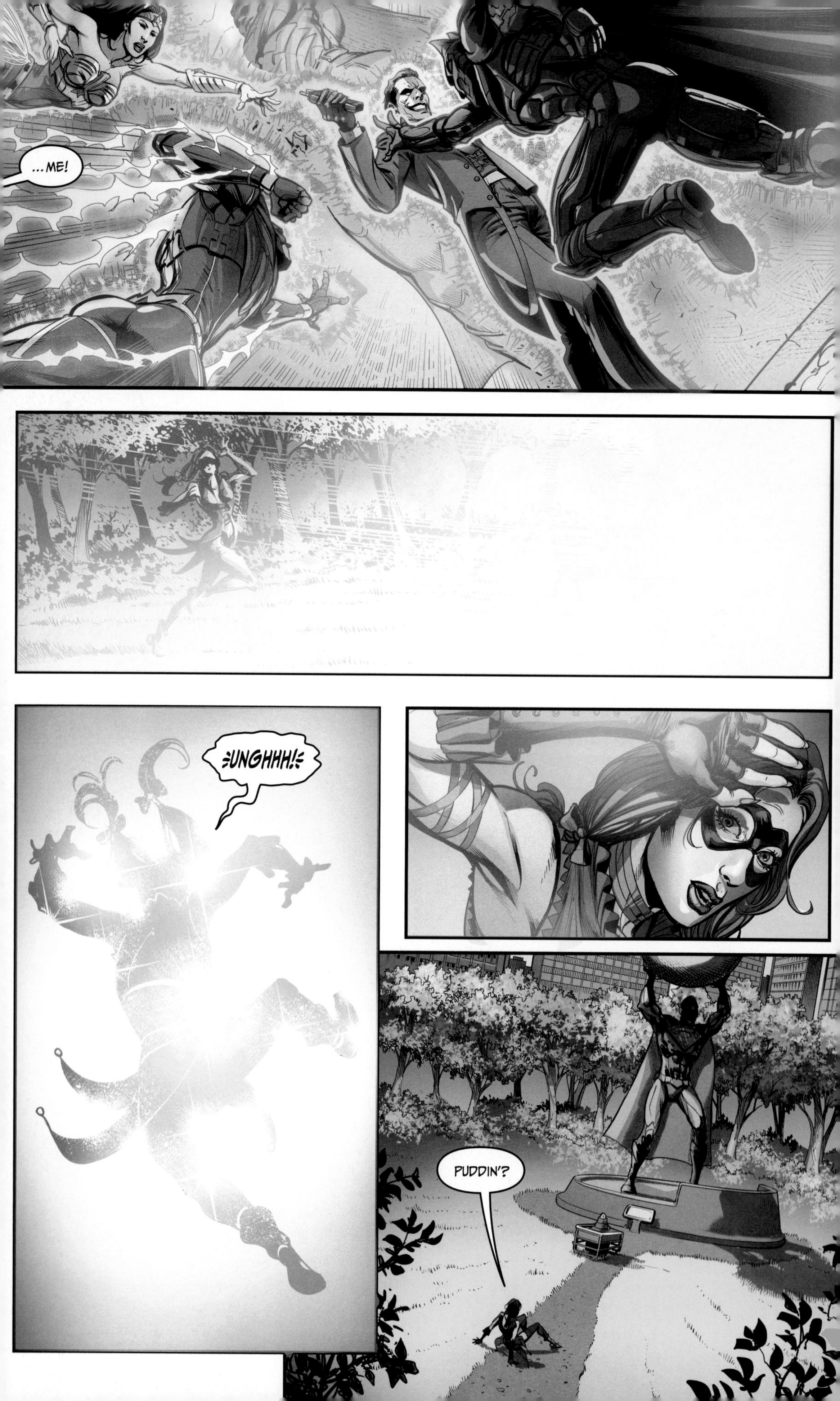
...ME!
UNGHHH!
PUDDIN'?

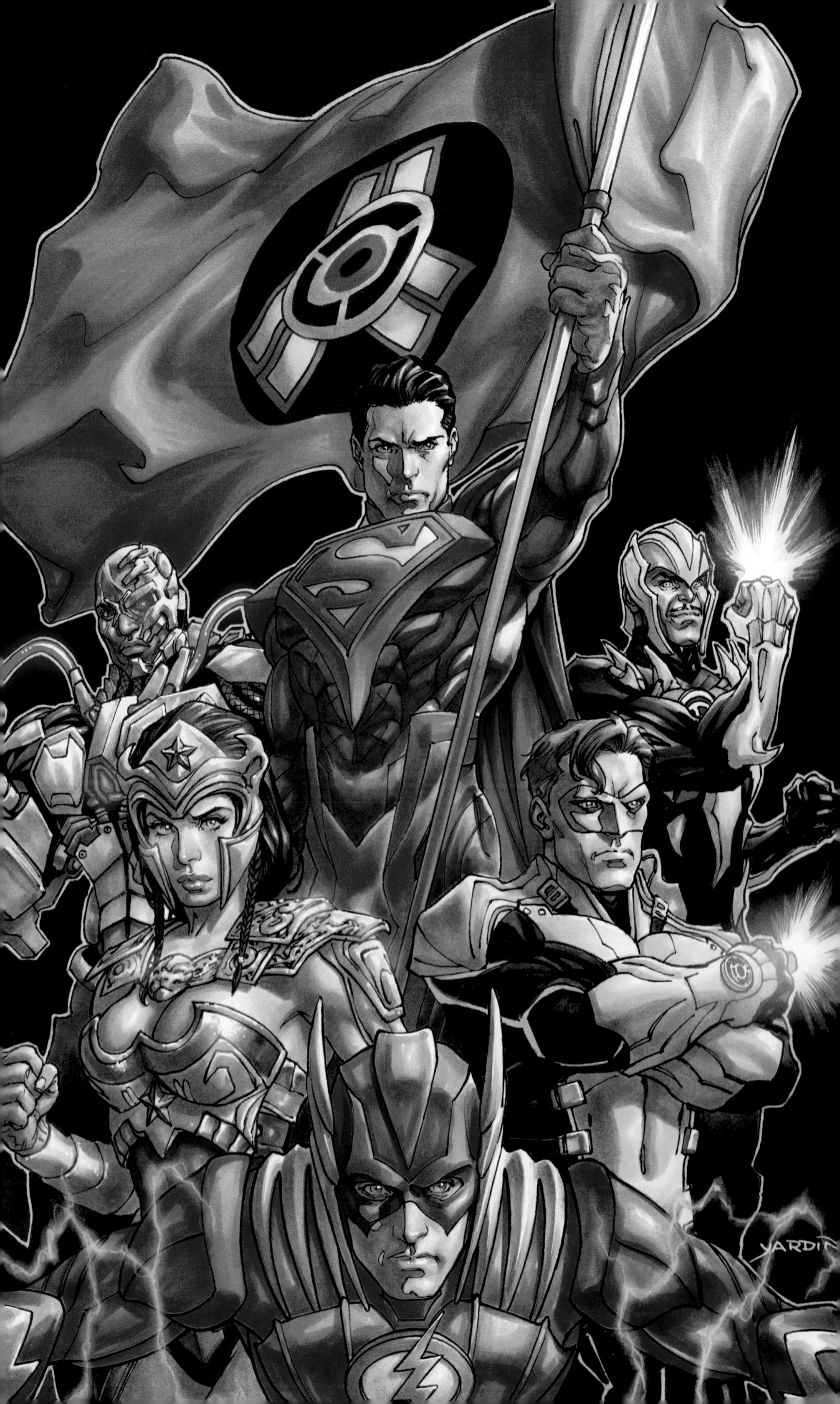

"The Final Gambit" **Mike S. Miller** Artist **J. Nanjan** Colorist

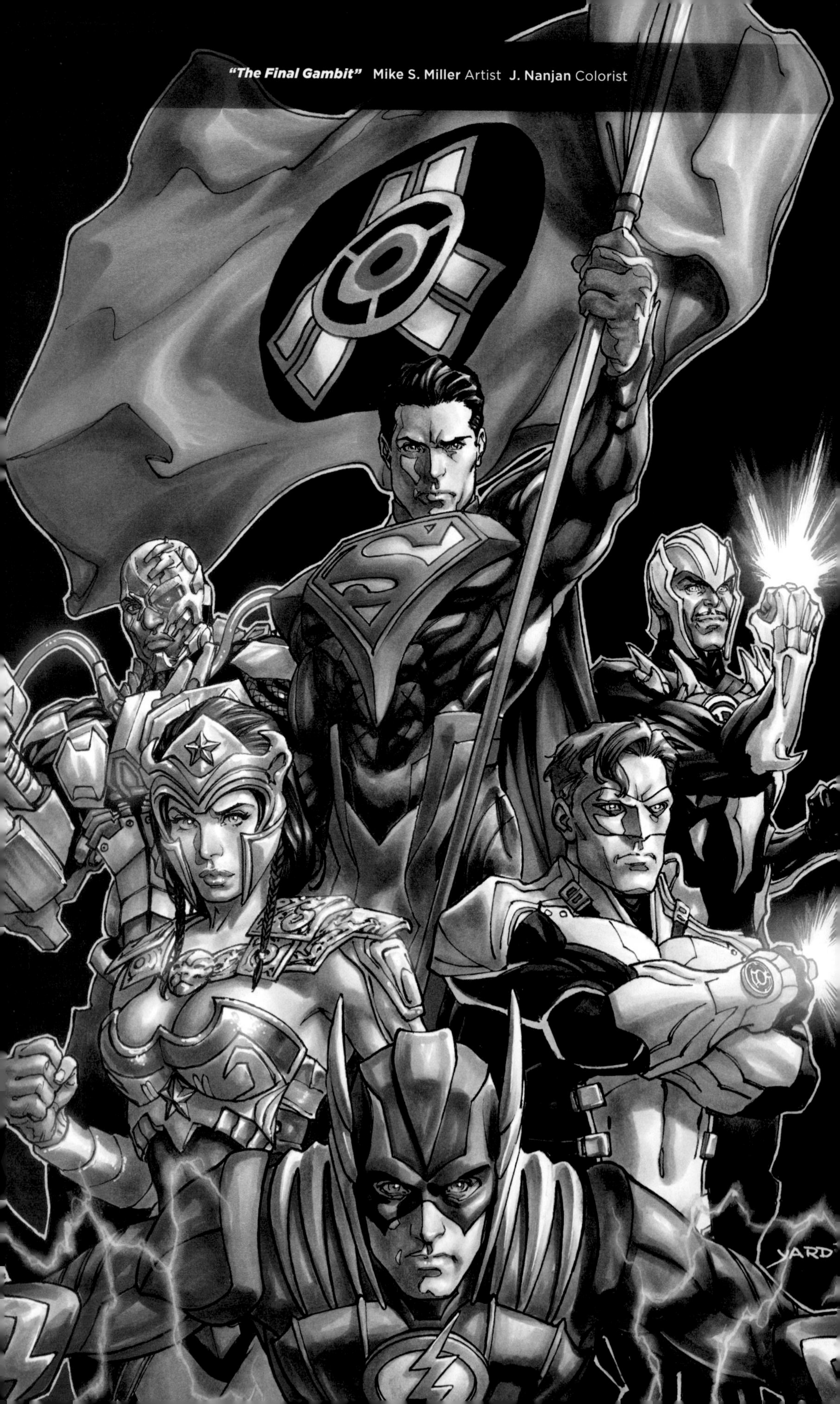

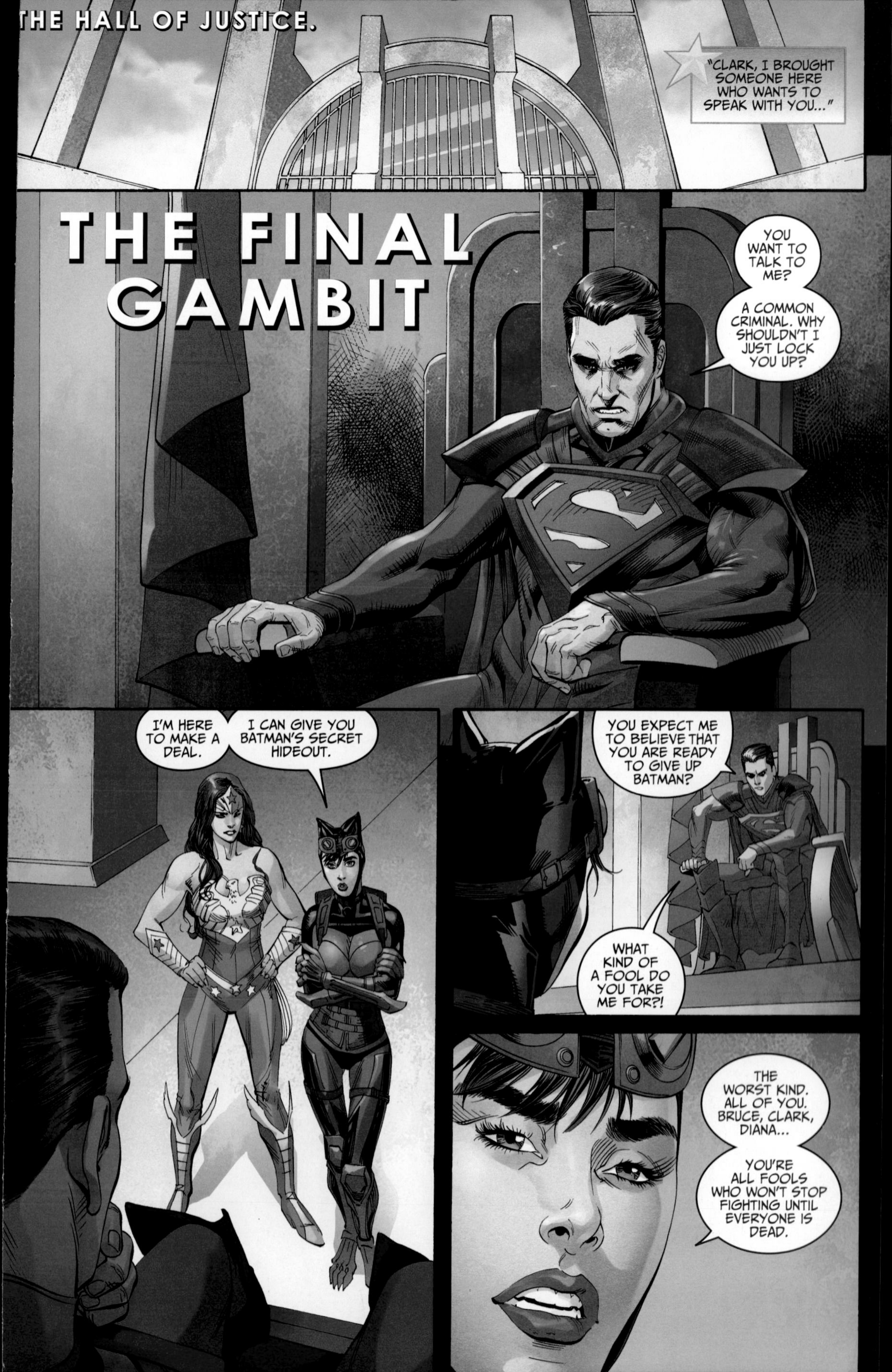
THE HALL OF JUSTICE.
"CLARK, I BROUGHT SOMEONE HERE WHO WANTS TO SPEAK WITH YOU..."
THE FINAL GAMBIT
YOU WANT TO TALK TO ME?
A COMMON CRIMINAL. WHY SHOULDN'T I JUST LOCK YOU UP?
I'M HERE TO MAKE A DEAL.
I CAN GIVE YOU BATMAN'S SECRET HIDEOUT.
YOU EXPECT ME TO BELIEVE THAT YOU ARE READY TO GIVE UP BATMAN?
WHAT KIND OF A FOOL DO YOU TAKE ME FOR?!
THE WORST KIND. ALL OF YOU. BRUCE, CLARK, DIANA...
YOU'RE ALL FOOLS WHO WON'T STOP FIGHTING UNTIL EVERYONE IS DEAD.

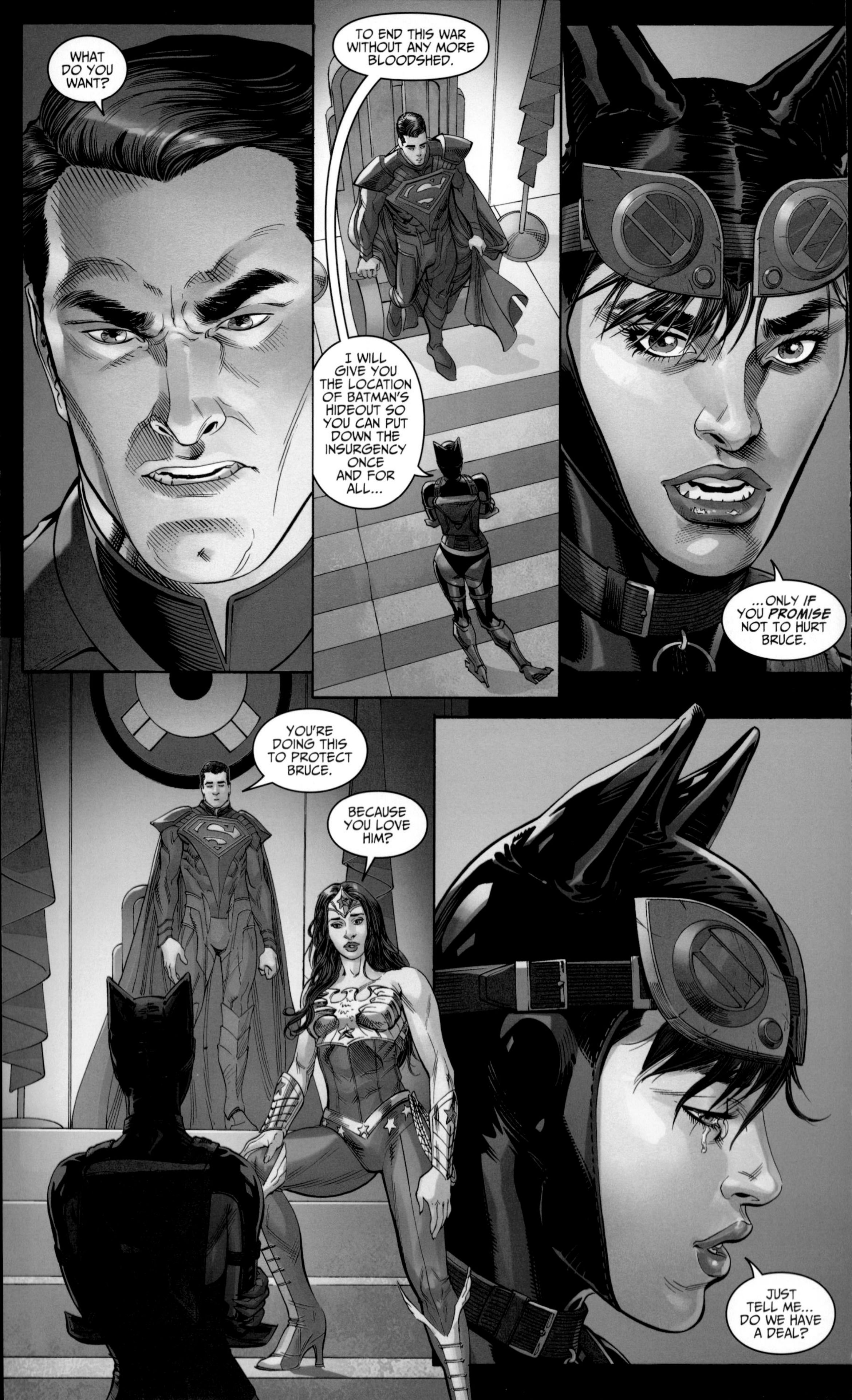
WHAT DO YOU WANT?
TO END THIS WAR WITHOUT ANY MORE BLOODSHED.
I WILL GIVE YOU THE LOCATION OF BATMAN'S HIDEOUT SO YOU CAN PUT DOWN THE INSURGENCY ONCE AND FOR ALL...
...ONLY *IF* YOU ***PROMISE*** NOT TO HURT BRUCE.
YOU'RE DOING THIS TO PROTECT BRUCE.
BECAUSE YOU LOVE HIM?
JUST TELL ME... DO WE HAVE A DEAL?

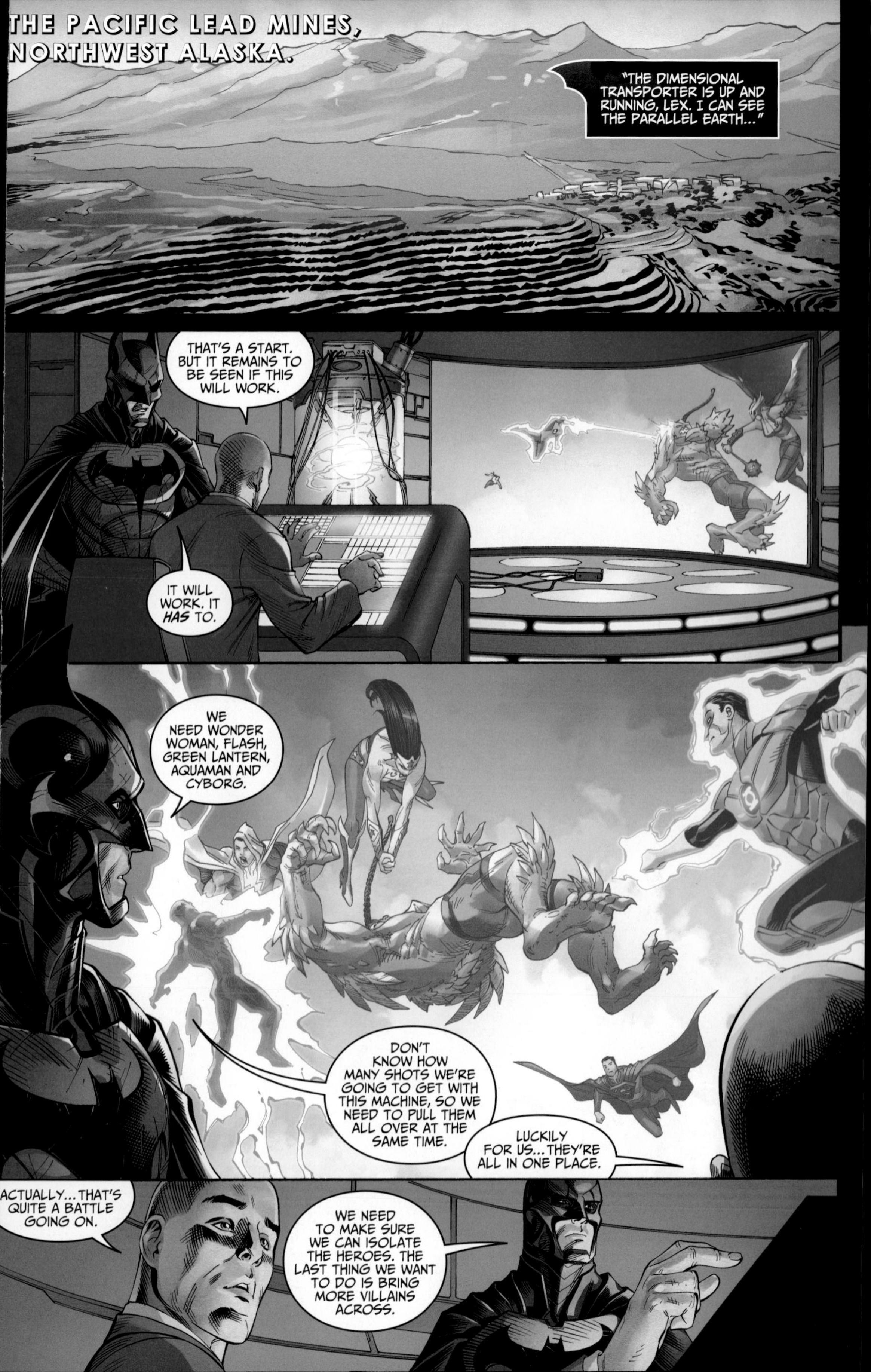
THE PACIFIC LEAD MINES, NORTHWEST ALASKA.
"THE DIMENSIONAL TRANSPORTER IS UP AND RUNNING, LEX. I CAN SEE THE PARALLEL EARTH..."
THAT'S A START. BUT IT REMAINS TO BE SEEN IF THIS WILL WORK.
IT WILL WORK. IT *HAS* TO.
WE NEED WONDER WOMAN, FLASH, GREEN LANTERN, AQUAMAN AND CYBORG.
DON'T KNOW HOW MANY SHOTS WE'RE GOING TO GET WITH THIS MACHINE, SO WE NEED TO PULL THEM ALL OVER AT THE SAME TIME.
LUCKILY FOR US... THEY'RE ALL IN ONE PLACE.
ACTUALLY... THAT'S QUITE A BATTLE GOING ON.
WE NEED TO MAKE SURE WE CAN ISOLATE THE HEROES. THE LAST THING WE WANT TO DO IS BRING MORE VILLAINS ACROSS.

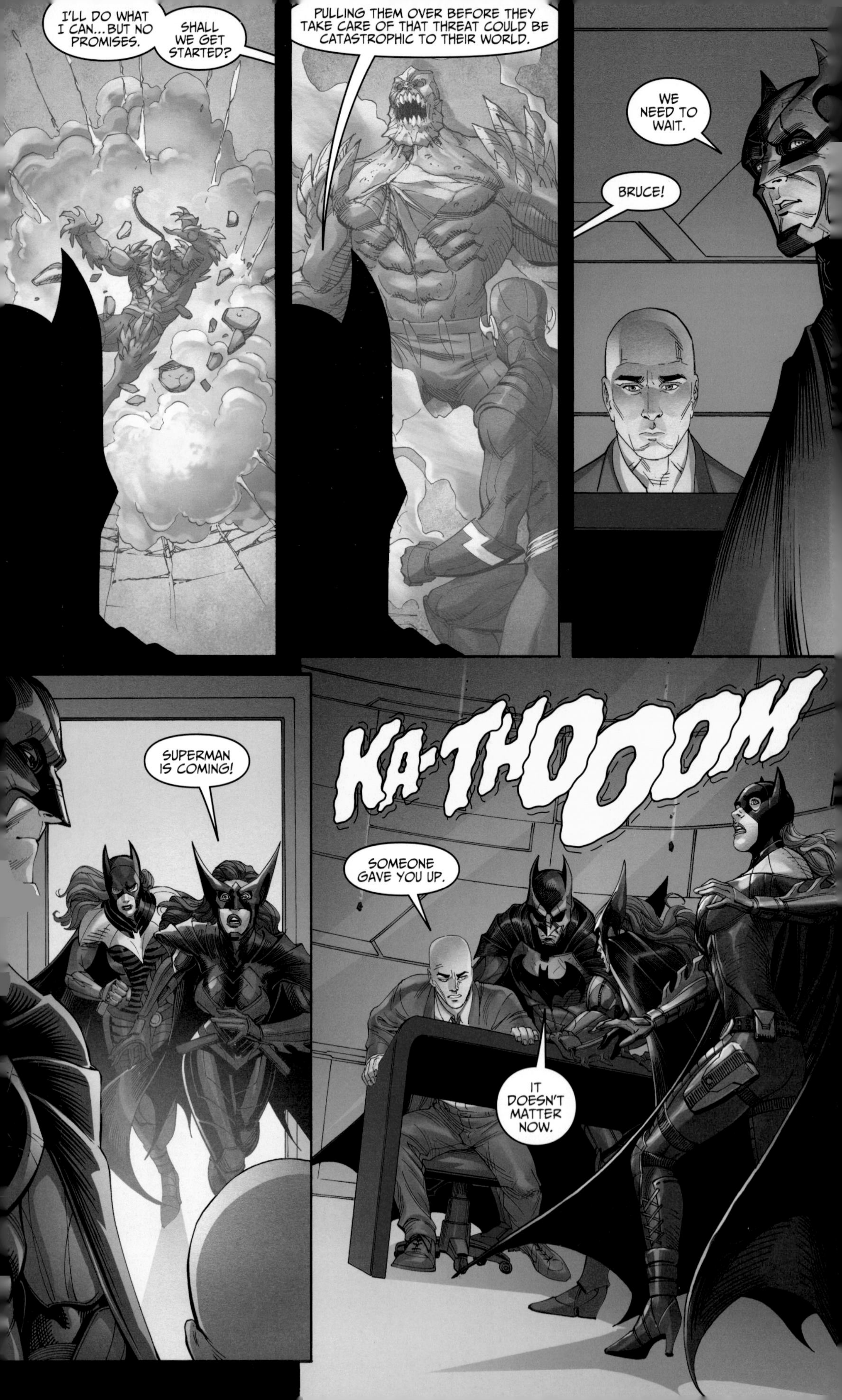
I'LL DO WHAT I CAN...BUT NO PROMISES.
SHALL WE GET STARTED?
PULLING THEM OVER BEFORE THEY TAKE CARE OF THAT THREAT COULD BE CATASTROPHIC TO THEIR WORLD.
WE NEED TO WAIT.
BRUCE!
SUPERMAN IS COMING!
KA-THOOOOM
SOMEONE GAVE YOU UP.
IT DOESN'T MATTER NOW.

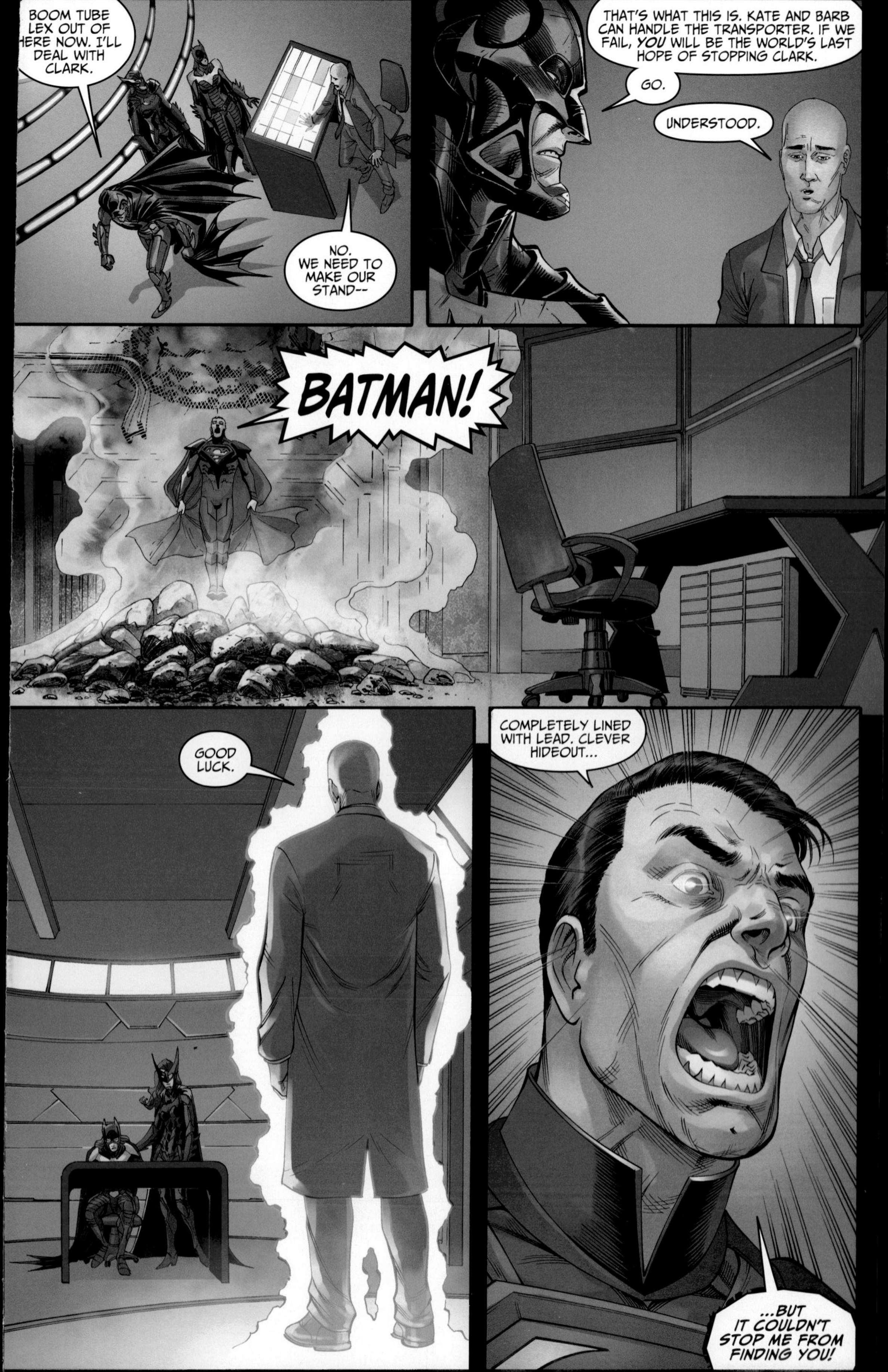
BOOM TUBE LEX OUT OF HERE NOW. I'LL DEAL WITH CLARK.
NO. WE NEED TO MAKE OUR STAND--
THAT'S WHAT THIS IS. KATE AND BARB CAN HANDLE THE TRANSPORTER. IF WE FAIL, *YOU* WILL BE THE WORLD'S LAST HOPE OF STOPPING CLARK.
GO.
UNDERSTOOD.
BATMAN!
GOOD LUCK.
COMPLETELY LINED WITH LEAD. CLEVER HIDEOUT...
...BUT IT COULDN'T STOP ME FROM FINDING YOU!

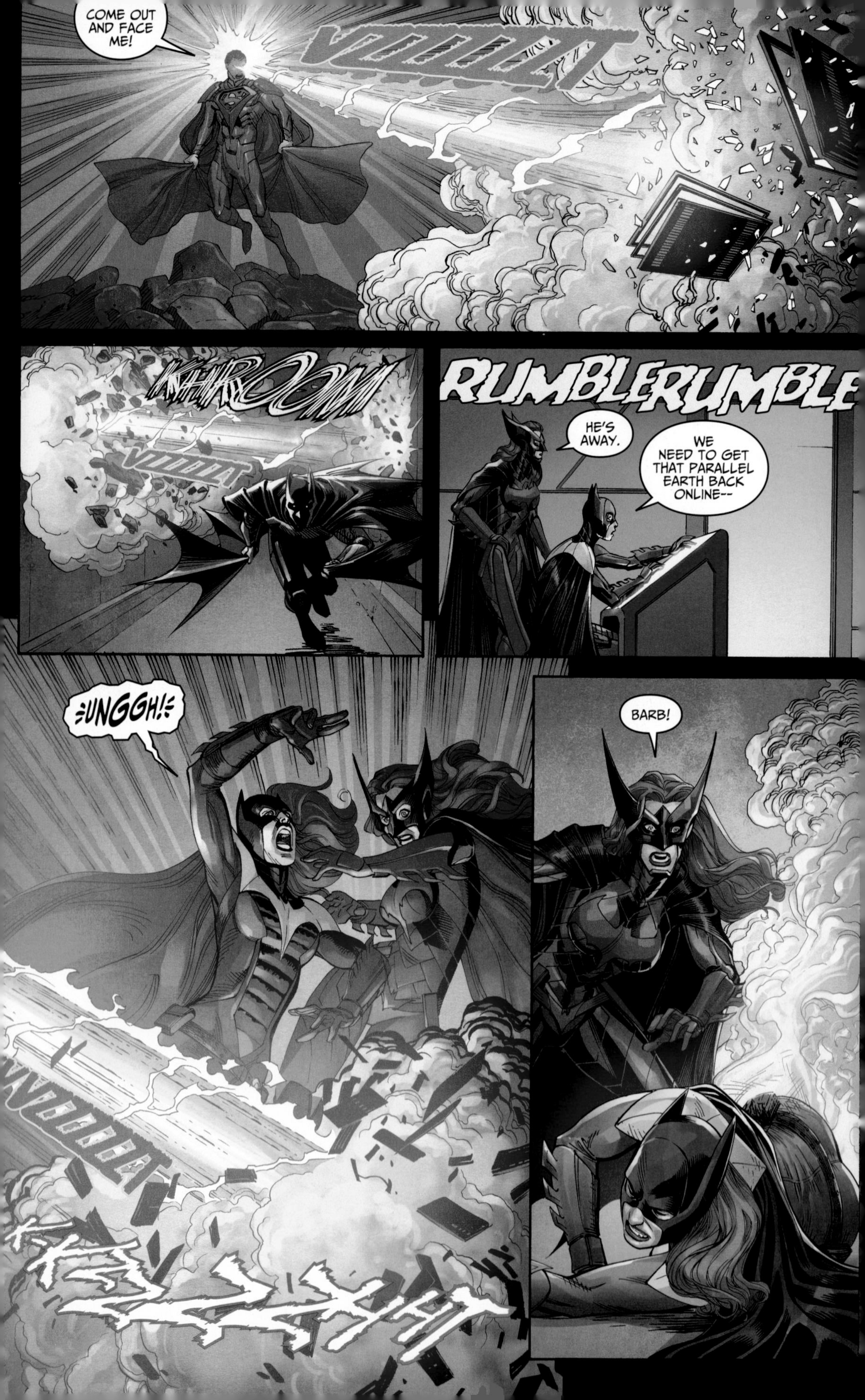
COME OUT AND FACE ME!
VZZZZZT
KHROOOM
VZZZZT
RUMBLERUMBLE
HE'S AWAY.
WE NEED TO GET THAT PARALLEL EARTH BACK ONLINE--
UNGGH!
VZZZZZT
KRSSHH
BARB!

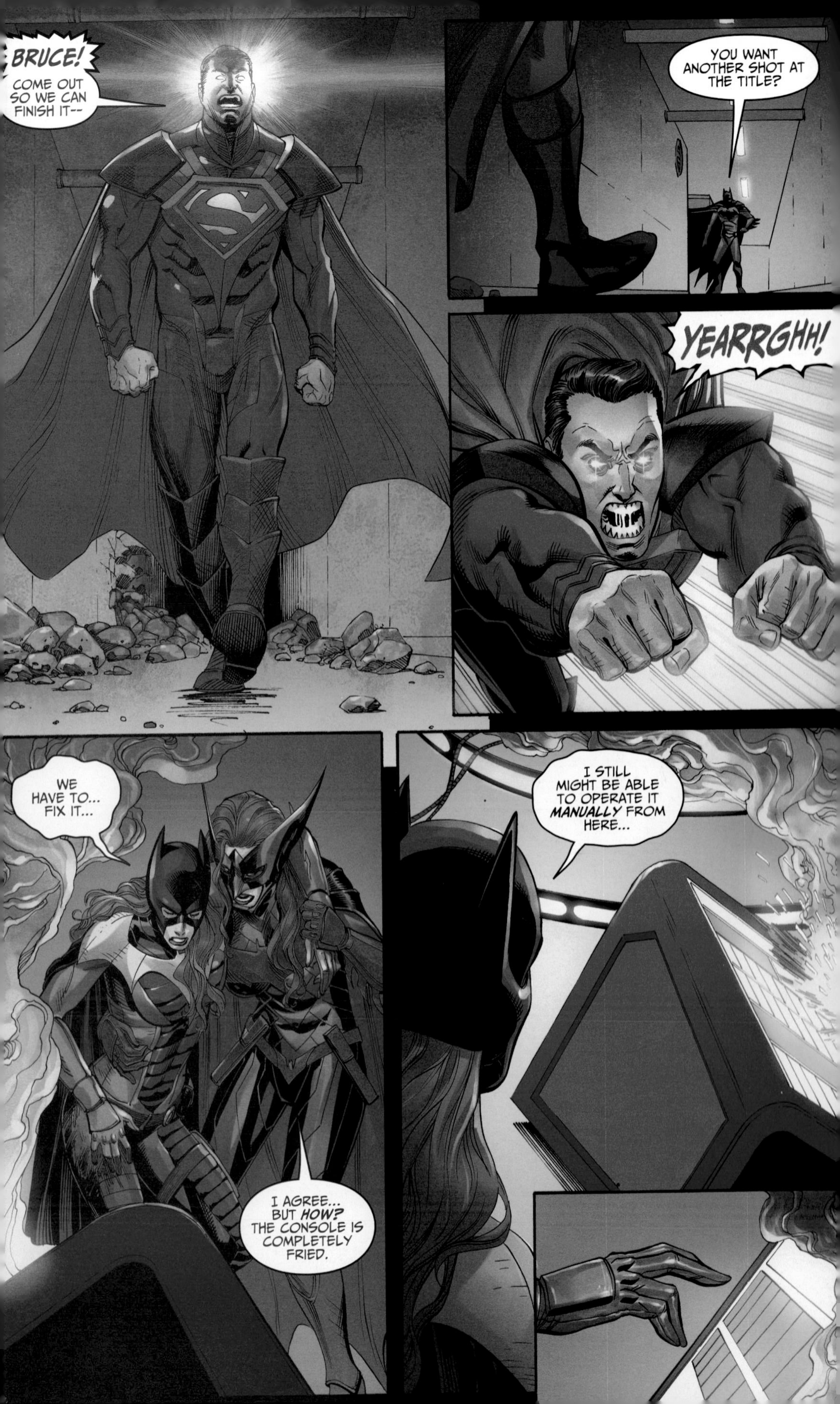
BRUCE!
COME OUT SO WE CAN FINISH IT--
YOU WANT ANOTHER SHOT AT THE TITLE?
YEARRGHH!
WE HAVE TO... FIX IT...
I AGREE... BUT *HOW?* THE CONSOLE IS COMPLETELY FRIED.
I STILL MIGHT BE ABLE TO OPERATE IT *MANUALLY* FROM HERE...

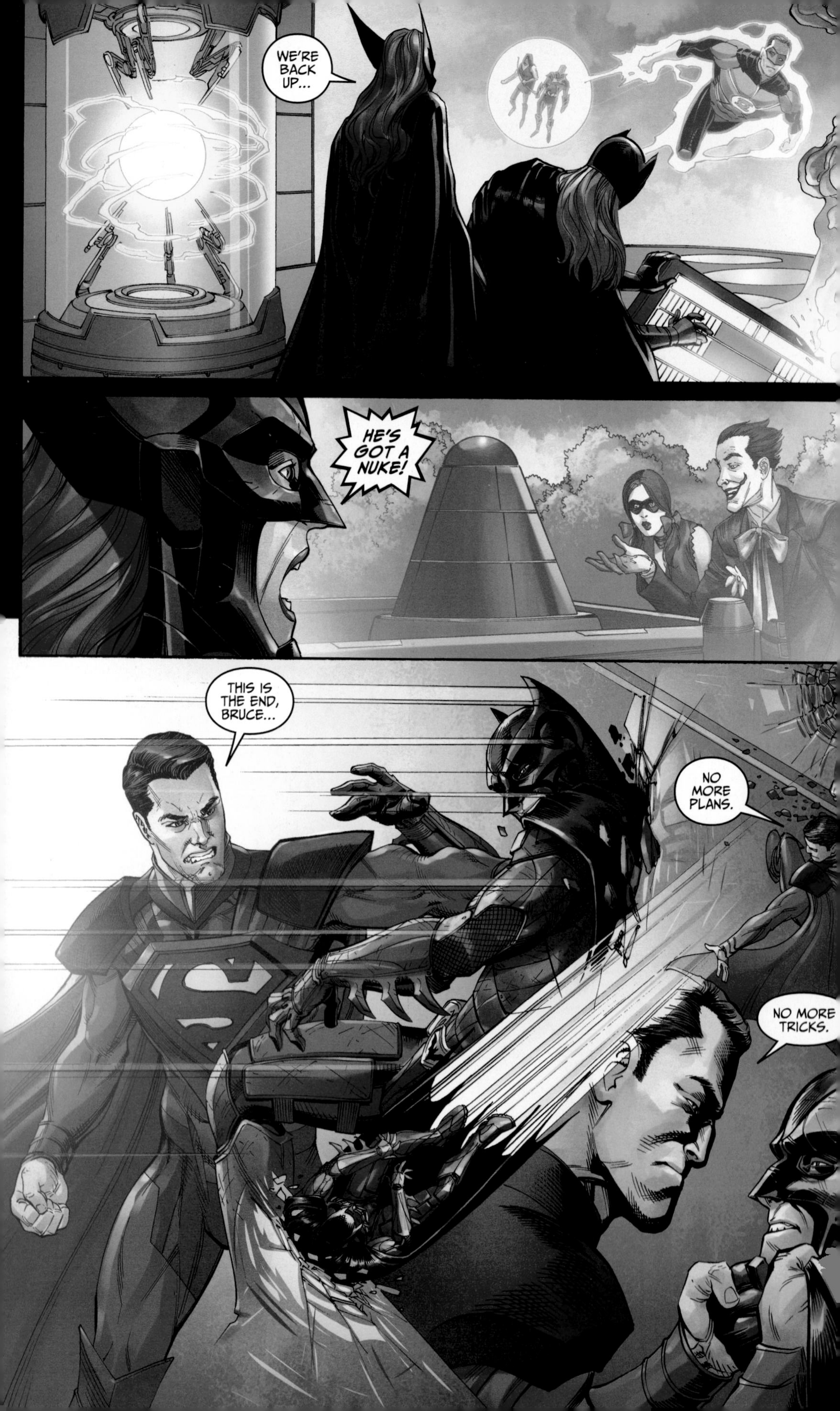
WE'RE BACK UP...
HE'S GOT A NUKE!
THIS IS THE END, BRUCE...
NO MORE PLANS.
NO MORE TRICKS.

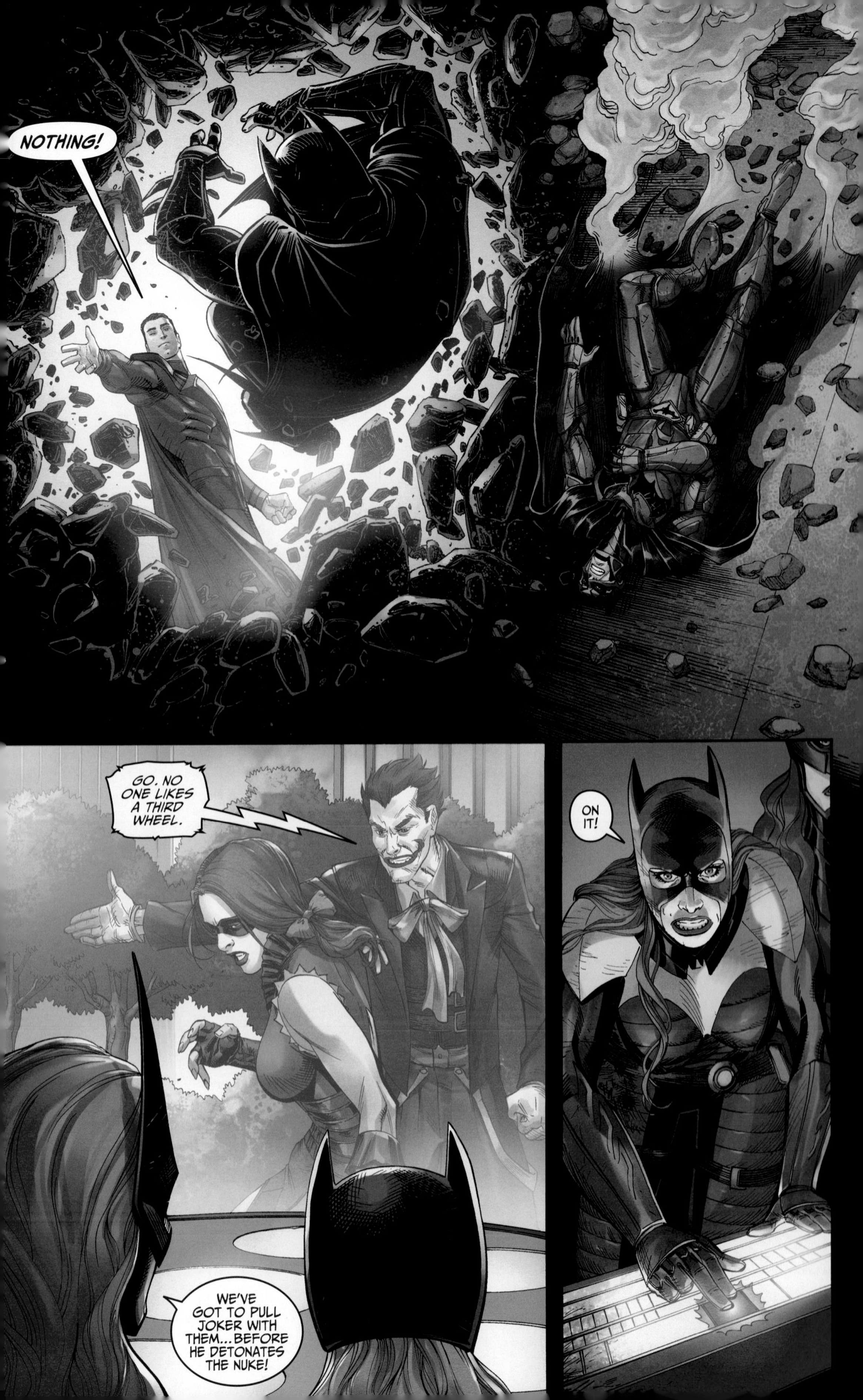
NOTHING!
GO. NO ONE LIKES A THIRD WHEEL.
WE'VE GOT TO PULL JOKER WITH THEM...BEFORE HE DETONATES THE NUKE!
ON IT!

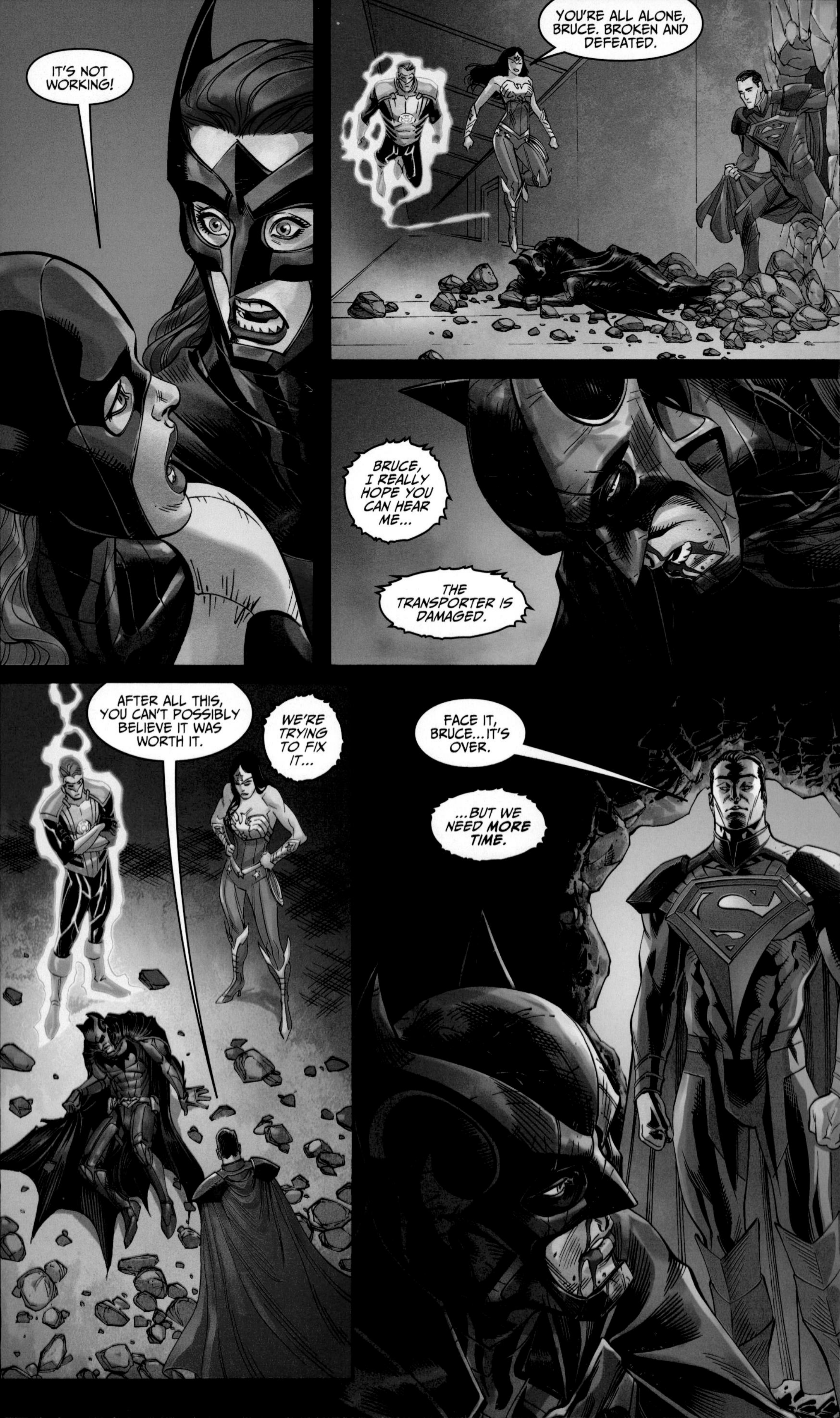
IT'S NOT WORKING!
YOU'RE ALL ALONE, BRUCE. BROKEN AND DEFEATED.
BRUCE, I REALLY HOPE YOU CAN HEAR ME...
THE TRANSPORTER IS DAMAGED.
AFTER ALL THIS, YOU CAN'T POSSIBLY BELIEVE IT WAS WORTH IT.
WE'RE TRYING TO FIX IT...
FACE IT, BRUCE...IT'S OVER.
...BUT WE NEED MORE TIME.

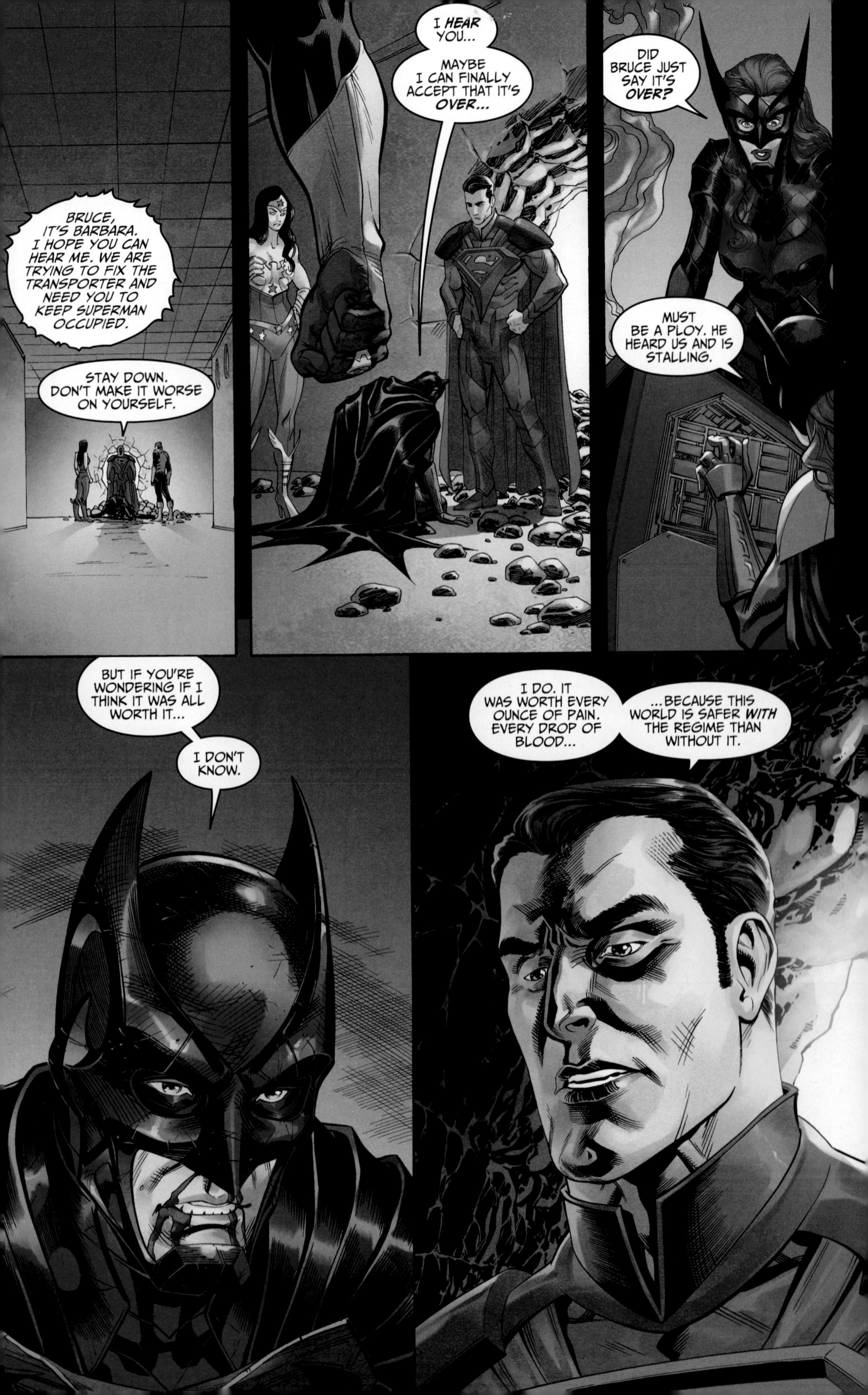
BRUCE, IT'S BARBARA. I HOPE YOU CAN HEAR ME. WE ARE TRYING TO FIX THE TRANSPORTER AND NEED YOU TO KEEP SUPERMAN OCCUPIED.
STAY DOWN. DON'T MAKE IT WORSE ON YOURSELF.
I HEAR YOU...
MAYBE I CAN FINALLY ACCEPT THAT IT'S OVER...
DID BRUCE JUST SAY IT'S OVER?
MUST BE A PLOY. HE HEARD US AND IS STALLING.
BUT IF YOU'RE WONDERING IF I THINK IT WAS ALL WORTH IT...
I DON'T KNOW.
I DO. IT WAS WORTH EVERY OUNCE OF PAIN. EVERY DROP OF BLOOD...
...BECAUSE THIS WORLD IS SAFER WITH THE REGIME THAN WITHOUT IT.

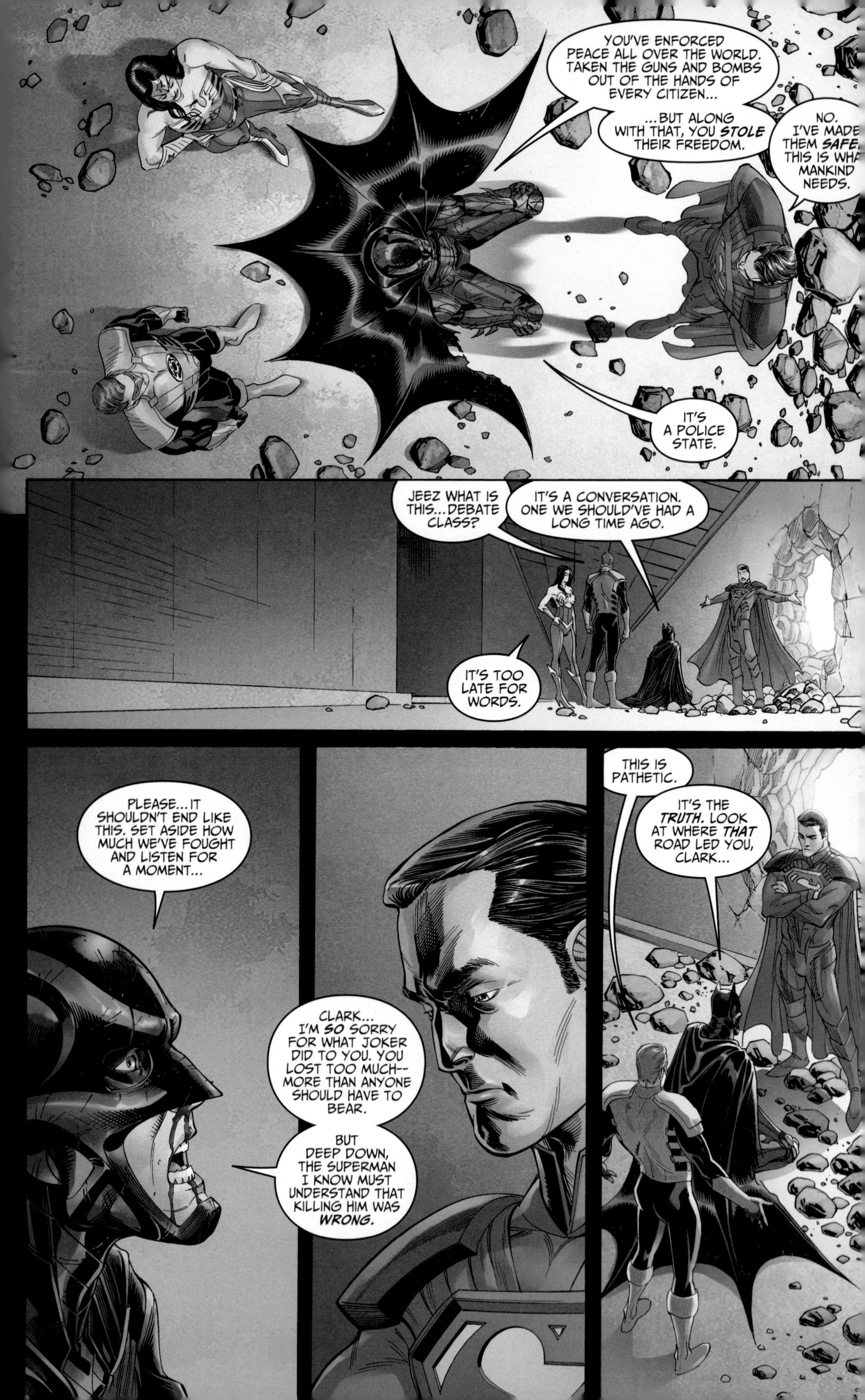
YOU'VE ENFORCED PEACE ALL OVER THE WORLD. TAKEN THE GUNS AND BOMBS OUT OF THE HANDS OF EVERY CITIZEN...
...BUT ALONG WITH THAT, YOU *STOLE* THEIR FREEDOM.
NO. I'VE MADE THEM *SAFE*. THIS IS WHAT MANKIND NEEDS.
IT'S A POLICE STATE.
JEEZ WHAT IS THIS...DEBATE CLASS?
IT'S A CONVERSATION. ONE WE SHOULD'VE HAD A LONG TIME AGO.
IT'S TOO LATE FOR WORDS.
PLEASE...IT SHOULDN'T END LIKE THIS. SET ASIDE HOW MUCH WE'VE FOUGHT AND LISTEN FOR A MOMENT...
CLARK... I'M *SO* SORRY FOR WHAT JOKER DID TO YOU. YOU LOST TOO MUCH-- MORE THAN ANYONE SHOULD HAVE TO BEAR.
BUT DEEP DOWN, THE SUPERMAN I KNOW MUST UNDERSTAND THAT KILLING HIM WAS *WRONG*.
THIS IS PATHETIC.
IT'S THE *TRUTH*. LOOK AT WHERE *THAT* ROAD LED YOU, CLARK...

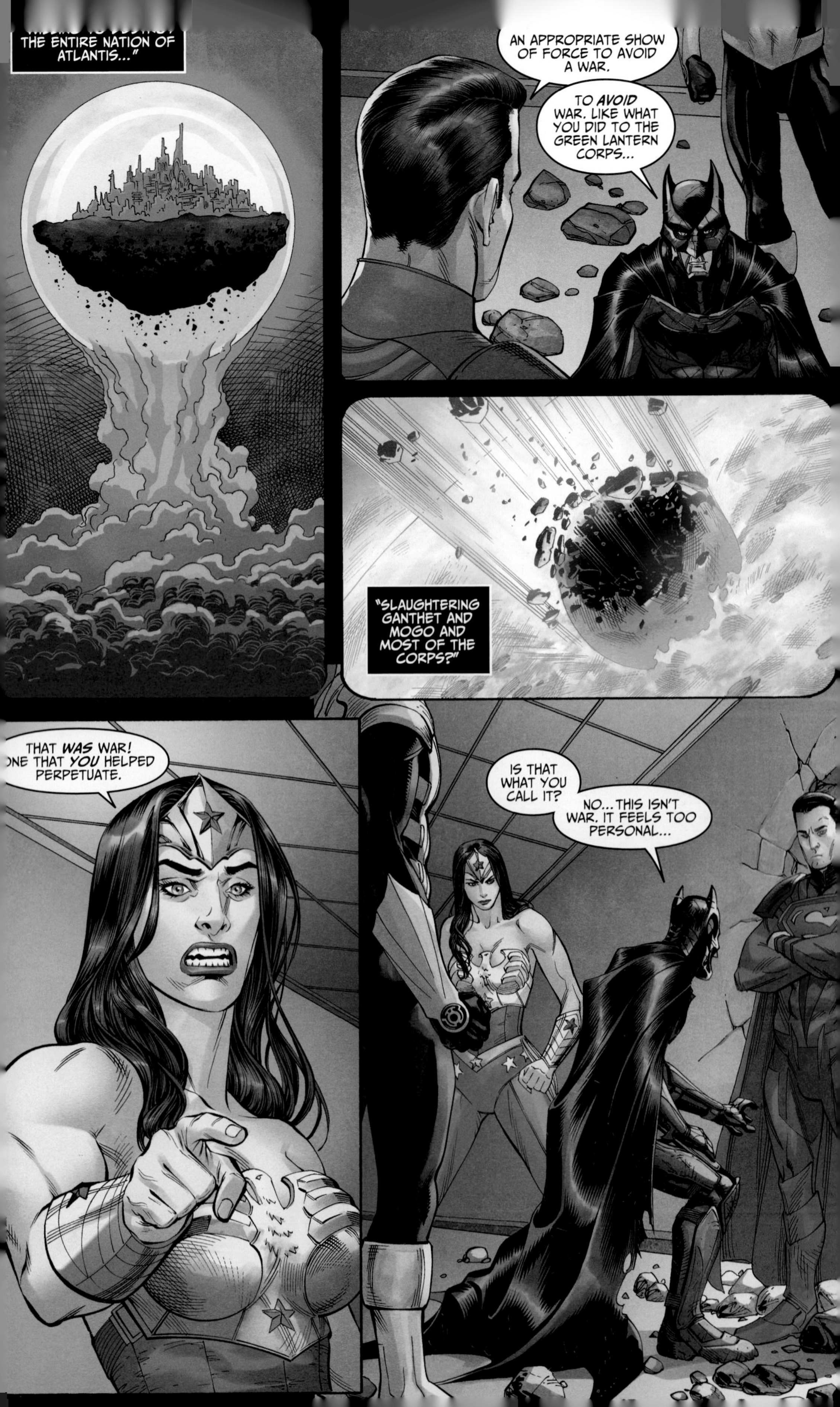
THE ENTIRE NATION OF ATLANTIS..."
AN APPROPRIATE SHOW OF FORCE TO AVOID A WAR.
TO AVOID WAR. LIKE WHAT YOU DID TO THE GREEN LANTERN CORPS...
"SLAUGHTERING GANTHET AND MOGO AND MOST OF THE CORPS?"
THAT WAS WAR! ONE THAT YOU HELPED PERPETUATE.
IS THAT WHAT YOU CALL IT?
NO... THIS ISN'T WAR. IT FEELS TOO PERSONAL...

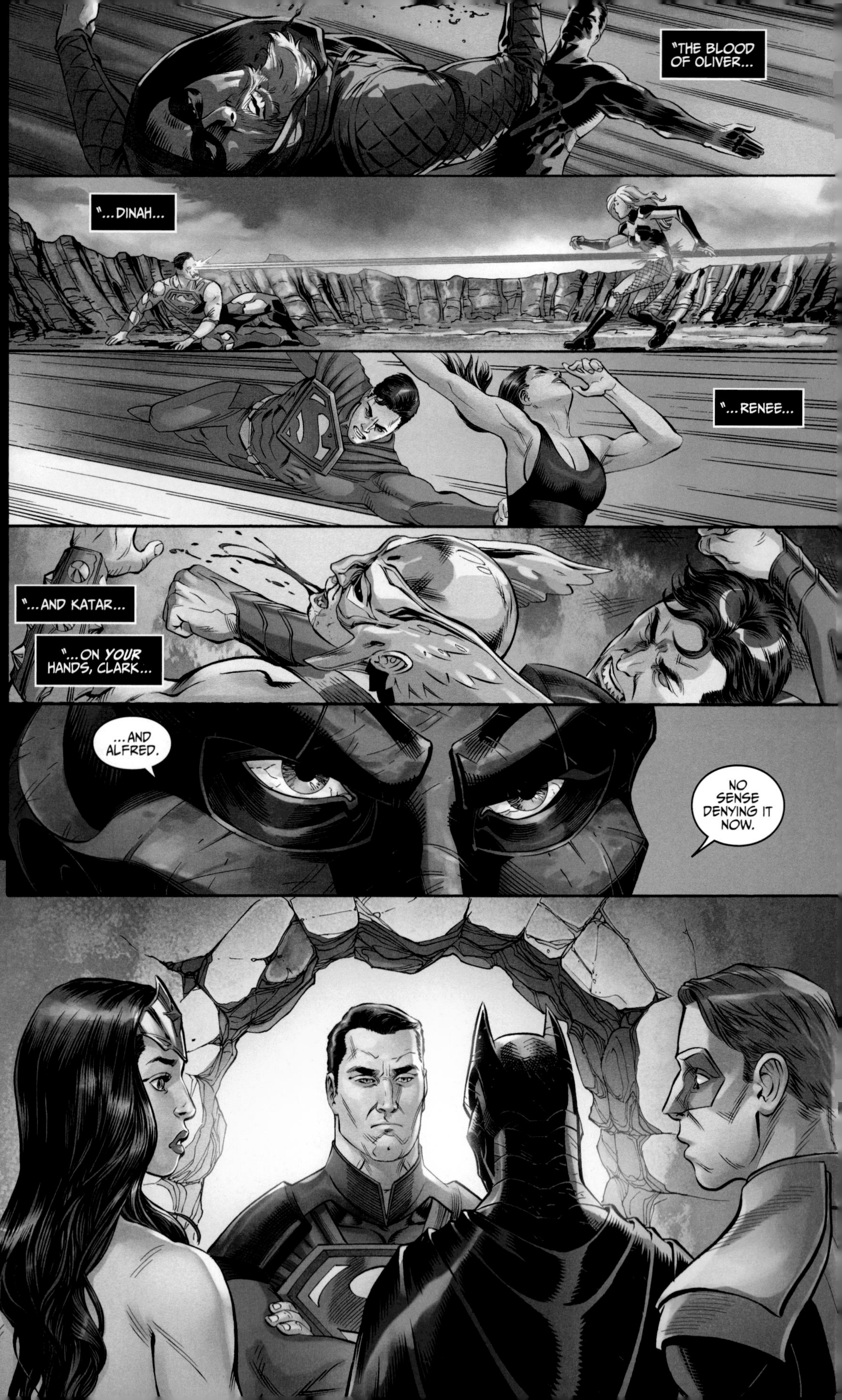
"THE BLOOD OF OLIVER...
"...DINAH...
"...RENEE...
"...AND KATAR...
"...ON *YOUR* HANDS, CLARK...
...AND ALFRED.
NO SENSE DENYING IT NOW.

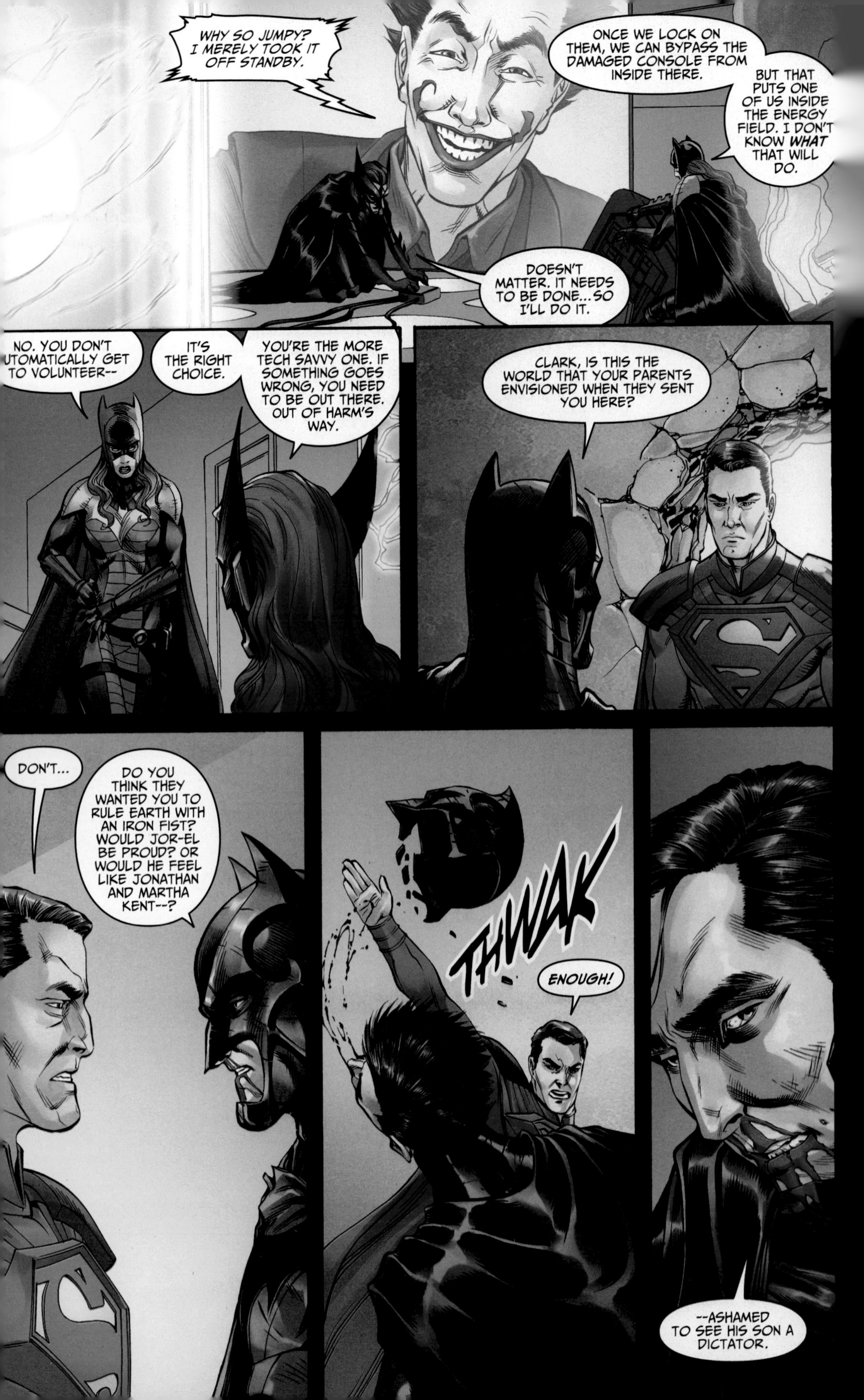
WHY SO JUMPY? I MERELY TOOK IT OFF STANDBY.
ONCE WE LOCK ON THEM, WE CAN BYPASS THE DAMAGED CONSOLE FROM INSIDE THERE.
BUT THAT PUTS ONE OF US INSIDE THE ENERGY FIELD. I DON'T KNOW *WHAT* THAT WILL DO.
DOESN'T MATTER. IT NEEDS TO BE DONE...SO I'LL DO IT.
NO. YOU DON'T UTOMATICALLY GET TO VOLUNTEER--
IT'S THE RIGHT CHOICE.
YOU'RE THE MORE TECH SAVVY ONE. IF SOMETHING GOES WRONG, YOU NEED TO BE OUT THERE. OUT OF HARM'S WAY.
CLARK, IS THIS THE WORLD THAT YOUR PARENTS ENVISIONED WHEN THEY SENT YOU HERE?
DON'T...
DO YOU THINK THEY WANTED YOU TO RULE EARTH WITH AN IRON FIST? WOULD JOR-EL BE PROUD? OR WOULD HE FEEL LIKE JONATHAN AND MARTHA KENT--?
THWAK
ENOUGH!
--ASHAMED TO SEE HIS SON A DICTATOR.

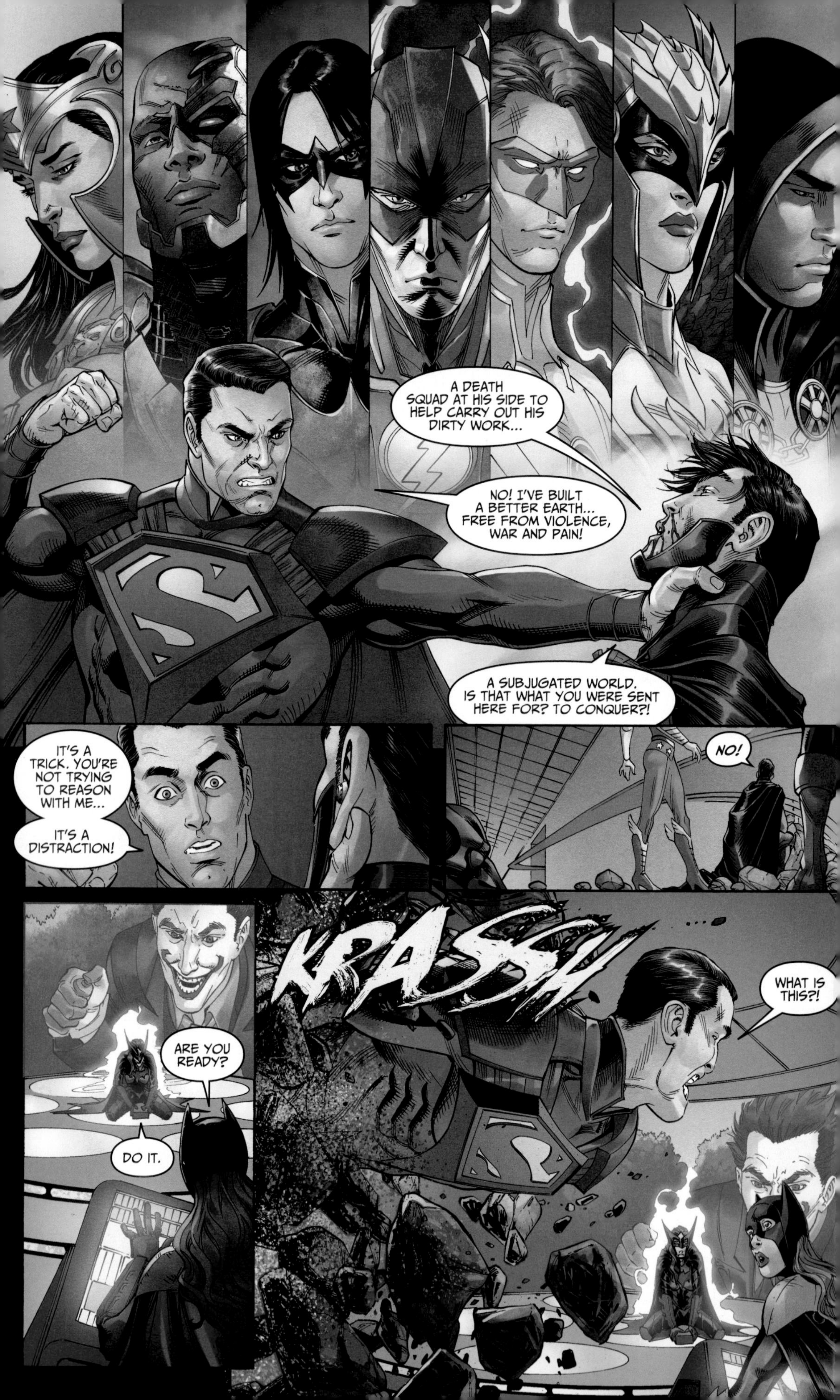

A DEATH SQUAD AT HIS SIDE TO HELP CARRY OUT HIS DIRTY WORK...
NO! I'VE BUILT A BETTER EARTH... FREE FROM VIOLENCE, WAR AND PAIN!
A SUBJUGATED WORLD. IS THAT WHAT YOU WERE SENT HERE FOR? TO CONQUER?!
IT'S A TRICK. YOU'RE NOT TRYING TO REASON WITH ME...
IT'S A DISTRACTION!
NO!
ARE YOU READY?
DO IT.
KRASH
WHAT IS THIS?!

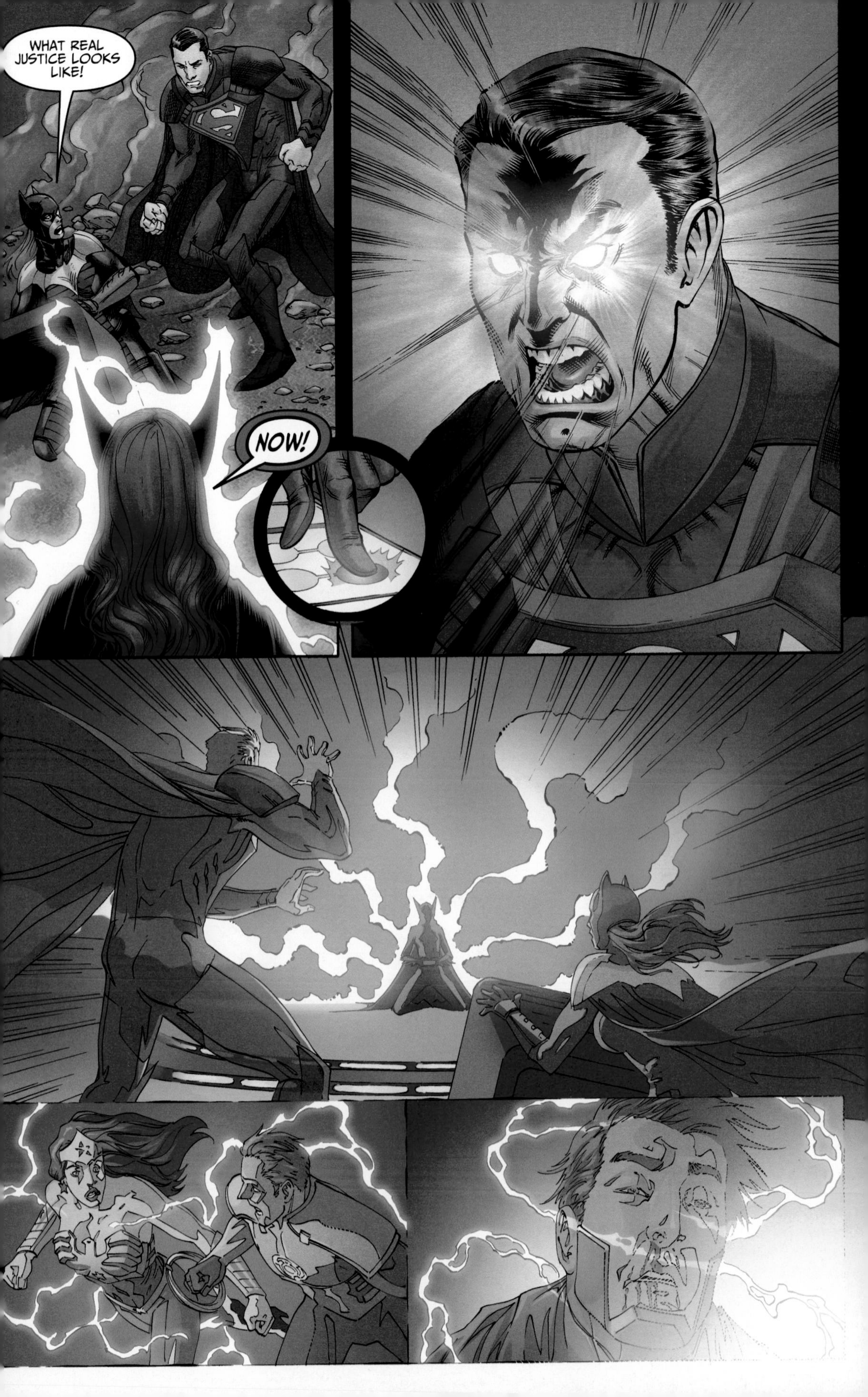
WHAT REAL JUSTICE LOOKS LIKE!
NOW!

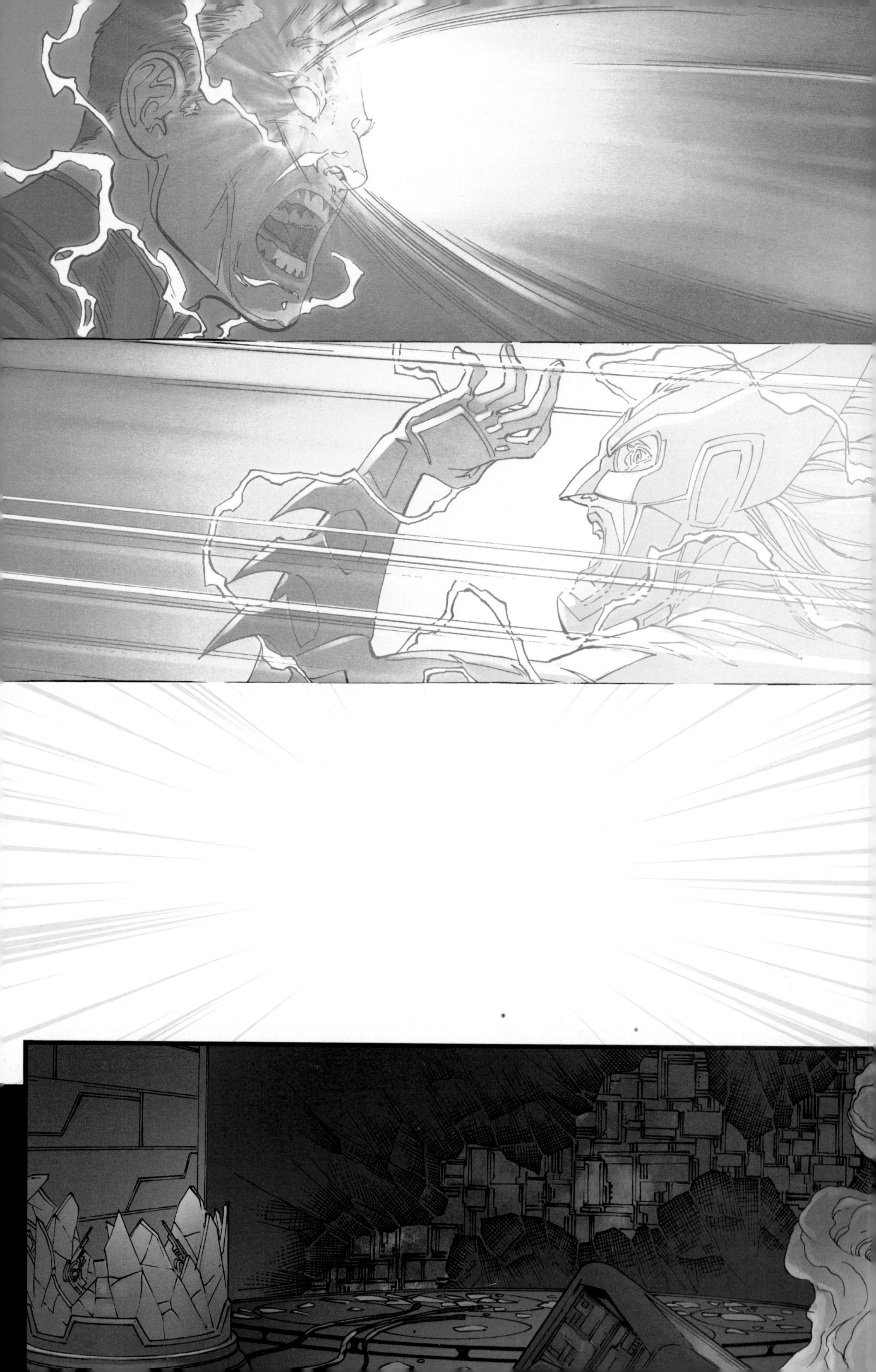

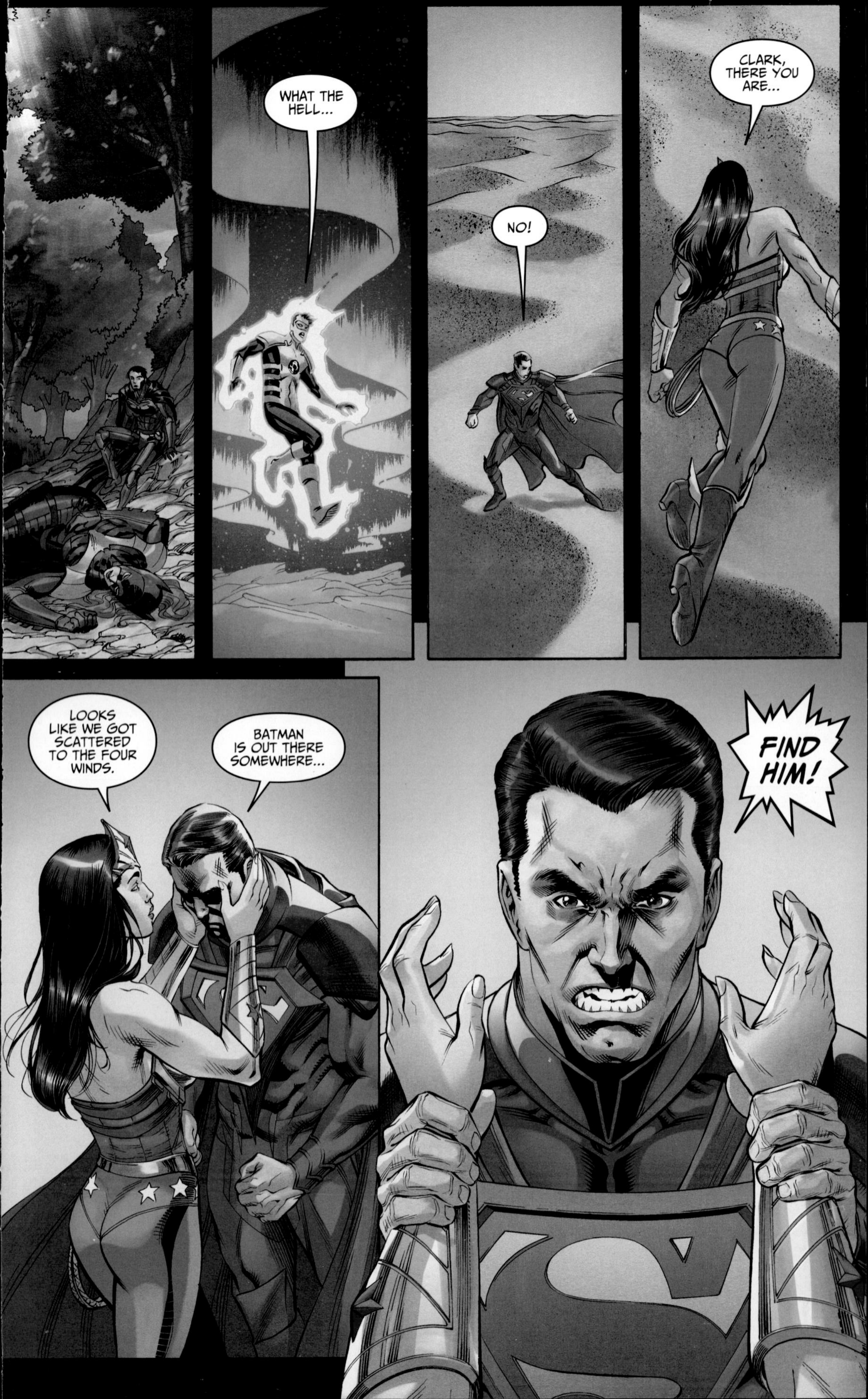
WHAT THE HELL...
NO!
CLARK, THERE YOU ARE...
LOOKS LIKE WE GOT SCATTERED TO THE FOUR WINDS.
BATMAN IS OUT THERE SOMEWHERE...
FIND HIM!

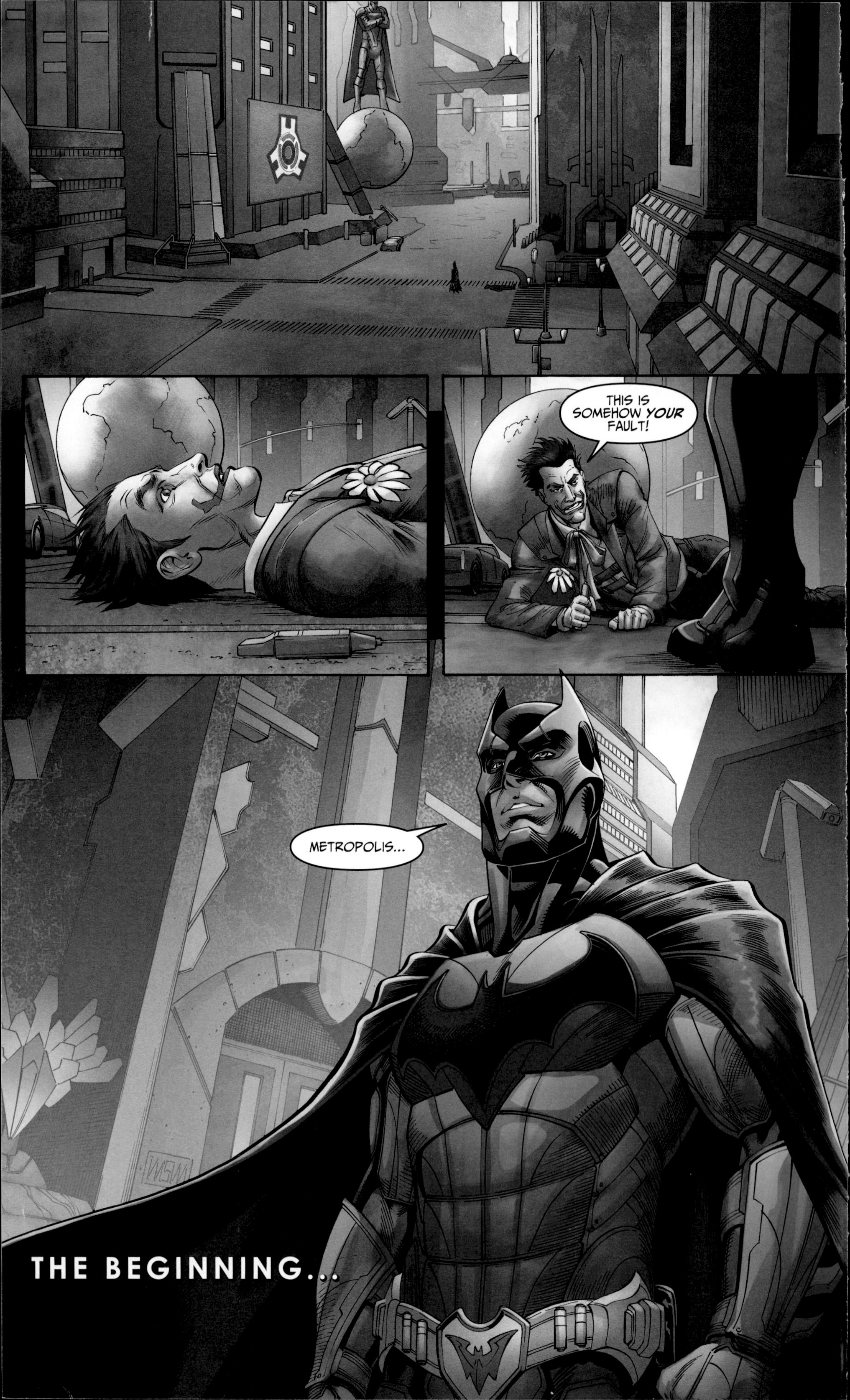

THIS IS SOMEHOW YOUR FAULT!
METROPOLIS...
THE BEGINNING...